W9-BSS-200

*The grass withers, and the flowers fade,*
*but the word of our God*
*stands forever.*

ISAIAH 40:8

# Presented to

_____

BY _____

_____

ON THE OCCASION OF

_____

_____

_____

DATE _____

*This explains why a man leaves*
*his father and mother*
*and is joined to his wife,*
*and the two are united into one.*

GENESIS 2:24

# Marriage

_____

AND _____

WERE UNITED IN MARRIAGE ON

_____

AT _____

BY _____

WITNESSED BY

MAID OF HONOR _____

BEST MAN _____

ATTENDANTS _____

_____

_____

_____

_____

*Children are a gift from the LORD;*

*they are a reward from him.*

PSALM 127:3

# Births

NAME _____ DATE _____

BIRTHPLACE _____

NAME _____ DATE _____

BIRTHPLACE _____

NAME _____ DATE _____

BIRTHPLACE _____

NAME _____ DATE _____

BIRTHPLACE _____

NAME _____ DATE _____

BIRTHPLACE _____

NAME _____ DATE _____

BIRTHPLACE _____

*There is only one Lord,*

*one faith, one baptism.*

EPHESIANS 4:5

# Baptisms

_____

WAS BAPTIZED ON _____

AT_____

BY_____


_____

WAS BAPTIZED ON _____

AT_____

BY_____


_____

WAS BAPTIZED ON _____

AT_____

BY_____


_____

WAS BAPTIZED ON _____

AT_____

BY_____

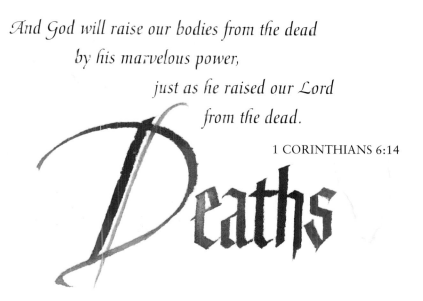

*And God will raise our bodies from the dead
by his marvelous power,
just as he raised our Lord
from the dead.*

1 CORINTHIANS 6:14

| NAME | DATE |
|------|------|
| NAME | DATE |
| NAME | DATE |
| NAME | DATE |
| NAME | DATE |
| NAME | DATE |
| NAME | DATE |

# Husband

NAME _____ BIRTHPLACE _____ DATES _____

BROTHERS AND SISTERS _____

## PARENTS

### FATHER

NAME _____

BIRTHPLACE _____ DATES _____

### MOTHER

NAME _____

BIRTHPLACE _____ DATES _____

## GRANDPARENTS

### PATERNAL

GRANDFATHER _____

BIRTHPLACE _____ DATES _____

GRANDMOTHER _____

BIRTHPLACE _____ DATES _____

### MATERNAL

GRANDFATHER _____

BIRTHPLACE _____ DATES _____

GRANDMOTHER _____

BIRTHPLACE _____ DATES _____

## GREAT-GRANDPARENTS

### PATERNAL

GRANDFATHER'S FATHER _____

BIRTHPLACE _____ DATES _____

GRANDFATHER'S MOTHER _____

BIRTHPLACE _____ DATES _____

GRANDMOTHER'S FATHER _____

BIRTHPLACE _____ DATES _____

GRANDMOTHER'S MOTHER _____

BIRTHPLACE _____ DATES _____

### MATERNAL

GRANDFATHER'S FATHER _____

BIRTHPLACE _____ DATES _____

GRANDFATHER'S MOTHER _____

BIRTHPLACE _____ DATES _____

GRANDMOTHER'S FATHER _____

BIRTHPLACE _____ DATES _____

GRANDMOTHER'S MOTHER _____

BIRTHPLACE _____ DATES _____

# ILY TREE

## Wife

NAME _____ BIRTHPLACE _____ DATES _____

BROTHERS AND SISTERS _____

## PARENTS

### FATHER

NAME _____

BIRTHPLACE _____ DATES _____

### MOTHER

NAME _____

BIRTHPLACE _____ DATES _____

## GRANDPARENTS

### PATERNAL

GRANDFATHER _____

BIRTHPLACE _____ DATES _____

GRANDMOTHER _____

BIRTHPLACE _____ DATES _____

### MATERNAL

GRANDFATHER _____

BIRTHPLACE _____ DATES _____

GRANDMOTHER _____

BIRTHPLACE _____ DATES _____

## GREAT-GRANDPARENTS

### PATERNAL

GRANDFATHER'S FATHER _____

BIRTHPLACE _____ DATES _____

GRANDFATHER'S MOTHER _____

BIRTHPLACE _____ DATES _____

GRANDMOTHER'S FATHER _____

BIRTHPLACE _____ DATES _____

GRANDMOTHER'S MOTHER _____

BIRTHPLACE _____ DATES _____

### MATERNAL

GRANDFATHER'S FATHER _____

BIRTHPLACE _____ DATES _____

GRANDFATHER'S MOTHER _____

BIRTHPLACE _____ DATES _____

GRANDMOTHER'S FATHER _____

BIRTHPLACE _____ DATES _____

GRANDMOTHER'S MOTHER _____

BIRTHPLACE _____ DATES _____

*Give thanks to the LORD,*
*for he is good!*
*His faithful love endures*
*forever.*

PSALM 118:29

# Special memories

EVENT

PLACE                                            DATE

EVENT

PLACE                                            DATE

EVENT

PLACE                                            DATE

EVENT

PLACE                                            DATE

EVENT

PLACE                                            DATE

# *life* APPLICATION® STUDY BIBLE

## NEW LIVING TRANSLATION

Tyndale House Publishers, Inc.
WHEATON, ILLINOIS

Tyndale House Publishers gratefully acknowledges the role of Youth for Christ/USA in preparing the Life Application Notes and Bible Helps.

The Bible text used in this edition of the *Life Application Bible* is the *Holy Bible,* New Living Translation.

*Life Application Study Bible* copyright © 1988, 1989, 1990, 1991, 1993, 1996 by Tyndale House Publishers, Inc., Wheaton, IL 60189. All rights reserved.

*Life Application* is a registered trademark of Tyndale House Publishers, Inc.

Notes and Bible Helps copyright © 1988, 1989, 1990, 1991, 1993, 1996 by Tyndale House Publishers, Inc. New Testament Notes and Bible Helps copyright © 1986 owned by assignment by Tyndale House Publishers, Inc. Harmony of the Gospels copyright © 1986 by James C. Galvin. Maps in text copyright © 1986, 1988 by Tyndale House Publishers, Inc. All rights reserved. Used by permission of Tyndale House Publishers. Inc.

Color maps, presentation pages, cross-references, and dictionary/concordance copyright © 1996 by Tyndale House Publishers, Inc. All rights reserved.

*Holy Bible,* New Living Translation, copyright © 1996 by Tyndale Charitable Trust. All rights reserved.

The text of the *Holy Bible,* New Living Translation, may be quoted in any form (written, visual, electronic, or audio) up to and inclusive of two hundred fifty (250) verses without express written permission of the publisher, provided that the verses quoted do not account for more than 20 percent of the work in which they are quoted, and provided that a complete book of the Bible is not quoted.

When the *Holy Bible,* New Living Translation, is quoted, one of the following credit lines must appear on the copyright page or title page of the work:

Scripture quotations marked (NLT) are taken from the *Holy Bible,* New Living Translation, copyright © 1996. Used by permission of Tyndale House Publishers, Inc., Wheaton, Illinois 60189. All rights reserved.

Scripture quotations are taken from the *Holy Bible,* New Living Translation, copyright © 1996. Used by permission of Tyndale House Publishers, Inc., Wheaton, Illinois 60189. All rights reserved.

Unless otherwise indicated, all Scripture quotations are taken from the *Holy Bible,* New Living Translation, copyright © 1996. Used by permission of Tyndale House Publishers, Inc., Wheaton, Illinois 60189. All rights reserved.

When quotations from the NLT text are used in nonsalable media, such as church bulletins, orders of service, newsletters, transparencies, or similar media, a complete copyright notice is not required, but the initials (NLT) must appear at the end of each quotation.

Quotations in excess of two hundred fifty (250) verses or 20 percent of the work, or other permission requests, must be directed to and approved in writing by Tyndale House Publishers, Inc., 351 Executive Drive, P.O. Box 80, Wheaton, Illinois 60189.

Publication of any commentary or other Bible reference work produced for commercial sale that uses the New Living Translation requires written permission for use of the NLT text.

*New Living Translation* and the New Living Translation logo are registered trademarks of Tyndale House Publishers, Inc.

Illustrated black and white icons for Timeline of Biblical Events copyright © 1996 by Corey Wilkinson.

ISBN 0-8423-3267-7 Hardcover
ISBN 0-8423-3300-2 Hardcover Indexed
ISBN 0-8423-5463-8 LeatherLike Black
ISBN 0-8423-5464-6 LeatherLike Black Indexed
ISBN 0-8423-5465-4 LeatherLike Burgundy
ISBN 0-8423-5466-2 LeatherLike Burgundy Indexed
ISBN 0-8423-5467-0 LeatherLike Navy
ISBN 0-8423-5468-9 LeatherLike Navy Indexed
ISBN-0-8423-3264-2 Bonded Leather Black

ISBN 0-8423-5222-8 Bonded Leather Black Indexed
ISBN 0-8423-3263-4 Bonded Leather Burgundy
ISBN 0-8423-3301-0 Bonded Leather Burgundy Indexed
ISBN-0-8423-5469-7 Bonded Leather Navy
ISBN 0-8423-5470-0 Bonded Leather Navy Indexed
ISBN 0-8423-3266-9 Genuine Leather Black
ISBN 0-8423-5474-3 Genuine Leather Black Indexed
ISBN 0-8423-3268-5 Genuine Leather Burgundy
ISBN 0-8423-5473-5 Genuine Leather Burgundy Indexed

*Life Application Study Bible,* NLT, also available in Large Print and Personal Edition sizes.

Printed in the United States of America

08  07  06  05  04  03  02
15  14  13  12  11  10  9   8

Each sale of the *Holy Bible,* New Living Translation, benefits Wycliffe Bible Translators, which completed its five hundredth New Testament in 1999 and plans to undertake translation work in every language that needs it by 2025. Tyndale House Publishers and Wycliffe Bible Translators share the vision for an understandable, accurate translation of the Bible for every person.

# CONTENTS

# CONTENTS

With 40 million copies in print, *The Living Bible* has been meeting a great need in people's hearts for more than thirty years. But even good things can be improved, so ninety evangelical scholars from various theological backgrounds and denominations were commissioned in 1989 to begin revising *The Living Bible*. The end result of this seven-year process is the *Holy Bible,* New Living Translation—a general-purpose translation that is accurate, easy to read, and excellent for study.

The goal of any Bible translation is to convey the meaning of the ancient Hebrew and Greek texts as accurately as possible to the modern reader. The New Living Translation is based on the most recent scholarship in the theory of translation. The challenge for the translators was to create a text that would make the same impact in the life of modern readers that the original text had for the original readers. In the New Living Translation, this is accomplished by translating entire thoughts (rather than just words) into natural, everyday English. The end result is a translation that is easy to read and understand and that accurately communicates the meaning of the original text.

We believe that this new translation, which combines the latest in scholarship with the best in translation style, will speak to your heart. We present the New Living Translation with the prayer that God will use it to speak his timeless truth to the church and to the world in a fresh, new way.

*The Publishers*
*July 1996*

*Translation Philosophy and Methodology*

There are two general theories or methods of Bible translation. The first has been called "formal equivalence." According to this theory, the translator attempts to render each word of the original language into the receptor language and seeks to preserve the original word order and sentence structure as much as possible. The second has been called "dynamic equivalence" or "functional equivalence." The goal of this translation theory is to produce in the receptor language the closest natural equivalent of the message expressed by the original-language text—both in meaning and in style. Such a translation attempts to have the same impact on modern readers as the original had on its own audience.

A dynamic-equivalence translation can also be called a thought-for-thought translation, as contrasted with a formal-equivalence or word-for-word translation. Of course, to translate the thought of the original language requires that the text be interpreted accurately and then be rendered in understandable idiom. So the goal of any thought-for-thought translation is to be both reliable and eminently readable. Thus, as a thought-for-thought translation, the New Living Translation seeks to be both exegetically accurate and idiomatically powerful.

In making a thought-for-thought translation, the translators must do their best to enter into the thought patterns of the ancient authors and to present the same ideas, connotations, and effects in the receptor language. In order to guard against personal biases and to ensure the accuracy of the message, a thought-for-thought translation should be created by a group of scholars who employ the best exegetical tools and who also understand the receptor language very well. With these concerns in mind, the Bible Translation Committee assigned each book of the Bible to three different scholars. Each scholar made a thorough review of the assigned book and submitted suggested revisions to the appropriate general reviewer. The general reviewer reviewed and summarized these suggestions and then proposed a first-draft revision of the text. This draft served as the basis for several additional phases of exegetical and stylistic committee review. Then the Bible Translation Committee jointly reviewed and approved every verse in the final translation.

A thought-for-thought translation prepared by a group of capable scholars has the potential to represent the intended meaning of the original text even more accurately than a word-for-word translation. This is illustrated by the various renderings of the Hebrew word *hesed*. This term cannot be adequately translated by any single English word because it can connote love, mercy, grace, kindness, faithfulness, and loyalty. The context—not the lexicon—must determine which English term is selected for translation.

The value of a thought-for-thought translation can be illustrated by comparing 1 Kings 2:10 in the King James Version, the New International Version, and the New Living Translation. "So David slept with his fathers, and was buried in the city of David" (KJV). "Then David rested with his fathers and was buried in the City of David" (NIV). "Then David died and was buried in the City of David" (NLT). Only the New Living Translation clearly translates the real meaning of the Hebrew idiom "slept with his fathers" into contemporary English.

*Written to Be Read Aloud*

It is evident in Scripture that the biblical documents were written to be read aloud, often in public worship (see Nehemiah 8; Luke 4:16-20; 1 Timothy 4:13; Revelation 1:3). It is still the case today that more people will hear the Bible read aloud in church than are likely to read it for themselves. Therefore, a new translation must communicate with clarity and

power when it is read aloud. For this reason, the New Living Translation is recommended as a Bible to be used for public reading. Its living language is not only easy to understand, but it also has an emotive quality that will make an impact on the listener.

## The Texts behind the New Living Translation

The translators of the Old Testament used the Masoretic Text of the Hebrew Bible as their standard text. They used the edition known as *Biblia Hebraica Stuttgartensia* (1977) with its up-to-date textual apparatus, a revision of Rudolf Kittel's *Biblia Hebraica* (Stuttgart, 1937). The translators also compared the Dead Sea Scrolls, the Septuagint and other Greek manuscripts, the Samaritan Pentateuch, the Syriac Peshitta, the Latin Vulgate, and any other versions or manuscripts that shed light on textual problems.

The translators of the New Testament used the two standard editions of the Greek New Testament: the *Greek New Testament,* published by the United Bible Societies (fourth revised edition, 1993), and *Novum Testamentum Graece,* edited by Nestle and Aland (twenty-seventh edition, 1993). These two editions, which have the same text but differ in punctuation and textual notes, represent the best in modern textual scholarship.

## Translation Issues

The translators have made a conscious effort to provide a text that can be easily understood by the average reader of modern English. To this end, we have used the vocabulary and language structures commonly used by the average person. The result is a translation of the Scriptures written generally at the reading level of a junior high school student. We have avoided using language that is likely to become quickly dated or that reflects a narrow subdialect of English, with the goal of making the New Living Translation as broadly useful as possible.

But our concern for readability goes beyond the concerns of vocabulary and sentence structure. We are also concerned about historical and cultural barriers to understanding the Bible, and we have sought to translate terms shrouded in history or culture in ways that can be immediately understood by the contemporary reader. Thus, our goal of easy readability expresses itself in a number of other ways:

- Rather than translating ancient weights and measures literally, which communicates little to the modern reader, we have expressed them by means of recognizable contemporary equivalents. We have converted ancient weights and measures to modern English (American) equivalents, and we have rendered the literal Hebrew or Greek measures, along with metric equivalents, in textual footnotes.
- Instead of translating ancient currency values literally, we have generally expressed them in terms of weights in precious metals. In some cases we have used other common terms to communicate the message effectively. For example, "three shekels of silver" might become "three silver coins" or "three pieces of silver" to convey the intended message. Again, a rendering of the literal Hebrew or Greek is given in textual footnotes.
- Since the Hebrew lunar calendar fluctuates from year to year in relation to the solar calendar used today, we have translated Hebrew dates in a way that communicates with our modern readership. It was clear that we could not use the names of the Hebrew months, such as *Abib,* which are meaningless to the modern reader. Nor could we use a simple designation such as "first month," because the months of the Hebrew lunar calendar do not correspond with the months of our calendar. Thus, we have often used seasonal references to communicate the time of year when something happened. For example, "the first month" (which occurs in March and April) might be translated "early spring." Where it is possible to define a specific ancient date in terms of our modern calendar, we use modern dates in the text. Textual footnotes then give the literal Hebrew date and state the rationale for our rendering. For example, Ezra 7:9 pinpoints the date when Ezra arrived in Jerusalem: "the first day of the fifth month." This was during the seventh year of King Artaxerxes' reign (Ezra 7:7). We translate that lunar date as August 4, with a footnote giving the Hebrew and identifying the year as 458 B.C.

- Since ancient references to the time of day differ from our modern methods of denoting time, we used renderings that are instantly understandable to the modern reader. Accordingly, we have rendered specific times of day by using approximate equivalents in terms of our common "o'clock" system. On occasion, translations such as "at dawn the next morning" or "as the sun began to set" have been used when the biblical reference is general.
- Many words in the original texts made sense to the original audience but communicate something quite different to the modern reader. In such cases, some liberty must be allowed in translation to communicate what was intended. Places identified by the term normally translated "city," for example, are often better identified as "towns" or "villages." Similarly, the term normally translated "mountain" is often better rendered "hill."
- Many words and phrases carry a great deal of cultural meaning that was obvious to the original readers but needs explanation in our own culture. For example, the phrase "they beat their breasts" (Luke 23:48) in ancient times meant that people were very upset. In our translation we chose to translate this phrase dynamically: "They went home *in deep sorrow.*" In some cases, however, we have simply illuminated the existing expression to make it immediately understandable. For example, we might have expanded the literal phrase to read "they beat their breasts *in sorrow.*"
- Metaphorical language is often difficult for contemporary readers to understand, so at times we have chosen to translate or illuminate the metaphor. For example, the ancient poet writes, "Your eyes are doves" (Song of Songs 1:15). To help the modern reader, who might be confused or distracted by a literal visualization of this image, we converted the metaphor to a simile to make the meaning immediately clear: "Your eyes are soft *like* doves." Here we also added the modifier "soft" to help the modern reader catch the significance of the metaphoric expression. A few chapters later, the poet writes, "Your neck is like the tower of David" (Song of Songs 4:4). We rendered it "Your neck is *as stately as* the tower of David" to clarify the intended positive meaning of the metaphor.
- We did not feel obligated to display all Hebrew poetry in English poetic form. Only the book of Psalms is set entirely in poetic lines. Other books, though poetic in nature, are set in prose for the sake of easier reading. Nonetheless, these prose renderings reflect the poetic language of the original Hebrew. Where a portion of text is explicitly said to be a poem or song, however, it has usually been set as such.
- One challenge we faced was in determining how to translate accurately the ancient biblical text that was originally written in a context where male-oriented terms were used to refer to humanity generally. We needed to respect the nature of the ancient context while also trying to make the translation clear to a modern audience that tends to read male-oriented language as applying only to males. Often the original text, though using masculine nouns and pronouns, clearly intends that the message be applied to both men and women. One example is found in the New Testament epistles, where the believers are called "brothers" *(adelphoi).* Yet it is clear that these epistles were addressed to all the believers—male and female. Thus, we have usually translated this Greek word "brothers and sisters" in order to represent the historical situation more accurately.

  We have also been sensitive to passages where the text applies generally to human beings or to the human condition. In many instances we have used plural pronouns (they, them) in place of the masculine singular (he, him). For example, a traditional rendering of Proverbs 22:6 is: "Train up a child in the way he should go, and when he is old he will not turn from it." We have rendered it: "Teach your children to choose the right path, and when they are older, they will remain upon it." At times we have also replaced third person pronouns with the second person to ensure clarity. A traditional rendering of Proverbs 26:27 is: "He who digs a pit will fall into it, and he who rolls a stone, it will come back on him." We have rendered it: "If you set a trap for others, you will get caught in it yourself. If you roll a boulder down on others, it will roll back and crush you."

All such decisions were driven by the concern to reflect accurately the intended meaning of the original texts of Scripture.

We should emphasize, however, that all masculine nouns and pronouns used to represent God (for example, "Father") have been maintained without exception. We believe that essential traits of God's revealed character can only be conveyed through the masculine language expressed in the original texts of Scripture.

### Lexical Consistency in Terminology

For the sake of clarity, we have maintained lexical consistency in areas such as divine names, synoptic passages, rhetorical structures, and nontheological technical terms (i.e., liturgical, cultic, zoological, botanical, cultural, and legal terms). For theological terms, we have allowed a greater semantic range of acceptable English words or phrases for a single Hebrew or Greek word. We avoided weighty theological terms that do not readily communicate to many modern readers. For example, we avoided using words such as "justification," "sanctification," and "regeneration." In place of these words (which are carryovers from Latin), we provided renderings such as "we are made right with God," "we are made holy," and "we are born anew."

### The Spelling of Proper Names

Many individuals in the Bible, especially the Old Testament, are known by more than one name or by a number of variant names (e.g., Uzziah/Azariah). For the sake of clarity, we have tried to use a single spelling for any one individual, footnoting the literal spelling whenever we differ from it. This is especially helpful in delineating the kings of Israel and Judah. King Joash/Jehoash of Israel has been consistently called Jehoash, while King Joash/Jehoash of Judah is called Joash. A similar distinction has been used to distinguish between Joram/Jehoram of Israel and Joram/Jehoram of Judah. All such decisions were made with the goal of clarifying the text for the reader. When the ancient biblical writers clearly had a theological purpose in their choice of a variant name (e.g., Eshbaal/Ishbosheth), the different names have been maintained with an explanatory footnote.

### The Rendering of Divine Names

All appearances of *'el, 'elohim,* or *'eloah* have been translated "God," except where the context demands the translation "god(s)." We have rendered the tetragrammaton (*YHWH*) consistently as "the LORD," utilizing a form with small capitals that is common among English translations. This will distinguish it from the name *'adonai,* which we render "Lord." When *'adonai* and *YHWH* appear in conjunction, we have rendered it "Sovereign LORD." This also distinguishes *'adonai YHWH* from cases where *YHWH* appears with *'elohim,* which is rendered "LORD God." When *YH* (the short form of *YHWH*) and *YHWH* appear together, we have rendered it "LORD GOD." The Hebrew word *'adon* is rendered "lord," or "master," or sometimes "sir."

In the New Testament, the Greek word *Christos* has been translated as "Messiah" when the context assumes a Jewish audience. When a Gentile audience can be assumed, *Christos* has been translated as "Christ." The Greek word *kurios* is consistently translated "Lord," except in four quotations of Psalm 110:1, where it is translated "LORD."

### Textual Footnotes

The New Living Translation provides several kinds of textual footnotes:

- All Old Testament passages that are clearly quoted in the New Testament are identified in a textual footnote in the New Testament.
- Some textual footnotes provide cultural and historical information on places, things, and people in the Bible that are probably obscure to modern readers. Such notes should aid the reader in understanding the message of the text. For example, in Acts 12:1, "King Herod" is named in this translation as "King Herod Agrippa" and is identified in a footnote as being "the nephew of Herod Antipas and a grandson of Herod the Great."
- When various ancient manuscripts contain different readings, these differences are often documented in footnotes. For instance, textual variants are footnoted when the variant reading is very familiar (usually through the King James

Version). We have used footnotes when we have selected variant readings that differ from the Hebrew and Greek editions normally followed.

- When the meaning of a proper name (or a wordplay inherent in a proper name) is relevant to the meaning of the text, it is illuminated with a textual footnote. For example, the footnote at Genesis 3:20 reads: "*Eve* sounds like a Hebrew term that means 'to give life.' " This wordplay in the Hebrew illuminates the meaning of the text, which goes on to say that Eve "would be the mother of all people everywhere." If the meaning of the name is more certain, it is stated more simply. For example, the footnote at Genesis 16:11 reads: "*Ishmael* means 'God hears.' " In this case, Hagar named her son Ishmael after realizing that God had heard her cry for help.

- When we translate the meaning of a place-name that is often simply transliterated from the Hebrew or Greek, we provide a textual footnote showing the transliteration that appears in many English translations. For example, the name usually transliterated "Havvoth-jair" in Judges 10:4 has been translated "the Towns of Jair," with a footnote that gives the traditional transliteration: "Hebrew *Havvoth-jair.*"

- Textual footnotes are also used to show alternative renderings. These are prefaced with the word "Or." On occasion, we also provide notes on words or phrases that represent a translation that departs from long-standing tradition. These notes are prefaced with the words "traditionally rendered." For example, a footnote to the translation "contagious skin disease" at Leviticus 13:2 says, "Traditionally rendered *leprosy.*"

AS WE SUBMIT this translation of the Bible for publication, we recognize that any translation of the Scriptures is subject to limitations and imperfections. Anyone who has attempted to communicate the richness of God's Word into another language will realize it is impossible to make a perfect translation. Recognizing these limitations, we sought God's guidance and wisdom throughout this project. Now we pray that he will accept our efforts and use this translation for the benefit of the Church and of all people.

We pray that the New Living Translation will overcome some of the barriers of history, culture, and language that have kept people from reading and understanding God's Word. We hope that readers unfamiliar with the Bible will find the words clear and easy to understand, and that readers well versed in the Scriptures will gain a fresh perspective. We pray that readers will gain insight and wisdom for living, but most of all that they will meet the God of the Bible and be forever changed by knowing him.

*The Bible Translation Committee*
*July 1996*

## PENTATEUCH

**Daniel I. Block,** General Reviewer
*The Southern Baptist Theological Seminary*

### GENESIS

**Allan Ross,** *Trinity Episcopal Seminary*
**John Sailhamer,** *Northwestern College*
**Gordon Wenham,** *The Cheltenham and Gloucester College of Higher Education*

### EXODUS

**Robert Bergen,** *Hannibal-LaGrange College*
**Daniel I. Block,** *The Southern Baptist Theological Seminary*
**Eugene Carpenter,** *Bethel College, Mishawaka, Indiana*

### LEVITICUS

**David Baker,** *Ashland Theological Seminary*
**Victor Hamilton,** *Asbury College*
**Kenneth Mathews,** *Beeson Divinity School, Samford University*

### NUMBERS

**Dale A. Brueggemann,** *Assemblies of God, Division of Foreign Missions*
**Roland K. Harrison** (deceased). *Wycliffe College*
**Gerald L. Mattingly.** *Johnson Bible College*

### DEUTERONOMY

**J. Gordon McConville,** *The Cheltenham and Gloucester College of Higher Education*
**Eugene H. Merrill,** *Dallas Theological Seminary*
**John A. Thompson,** *University of Melbourne*

## HISTORICAL BOOKS

**Barry J. Beitzel,** General Reviewer
*Trinity Evangelical Divinity School*

### JOSHUA/ JUDGES

**Carl E. Armerding,** *Schloss Mittersill Study Centre*
**Barry J. Beitzel,** *Trinity Evangelical Divinity School*
**Lawson Stone,** *Asbury Theological Seminary*

### 1 & 2 SAMUEL

**Barry J. Beitzel,** *Trinity Evangelical Divinity School*
**V. Philips Long,** *Covenant Theological Seminary*
**J. Robert Vannoy,** *Biblical Theological Seminary*

### 1 & 2 KINGS

**Bill T. Arnold,** *Asbury Theological Seminary*

**William H. Barnes,** *North Central University*
**Frederic W. Bush,** *Fuller Theological Seminary*

### 1 & 2 CHRONICLES

**Raymond B. Dillard** (deceased), *Westminster Theological Seminary*
**David A. Dorsey,** *Evangelical School of Theology*
**Terry Eves,** *Calvin College*

### EZRA/ NEHEMIAH/ ESTHER/ RUTH

**William C. Williams,** *Southern California College*
**Hugh G. M. Williamson,** *Oxford University*

## POETRY

**Tremper Longman III,** General Reviewer
*Westminster Theological Seminary*

### JOB

**August Konkel,** *Providence Theological Seminary*
**Tremper Longman III,** *Westminster Theological Seminary*
**Al Wolters,** *Redeemer College*

### PSALMS 1–75

**Mark D. Futato,** *Westminster Theological Seminary in California*
**Douglas Green,** *Westminster Theological Seminary*
**Richard Pratt,** *Reformed Theological Seminary*

### PSALMS 76–150

**David M. Howard Jr.,** *Trinity Evangelical Divinity School*
**Raymond C. Ortlund Jr.,** *Trinity Evangelical Divinity School*
**Willem VanGemeren,** *Trinity Evangelical Divinity School*

### PROVERBS

**Ted Hildebrandt,** *Grace College*
**Richard Schultz,** *Wheaton College*
**Raymond C. Van Leeuwen,** *Eastern College*

### ECCLESIASTES/ SONG OF SONGS

**Daniel C. Fredericks,** *Belhaven College*
**David Hubbard (deceased),** *Fuller Theological Seminary*
**Tremper Longman III,** *Westminster Theological Seminary*

## PROPHETS

**John N. Oswalt,** General Reviewer
*Asbury Theological Seminary*

ISAIAH
**John N. Oswalt,** *Asbury Theological Seminary*
**Gary Smith,** *Bethel Theological Seminary*
**John Walton,** *Moody Bible Institute*

JEREMIAH/ LAMENTATIONS
**G. Herbert Livingston,** *Asbury Theological Seminary*
**Elmer A. Martens,** *Mennonite Brethren Biblical Seminary*

EZEKIEL
**Daniel I. Block,** *The Southern Baptist Theological Seminary*
**David H. Engelhard,** *Calvin Theological Seminary*
**David Thompson,** *Asbury Theological Seminary*

DANIEL/ HAGGAI/ ZECHARIAH/ MALACHI
**Joyce Baldwin Caine** (deceased), *Trinity College, Bristol*
**Douglas Gropp,** *Catholic University of America*
**Roy Hayden,** *Oral Roberts School of Theology*

HOSEA–ZEPHANIAH
**Joseph Coleson,** *Nazarene Theological Seminary*
**Andrew Hill,** *Wheaton College*
**Richard Patterson,** *Professor Emeritus, Liberty University*

## GOSPELS AND ACTS

**Grant R. Osborne,** General Reviewer
*Trinity Evangelical Divinity School*

MATTHEW
**Craig Blomberg,** *Denver Conservative Baptist Seminary*
**Donald A. Hagner,** *Fuller Theological Seminary*
**David Turner,** *Grand Rapids Baptist Seminary*

MARK
**Robert Guelich** (deceased), *Fuller Theological Seminary*
**Grant R. Osborne,** *Trinity Evangelical Divinity School*

LUKE
**Darrell Bock,** *Dallas Theological Seminary*
**Scot McKnight,** *North Park College*
**Robert Stein,** *Bethel Theological Seminary*

JOHN
**Gary M. Burge,** *Wheaton College*
**Philip W. Comfort,** *Wheaton College*
**Marianne Meye Thompson,** *Fuller Theological Seminary*

## ACTS

**D. A. Carson,** *Trinity Evangelical Divinity School*
**William J. Larkin,** *Columbia Biblical Seminary*
**Roger Mohrlang,** *Whitworth College*

## LETTERS AND REVELATION

**Norman R. Ericson,** General Reviewer
*Wheaton College*

ROMANS/ GALATIANS
**Gerald Borchert,** *The Southern Baptist Theological Seminary*
**Douglas J. Moo,** *Trinity Evangelical Divinity School*
**Thomas R. Schreiner,** *Bethel Theological Seminary*

1 & 2 CORINTHIANS
**Joseph Alexanian,** *Trinity International University*
**Linda Belleville,** *North Park Theological Seminary*
**Douglas A. Oss,** *Central Bible College*
**Robert Sloan,** *Baylor University*

EPHESIANS–PHILEMON
**Harold W. Hoehner,** *Dallas Theological Seminary*
**Moises Silva,** *Gordon-Conwell Theological Seminary*
**Klyne Snodgrass,** *North Park Theological Seminary*

HEBREWS/ JAMES/ 1 & 2 PETER/ JUDE
**Peter Davids,** *Canadian Theological Seminary*
**Norman R. Ericson,** *Wheaton College*
**William Lane** (deceased), *Seattle Pacific University*
**J. Ramsey Michaels,** *S. W. Missouri State University*

1–3 JOHN/ REVELATION
**Greg Beale,** *Gordon-Conwell Theological Seminary*
**Robert Mounce,** *Whitworth College*
**M. Robert Mulholland Jr.,** *Asbury Theological Seminary*

## SPECIAL REVIEWERS

**F. F. Bruce** (deceased), *University of Manchester*
**Kenneth N. Taylor,** *Tyndale House Publishers*

## COORDINATING TEAM

**Mark R. Norton,** Managing Editor and O.T. Coordinating Editor
**Philip W. Comfort,** N.T. Coordinating Editor
**Ronald A. Beers,** Executive Director and Stylist
**Mark D. Taylor,** Director and Chief Stylist
**Daniel W. Taylor,** Consultant

*Senior Editorial Team*
Dr. Bruce B. Barton
Ronald A. Beers
Dr. James C. Galvin
LaVonne Neff
Linda Chaffee Taylor
David R. Veerman

*General Editor*
Ronald A. Beers

*Tyndale House Bible Editors*
Dr. Philip W. Comfort
Virginia Muir
Robert Brown
Del Lankford
Mark Norton
Steve Benson

*Book Introductions*
David R. Veerman

*Book Outlines, Blueprints,*
*Harmony*
Dr. James C. Galvin

*Megathemes*
Dr. Bruce B. Barton

*Map Development &*
*Computer Operation*
Linda Chaffee Taylor

*Color Map Consultant*
Dr. Barry Beitzel

*Charts & Diagrams*
Neil S. Wilson
Ronald A. Beers
David R. Veerman
Pamela York

*Dictionary/Concordance*
Dietrich Gruen

*Personality Profiles*
Neil S. Wilson

*Design & Development Team*
Dr. Bruce B. Barton
Ronald A. Beers
Dr. James C. Galvin
David R. Veerman

*Tyndale House Production*
Joan Major
Marlene Muller
Julee Schwarzburg
Jim Boltor
Linda Walz
Lois Rusch
Gwen Elliott

*Tyndale House Graphic Design*
Timothy R. Botts

*A Chronology of Bible Events*
*and World Events*
Dr. David Maas

*Theological Reviewers*

Dr. Kenneth S. Kantzer
*General Theological Reviewer*
Dean Emeritus and
Distinguished Professor of Bible
and Systematic Theology
Trinity Evangelical Divinity School

Dr. V. Gilbert Beers
President of
Scripture Press Ministries

Dr. Barry Beitzel
Associate Academic Dean
and Professor of Old Testament
and Semitic Languages
Trinity Evangelical Divinity School

Dr. Edwin A. Blum
Associate Professor of
Historical Theology
Dallas Theological Seminary

Dr. Geoffrey W. Bromiley
Professor
Fuller Theological Seminary

Dr. George K. Brushaber
President
Bethel College & Seminary

Dr. L. Russ Bush
Associate Professor
Philosophy & Religion
Southwestern Baptist
Theological Seminary

C. Donald Cole
Pastor, Moody Radio Network

Mrs. Naomi E. Cole
Speaker & Seminar Leader

Dr. Walter A. Elwell
Dean
Wheaton College Graduate School

Dr. Gerald F. Hawthorne
Professor of Greek
Wheaton College

Dr. Howard G. Hendricks
Professor-at-Large
Chairman
Center for Christian Leadership
Dallas Theological Seminary

Dr. Grant R. Osborne
Professor of New Testament
Trinity Evangelical Divinity School

A special thanks to the nationwide
staff of Youth for Christ/USA for
their suggestions and field testing,
and to the following additional
contributing writers: V. Gilbert
Beers, Neil Wilson, John Crosby,
Joan Young, Jack Crabtree, Philip
Craven, Bob Black, Bur Shilling,
Arthur Deyo, Annie Lafrentz,
Danny Sartin, William Hanawalt,
William Bonikowsky, Brian
Rathbun, Pamela Barden, Thomas
Stobie, Robert Arnold, Greg
Monaco, Larry Dunn, Lynn
Ziegenfuss, Mitzie Barton, Mari-
jean Hamilton, Larry Kreider, Gary
Dausey, William Roland, Kathy
Howell, Philip Steffeck, James
Coleman, Marty Grasley, O'Ann
Steere, Julia Amstutz.

A special thanks also to the following people whose personal counsel,
encouragement, and determination
helped make this product a reality:

Dr. Kenneth N. Taylor
Translator of *The Living Bible*
Chairman of the Board
Tyndale House Publishers, Inc.

Mark D. Taylor
President
Tyndale House Publishers, Inc.

Dr. Wendell C. Hawley
Senior Vice President
Editorial
Tyndale House Publishers, Inc.

Virginia Muir
Retired Assistant Editor-in-Chief
Tyndale House Publishers, Inc.

Richard R. Wynn
Youth for Christ/Area Director
for Asia and Pacific

Dr. Jay L. Kesler
President, Taylor University

# A CHRONOLOGY OF BIBLE EVENTS AND WORLD EVENTS

Creation
**undated**

Noah builds the ark
**undated**

Abraham born
**2166**

Abraham enters Canaan
**2091**

**2500 BC.**
Egyptians discover papyrus and ink for writing and build the first libraries; iron objects manufactured in the ancient Near East

**2400**
Egyptians import gold from other parts of Africa

**2331**
Semitic chieftain, Sargon, conquers Sumer to become first "world conqueror"

**2300**
Horses domesticated in Egypt; chickens domesticated in Babylon; bows & arrows used in wars

**2100**
Glass made by the Mesopotamians; ziggurats (like the tower of Babel) built in Mesopotamia; earliest discovered drug, ethyl alcohol, used to alleviate pain

Have you ever opened your Bible and asked the following:

- What does this passage really mean?
- How does it apply to my life?
- Why does some of the Bible seem irrelevant?
- What do these ancient cultures have to do with today?
- I love God; why can't I understand what he is saying to me through his Word?
- What's going on in the lives of these Bible people?

Many Christians do not read the Bible regularly. Why? Because in the pressures of daily living, they cannot find a connection between the timeless principles of Scripture and the ever-present problems of day-by-day living.

God urges us to apply his Word (Isaiah 42:23; 1 Corinthians 10:11; 2 Thessalonians 3:4), but too often we stop at accumulating Bible knowledge. This is why the *Life Application Study Bible* was developed—to show how to put into practice what we have learned.

Applying God's Word is a vital part of one's relationship with God; it is the evidence that we are obeying him. The difficulty in applying the Bible is not with

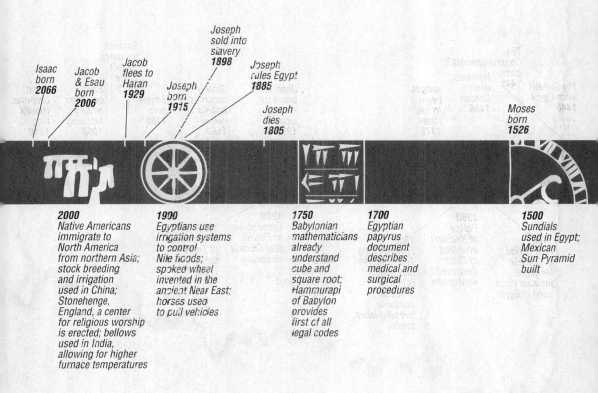

Isaac
born
**2066**

Jacob
& Esau
born
**2006**

Jacob
flees to
Haran
**1929**

Joseph
born
**1915**

Joseph
sold into
slavery
**1898**

Joseph
rules Egypt
**1885**

Joseph
dies
**1805**

Moses
born
**1526**

**2000**
Native Americans immigrate to North America from northern Asia; stock breeding and irrigation used in China; Stonehenge, England, a center for religious worship is erected; bellows used in India, allowing for higher furnace temperatures

**1900**
Egyptians use irrigation systems to control Nile floods; spoked wheel invented in the ancient Near East; horses used to pull vehicles

**1750**
Babylonian mathematicians already understand cube and square root; Hammurapi of Babylon provides first of all legal codes

**1700**
Egyptian papyrus document describes medical and surgical procedures

**1500**
Sundials used in Egypt; Mexican Sun Pyramid built

the Bible itself, but with the reader's inability to bridge the gap between the past and present, the conceptual and practical. When we don't or can't do this, spiritual dryness, shallowness, and indifference are the results.

The words of Scripture itself cry out to us, "And remember, it is a message to obey, not just to listen to. If you don't obey, you are only fooling yourself" (James 1:22). The *Life Application Study Bible* does just that. Developed by an interdenominational team of pastors, scholars, family counselors, and a national organization dedicated to promoting God's Word and spreading the gospel, the *Life Application Study Bible* took many years to complete, and all the work was reviewed by several renowned theologians under the directorship of Dr. Kenneth Kantzer.

The *Life Application Study Bible* does what a good resource Bible should—it helps you understand the context of a passage, gives important background and historical information, explains difficult words and phrases, and helps you see the interrelationships within Scripture. But it does much more. The *Life Application Study Bible* goes deeper into God's Word, helping you discover the timeless truth being communicated, see the relevance for your life, and make a personal application. While some study Bibles attempt application, over 75% of this Bible is application-oriented. The notes answer the questions, "So what?" and "What does this passage mean to me, my family, my friends, my job, my neighborhood, my church, my country?"

Imagine reading a familiar passage of Scripture and gaining fresh insight, as if it were the first time you had ever read it. How much richer your life would be if you left each Bible reading with a new perspective and a small change for the better. A small change every day adds up to a changed life—and that is the very purpose of Scripture.

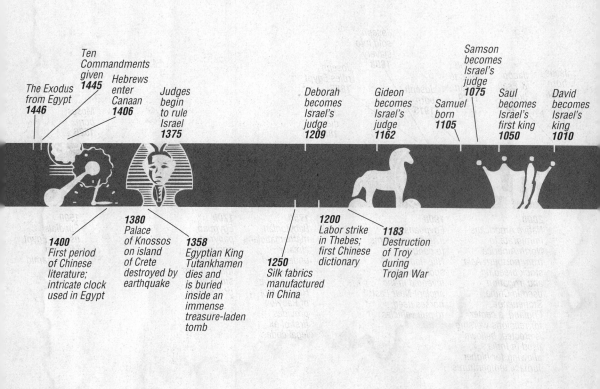

Ten Commandments given **1445**
Hebrews enter Canaan **1406**

The Exodus from Egypt **1446**

Judges begin to rule Israel **1375**

Deborah becomes Israel's judge **1209**

Gideon becomes Israel's judge **1162**

Samuel born **1105**

Samson becomes Israel's judge **1075**

Saul becomes Israel's first king **1050**

David becomes Israel's king **1010**

**1400** First period of Chinese literature; intricate clock used in Egypt

**1380** Palace of Knossos on island of Crete destroyed by earthquake

**1358** Egyptian King Tutankhamen dies and is buried inside an immense treasure-laden tomb

**1250** Silk fabrics manufactured in China

**1200** Labor strike in Thebes; first Chinese dictionary

**1183** Destruction of Troy during Trojan War

The best way to define application is to first determine what it is *not*. Application is *not* just accumulating knowledge. This helps us discover and understand facts and concepts. but it stops there. History is filled with philosophers who knew what the Bible said but failed to apply it to their lives, keeping them from believing and changing. Many think that understanding is the end goal of Bible study, but it is really only the beginning.

Application is *not* just illustration. Illustration only tells us how someone else handled a similar situation. While we may empathize with that person, we still have little direction for our personal situation.

Application is *not* just making a passage "relevant." Making the Bible relevant only helps us to see that the same lessons that were true in Bible times are true today; it does not show us how to apply them to the problems and pressures of our individual lives.

What, then, is application? Application begins by knowing and understanding God's Word and its timeless truths. *But you cannot stop there.* If you do, God's Word may not change your life, and it may become dull, difficult, tedious, and tiring. A good application focuses the truth of God's Word, shows the reader what to do about what is being read, and motivates the reader to respond to what God is teaching. All three are essential to application.

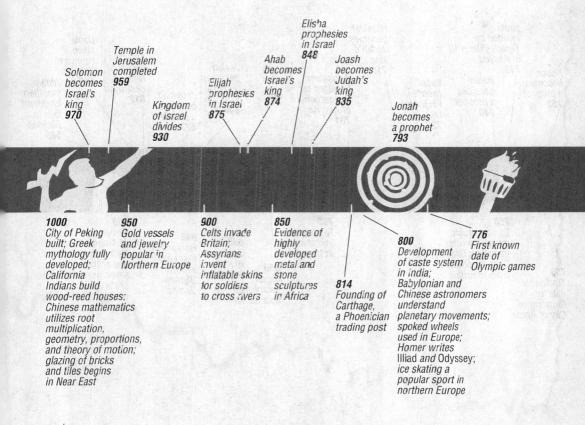

Solomon becomes Israel's king **970**

Temple in Jerusalem completed **959**

Kingdom of Israel divides **930**

Elijah prophesies in Israel **875**

Ahab becomes Israel's king **874**

Elisha prophesies in Israel **848**

Joash becomes Judah's king **835**

Jonah becomes a prophet **793**

**1000** City of Peking built; Greek mythology fully developed; California Indians build wood-reed houses; Chinese mathematics utilizes root multiplication, geometry, proportions, and theory of motion; glazing of bricks and tiles begins in Near East

**950** Gold vessels and jewelry popular in Northern Europe

**900** Celts invade Britain; Assyrians invent inflatable skins for soldiers to cross rivers

**850** Evidence of highly developed metal and stone sculptures in Africa

**814** Founding of Carthage, a Phoenician trading post

**800** Development of caste system in India; Babylonian and Chinese astronomers understand planetary movements; spoked wheels used in Europe; Homer writes Illiad and Odyssey; ice skating a popular sport in northern Europe

**776** First known date of Olympic games

Application is putting into practice what we already know (see Mark 4:24 and Hebrews 5:14) and answering the question, "So what?" by confronting us with the right questions and motivating us to take action (see 1 John 2:5, 6 and James 2:17). Application is deeply personal—unique for each individual. It is making a relevant truth a personal truth, and involves developing a strategy and action plan to live your life in harmony with the Bible. It is the Biblical "how to" of life.

You may ask, "How can your application notes be relevant to my life?" Each application note has three parts: (1) an *explanation* that ties the note directly to the Scripture passage and sets up the truth that is being taught, (2) the *bridge* that explains the timeless truth and makes it relevant for today, (3) the *application* that shows you how to take the timeless truth and apply it to your personal situation. No note, by itself, can apply Scripture directly to your life. It can only teach, direct, lead, guide, inspire, recommend, and urge. It can give you the resources and direction you need to apply the Bible; but only *you* can take these resources and put them into practice.

A good note, therefore, should not only give you knowledge and understanding, but point you to application. Before you buy any kind of resource Bible, you should evaluate the notes and ask the following questions: (1) Does the note contain enough information to help me understand the point of the Scripture passage? (2) Does the note assume I know too much? (3) Does the note avoid denominational bias? (4) Do the notes touch most of life's experiences? (5) Does the note help me *apply* God's Word?

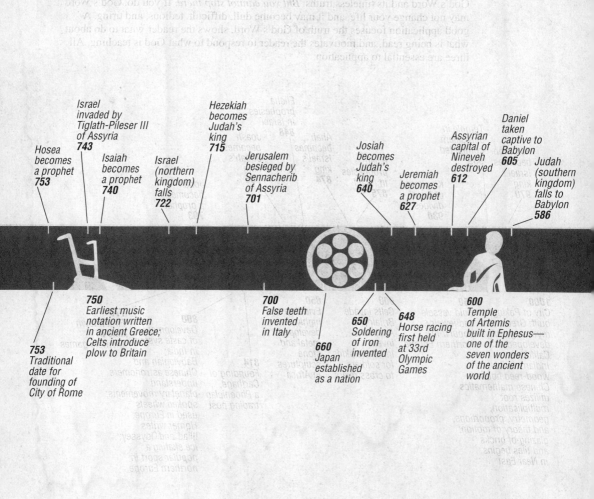

## NOTES

In addition to providing the reader with many application notes, the *Life Application Study Bible* offers several explanatory notes, which are notes that help the reader understand culture, history, context, difficult-to-understand passages, background, places, theological concepts, and the relationship of various passages in Scripture to other passages. Maps, charts, and diagrams are also found on the same page as the passages to which they relate. For an example of an application note, see Mark 15:47. For an example of an explanatory note, see Mark 11:1, 2. The abbreviation *ff* appears in some notes to indicate that the comments apply not only to the verse referenced, but to the following passage as well.

## BOOK INTRODUCTIONS

The Book Introductions are divided into several easy-to-find parts:

*Timeline.* This puts the Bible book into its historical setting. It lists the key events of each book and the date when they occurred. The alternative dates in parenthesis are based on a later dating of the Exodus.

*Vital Statistics.* This is a list of straight facts about the book—those pieces of information you need to know at a glance.

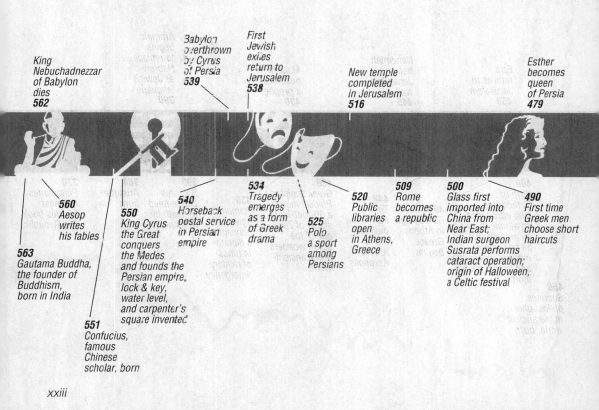

King
Nebuchadnezzar
of Babylon
dies
**562**

Babylon
overthrown
by Cyrus
of Persia
**539**

First
Jewish
exiles
return to
Jerusalem
**538**

New temple
completed
in Jerusalem
**516**

Esther
becomes
queen
of Persia
**479**

**563**
Gautama Buddha,
the founder of
Buddhism,
born in India

**560**
Aesop
writes
his fables

**551**
Confucius,
famous
Chinese
scholar, born

**550**
King Cyrus
the Great
conquers
the Medes
and founds the
Persian empire,
lock & key,
water level,
and carpenter's
square invented

**540**
Horseback
postal service
in Persian
empire

**534**
Tragedy
emerges
as a form
of Greek
drama

**525**
Polo
a sport
among
Persians

**520**
Public
libraries
open
in Athens,
Greece

**509**
Rome
becomes
a republic

**500**
Glass first
imported into
China from
Near East;
Indian surgeon
Susrata performs
cataract operation;
origin of Halloween,
a Celtic festival

**490**
First time
Greek men
choose short
haircuts

*Overview.* This is a summary of the book with general lessons and application that can be learned from the book as a whole.

*Blueprint.* This is the outline of the book. It is printed in easy-to-understand language and is designed for easy memorization. To the right of each main heading is a key lesson that is taught in that particular section.

*Megathemes.* This section gives the main themes of the Bible book, explains their significance, and then tells why they are still important for us today.

*Map.* This shows the key places found in that book and retells the story of the book from a geographical point of view.

## OUTLINE
The *Life Application Study Bible* has a new, custom-made outline that was designed specifically from an application point of view. Several unique features should be noted:

1. To avoid confusion and to aid memory work, each book outline has only three levels for headings. Main outline heads are marked with a capital letter. Subheads are marked by a number. Minor explanatory heads have no letter or number.

2. Each main outline head marked by a letter also has a brief paragraph below it summarizing the Bible text and offering a general application.

3. Parallel passages are listed where they apply in the Gospels.

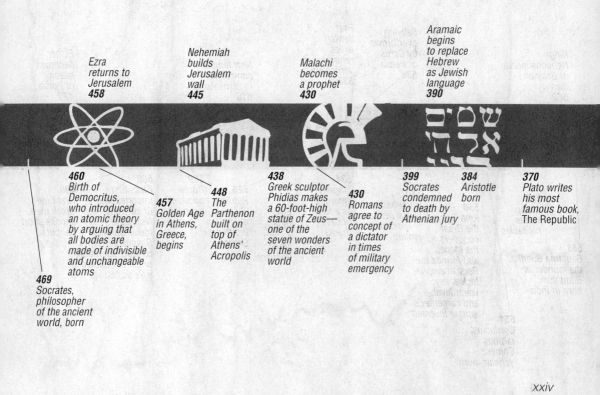

Ezra returns to Jerusalem **458**

Nehemiah builds Jerusalem wall **445**

Malachi becomes a prophet **430**

Aramaic begins to replace Hebrew as Jewish language **390**

**460** Birth of Democritus, who introduced an atomic theory by arguing that all bodies are made of indivisible and unchangeable atoms

**457** Golden Age in Athens, Greece, begins

**448** The Parthenon built on top of Athens' Acropolis

**438** Greek sculptor Phidias makes a 60-foot-high statue of Zeus—one of the seven wonders of the ancient world

**430** Romans agree to concept of a dictator in times of military emergency

**399** Socrates condemned to death by Athenian jury

**384** Aristotle born

**370** Plato writes his most famous book, The Republic

**469** Socrates, philosopher of the ancient world, born

## HARMONY OF THE GOSPELS

A harmony of the Gospels was developed specifically for this Bible. It is the first harmony that has ever been incorporated into the Bible text. Through a unique and simple numbering system (found both in the harmony feature and parenthesized in the subheads throughout the gospels), you can read any Gospel account and see just where you are in relation to other events in the life of Christ. The harmony feature is located after the Gospel of John and explained in detail there.

## PROFILE NOTES

Another unique feature of this Bible is the profiles of many Bible people, including their strengths and weaknesses, greatest accomplishments and mistakes, and key lessons from their lives. The profiles of these people are found in the Bible books where their stories occur.

## MAPS

The *Life Application Study Bible* has more maps than any other Bible. A thorough and comprehensive Bible atlas is built right into each Bible book. There are two kinds of maps: (1) A book introduction map, telling the story of that Bible book. (2) Thumb-nail maps in the notes, plotting most geographic movements in the Bible. In addition to these numerous black-and-white maps, there is an entirely new and comprehensive set of color maps and diagrams at the back of this Bible.

## CHARTS AND DIAGRAMS

Hundreds of charts and diagrams are included to help the reader better visualize difficult concepts or relationships. Most charts not only present the needed information but show the significance of the information as well.

*Temple of Jerusalem plundered by Antiochus IV*
**169**

*Judas Maccabeus begins a revolt against Antiochus IV*
**165**

**312**
Romans build first paved road, the "Appian Way," from Rome to Capua

**330**
Alexander the Great defeats the Persian empire

**241**
Romans conquer Sicily and add their first non-Italian territory to the Roman empire

**255**
Hebrew Old Testament translated into Greek and called the Septuagint

**215**
Great Wall of China built

**139**
Jews and astrologers banished from Rome

**102**
First Chinese ships reach east coast of India; ball bearings used in Danish cart wheels

**100**
Julius Caesar, first emperor of Rome, born

**51**
Cleopatra becomes last independent Egyptian ruler of the ancient world

**55**
Romans conquer England and make it part of Roman empire until A.D. 442

## CROSS-REFERENCES

A carefully organized cross-reference system in the margins of the Bible text helps the reader find related passages quickly. A cross-reference marked by two slashes (//) indicates that the cross-reference is a parallel passage, largely identical to the identified text in content and wording. A cross-reference marked by a dagger (†) indicates that the identified text either quotes from the cross-reference or the cross-referenced text quotes the identified text.

## TEXTUAL NOTES AND SECTIONAL HEADINGS

Directly related to the New Living Translation text, the textual notes examine such things as alternate translations, meaning of Hebrew and Greek terms, Old Testament quotations, and variant readings in ancient Biblical manuscripts. The NLT text also contains sectional headings in order to help you more easily understand the subject and content of each section. The headings throughout the gospels also include a parenthesized number, relating each passage to the Harmony of the Gospels feature.

## INDEX

This book contains a complete index to all the notes, charts, maps, and personality profiles. With its emphasis on application, it is helpful for group Bible study, sermon preparation, teaching, or personal study.

## DICTIONARY/CONCORDANCE

A concise concordance identifies terms of special interest and lists the important occurrences in context. Each word is followed by a brief definition.

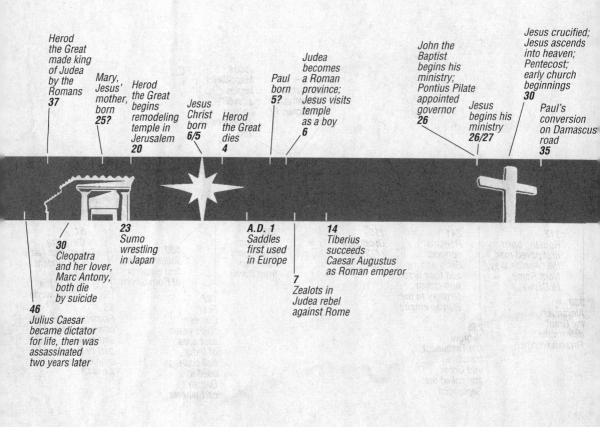

Herod the Great made king of Judea by the Romans
**37**

Mary, Jesus' mother, born
**25?**

Herod the Great begins remodeling temple in Jerusalem
**20**

Jesus Christ born
**6/5**

Herod the Great dies
**4**

Paul born
**5?**

Judea becomes a Roman province; Jesus visits temple as a boy
**6**

John the Baptist begins his ministry; Pontius Pilate appointed governor
**26**

Jesus begins his ministry
**26/27**

Jesus crucified; Jesus ascends into heaven; Pentecost; early church beginnings
**30**

Paul's conversion on Damascus road
**35**

**30**
Cleopatra and her lover, Marc Antony, both die by suicide

**46**
Julius Caesar became dictator for life, then was assassinated two years later

**23**
Sumo wrestling in Japan

**A.D. 1**
Saddles first used in Europe

**7**
Zealots in Judea rebel against Rome

**14**
Tiberius succeeds Caesar Augustus as Roman emperor

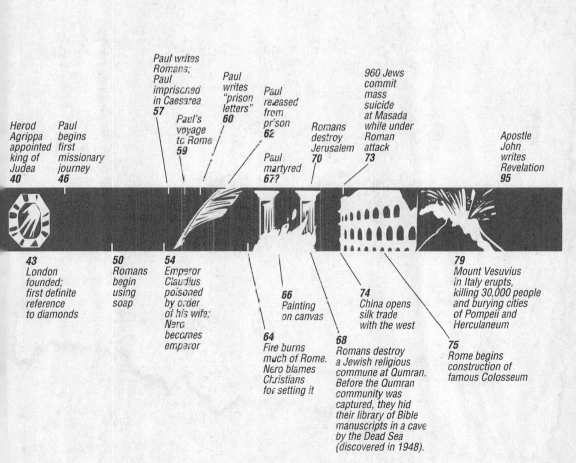

Paul writes
Romans;
Paul
imprisoned
in Caesarea
**57**

Paul
writes
"prison
letters"
**60**

Paul
released
from
prison
**62**

960 Jews
commit
mass
suicide
at Masada
while under
Roman
attack
**73**

Herod
Agrippa
appointed
king of
Judea
**40**

Paul
begins
first
missionary
journey
**46**

Paul's
voyage
to Rome
**59**

Paul
martyred
**67?**

Romans
destroy
Jerusalem
**70**

Apostle
John
writes
Revelation
**95**

**43**
London
founded;
first definite
reference
to diamonds

**50**
Romans
begin
using
soap

**54**
Emperor
Claudius
poisoned
by order
of his wife;
Nero
becomes
emperor

**66**
Painting
on canvas

**74**
China opens
silk trade
with the west

**79**
Mount Vesuvius
in Italy erupts,
killing 30,000 people
and burying cities
of Pompeii and
Herculaneum

**64**
Fire burns
much of Rome.
Nero blames
Christians
for setting it

**68**
Romans destroy
a Jewish religious
commune at Qumran.
Before the Qumran
community was
captured, they hid
their library of Bible
manuscripts in a cave
by the Dead Sea
(discovered in 1948).

**75**
Rome begins
construction of
famous Colosseum

Apostle John writes Revelation
95

960 Jews commit mass suicide at Masada while under Roman attack
73

Romans destroy Jerusalem
70

Paul released from prison
62

Paul writes Prison letters
60

Paul martyred
67?

Paul imprisoned in Caesarea
57

Paul's voyage to Rome
59

Paul writes Romans; Paul imprisoned in Caesarea
57

Herod Agrippa appointed first king of Judea
40?

79 Mount Vesuvius in Italy erupts, killing 20,000 people and burying cities of Pompeii and Herculaneum

75 Rome begins construction of famous Colosseum

74 China opens silk trade with the west

68 Romans destroy a Jewish religious commune at Qumran. Before the Qumran community was captured, they hid their library of Bible manuscripts in a cave by the Dead Sea (discovered in 1946-8)

58 Painting on canvas

64 Fire burns much of Rome. Nero blames Christians for setting it

54 Emperor Claudius poisoned by order of his wife. Nero becomes emperor

50 Romans begin using soap

43 London founded; first definite reference to diamonds

# THE OLD TESTAMENT

# GENESIS

## VITAL STATISTICS

**PURPOSE:**
To record God's creation of the world and his desire to have a people set apart to worship him

**AUTHOR:**
Moses

**TO WHOM WRITTEN:**
The people of Israel

**DATE WRITTEN:**
1450–1410 B.C.

**SETTING:**
The region presently known as the Middle East

**KEY VERSES:**
"So God created people in his own image; God patterned them after himself; male and female he created them" (1:27). " 'I will cause you to become the father of a great nation. I will bless you and make you famous, and I will make you a blessing to others. I will bless those who bless you and curse those who curse you. All the families of the earth will be blessed through you' " (12:2, 3).

**KEY PEOPLE:**
Adam, Eve, Noah, Abraham, Sarah, Isaac, Rebekah, Jacob, Joseph

BEGIN . . . start . . . commence . . . open. . . . There's something refreshing and optimistic about these words, whether they refer to the dawn of a new day, the birth of a child, the prelude of a symphony, or the first miles of a family vacation. Free of problems and full of promise, beginnings stir hope and imaginative visions of the future. *Genesis* means "beginnings" or "origin," and it unfolds the record of the beginning of the world, of human history, of family, of civilization, of salvation. It is the story of God's purpose and plan for his creation. As the book of beginnings, Genesis sets the stage for the entire Bible. It reveals the person and nature of God (Creator, Sustainer, Judge, Redeemer); the value and dignity of human beings (made in God's image, saved by grace, used by God in the world); the tragedy and consequences of sin (the Fall, separation from God, judgment); and the promise and assurance of salvation (covenant, forgiveness, promised Messiah).

God. That's where Genesis begins. All at once we see him creating the world in a majestic display of power and purpose, culminating with a man and woman made like himself (1:26, 27). But before long, sin entered the world, and Satan was unmasked. Bathed in innocence, creation was shattered by the Fall (the willful disobedience of Adam and Eve). Fellowship with God was broken, and evil began weaving its destructive web. In rapid succession, we read how Adam and Eve were expelled from the beautiful garden, their first son turned murderer, and evil bred evil until God finally destroyed everyone on earth except a small family led by Noah, the only godly person left.

As we come to Abraham on the plains of Canaan, we discover the beginning of God's covenant people and the broad strokes of his salvation plan: Salvation comes by faith, Abraham's descendants will be God's people, and the Savior of the world will come through this chosen nation. The stories of Isaac, Jacob, and Joseph that follow are more than interesting biographies. They emphasize the promises of God and the proof that he is faithful. The people we meet in Genesis are simple, ordinary people, yet through them, God did great things. These are vivid pictures of how God can and does use all kinds of people to accomplish his good purposes—even people like you and me.

Read Genesis and be encouraged. There is hope! No matter how dark the world situation seems, God has a plan. No matter how insignificant or useless you feel, God loves you and wants to use you in his plan. No matter how sinful and separated from God you are, his salvation is available. Read Genesis . . . and hope!

## THE BLUEPRINT

**A. THE STORY OF CREATION (1:1—2:4)**

God created the sky, seas, and land. He created the plants, animals, fish, and birds. But he created human beings in his own image. At times, others may treat us disrespectfully. But we can be certain of our dignity and worth because we have been created in the image of God.

**B. THE STORY OF ADAM (2:4—5:32)**
1. Adam and Eve
2. Cain and Abel
3. Adam's descendants

When Adam and Eve were created by God, they were without sin. But they became sinful when they disobeyed God and ate some fruit from the tree. Through Adam and Eve we learn about the destructive power of sin and its bitter consequences.

**C. THE STORY OF NOAH (6:1—11:32)**
1. The Flood
2. Repopulating the earth
3. The tower of Babel

Noah was spared from the destruction of the Flood because he obeyed God and built the boat. Just as God protected Noah and his family, he still protects those who are faithful to him today.

**D. THE STORY OF ABRAHAM (12:1—25:18)**
1. God promises a nation to Abram
2. Abram and Lot
3. God promises a son to Abram
4. Sodom and Gomorrah
5. Birth and near sacrifice of Isaac
6. Isaac and Rebekah
7. Abraham dies

Abraham was asked to leave his country, wander in Canaan, wait years for a son, and then sacrifice him as a burnt offering. Through these periods of sharp testing, Abraham remained faithful to God. His example teaches us what it means to live a life of faith.

**E. THE STORY OF ISAAC (25:19—28:9)**
1. Jacob and Esau
2. Isaac and Abimelech
3. Jacob gets Isaac's blessing

Isaac did not demand his own way. He did not resist when he was about to be sacrificed, and he gladly accepted a wife chosen for him by others. Like Isaac, we must learn to put God's will ahead of our own.

**F. THE STORY OF JACOB (28:10—36:43)**
1. Jacob starts a family
2. Jacob returns home

Jacob did not give up easily. He faithfully served Laban for over 14 years. Later, he wrestled with God. Although Jacob made many mistakes, his hard work teaches us about living a life of service for our Lord.

**G. THE STORY OF JOSEPH (37:1—50:26)**
1. Joseph is sold into slavery
2. Judah and Tamar
3. Joseph is thrown into prison
4. Joseph is placed in charge of Egypt
5. Joseph and his brothers meet in Egypt
6. Jacob's family moves to Egypt
7. Jacob and Joseph die in Egypt

Joseph was sold into slavery by his brothers and unjustly thrown into prison by his master. Through the life of Joseph, we learn that suffering, no matter how unfair, can develop strong character in us.

## MEGATHEMES

| THEME | EXPLANATION | IMPORTANCE |
| --- | --- | --- |
| *Beginnings* | Genesis explains the beginning of many important realities: the universe, the earth, people, sin, and God's plan of salvation. | Genesis teaches us that the earth is well made and good. People are special to God and unique. God creates and sustains all life. |
| *Disobedience* | People are always facing great choices. Disobedience occurs when people choose not to follow God's plan of living. | Genesis explains why people are evil: They choose to do wrong. Even great Bible heroes failed God and disobeyed. |
| *Sin* | Sin ruins people's lives. It happens when we disobey God. | Living God's way makes life productive and fulfilling. |

| Promises | God makes promises to help and protect people. This kind of promise is called a "covenant." | God kept his promises then, and he keeps them now. He promises to love us, accept us, forgive us. |
| Obedience | The opposite of sin is obedience. Obeying God restores our relationship to him. | The only way to enjoy the benefits of God's promises is to obey him. |
| Prosperity | Prosperity is deeper than mere material wealth. True prosperity and fulfillment come as a result of obeying God. | When people obey God, they find peace with him, with others, and with themselves. |
| Israel | God started the nation of Israel in order to have a dedicated people who would (1) keep his ways alive in the world, (2) proclaim to the world what he is really like, and (3) prepare the world for the birth of Christ. | God is looking for people today to follow him. We are to proclaim God's truth and love to all nations, not just our own. We must be faithful to carry out the mission God has given us. |

# KEY PLACES IN GENESIS

Modern names and boundaries are shown in gray.

God created the universe and the earth. Then he made man and woman, giving them a home in a beautiful garden. Unfortunately, Adam and Eve disobeyed God and were banished from the garden (3:23).

**1 Mountains of Ararat** Adam and Eve's sin brought sin into the human race. Years later, sin had run rampant and God decided to destroy the earth with a great flood. But Noah, his family, and two of each animal were safe in the boat. When the floods receded, the boat rested on the mountains of Ararat (8:4).

**2 Babel** People never learn. Again sin abounded, and the pride of the people led them to build a huge tower as a monument to their own greatness—obviously they had no thought of God. As punishment, God scattered the people by giving them different languages (11:8, 9).

**3 Ur of the Chaldeans** Abram, a descendant of Shem and father of the Hebrew nation, was born in this great city (11:27, 28).

**4 Haran** Terah, Abram, Lot, and Sarai left Ur and, following the fertile crescent of the Euphrates River, headed toward the land of Canaan. Along the way, they settled in the city of Haran for a while (11:31).

**5 Shechem** God urged Abram to leave Haran and go to a place where he would become the father of a great nation (12:1, 2). So Abram, Lot, and Sarai traveled to the land of Canaan and settled near a city called Shechem (12:6).

**6 Hebron** Abraham moved on to Hebron where he put down his deepest roots (13:18).

Abraham, Isaac, and Jacob all lived and were buried here.

**7 Beersheba** The well at Beersheba was a source of conflict between Abraham and King Abimelech and later became a sign of the oath that they swore there (21:31). Years later, as Isaac was moving from place to place, God appeared to him here and passed on to him the covenant he had made with his father, Abraham (26:23–25).

**8 Bethel** After deceiving his brother, Jacob left Beersheba and fled to Haran. Along the way, God revealed himself to Jacob in a dream and passed on the covenant he had made with Abraham and Isaac (28:10–22). Jacob lived in Haran, worked for Laban, and married Leah and Rachel (29:15–30). After a tense meeting with his brother, Esau, Jacob returned to Bethel (35:1).

**9 Egypt** Jacob had 12 sons, including Joseph, Jacob's favorite. Joseph's 10 older brothers grew jealous, until one day the brothers sold him to Ishmaelite traders going to Egypt. Eventually, Joseph rose from Egyptian slave to Pharaoh's "right-hand man," saving Egypt from famine. His entire family moved from Canaan to Egypt and settled there (46:3–7).

## A. THE STORY OF CREATION (1:1—2:4)

We sometimes wonder how our world came to be. But here we find the answer. God created the earth and everything in it, and made humans like himself. Although we may not understand the complexity of just how he did it, it is clear that God did create all life. This shows not only God's authority over humanity, but his deep love for all people.

*The Account of Creation*

**1:1**
Pss 89:11; 102:25
John 1:1-2

**1:2**
Ps 104:30
Isa 45:18

**1:3**
Pss 33:9; 104:2
2 Cor 4:6

**1** In the beginning God created* the heavens and the earth. 2The earth was empty, a formless mass cloaked in darkness. And the Spirit of God was hovering over its surface. 3Then God said, "Let there be light," and there was light. 4And God saw that it was good. Then he separated the light from the darkness. 5God called the light "day" and the darkness "night." Together these made up one day.

**1:1** Or *In the beginning when God created,* or *When God began to create.*

**BEGINNINGS**

The Bible does not discuss the subject of evolution. Rather, its worldview assumes God created the world. The biblical view of creation is not in conflict with science; rather, it is in conflict with any worldview that starts without a creator.

Equally committed and sincere Christians have struggled with the subject of beginnings and come to differing conclusions. This, of course, is to be expected because the evidence is very old and, due to the ravages of the ages, quite fragmented. Students of the Bible and of science should avoid polarizations and black/white thinking. Students of the Bible must be careful not to make the Bible say what it doesn't say, and students of science must not make science say what it doesn't say.

The most important aspect of the continuing discussion is not the *process* of creation, but the *origin* of creation. The world is not a product of blind chance and probability; God created it.

The Bible not only tells us that the world was created by God; more important, it tells us who this God is. It reveals God's personality, his character, and his plan for his creation. It also reveals God's deepest desire: to relate to and fellowship with the people he created. God took the ultimate step toward fellowship with us through his historic visit to this planet in the person of his Son, Jesus Christ. We can know in a very personal way this God who created the universe.

The heavens and the earth are here. We are here. God created all that we see and experience. The book of Genesis begins, "God created the heavens and the earth."

Here we begin the most exciting and fulfilling journey imaginable.

**1:1** The simple statement that God created the heavens and the earth is one of the most challenging concepts confronting the modern mind. The vast galaxy we live in is spinning at the incredible speed of 490,000 miles an hour. But even at this break-neck speed, our galaxy still needs 200 million years to make one rotation. And there are over one billion other galaxies just like ours in the universe.

Some scientists say that the number of stars in creation is equal to all the grains of all the sands on all the beaches of the world. Yet this complex sea of spinning stars functions with remarkable order and efficiency. To say that the universe "just happened" or "evolved" requires more faith than to believe that God is behind these amazing statistics. God truly did create a wonderful universe.

God did not *need* to create the universe; he *chose* to create it. Why? God is love, and love is best expressed toward something or someone else—so God created the world and people as an expression of his love. We should avoid reducing God's creation to merely scientific terms. Remember that God created the universe because he loves each of us.

**1:1ff** The creation story teaches us much about God and ourselves. First, we learn about God: (1) He is creative; (2) as the Creator, he is distinct from his creation; (3) he is eternal and in control of the world. We also learn about ourselves: (1) Since God chose to create us, we are valuable in his eyes; (2) we are more important than the animals. (See 1:28 for more on our role in the created order.)

**1:1ff** Just how did God create the earth? This is still a subject of great debate. Some say that there was a sudden explosion and the universe appeared. Others say that God started the process and the universe evolved over billions of years. Almost every ancient

religion has its own story to explain how the earth came to be. And almost every scientist has an opinion on the origin of the universe. But only the Bible shows one supreme God creating the earth out of his great love and giving all people a special place in it. We will never know all the answers to how God created the earth, but the Bible tells us that God did create it. That fact alone gives worth and dignity to all people.

**1:2** The statement "the earth was empty, a formless mass" provides the setting for the creation narrative that follows. During the second and third days of creation, God gave *form* to the universe; during the next three days, God *filled* the earth with living beings. The "darkness" was dispelled on the first day, when God created light.

**1:2** The image of the Spirit of God hovering over the earth's surface is similar to a mother bird caring for and protecting its young (see Deuteronomy 32:11, 12; Isaiah 31:5). God's Spirit was actively involved in the creation of the world (see Job 33:4; Psalm 104:30). God's care and protection are still active.

**1:3—2:7** How long did it take God to create the world? There are two basic views about the days of creation: (1) Each day was a literal 24-hour period; (2) each day represents an indefinite period of time (even millions of years).

The Bible does not say how long these time periods were. The real question, however, is not how long God took, but how he did it. God created the earth in an orderly fashion (he did not make plants before light), and he created men and women as unique beings capable of communication with him. No other part of creation can claim that remarkable privilege. It is not important how long it took God to create the world, whether a few days or a few billion years, but that he created it just the way he wanted it.

⁶And God said, "Let there be space between the waters, to separate water from water." ⁷And so it was. God made this space to separate the waters above from the waters below. ⁸And God called the space "sky." This happened on the second day.

⁹And God said, "Let the waters beneath the sky be gathered into one place so dry ground may appear." And so it was. ¹⁰God named the dry ground "land" and the water "seas." And God saw that it was good. ¹¹Then God said, "Let the land burst forth with every sort of grass and seed-bearing plant. And let there be trees that grow seed-bearing fruit. The seeds will then produce the kinds of plants and trees from which they came." And so it was. ¹²The land was filled with seed-bearing plants and trees, and their seeds produced plants and trees of like kind. And God saw that it was good. ¹³This all happened on the third day.

¹⁴And God said, "Let bright lights appear in the sky to separate the day from the night. They will be signs to mark off the seasons, the days, and the years. ¹⁵Let their light shine down upon the earth." And so it was. ¹⁶For God made two great lights, the sun and the moon, to shine down upon the earth. The greater one, the sun, presides during the day; the lesser one, the moon, presides through the night. He also made the stars. ¹⁷God set these lights in the heavens to light the earth, ¹⁸to govern the day and the night, and to separate the light from the darkness. And God saw that it was good. ¹⁹This all happened on the fourth day.

²⁰And God said, "Let the waters swarm with fish and other life. Let the skies be filled with birds of every kind." ²¹So God created great sea creatures and every sort of fish and every kind of bird. And God saw that it was good. ²²Then God blessed them, saying, "Let the fish multiply and fill the oceans. Let the birds increase and fill the earth." ²³This all happened on the fifth day.

²⁴And God said, "Let the earth bring forth every kind of animal—livestock, small animals, and wildlife." And so it was. ²⁵God made all sorts of wild animals, livestock, and small animals, each able to reproduce more of its own kind. And God saw that it was good.

²⁶Then God said, "Let us make people* in our image, to be like ourselves. They will

**1:26a** Hebrew *man;* also in 1:27.

**1:6**
Job 26:10
Ps 136:5-6
Isa 40:22
Jer 10:12

**1:7**
Job 38:8-11
Ps 148:4

**1:9**
Job 26:7
Ps 95:5
Jer 5:22
2 Pet 3:5

**1:10**
Pss 33:7; 95:5

**1:11**
Gen 2:9
Ps 104:14
Matt 6:30

**1:14**
Pss 74:16; 104:19

**1:16**
Pss 8:3; 19:1-6;
136:8-9
1 Cor 15:41

**1:18**
Jer 33:20, 25

**1:20**
Gen 2:19
Ps 146:6

**1:21**
Ps 104:25-28

**1:24**
Gen 2:19

**1:26**
Gen 5:1; 9:6
Ps 8:6-8
Acts 17:28-29

---

| | | **DAYS OF** |
| --- | --- | --- |
| First Day . . . . . . . | Light (so there was light and darkness) | **CREATION** |
| Second Day . . . . | Sky and water (waters separated) | |
| Third Day . . . . . . | Land and seas (waters gathered); vegetation | |
| Fourth Day . . . . . | Sun, moon, and stars (to govern the day and the night and to mark seasons, days, and years) | |
| Fifth Day . . . . . . . | Fish and birds (to fill the waters and the sky) | |
| Sixth Day . . . . . . | Animals (to fill the earth) Man and woman (to care for the earth and to commune with God) | |
| Seventh Day . . . . | God rested and declared all he had made to be very good | |

---

**1:6** The "space between the waters" was a separation between the sea and the mists of the skies.

**1:25** God saw that his work was good. People sometimes feel guilty for having a good time or for feeling good about an accomplishment. This need not be so. Just as God felt good about his work, we can be pleased with ours. However, we should not feel good about our work if God would not be pleased with it. What are you doing that pleases both you and God?

**1:26** Why does God use the plural form, "Let *us* make people in *our* image"? One view says this is a reference to the Trinity—God the Father, Jesus Christ his Son, and the Holy Spirit—all of whom are God. Another view is that the plural wording is used to denote majesty. Kings traditionally use the plural form in speaking of themselves. From Job 33:4 and Psalm 104:30, we do know that God's Spirit was present in the Creation. From Colossians 1:16 we know that Christ, God's Son, was at work in the Creation.

**1:26** In what ways are we made in God's image? God obviously did not create us exactly like himself because God has no physical body. Instead, we are reflections of God's glory. Some feel that our reason, creativity, speech, or self-determination is the image of God. More likely, it is our entire self that reflects the image of God. We will never be totally like God because he is our supreme Creator. But we do have the ability to reflect his character in our love, patience, forgiveness, kindness, and faithfulness.

Knowing that we are made in God's image and thus share many of his characteristics provides a solid basis for self-worth. Human worth is not based on possessions, achievements, physical attractiveness, or public acclaim. Instead, it is based on being made in God's image. Because we bear God's image, we can feel positive about ourselves. Criticizing or downgrading ourselves is criticizing what God has made and the abilities he has given us. Knowing that you are a person of worth helps you love God, know him personally, and make a valuable contribution to those around you.

be masters over all life—the fish in the sea, the birds in the sky, and all the livestock, wild animals,* and small animals."

**1:27**
†Matt 19:4
†Mark 10:6

27 So God created people in his own image;
    God patterned them after himself;
    male and female he created them.

**1:29**
Gen 9:3
Pss 104:13; 136:25

**1:30**
Ps 104:14; 145:15

**1:31**
Ps 104:24

28 God blessed them and told them, "Multiply and fill the earth and subdue it. Be masters over the fish and birds and all the animals." 29 And God said, "Look! I have given you the seed-bearing plants throughout the earth and all the fruit trees for your food. 30 And I have given all the grasses and other green plants to the animals and birds for their food." And so it was. 31 Then God looked over all he had made, and he saw that it was excellent in every way. This all happened on the sixth day.

**2:2**
Exod 20:11; 31:17
†Heb 4:4

**2:4**
Gen 1:3-31; 5:1;
6:9; 10:1
Job 38:4-11

**2** So the creation of the heavens and the earth and everything in them was completed. 2 On the seventh day, having finished his task, God rested from all his work. 3 And God blessed the seventh day and declared it holy, because it was the day when he rested from his work of creation.

    4 This is the account of the creation of the heavens and the earth.

### B. THE STORY OF ADAM (2:4—5:32)

Learning about our ancestors often helps us understand ourselves. Adam and Eve, our first ancestors, were the highlight of God's creation—the very reason God made the world. But they didn't always live the way God intended. Through their mistakes, we can learn important lessons about the way God wants us to live. Adam and Eve teach us much about the nature of sin and its consequences.

**2:5**
Gen 1:11

### 1. Adam and Eve

When the LORD God made the heavens and the earth, 5 there were no plants or grain growing on the earth, for the LORD God had not sent any rain. And no one was there

**1:26b** As in Syriac version; Hebrew reads all the earth.

---

**WHAT THE BIBLE SAYS ABOUT MARRIAGE**

| | |
|---|---|
| Genesis 2:18–24 | Marriage is God's idea |
| Genesis 24:58–60 | Commitment is essential to a successful marriage |
| Genesis 29:10-11 | Romance is important |
| Jeremiah 7:34 | Marriage holds times of great joy |
| Malachi 2:14, 15 | Marriage creates the best environment for raising children |
| Matthew 5:32 | Unfaithfulness breaks the bond of trust, the foundation of all relationships |
| Matthew 19:6 | Marriage is permanent |
| Romans 7:2, 3 | Ideally, only death should dissolve marriage |
| Ephesians 5:21–33 | Marriage is based on the principled practice of love, not on feelings |
| Ephesians 5:23–32 | Marriage is a living symbol of Christ and the church |
| Hebrews 13:4 | Marriage is good and honorable |

---

**1:27** God made both man and woman in his image. Neither man nor woman is made more in the image of God than the other. From the beginning the Bible places both man and woman at the pinnacle of God's creation. Neither sex is exalted, and neither is depreciated.

**1:28** To "be masters over" something is to have absolute authority and control over it. God has ultimate rule over the earth, and he exercises his authority with loving care. When God delegated some of his authority to the human race, he expected us to take responsibility for the environment and the other creatures that share our planet. We must not be careless and wasteful as we fulfill this charge. God was careful how he made this earth. We must not be careless about how we take care of it.

**1:31** God saw that all he had created was excellent in every way.

You are part of God's creation, and he is pleased with how he made you. If at times you feel worthless or of little value, remember that God made you for a good reason. You are valuable to him.

**2:2, 3** We live in an action-oriented world! There always seems to be something to do and no time to rest. Yet God demonstrated that rest is appropriate and right. If God himself rested from his work, then it should not amaze us that we also need rest. Jesus demonstrated this principle when he and his disciples left in a boat to get away from the crowds (see Mark 6:31, 32). Our times of rest refresh us for times of service.

**2:3** That God *blessed* the seventh day means that he set it apart for holy use. This act is picked up in the Ten Commandments (Exodus 20:1-17), in which God commanded the observance of the Sabbath.

to cultivate the soil. [6] But water came up out of the ground and watered all the land. [7] And the LORD God formed a man's body from the dust of the ground and breathed into it the breath of life. And the man became a living person.

[8] Then the LORD God planted a garden in Eden, in the east, and there he placed the man he had created. [9] And the LORD God planted all sorts of trees in the garden—beautiful trees that produced delicious fruit. At the center of the garden he placed the tree of life and the tree of the knowledge of good and evil.

[10] A river flowed from the land of Eden, watering the garden and then dividing into four branches. [11] One of these branches is the Pishon, which flows around the entire land of Havilah, where gold is found. [12] The gold of that land is exceptionally pure; aromatic resin and onyx stone are also found there. [13] The second branch is the Gihon, which flows around the entire land of Cush. [14] The third branch is the Tigris, which flows to the east of Asshur. The fourth branch is the Euphrates.

[15] The LORD God placed the man in the Garden of Eden to tend and care for it. [16] But the LORD God gave him this warning: "You may freely eat any fruit in the garden [17] except fruit from the tree of the knowledge of good and evil. If you eat of its fruit, you will surely die."

[18] And the LORD God said, "It is not good for the man to be alone. I will make a companion who will help him." [19] So the LORD God formed from the soil every kind of animal and bird. He brought them to Adam* to see what he would call them, and Adam chose a name for each one. [20] He gave names to all the livestock, birds, and wild animals. But still there was no companion suitable for him. [21] So the LORD God caused Adam to fall into a deep sleep. He took one of Adam's ribs* and closed up the place from which he had taken it. [22] Then the LORD God made a woman from the rib and brought her to Adam.

[23] "At last!" Adam exclaimed. "She is part of my own flesh and bone! She will be called 'woman,' because she was taken out of a man." [24] This explains why a man

2:19 Hebrew *the man,* and so throughout this chapter.    2:21 Or *took a part of Adam's side.*

**2:7**
Gen 3:19
Job 33:4
Ps 103:14
John 20:22
†1 Cor 15:45

**2:8**
Gen 3:23; 13:10
Ezek 28:13

**2:9**
Gen 3:22
Ezek 47:12
Rev 2:7; 22:2, 14

**2:10**
Rev 22:1, 17

**2:11**
Gen 25:18

**2:14**
Gen 15:18
Deut 1:7

**2:16**
Gen 3:1-3

**2:17**
Deut 30:15, 19-20
Rom 6:23
Jas 1:15

**2:18**
Gen 3:12
Prov 18:22

**2:22**
1 Cor 11:8-9
1 Tim 2:13

**2:23**
Gen 29:14
Eph 5:28-30

**2:24**
†Matt 19:5
†1 Cor 6:16
Eph 5:31

---

**2:7** "From the dust of the ground" implies that there is nothing fancy about the chemical elements making up our bodies. The body is a lifeless shell until God brings it alive with his "breath of life." When God removes his life-giving breath, our bodies once again return to dust. Therefore, our life and worth come from God's Spirit. Many boast of their achievements and abilities as though they were the originator of their own strengths. Others feel worthless because their abilities do not stand out. In reality, our worth comes not from our achievements but from the God of the universe, who chooses to give us the mysterious and miraculous gift of life. Value life, as he does.

**2:9** The name of the tree of the knowledge of good and evil implies that evil had already occurred, if not in the garden, then at the time of Satan's fall.

**2:9, 16, 17** Were the tree of life and the tree of the knowledge of good and evil real trees? Two views are often expressed:

(1) *The trees were real, but symbolic.* Eternal life with God was pictured as eating from the tree of life.

(2) *The trees were real, possessing special properties.* By eating the fruit from the tree of life, Adam and Eve could have had eternal life, enjoying a permanent relationship as God's children.

In either case, Adam and Eve's sin separated them from the tree of life and thus kept them from obtaining eternal life. Interestingly, the tree of life again appears in a description in Revelation 22 of people enjoying eternal life with God.

**2:15-17** God gave Adam responsibility for the garden and told him not to eat from the tree of the knowledge of good and evil. Rather than physically preventing him from eating, God gave Adam a choice and, thus, the possibility of choosing wrongly. God still gives us choices, and we, too, often choose wrongly. These wrong choices may cause us pain, but they can help us learn and grow and make better choices in the future. Living with the consequences of our choices teaches us to think and choose more carefully.

**2:16, 17** Why would God place a tree in the garden and then forbid Adam to eat from it? God wanted Adam to obey, but God gave Adam the freedom to choose. Without choice, Adam would have been like a prisoner, and his obedience would have been hollow. The two trees provided an exercise in choice, with rewards for choosing to obey and sad consequences for choosing to disobey. When you are faced with the choice, always choose to obey God.

**2:18-24** God's creative work was not complete until he made woman. He could have made her from the dust of the ground, as he made man. God chose, however, to make her from the man's flesh and bone. In so doing, he illustrated for us that in marriage man and woman symbolically are united into one. This is a mystical union of the couple's hearts and lives. Throughout the Bible, God treats this special partnership seriously. If you are married or planning to be married, are you willing to keep the commitment that makes the two of you one? The goal in marriage should be more than friendship; it should be oneness.

**2:21-23** God forms and equips men and women for various tasks, but all these tasks lead to the same goal—honoring God. Man gives life to woman; woman gives life to the world. Each role carries exclusive privileges; there is no room for thinking that one sex is superior to the other.

**2:24** God gave marriage as a gift to Adam and Eve. They were created perfect for each other. Marriage was not just for convenience, nor was it brought about by any culture. It was instituted by God and has three basic aspects: (1) the man leaves his parents and, in a public act, promises himself to his wife; (2) the man and woman are joined together by taking responsibility for each other's welfare and by loving the mate above all others; (3) the two are united into one in the intimacy and commitment of sexual union that is reserved for marriage. Strong marriages include all three of these aspects.

**2:25**
Gen 3:7, 10-11

leaves his father and mother and is joined to his wife, and the two are united into one. 25 Now, although Adam and his wife were both naked, neither of them felt any shame.

### Adam and Eve Sin

**3:1**
2 Cor 11:3
Rev 12:9; 20:2

**3** Now the serpent was the shrewdest of all the creatures the LORD God had made. "Really?" he asked the woman. "Did God really say you must not eat any of the fruit in the garden?"

---

We can hardly imagine what it must have been like to be the first and only person on earth. It's one thing for us to be lonely; it was another for Adam, who had never known another human being. He missed much that makes us who we are—he had no childhood, no parents, no family or friends. He had to learn to be human on his own. Fortunately God didn't let him struggle too long before presenting him with an ideal companion and mate, Eve. Theirs was a complete, innocent, and open oneness, without a hint of shame.

One of Adam's first conversations with his delightful new companion must have been about the rules of the garden. Before God made Eve, he had already given Adam complete freedom in the garden, with the responsibility to tend and care for it. But one tree was off-limits, the tree of the knowledge of good and evil. Adam would have told Eve all about this. She knew, when Satan approached her, that the tree's fruit was not to be eaten. However, she decided to eat the forbidden fruit. Then she offered some to Adam. At that moment, the fate of creation was on the line. Sadly, Adam didn't pause to consider the consequences. He went ahead and ate.

In that moment of small rebellion on something large, beautiful, and free was shattered . . . God's perfect creation. Adam was separated from God by his desire to act on his own. The effect on a plate glass window is the same whether a pebble or a boulder is hurled at it—the thousands of fragments can never be regathered.

In the case of Adam's sin, however, God already had a plan in motion to overcome the effects of the rebellion. The entire Bible is the story of how that plan unfolds, ultimately leading to God's own visit to earth through his Son, Jesus. His sinless life and death made it possible for God to offer forgiveness to all who want it. Our small and large acts of rebellion prove that we are descendants of Adam. Only by asking forgiveness of Jesus Christ can we become children of God.

| | |
|---|---|
| **Strengths and accomplishments** | ▪ The first zoologist—namer of animals<br>▪ The first landscape architect, placed in the garden to care for it<br>▪ Father of the human race<br>▪ The first person made in the image of God, and the first human to share an intimate personal relationship with God |
| **Weaknesses and mistakes** | ● Avoided responsibility and blamed others; chose to hide rather than to confront; made excuses rather than admitting the truth<br>● Greatest mistake: teamed up with Eve to bring sin into the world |
| **Lessons from his life** | ● As Adam's descendants, we all reflect to some degree the image of God<br>● God wants people who, though free to do wrong, choose instead to love him<br>● We should not blame others for our faults<br>● We cannot hide from God |
| **Vital statistics** | ● Where: Garden of Eden<br>● Occupation: Caretaker, gardener, farmer<br>● Relatives: Wife: Eve. Sons: Cain, Abel, Seth. Numerous other children. The only man who never had an earthly mother or father |
| **Key verses** | "It was the woman you gave me who brought me the fruit, and I ate it" (Genesis 3:12). "Everyone dies because all of us are related to Adam, the first man. But all who are related to Christ, the other man, will be given new life" (1 Corinthians 15:22). |

Adam's story is told in Genesis 1:26—5:5. He is also mentioned in 1 Chronicles 1:1; Luke 3:38; Romans 5:14; 1 Corinthians 15:22, 45; 1 Timothy 2:13, 14.

---

**2:25** Have you ever noticed how a little child can run naked through a room full of strangers without embarrassment? He is not aware of his nakedness, just as Adam and Eve were not embarrassed in their innocence. But after Adam and Eve sinned, shame and awkwardness followed, creating barriers between themselves and God. We often experience these same barriers in marriage. Ideally a husband and wife have no barriers, feeling no embarrassment in exposing themselves to each other or to God. But, like

Adam and Eve (3:7), we put on fig leaves (barriers) because we have areas we don't want our spouse, or God, to know about. Then we hide, just as Adam and Eve hid from God. In marriage, lack of spiritual, emotional, and intellectual intimacy usually precedes a breakdown of physical intimacy. In the same way, when we fail to expose our secret thoughts to God, we break our lines of communication with him.

2"Of course we may eat it," the woman told him. 3"It's only the fruit from the tree at the center of the garden that we are not allowed to eat. God says we must not eat it or even touch it, or we will die."

**3:3**
Gen 2:17
Exod 19:12

4"You won't die!" the serpent hissed. 5"God knows that your eyes will be opened when you eat it. You will become just like God, knowing everything, both good and evil."

**3:4**
John 8:44
2 Cor 11:3

**3:5**
Isa 14:14
Ezek 28:2

6The woman was convinced. The fruit looked so fresh and delicious, and it would make her so wise! So she ate some of the fruit. She also gave some to her husband, who was with her. Then he ate it, too. 7At that moment, their eyes were opened, and they suddenly felt shame at their nakedness. So they strung fig leaves together around their hips to cover themselves.

**3:6**
2 Cor 11:3
1 Tim 2:14
Jas 1:14-15
1 John 2:16

8Toward evening they heard the LORD God walking about in the garden, so they hid themselves among the trees. 9The LORD God called to Adam,* "Where are you?"

**3:8**
Lev 26:12
Deut 23:14

**3:9** Hebrew *the man,* and so throughout this chapter.

---

**3:1** Disguised as a shrewd serpent, Satan came to tempt Eve. Satan at one time was an angel who rebelled against God and was thrown out of heaven. As a created being, Satan has definite limitations. Although he is trying to tempt everyone away from God, he will not be the final victor. In 3:14, 15, God promises that Satan will be crushed by one of the woman's offspring, the Messiah.

**3:1-6** Why does Satan tempt us? Temptation is Satan's invitation to give in to his kind of life and give up on God's kind of life. Satan tempted Eve and succeeded in getting her to sin. Ever since then, he's been busy getting people to sin. He even tempted Jesus (Matthew 4:1-11). But Jesus did not sin!

How could Eve have resisted temptation? By following the same guidelines we can follow. First, we must realize that *being tempted* is not a sin. We have not sinned until we *give in* to the temptation. Then, to resist temptation, we must (1) pray for strength to resist, (2) run, sometimes literally, and (3) say no when confronted with what we know is wrong. James 1:12 tells of the blessings and rewards for those who don't give in when tempted.

**3:1-6** The serpent, Satan, tempted Eve by getting her to doubt God's goodness. He implied that God was strict, stingy, and selfish for not wanting Eve to share his knowledge of good and evil. Satan made Eve forget all that God had given her and, instead, focus on the one thing she couldn't have. We fall into trouble, too, when we dwell on the few things we don't have rather than on the countless things God has given us. The next time you are feeling sorry for yourself and what you don't have, consider all you *do* have and thank God. Then your doubts won't lead you into sin.

**3:5** Adam and Eve got what they wanted: an intimate knowledge of both good and evil. But they got it by doing evil, and the results were disastrous. Sometimes we have the illusion that freedom is doing anything we want. But God says that true freedom comes from obedience and knowing what *not* to do. The restrictions he gives us are for our good, helping us avoid evil. We have the freedom to walk in front of a speeding car, but we don't need to be hit to realize it would be foolish to do so. Don't listen to Satan's temptations. You don't have to do evil to gain more experience and learn more about life.

**3:5** Satan used a sincere motive to tempt Eve: "You will become just like God." It wasn't wrong of Eve to want to be like God. To become more like God is humanity's highest goal. It is what we are supposed to do. But Satan misled Eve concerning the right way to accomplish this goal. He told her that she could become more like God by defying God's authority, by taking God's place and deciding for herself what was best for her life. In effect, he told her to become her own god.

But to become like God is not the same as trying to become God. Rather, it is to reflect his characteristics and to recognize his authority over your life. Like Eve, we often have a worthy goal but try to achieve it in the wrong way. We act like a political candidate

who pays off an election judge to be "voted" into office. When he does this, serving the people is no longer his highest goal.

Self-exaltation leads to rebellion against God. As soon as we begin to leave God out of our plans, we are placing ourselves above him. This is exactly what Satan wants us to do.

**3:6** Satan tried to make Eve think that sin is good, pleasant, and desirable. A knowledge of both good and evil seemed harmless to her. People usually choose wrong things because they have become convinced that those things are good, at least for themselves. Our sins do not always appear ugly to us, and the pleasant sins are the hardest to avoid. So prepare yourself for the attractive temptations that may come your way. We cannot always prevent temptation, but there is always a way of escape (1 Corinthians 10:13). Use God's Word and God's people to help you stand against it.

**3:6, 7** Notice what Eve did: She looked, she took, she ate, and she gave. The battle is often lost at the first look. Temptation often begins by simply seeing something you want. Are you struggling with temptation because you have not learned that looking is the first step toward sin? You would win over temptation more often if you followed Paul's advice to run from those things that produce evil thoughts (2 Timothy 2:22).

**3:6, 7** One of the realities of sin is that its effects spread. After Eve sinned, she involved Adam in her wrongdoing. When we do something wrong, often we try to relieve our guilt by involving someone else. Like toxic waste spilled in a river, sin swiftly spreads. Recognize and confess your sin to God before you are tempted to pollute those around you.

**3:7, 8** After sinning, Adam and Eve felt guilt and embarrassment over their nakedness. Their guilty feelings made them try to hide from God. A guilty conscience is a warning signal God placed inside you that goes off when you've done wrong. The worst step you can take is to eliminate the guilty feelings without eliminating the cause. That would be like using a painkiller but not treating the disease. Be glad those guilty feelings are there. They make you aware of your sin so you can ask God's forgiveness and then correct your wrongdoing.

**3:8** The thought of two humans covered with fig leaves trying to hide from the all-seeing, all-knowing God is humorous. How could they be so silly as to think they could actually hide? Yet we do the same, acting as though God doesn't know what we're doing. Have the courage to share all you do and think with him. And don't try to hide—it can't be done. Honesty will strengthen your relationship with God.

**3:8, 9** These verses show God's desire to have fellowship with us. They also show why we are afraid to have fellowship with him. Adam and Eve hid from God when they heard him approaching. God wanted to be with them, but because of their sin, they were afraid to show themselves. Sin had broken their close relationship with God, just as it has broken ours.

**5:21**
1 Chr 1:3
Luke 3:37

**5:24**
2 Kgs 2:1, 11
Ps 73:24
Heb 11:5

**5:25**
1 Chr 1:3
Luke 3:36

**5:29**
Gen 3:17
1 Chr 1:3
Luke 3:36
Rom 8:20

**5:32**
Gen 7:6; 9:18

<sup>21</sup>When Enoch was 65 years old, his son Methuselah was born. <sup>22</sup>After the birth of Methuselah, Enoch lived another 300 years in close fellowship with God, and he had other sons and daughters. <sup>23</sup>Enoch lived 365 years in all. <sup>24</sup>He enjoyed a close relationship with God throughout his life. Then suddenly, he disappeared because God took him.

<sup>25</sup>When Methuselah was 187 years old, his son Lamech was born. <sup>26</sup>After the birth of Lamech, Methuselah lived another 782 years, and he had other sons and daughters. <sup>27</sup>He died at the age of 969.

<sup>28</sup>When Lamech was 182 years old, his son Noah was born. <sup>29</sup>Lamech named his son Noah,* for he said, "He will bring us relief from the painful labor of farming this ground that the LORD has cursed." <sup>30</sup>After the birth of Noah, Lamech lived 595 years, and he had other sons and daughters. <sup>31</sup>He died at the age of 777.

<sup>32</sup>By the time Noah was 500 years old, he had three sons: Shem, Ham, and Japheth.

## C. THE STORY OF NOAH (6:1—11:32)

Earth was no longer the perfect paradise that God had intended. It is frightening to see how quickly all of humanity forgot about God. Incredibly, in all the world, only one man and his family still worshiped God. That man was Noah. Because of his faithfulness and obedience, God saved him and his family from a vast flood that destroyed every other human being on earth. This section shows us how God hates sin and judges those who enjoy it.

### 1. The Flood

**6:1**
Gen 1:28

**6:3**
Ps 78:39
1 Pet 3:20

**6** When the human population began to grow rapidly on the earth, <sup>2</sup>the sons of God saw the beautiful women of the human race and took any they wanted as their wives. <sup>3</sup>Then the LORD said, "My Spirit will not put up with humans for such a long

**5:29** *Noah* sounds like a Hebrew term that can mean "relief" or "comfort."

---

Abel was the second child born into the world, but the first one to obey God. All we know about this man is that his parents were Adam and Eve, he was a shepherd, he presented pleasing offerings to God, and his short life was ended at the hands of his jealous older brother, Cain.

The Bible doesn't tell us why God liked Abel's gift and disliked Cain's, but both Cain and Abel knew what God expected. Only Abel obeyed. Throughout history, Abel is remembered for his obedience and faith (Hebrews 11:4), and he is called "righteous" (Matthew 23:35).

The Bible is filled with God's general guidelines and expectations for our lives. It is also filled with more specific directions. Like Abel, we must obey regardless of the cost and trust God to make things right.

| | |
|---|---|
| **Strengths and accomplishments** | • First member of the Hall of Faith in Hebrews 11<br>• First shepherd<br>• First martyr for truth (Matthew 23:35) |
| **Lessons from his life** | • God hears those who come to him<br>• God recognizes the innocent person and sooner or later punishes the guilty |
| **Vital statistics** | • Where: Just outside of Eden<br>• Occupation: Shepherd<br>• Relatives: Parents: Adam and Eve. Brother: Cain |
| **Key verse** | "It was by faith that Abel brought a more acceptable offering to God than Cain did. God accepted Abel's offering to show that he was a righteous man. And although Abel is long dead, he still speaks to us because of his faith" (Hebrews 11:4). |

Abel's story is told in Genesis 4:1-8. He is also mentioned in Matthew 23:35; Luke 11:51; Hebrews 11:4 and 12:24.

---

**5:25-27** How did these people live so long? Some believe that the ages listed here were lengths of family dynasties rather than ages of individual men. Those who think these were actual ages offer three explanations: (1) The human race was more genetically pure in this early time period, so there was less disease to shorten life spans; (2) no rain had yet fallen on the earth, and the expanse of water "above" (1:7) kept out harmful cosmic rays and shielded people from environmental factors that hasten aging; (3) God gave people longer lives so they would have time to "fill the earth" (1:28).

**6:1-4** Some people believe that the "sons of God" were fallen angels (see 2 Peter 2:4-6; Jude 6-7). Others believe this could not have happened (see Matthew 22:30; Mark 12:25) and that this phrase refers to the descendants of Seth who intermarried with Cain's descendants. Either way, the result would have weakened the good influence of the faithful and increased moral depravity in the world, resulting in an explosion of evil.

time, for they are only mortal flesh. In the future, they will live no more than 120 years."

$^4$In those days, and even afterward, giants* lived on the earth, for whenever the sons of God had intercourse with human women, they gave birth to children who became the heroes mentioned in legends of old.

$^5$Now the LORD observed the extent of the people's wickedness, and he saw that all their thoughts were consistently and totally evil. $^6$So the LORD was sorry he had ever made them. It broke his heart. $^7$And the LORD said, "I will completely wipe out this human race that I have created. Yes, and I will destroy all the animals and birds, too. I am sorry I ever made them." $^8$But Noah found favor with the LORD.

$^9$This is the history of Noah and his family. Noah was a righteous man, the only blameless man living on earth at the time. He consistently followed God's will and enjoyed a close relationship with him. $^{10}$Noah had three sons: Shem, Ham, and Japheth.

$^{11}$Now the earth had become corrupt in God's sight, and it was filled with violence. $^{12}$God observed all this corruption in the world, and he saw violence and depravity everywhere. $^{13}$So God said to Noah, "I have decided to destroy all living creatures, for the earth is filled with violence because of them. Yes, I will wipe them all from the face of the earth!

$^{14}$"Make a boat* from resinous wood and seal it with tar, inside and out. Then construct decks and stalls throughout its interior. $^{15}$Make it 450 feet long, 75 feet wide, and 45 feet high.* $^{16}$Construct an opening all the way around the boat, 18 inches* below the roof. Then put three decks inside the boat—bottom, middle, and upper—and put a door in the side.

$^{17}$"Look! I am about to cover the earth with a flood that will destroy every living thing. Everything on earth will die! $^{18}$But I solemnly swear to keep you safe in the boat, with your wife and your sons and their wives. $^{19}$Bring a pair of every kind of animal—a male and a female—into the boat with you to keep them alive during the flood. $^{20}$Pairs of each kind of bird and each kind of animal, large and small alike, will come to you to be kept alive. $^{21}$And remember, take enough food for your family and for all the animals."

$^{22}$So Noah did everything exactly as God had commanded him.

**6:4** Num 13:33
**6:5** Ps 14:1-3
**6:6** Exod 32:14
Num 23:19
1 Sam 15:11, 35
2 Sam 24:16
**6:7** Deut 29:20
**6:8** Exod 33:17
**6:9** Job 1:1
Ezek 14:14
**6:11** Deut 31:29
Judg 2:19
Ezek 8:17
**6:12** Ps 14:1-3
**6:13** Isa 34:1-4
Ezek 7:2-3
**6:14** Exod 2:3
1 Pet 3:20
**6:17** Ps 29:10
2 Pet 2:5
**6:18** Gen 9:9-16; 17:7; 19:12
**6:20** Gen 7:3
**6:21** Gen 1:29
**6:22** Gen 7:5
Exod 40:16

**6:4** Hebrew *Nephilim.*   **6:14** Traditionally rendered *an ark.*   **6:15** Hebrew *300 cubits* [135 meters] *long, 50 cubits* [22.5 meters] *wide, and 30 cubits* [13.5 meters] *high.*   **6:16** Hebrew *1 cubit* [45 centimeters].

---

**6:3** "They will live no more than 120 years" has been interpreted by some commentators to mean that God was allowing the people of Noah's day 120 years to change their sinful ways. God shows his great patience with us as well. He is giving us time to quit living our way and begin living his way, the way he shows us in his Word. While 120 years seems like a long time, eventually the time ran out, and the floodwaters swept across the earth. Your time also may be running out. Turn to God to forgive your sins. You can't see the stopwatch of God's patience, and there is no bargaining for additional time.

**6:4** These "giants" were people probably nine or ten feet tall. This same Hebrew term was used to name a tall race of people in Numbers 13:33. Goliath, who was nine feet tall, appears in 1 Samuel 17. The giants used their physical advantage to oppress the people around them.

**6:6, 7** Does this mean that God regretted creating humanity? Was he admitting he made a mistake? No, God does not change his mind (1 Samuel 15:29). Instead, he was expressing sorrow for what the people had done to themselves, as a parent might express sorrow over a rebellious child. God was sorry that the people chose sin and death instead of a relationship with him.

**6:6-8** The people's sin grieved God. Our sins break God's heart as much as sin did in Noah's day. Noah, however, pleased God, although he was far from perfect. We can follow Noah's example and find "favor with the LORD" in spite of the sin that surrounds us.

**6:9** To say that Noah was "righteous" and "blameless" does not mean that he never sinned (the Bible records one of his

sins in 9:20ff). Rather, it means that he wholeheartedly loved and obeyed God. For a lifetime he walked step by step in faith as a living example to his generation. Like Noah, we live in a world filled with evil. Are we influencing others or being influenced by them?

**6:15** The boat Noah built was no canoe! Picture yourself building a boat the length of one and a half football fields and as high as a four-story building. The boat was exactly six times longer than it was wide—the same ratio used by modern shipbuilders. This huge boat was probably built miles from any body of water by only a few faithful men who believed God's promises and obeyed his commands.

**6:18** When God said, "I solemnly swear," he was making a promise or a *covenant.* This is a familiar theme in Scripture— God making covenants with his people. How reassuring it is to know God's covenant is established with us. He is still our salvation, and we are kept safe through our relationship with him. For more on covenants, see 9:8-17; 12:1-3; and 15:17-21.

**6:22** Noah got right to work when God told him to build the huge boat. Other people must have been warned about the coming disaster (1 Peter 3:20), but apparently they did not expect it to happen. Today things haven't changed much. Each day thousands of people are warned of God's inevitable judgment, yet most of them don't really believe it will happen. Don't expect people to welcome or accept your message of God's coming judgment on sin. Those who don't believe in God will deny his judgment and try to get you to deny God as well. But remember God's promise to Noah to keep him safe. This can inspire you to trust God for deliverance in the judgment that is sure to come.

*The Flood Covers the Earth*

**7:1**
Gen 6:18
Matt 24:38
Luke 17:26-27
Heb 11:7
1 Pet 3:20

**7:2**
Lev 11:1-47
Deut 14:3-20
Ezek 44:23

**7:4**
Gen 6:7, 13

**7:6**
Gen 5:32

**7:7**
Gen 6:18

**7:9**
Gen 6:22

**7:11**
Ps 78:23
Ezek 26:19
Mal 3:10

**7:13**
1 Pet 3:20
2 Pet 2:5

**7** Finally, the day came when the LORD said to Noah, "Go into the boat with all your family, for among all the people of the earth, I consider you alone to be righteous. ²Take along seven pairs of each animal that I have approved for eating and for sacrifice, and take one pair of each of the others. ³Then select seven pairs of every kind of bird. There must be a male and a female in each pair to ensure that every kind of living creature will survive the flood. ⁴One week from today I will begin forty days and forty nights of rain. And I will wipe from the earth all the living things I have created."

⁵So Noah did exactly as the LORD had commanded him. ⁶He was 600 years old when the flood came, ⁷and he went aboard the boat to escape—he and his wife and his sons and their wives. ⁸With them were all the various kinds of animals—those approved for eating and sacrifice and those that were not—along with all the birds and other small animals. ⁹They came into the boat in pairs, male and female, just as God had commanded Noah ¹⁰One week later, the flood came and covered the earth.

¹¹When Noah was 600 years old, on the seventeenth day of the second month, the underground waters burst forth on the earth, and the rain fell in mighty torrents from the sky. ¹²The rain continued to fall for forty days and forty nights. ¹³But Noah had gone into the boat that very day with his wife and his sons—Shem, Ham, and Japheth—and their wives. ¹⁴With them in the boat were pairs of every kind of breathing animal—domestic and wild, large and small—along with birds and flying

In spite of parents' efforts and worries, conflicts between children in a family seem inevitable. Sibling relationships allow both competition and cooperation. In most cases, the mixture of loving and fighting eventually creates a strong bond between brothers and sisters. It isn't unusual, though, to hear parents say, "They fight so much I hope they don't kill each other before they grow up." In Cain's case, the troubling potential became a reality. And while we don't know many details of this first child's life, his story can still teach us.

Cain got angry. Furious. Both he and his brother Abel had given offerings to God, and his had been rejected. Cain's reaction gives us a clue that his attitude was probably wrong from the start. Cain had a choice to make. He could correct his attitude about his offering to God, or he could take out his anger on his brother. His decision is a clear reminder of how often we are aware of opposite choices, yet choose the wrong just as Cain did. We may not be choosing to murder, but we are still intentionally choosing what we shouldn't.

The feelings motivating our behavior can't always be changed by simple thought-power. But here we can begin to experience God's willingness to help. Asking for his help to do what is right can prevent us from setting into motion actions that we will later regret.

| | |
|---|---|
| **Strengths and accomplishments** | • First human child<br>• First to follow in father's profession, farming |
| **Weaknesses and mistakes** | • When disappointed, reacted in anger<br>• Took the negative option even when a positive possibility was offered<br>• Was the first murderer |
| **Lessons from his life** | • Anger is not necessarily a sin, but actions motivated by anger can be sinful. Anger should be the energy behind good action, not evil action<br>• What we offer to God must be from the heart—the best we are and have<br>• The consequences of sin may last a lifetime |
| **Vital statistics** | • Where: Near Eden, which was probably located in present-day Iraq or Iran<br>• Occupation: Farmer, then wanderer<br>• Relatives: Parents: Adam and Eve. Brothers: Abel, Seth, and others not mentioned by name |
| **Key verse** | "You will be accepted if you respond in the right way. But if you refuse to respond correctly, then watch out! Sin is waiting to attack and destroy you, and you must subdue it" (Genesis 4:7). |

Cain's story is told in Genesis 4:1–17. He is also mentioned in Hebrews 11:4; 1 John 3:12; Jude 1:11.

**7:1ff** Pairs of every animal joined Noah in the boat, seven pairs were taken of those animals used for sacrifice. Scholars have estimated that almost 45,000 animals could have fit into the boat.

insects of every kind. ¹⁵Two by two they came into the boat, ¹⁶male and female, just as God had commanded. Then the LORD shut them in.

¹⁷For forty days the floods prevailed, covering the ground and lifting the boat high above the earth. ¹⁸As the waters rose higher and higher above the ground, the boat floated safely on the surface. ¹⁹Finally, the water covered even the highest mountains on the earth, ²⁰standing more than twenty-two feet* above the highest peaks. ²¹All the living things on earth died—birds, domestic animals, wild animals, all kinds of small animals, and all the people. ²²Everything died that breathed and lived on dry land. ²³Every living thing on the earth was wiped out—people, animals both large and small, and birds. They were all destroyed, and only Noah was left alive, along with those who were with him in the boat. ²⁴And the water covered the earth for 150 days.

### The Flood Recedes

**8** But God remembered Noah and all the animals in the boat. He sent a wind to blow across the waters, and the floods began to disappear. ²The underground water sources ceased their gushing, and the torrential rains stopped. ³So the flood gradually began to recede. After 150 days, ⁴exactly five months from the time the flood began,* the boat came to rest on the mountains of Ararat. ⁵Two and a half months later,* as the waters continued to go down, other mountain peaks began to appear.

⁶After another forty days, Noah opened the window he had made in the boat ⁷and released a raven that flew back and forth until the earth was dry. ⁸Then he sent out a dove to see if it could find dry ground. ⁹But the dove found no place to land because the water was still too high. So it returned to the boat, and Noah held out his hand and drew the dove back inside. ¹⁰Seven days later, Noah released the dove again. ¹¹This time, toward evening, the bird returned to him with a fresh olive leaf in its beak. Noah now knew that the water was almost gone. ¹²A week later, he released the dove again, and this time it did not come back.

¹³Finally, when Noah was 601 years old, ten and a half months after the flood began,* Noah lifted back the cover to look. The water was drying up. ¹⁴Two more months went by,* and at last the earth was dry! ¹⁵Then God said to Noah, ¹⁶"Leave the boat, all of you. ¹⁷Release all the animals and birds so they can breed and reproduce in great numbers." ¹⁸So Noah, his wife, and his sons and their wives left the boat. ¹⁹And all the various kinds of animals and birds came out, pair by pair.

²⁰Then Noah built an altar to the LORD and sacrificed on it the animals and birds that

**7:20** Hebrew *15 cubits* [6.8 meters]. **8:4** Hebrew *on the seventeenth day of the seventh month;* see 7:11. **8:5** Hebrew *On the first day of the tenth month;* see 7:11 and note on 8:4. **8:13** Hebrew *on the first day of the first month;* see 7:11. **8:14** Hebrew *The twenty-seventh day of the second month arrived;* see note on 8:13.

**7:15**
Gen 6:19; 7:9

**7:19**
Ps 104:6

**7:20**
2 Pet 3:6

**7:23**
Matt 24:38-39
Luke 17:26-27
1 Pet 3:20
2 Pet 2:5

**7:24**
Gen 8:3

**8:1**
Gen 19:29; 30:22
Exod 2:24; 14:21
Job 12:15
Isa 44:27

**8:2**
Gen 7:4, 12

**8:4**
Gen 7:20

**8:7**
Lev 11:15
Deut 14:14
1 Kgs 17:4
Luke 12:24

**8:8**
Isa 60:8
Hos 11:11
Matt 10:16

**8:13**
Gen 5:32

**8:16**
Gen 7:13

**8:17**
Gen 1:22

**8:20**
Gen 4:4; 12:7;
13:18; 22:2

---

**7:16** Many have wondered how this animal kingdom roundup happened. Did Noah and his sons spend years collecting all the animals? In reality the creation, along with Noah, was doing just as God had commanded. There seemed to be no problem gathering the animals—God took care of the details of that job while Noah was doing his part by building the boat. Often we do just the opposite of Noah. We worry about details over which we have no control, while neglecting specific areas (such as attitudes, relationships, responsibilities) that *are* under our control. Like Noah, concentrate on what God has given you to do, and leave the rest to God.

**7:17-24** Was the Flood a local event, or did it cover the entire earth? A universal flood was certainly possible. There is enough water on the earth to cover all dry land (the earth began that way; see 1:9, 10). Afterward God promised never again to destroy the earth with a flood. Thus, this Flood must have either covered the entire earth or destroyed all the inhabitants of the earth. Remember, God's reason for sending the Flood was to destroy all the earth's wickedness. It would have taken a major flood to accomplish this.

**8:6-16** Occasionally Noah would send a bird out to test the earth and see if it was dry. But Noah didn't get out of the boat until God told him to. He was waiting for God's timing. God knew that even though the water was gone, the earth was not dry

enough for Noah and his family to venture out. What patience Noah showed, especially after spending an entire year inside his boat! We, like Noah, must trust God to give us patience during those difficult times when we must wait.

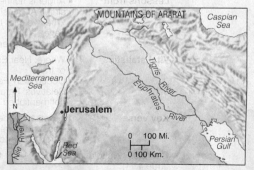

**MOUNTAINS OF ARARAT** The boat touched land in the mountains of Ararat, located in present-day Turkey. There it rested for almost eight months before Noah, his family, and the animals stepped onto dry land.

**8:21**
Gen 3:17
Exod 29:18, 25
Lev 1:9, 13
Isa 54:9

**8:22**
Ps 74:17

had been approved for that purpose. <sup>21</sup>And the LORD was pleased with the sacrifice and said to himself, "I will never again curse the earth, destroying all living things, even though people's thoughts and actions are bent toward evil from childhood. <sup>22</sup>As long as the earth remains, there will be springtime and harvest, cold and heat, winter and summer, day and night."

## 2. Repopulating the earth

*God's Covenant with Noah*

**9:1**
Gen 1:22

**9:2**
Gen 1:26-29

**9:4**
Lev 3:17; 7:26;
17:10
Deut 12:16

**9:5**
Exod 21:28-32

**9:6**
Exod 20:13; 21:12
Num 35:33

**9** God blessed Noah and his sons and told them, "Multiply and fill the earth. <sup>2</sup>All the wild animals, large and small, and all the birds and fish will be afraid of you. I have placed them in your power. <sup>3</sup>I have given them to you for food, just as I have given you grain and vegetables. <sup>4</sup>But you must never eat animals that still have their lifeblood in them. <sup>5</sup>And murder is forbidden. Animals that kill people must die, and any person who murders must be killed <sup>6</sup>Yes, you must execute anyone who murders another person, for to kill a person is to kill a living being made in God's image. <sup>7</sup>Now you must have many children and repopulate the earth. Yes, multiply and fill the earth!"

---

**NOAH**

The story of Noah's life involves not one, but two great and tragic floods. The world in Noah's day was flooded with evil. The number of those who remembered the God of creation, perfection, and love had dwindled to one. Of God's people, only Noah was left. God's response to the severe situation was a 120-year-long last chance, during which he had Noah build a graphic illustration of the message of his life. Nothing like a huge boat on dry land to make a point! For Noah, obedience meant a long-term commitment to a project.

Many of us have trouble sticking to any project, whether or not it is directed by God. It is interesting that the length of Noah's obedience was greater than the lifespan of people today. The only comparable long-term project is our very lives. But perhaps this is one great challenge Noah's life gives us—to live, in acceptance of God's grace, an entire lifetime of obedience and gratitude.

| | |
|---|---|
| **Strengths and accomplishments** | • Only follower of God left in his generation<br>• Second father of the human race<br>• Man of patience, consistency, and obedience<br>• First major shipbuilder |
| **Weakness and mistake** | • Got drunk and embarrassed himself in front of his sons |
| **Lessons from his life** | • God is faithful to those who obey him<br>• God does not always protect us from trouble, but cares for us in spite of trouble<br>• Obedience is a long-term commitment<br>• A man may be faithful, but his sinful nature always travels with him |
| **Vital statistics** | • Where: We're not told how far from the Garden of Eden people had settled<br>• Occupation: Farmer, shipbuilder, preacher<br>• Relatives: Grandfather: Methuselah. Father: Lamech. Sons: Ham, Shem, and Japheth |
| **Key verse** | "So Noah did everything exactly as God had commanded him" (Genesis 6:22). |

Noah's story is told in Genesis 5:28—10:32. He is also mentioned in 1 Chronicles 1:3, 4; Isaiah 54:9; Ezekiel 14:14, 20; Matthew 24:37, 38; Luke 3:36; 17:26, 27; Hebrews 11:7; 1 Peter 3:20; 2 Peter 2:5.

---

**8:21, 22** Countless times throughout the Bible we see God showing his love and patience toward men and women in order to save them. Although he realizes that their hearts are evil, he continues to try to reach them. When we sin or fall away from God, we surely deserve to be destroyed by his judgment. But God has promised never again to destroy everything on earth until the judgment day when Christ returns to destroy evil forever. Now every change of season is a reminder of his promise.

**9:5** God will require each person to account for his or her actions. We cannot harm or kill another human being with-

out answering to God. A penalty must be paid. Justice will be served.

**9:5, 6** Here God explains why murder is so wrong: To kill a person is to kill one made in God's image. Because all human beings are made in God's image, all people possess the qualities that distinguish them from animals: morality, reason, creativity, and self-worth. When we interact with others, we are interacting with beings made by God, beings to whom God offers eternal life. God wants us to recognize his image in all people.

8 Then God told Noah and his sons, 9 "I am making a covenant with you and your descendants, 10 and with the animals you brought with you—all these birds and livestock and wild animals. 11 I solemnly promise never to send another flood to kill all living creatures and destroy the earth." 12 And God said, "I am giving you a sign as evidence of my eternal covenant with you and all living creatures. 13 I have placed my rainbow in the clouds. It is the sign of my permanent promise to you and to all the earth. 14 When I send clouds over the earth, the rainbow will be seen in the clouds, 15 and I will remember my covenant with you and with everything that lives. Never again will there be a flood that will destroy all life. 16 When I see the rainbow in the clouds, I will remember the eternal covenant between God and every living creature on earth." 17 Then God said to Noah, "Yes, this is the sign of my covenant with all the creatures of the earth."

**9:11**
Isa 24:5

**9:12**
Gen 17:11

**9:13**
Ezek 1:28

**9:15**
Deut 7:9

### Noah's Sons

18 Shem, Ham, and Japheth, the three sons of Noah, survived the Flood with their father. (Ham is the ancestor of the Canaanites.) 19 From these three sons of Noah came all the people now scattered across the earth.

20 After the Flood, Noah became a farmer and planted a vineyard. 21 One day he became drunk on some wine he had made and lay naked in his tent. 22 Ham, the father of Canaan, saw that his father was naked and went outside and told his brothers. 23 Shem and Japheth took a robe, held it over their shoulders, walked backward into the tent, and covered their father's naked body. As they did this, they looked the other way so they wouldn't see him naked. 24 When Noah woke up from his drunken stupor, he learned what Ham, his youngest son, had done. 25 Then he cursed the descendants of Canaan, the son of Ham:

**9:21**
Gen 19:35

**9:22**
Hab 2:15

**9:25**
Deut 27:16

"A curse on the Canaanites!
May they be the lowest of servants
to the descendants of Shem and Japheth."

26 Then Noah said,

**9:26**
Gen 14:20

"May Shem be blessed by the LORD my God;
and may Canaan be his servant.
27 May God enlarge the territory of Japheth,
and may he share the prosperity of Shem;*
and let Canaan be his servant."

**9:27**
Gen 10:2-5
Isa 66:19

28 Noah lived another 350 years after the Flood. 29 He was 950 years old when he died.

**9:29**
Gen 2:17

**10** This is the history of the families of Shem, Ham, and Japheth, the three sons of Noah. Many children were born to them after the Flood.

**10:1**
Gen 9:18
1 Chr 1:4

### Descendants of Japheth

2 The descendants of Japheth were Gomer, Magog, Madai, Javan, Tubal, Meshech, and Tiras.
3 The descendants of Gomer were Ashkenaz, Riphath, and Togarmah.
4 The descendants of Javan were Elishah, Tarshish, Kittim, and Rodanim.* 5 Their

**10:2**
1 Chr 1:5-7
Isa 66:19
Ezek 27:13;
38:2-3, 6

**10:4**
1 Chr 1:6-7

**9:27** Hebrew *may he live in the tents of Shem.*   **10:4** As in some Hebrew manuscripts and Greek version (see also 1 Chr 1:7); most Hebrew manuscripts read *Dodanim.*

---

**9:8-17** Noah stepped out of the boat onto an earth devoid of human life. But God gave him a reassuring promise. This covenant had three parts: (1) Never again will a flood do such destruction; (2) as long as the earth remains, the seasons will always come as expected; (3) a rainbow will be visible when it rains as a sign to all that God will keep his promises. The earth's order and seasons are still preserved, and rainbows still remind us of God's faithfulness to his word.

**9:20-27** Noah, the great hero of faith, got drunk—a poor example of godliness to his sons. Perhaps this story is included to show us that even godly people can sin and

that their bad influence affects their families. Although the wicked people had all been killed, the possibility of evil still existed in the hearts of Noah and his family. Ham's mocking attitude revealed a severe lack of respect for his father and for God.

**9:25** This verse has been wrongly used to support racial prejudice and even slavery. Noah's curse, however, wasn't directed toward any particular race, but rather at the Canaanite nation—a nation God knew would become wicked. The curse was fulfilled when the Israelites entered the Promised Land and drove the Canaanites out (see the book of Joshua).

descendants became the seafaring peoples in various lands, each tribe with its own language.

### Descendants of Ham

**10:6**
1 Chr 1:8-10

6 The descendants of Ham were Cush, Mizraim,* Put, and Canaan.

**10:7**
Isa 43:3
Ezek 27:15, 20, 22

7 The descendants of Cush were Seba, Havilah, Sabtah, Raamah, and Sabteca. The descendants of Raamah were Sheba and Dedan.

8 One of Cush's descendants was Nimrod, who became a heroic warrior. 9 He was a mighty hunter in the LORD's sight.* His name became proverbial, and people would speak of someone as being "like Nimrod, a mighty hunter in the LORD's

**10:10**
Gen 11:9

sight." 10 He built the foundation for his empire in the land of Babylonia,* with the

**10:11**
Mic 5:6

cities of Babel, Erech, Akkad, and Calneh. 11 From there he extended his reign to Assyria, where he built Nineveh, Rehoboth-ir, Calah, 12 and Resen—the main city of the empire, located between Nineveh and Calah.

**10:13**
Jer 46:9

13 Mizraim was the ancestor of the Ludites, Anamites, Lehabites, Naphtuhites,

**10:14**
1 Chr 1:12

14 Pathrusites, Casluhites, and the Caphtorites, from whom the Philistines came.*

**10:15**
Gen 15:20; 23:3
1 Chr 1:13
Jer 47:4

15 Canaan's oldest son was Sidon, the ancestor of the Sidonians. Canaan was also the ancestor of the Hittites, 16 Jebusites, Amorites, Girgashites, 17 Hivites, Arkites,

**10:16**
Gen 15:18-21

Sinites, 18 Arvadites, Zemarites, and Hamathites. 19 Eventually the territory of Canaan spread from Sidon to Gerar, near Gaza, and to Sodom, Gomorrah, Admah,

**10:19**
Gen 14:2

and Zeboiim, near Lasha.

20 These were the descendants of Ham, identified according to their tribes, languages, territories, and nations.

### Descendants of Shem

**10:22**
2 Kgs 15:29
Isa 66:19

21 Sons were also born to Shem, the older brother of Japheth.* Shem was the ancestor of all the descendants of Eber. 22 The descendants of Shem were Elam, Asshur,

**10:23**
Job 1:1

Arphaxad, Lud, and Aram.

23 The descendants of Aram were Uz, Hul, Gether, and Mash.

**10:24**
Luke 3:35

24 Arphaxad was the father of Shelah,* and Shelah was the father of Eber. 25 Eber had two sons. The first was named Peleg—"division"—for during his lifetime the people of the world were divided into different language groups and dispersed. His brother's name was Joktan.

26 Joktan was the ancestor of Almodad, Sheleph, Hazarmaveth, Jerah, 27 Hadoram, Uzal, Diklah, 28 Obal, Abimael, Sheba, 29 Ophir, Havilah, and Jobab. 30 The descendants of Joktan lived in the area extending from Mesha toward the eastern hills of Sephar.

31 These were the descendants of Shem, identified according to their tribes, languages, territories, and nations.

**10:32**
Gen 9:19; 10:1

32 These are the families that came from Noah's sons, listed nation by nation according to their lines of descent. The earth was populated with the people of these nations after the Flood.

**10:6** Or *Egypt;* also in 10:13. **10:9** Hebrew *a mighty hunter before the LORD;* also in 10:9b. **10:10** Hebrew *Shinar.* **10:14** Hebrew *Casluhites, from whom the Philistines came, Caphtorites.* Compare Jer 47:4; Amos 9:7. **10:21** Or *Shem, whose older brother was Japheth.* **10:24** Greek version reads *Arphaxad was the father of Cainan, Cainan was the father of Shelah.*

---

| **BIBLE NATIONS DESCENDED FROM NOAH'S SONS** | *Shem* | *Ham* | *Japheth* | Shem's descendants were called Semites. |
|---|---|---|---|---|
| | Hebrews | Canaanites | Greeks | Abraham, David, and Jesus descended from |
| | Chaldeans | Egyptians | Thracians | Shem. Ham's descendants settled in Canaan, |
| | Assyrians | Philistines | Scythians | Egypt, and the rest of Africa. Japheth's |
| | Persians | Hittites | | descendants settled for the most part in |
| | Syrians | Amorites | | Europe and As a Minor. |

---

**10:8, 9** Who was Nimrod? Not much is known about him except that he was a heroic warrior. But people with great gifts can become proud, and that is probably what happened to Nimrod. Some consider him the founder of the great, godless Babylonian Empire.

## 3. The tower of Babel

**11** At one time the whole world spoke a single language and used the same words. ²As the people migrated eastward, they found a plain in the land of Babylonia* and settled there. ³They began to talk about construction projects. "Come," they said, "let's make great piles of burnt brick and collect natural asphalt to use as mortar. ⁴Let's build a great city with a tower that reaches to the skies—a monument to our greatness! This will bring us together and keep us from scattering all over the world."

⁵But the LORD came down to see the city and the tower the people were building. ⁶"Look!" he said. "If they can accomplish this when they have just begun to take advantage of their common language and political unity, just think of what they will do later. Nothing will be impossible for them! ⁷Come, let's go down and give them different languages. Then they won't be able to understand each other."

⁸In that way, the LORD scattered them all over the earth; and that ended the building of the city. ⁹That is why the city was called Babel,* because it was there that the LORD confused the people by giving them many languages, thus scattering them across the earth.

*From Shem to Abram*

¹⁰This is the history of Shem's family.

When Shem was 100 years old, his son Arphaxad was born. This happened two years after the Flood. ¹¹After the birth of Arphaxad, Shem lived another 500 years and had other sons and daughters.

¹²When Arphaxad was 35 years old, his son Shelah was born.* ¹³After the birth of Shelah, Arphaxad lived another 403 years and had other sons and daughters.*

¹⁴When Shelah was 30 years old, his son Eber was born. ¹⁵After the birth of Eber, Shelah lived another 403 years and had other sons and daughters.

¹⁶When Eber was 34 years old, his son Peleg was born. ¹⁷After the birth of Peleg, Eber lived another 430 years and had other sons and daughters.

¹⁸When Peleg was 30 years old, his son Reu was born. ¹⁹After the birth of Reu, Peleg lived another 209 years and had other sons and daughters.

²⁰When Reu was 32 years old, his son Serug was born. ²¹After the birth of Serug, Reu lived another 207 years and had other sons and daughters.

²²When Serug was 30 years old, his son Nahor was born. ²³After the birth of Nahor, Serug lived another 200 years and had other sons and daughters.

²⁴When Nahor was 29 years old, his son Terah was born. ²⁵After the birth of Terah, Nahor lived another 119 years and had other sons and daughters.

**11:2** Gen 10:10; 14:1 Isa 11:11

**11:3** Gen 14:10

**11:4** 2 Sam 8:13

**11:5** Gen 18:21 Exod 19:11

**11:6** Gen 9:19; 11:1

**11:7** Gen 1:26

**11:8** Gen 9:19

**11:9** Gen 10:10

**11:10** Gen 10:22-25 Luke 3:36

**11:12** Luke 3:36

**11:13** 1 Chr 1:17

**11:14** Luke 3:35

**11:16** Luke 3:35

**11:18** Luke 3:35

**11:20** Luke 3:35

**11:22** Luke 3:34

**11:24** Josh 24:2 Luke 3:34

**11:2** Hebrew *Shinar.*   **11:9** *Babel* sounds like a Hebrew term that means "confusion."   **11:12** Or *his son, the ancestor of Shelah, was born;* similarly in 11:14, 16, 18, 20, 22, 24.   **11:12-13** Greek version reads ¹²*When Arphaxad was 135 years old, his son Cainan was born.* ¹³*After the birth of Cainan, Arphaxad lived another 430 years and had other sons and daughters, and then he died. When Cainan was 130 years old, his son Shelah was born. After the birth of Shelah, Cainan lived another 330 years and had other sons and daughters, and then he died.*

---

**11:3** The brick used to build this tower was man made and not as hard as stone.

**11:3, 4** The tower of Babel was most likely a ziggurat, a common structure in Babylonia at this time. Most often built as temples, ziggurats looked like pyramids with steps or ramps leading up the sides. Ziggurats stood as high as 300 feet and were often just as wide; thus they were the focal point of the city. The people in this story built their tower as a monument to their own greatness, something for the whole world to see.

**11:4** The tower of Babel was a great human achievement, a wonder of the world. But it was a monument to the people themselves rather than to God. We may build monuments to ourselves (expensive clothes, big house, fancy car, important job) to call attention to our achievements. These may not be wrong in themselves, but when we use them to give us identity and self-worth, they take God's place in our lives. We are free to develop in many areas, but we are not free to think we have replaced God. What "towers" have you built in your life?

**11:10-27** In 9:25 we read Noah's curse on Canaan, Ham's son, ancestor of the evil Canaanites. Here and in 10:22-31 we have a list of Shem's descendants, who were blessed (9:26). From

Shem's line came Abram and the entire Jewish nation, which would eventually conquer the land of Canaan in the days of Joshua.

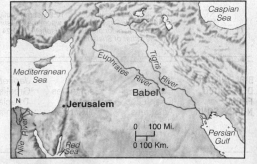

**THE TOWER OF BABEL** The plain between the Tigris and Euphrates Rivers offered a perfect location for the city and tower "that reaches to the skies."

**11:26**
Gen 22:20
1 Chr 1:26-27
Luke 3:34

²⁶When Terah was 70 years old, he became the father of Abram, Nahor, and Haran.

*The Family of Terah*

**11:29**
Gen 17:15;
20:11-12; 22:20

²⁷This is the history of Terah's family. Terah was the father of Abram, Nahor, and Haran; and Haran had a son named Lot. ²⁸But while Haran was still young, he died in Ur of the Chaldeans, the place of his birth. He was survived by Terah, his father. ²⁹Meanwhile, Abram married Sarai, and his brother Nahor married Milcah, the daughter of their brother Haran.

**11:30**
Gen 16:1; 18:11;
25:21
1 Sam 1:5
Luke 1:7

(Milcah had a sister named Iscah.) ³⁰Now Sarai was not able to have any children.

**11:31**
Gen 27:43
Josh 24:2
Acts 7:4

³¹Terah took his son Abram, his daughter-in-law Sarai, and his grandson Lot (his son Haran's child) and left Ur of the Chaldeans to go to the land of Canaan. But they stopped instead at the village of Haran and settled there. ³²Terah lived for 205 years* and died while still at Haran.

## D. THE STORY OF ABRAHAM (12:1—25:18)

Despite God's swift judgment of sin, most people ignored him and continued to sin. But a handful of people really tried to follow him. One of these was Abraham. God appeared to Abraham one day and promised to make his descendants into a great nation. Abraham's part of the agreement was to obey God. Through sharp testing and an incident that almost destroyed his family, Abraham remained faithful to God. Throughout this section we discover how to live a life of faith.

### 1. God promises a nation to Abram

*The Call of Abram*

**12:1**
Gen 15:7
†Acts 7:3
Heb 11:8

**12** Then the LORD told Abram. "Leave your country, your relatives, and your father's house, and go to the land that I will show you. ²I will cause you to become the father of a great nation. I will bless you and make you famous, and I will make you a blessing to others. ³I will bless those who bless you and curse those who curse you. All the families of the earth will be blessed through you."

**12:2**
Gen 13:16; 15:5;
17:4; 18:18; 22:17
Zech 8:13

**12:3**
Gen 22:18; 26:4
Exod 23:22
†Gal 3:8

⁴So Abram departed as the LORD had instructed him, and Lot went with him. Abram was seventy-five years old when he left Haran. ⁵He took his wife, Sarai, his nephew Lot, and all his wealth—his livestock and all the people who had joined his household

**11:32** Some ancient versions read *145 years;* compare 11:26; 12:4.

---

**11:27-28** Abram grew up in Ur of the Chaldeans, an important city in the ancient world. Archaeologists have discovered evidence of a flourishing civilization there in Abram's day. The city carried on an extensive trade with its neighbors and had a vast library. Growing up in Ur, Abram was probably well educated.

**11:31** Terah left Ur to go to Canaan but settled in Haran instead. Why did he stop halfway? It may have been his health, the climate, or even fear. But this did not change Abram's calling ("the LORD told Abram," 12:1). He had respect for his father's leadership, but when Terah died, Abram moved on to Canaan. God's will may come in stages. Just as the time in Haran was a transition period for Abram, so God may give us transition periods and times of waiting to help us depend on him and trust his timing. If we patiently go his will during the transition times, we will be better prepared to serve him as we should when he calls us.

**12:1-3** When God called him, Abram moved out in faith from Ur to Haran and finally to Canaan. God then established a covenant with Abram, telling him that he would found a great nation. Not only would this nation be blessed, God said, but the other nations of the earth would be blessed through Abram's descendants. Israel, the nation that would come from Abram was to follow God and influence those with whom it came in contact. Through Abram's family tree, Jesus Christ was born to save humanity. Through Christ, people can have a personal relationship with God and be blessed beyond measure.

**12:2** God promised to bless Abram and make him famous, but there was one condition. Abram had to do what God wanted him to do. This meant leaving his home and friends and traveling to a new land where God promised to build a great nation from Abram's family. Abram obeyed, walking away from his

home for God's promise of even greater blessings in the future. God may be trying to lead you to a place of greater service and usefulness for him. Don't let the comfort and security of your present position make you miss God's plan for you.

**12:5** God planned to develop a nation of people he would call his own. He called Abram from the godless, self-centered city of Ur to a fertile region called Canaan, where a God-centered, moral nation could be established. Though small in dimension, the land of Canaan was the focal point for most of the history of Israel as well as for the rise of Christianity. This small land given to one man, Abram, has had a tremendous impact on world history.

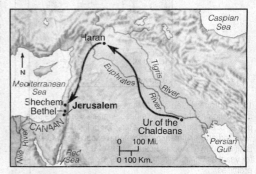

**ABRAM'S JOURNEY TO CANAAN** Abram, Sarai, and Lot traveled from Ur of the Chaldeans to Canaan by way of Haran. Though indirect, this route followed the rivers rather than attempting to cross the vast desert.

at Haran—and finally arrived in Canaan. ⁶Traveling through Canaan, they came to a place near Shechem and set up camp beside the oak at Moreh. At that time, the area was inhabited by Canaanites.

**12:6**
Gen 33:18; 35:4
Deut 11:30

⁷Then the LORD appeared to Abram and said, "I am going to give this land to your offspring.*" And Abram built an altar there to commemorate the LORD's visit. ⁸After that, Abram traveled southward and set up camp in the hill country between Bethel on the west and Ai on the east. There he built an altar and worshiped the LORD. ⁹Then Abram traveled south by stages toward the Negev.

**12:7**
Gen 13:15
†Gal 3:16

**12:8**
Gen 4:26; 8:20;
22:9

**12:9**
Gen 13:1; 20:1

### Abram and Sarai in Egypt

¹⁰At that time there was a severe famine in the land, so Abram went down to Egypt to wait it out. ¹¹As he was approaching the borders of Egypt, Abram said to Sarai, "You are a very beautiful woman. ¹²When the Egyptians see you, they will say, 'This is his wife. Let's kill him; then we can have her!' ¹³But if you say you are my sister, then the Egyptians will treat me well because of their interest in you, and they will spare my life."

**12:10**
Gen 26:1; 42:5

**12:11**
Gen 29:17

**12:12**
Gen 20:11

¹⁴And sure enough, when they arrived in Egypt, everyone spoke of her beauty. ¹⁵When the palace officials saw her, they sang her praises to their king, the pharaoh, and she was taken into his harem. ¹⁶Then Pharaoh gave Abram many gifts because of her—sheep, cattle, donkeys, male and female servants, and camels.

**12:16**
Gen 20:14; 24:35

¹⁷But the LORD sent a terrible plague upon Pharaoh's household because of Sarai, Abram's wife. ¹⁸So Pharaoh called for Abram and accused him sharply. "What is this you have done to me?" he demanded. "Why didn't you tell me she was your wife? ¹⁹Why were you willing to let me marry her, saying she was your sister? Here is your wife! Take her and be gone!" ²⁰Pharaoh then sent them out of the country under armed escort—Abram and his wife, with all their household and belongings.

**12:17**
1 Chr 16:21
Ps 105:14

**12:18**
Gen 20:9-10

**12:19**
Gen 20:5; 26:9

**12:7** Hebrew *seed.*

---

**ABRAM'S
JOURNEY
TO EGYPT**
A famine could cause the loss of a shepherd's wealth. So Abram traveled through the Negev to Egypt, where there was plenty of food and good land for his flocks.

Abram regularly built altars to God for two reasons: (1) for prayer and worship, and (2) as reminders of God's promise to bless him. Abram couldn't survive spiritually without regularly renewing his love and loyalty to God. Building altars helped Abram remember that God was at the center of his life. Regular worship helps us remember what God desires and motivates us to obey him.

**12:10** When famine struck, Abram went to Egypt where there was food. Why would there be a famine in the land where God had just called Abram? This was a test of Abram's faith, and Abram passed. He didn't question God's leading when facing this difficulty. Many believers find that when they determine to follow God, they immediately encounter great obstacles. The next time you face such a test, don't try to second-guess what God is doing. Use the intelligence God gave you, as Abram did when he temporarily moved to Egypt, and wait for new opportunities.

**12:11-13** Abram, acting out of fear, asked Sarai to tell a half-truth by saying she was his sister. She *was* his half sister (see 20:12), but she was also his wife.

Abram's intent was to deceive the Egyptians. He feared that if they knew the truth, they would kill him to get Sarai. She would have been a desirable addition to Pharaoh's harem because of her wealth, beauty, and potential for political alliance. As Sarai's brother, Abram would have been given a place of honor. As her husband, however, his life would be in danger because Sarai could not enter Pharaoh's harem unless Abram was dead. So Abram lost faith in God's protection, even after all God had promised him, and told a half-truth. This shows how lying compounds the effects of sin. When he lied, Abram's problems multiplied.

**12:7** Abram built an altar to the Lord. Altars were used in many religions, but for God's people, altars were more than places of sacrifice. For them, altars symbolized communion with God and commemorated notable encounters with him. Built of rough stones and earth, altars often remained in place for years as continual reminders of God's protection and promises.

## 2. Abram and Lot

*Abram and Lot Separate*

**13** So they left Egypt and traveled north into the Negev—Abram with his wife and Lot and all that they owned, 2for Abram was very rich in livestock, silver, and gold. 3Then they continued traveling by stages toward Bethel, to the place between Bethel and Ai where they had camped before. 4This was the place where Abram had built the altar, and there he again worshiped the LORD.

5Now Lot, who was traveling with Abram, was also very wealthy with sheep, cattle, and many tents. 6But the land could not support both Abram and Lot with all their flocks and herds living so close together. There were too many animals for the available pastureland. 7So an argument broke out between the herdsmen of Abram and Lot. At that time Canaanites and Perizzites were also living in the land.

8Then Abram talked it over with Lot. "This arguing between our herdsmen has got to stop," he said. "After all, we are close relatives! 9I'll tell you what we'll do. Take your choice of any section of the land you want, and we will separate. If you want that area over there, then I'll stay here. If you want to stay in this area, then I'll move on to another place."

10Lot took a long look at the fertile plains of the Jordan Valley in the direction of Zoar. The whole area was well watered everywhere, like the garden of the LORD or the beautiful land of Egypt. (This was before the LORD had destroyed Sodom and Gomorrah.) 11Lot chose that land for himself—the Jordan Valley to the east of them. He went there with his flocks and servants and parted company with his uncle Abram. 12So while Abram stayed in the land of Canaan, Lot moved his tents to a place near Sodom, among the cities of the plain. 13The people of this area were unusually wicked and sinned greatly against the LORD.

14After Lot was gone, the LORD said to Abram, "Look as far as you can see in every direction. 15I am going to give all this land to you and your offspring* as a permanent possession. 16And I am going to give you so many descendants that, like dust, they cannot be counted! 17Take a walk in every direction and explore the new possessions I am giving you." 18Then Abram moved his camp to the oak grove owned by Mamre, which is at Hebron. There he built an altar to the LORD.

*Abram Rescues Lot*

**14** About this time war broke out in the region. King Amraphel of Babylonia,* King Arioch of Ellasar, King Kedorlaomer of Elam, and King Tidal of Goiim 2fought against King Bera of Sodom, King Birsha of Gomorrah, King Shinab of Admah, King Shemeber of Zeboiim, and the king of Bela (now called Zoar).

**13:15** Hebrew *seed.*   **14:1** Hebrew *Shinar;* also in 14:9.

---

**13:1, 2**  In Abram's day, sheep and cattle owners could acquire great wealth. Abram's wealth not only included silver and gold, but also livestock. These animals were a valuable commodity used for food, clothing, tent material, and sacrifices. They were often traded for other goods and services. Abram was able to watch his wealth grow and multiply daily.

**13:5-9**  Facing a potential conflict with his nephew Lot, Abram took the initiative in settling the dispute. He gave Lot first choice, even though Abram, being older, had the right to choose first. Abram also showed a willingness to risk being cheated. Abram's example shows us how to respond to difficult family situations: (1) Take the initiative in resolving conflicts; (2) let others have first choice, even if that means not getting what we want; (3) put family peace above personal desires.

**13:7, 8**  Surrounded by hostile neighbors, the herdsmen of Abram and Lot should have pulled together. Instead, they let petty jealousy tear them apart. Similar situations exist today. Christians often bicker while Satan is at work all around them.

Rivalries, arguments, and disagreements among believers can be destructive in three ways: (1) They damage goodwill, trust, and peace—the foundations of good human relations; (2) they hamper progress toward important goals; (3) they make

us self-centered rather than love-centered. Jesus understood how destructive arguments among brothers could be. In his final prayer before being betrayed and arrested, Jesus asked God that his followers be "one" (John 17).

**13:10, 11**  Lot's character is revealed by his choices. He took the best share of the land even though it meant living near Sodom, a city known for its sin. He was greedy, wanting the best for himself, without thinking about his uncle Abram's needs or what was fair.

Life is a series of choices. We, too, can choose the best while ignoring the needs and feelings of others. But this kind of choice, as Lot's life shows, leads to problems. When we stop making choices in God's direction, all that is left is to make choices in the wrong direction.

**13:12, 13**  Good pasture and available water seemed like a wise choice to Lot at first. But he failed to recognize that wicked Sodom could provide temptations strong enough to destroy his family. Have you chosen to live or work in a Sodom? Even though you may be strong enough to resist the temptations, other members of your family may not. While God commands us to reach people in the "Sodom" near us, we must be careful not to become like the very people we are trying to reach.

³The kings of Sodom, Gomorrah, Admah, Zeboiim, and Bela formed an alliance and mobilized their armies in Siddim Valley (that is, the valley of the Dead Sea*). ⁴For twelve years they had all been subject to King Kedorlaomer, but now in the thirteenth year they rebelled.

⁵One year later, Kedorlaomer and his allies arrived. They conquered the Rephaites in Ashteroth-karnaim, the Zuzites in Ham, the Emites in the plain of Kiriathaim, ⁶and the Horites in Mount Seir, as far as El-paran at the edge of the wilderness. ⁷Then they swung around to En-mishpat (now called Kadesh) and destroyed the Amalekites, and also the Amorites living in Hazazon-tamar.

⁸But now the army of the kings of Sodom, Gomorrah, Admah, Zeboiim, and Bela (now called Zoar) prepared for battle in the valley of the Dead Sea* ⁹against King Kedorlaomer of Elam and the kings of Goiin, Babylonia, and Ellasar—four kings against five. ¹⁰As it happened, the valley was filled with tar pits. And as the army of the kings of Sodom and Gomorrah fled, some slipped into the tar pits, while the rest escaped into the mountains. ¹¹The victorious invaders then plundered Sodom and Gomorrah and began their long journey home, taking all the wealth and food with them. ¹²They also captured Lot—Abram's nephew who lived in Sodom—and took everything he owned. ¹³One of the men who escaped came and told Abram the Hebrew, who was camped at the oak grove belonging to Mamre the Amorite. Mamre and his relatives, Eshcol and Aner, were Abram's allies.

¹⁴When Abram learned that Lot had been captured, he called together the men born into his household, 318 of them in all. He chased after Kedorlaomer's army until he caught up with them in Dan. ¹⁵There he divided his men and attacked during the night from several directions. Kedorlaome's army fled, but Abram chased them to Hobah, north of Damascus. ¹⁶Abram and his alies recovered everything—the goods that had been taken, Abram's nephew Lot with his possessions, and all the women and other captives.

### Melchizedek Blesses Abram

¹⁷As Abram returned from his victory over Kedorlaomer and his allies, the king of Sodom came out to meet him in the valley of Shaveh (that is, the King's Valley). ¹⁸Then Melchizedek, the king of Salem and a priest of God Most High, brought him bread and wine. ¹⁹Melchizedek blessed Abram with this blessing:

14:3 Hebrew *Salt Sea.*   14 Hebrew *in Siddim Valley;* see 14:3.

**14:3**
Num 34:3, 12
Deut 3:17
Josh 3:16

**14:5**
Gen 15:20
Deut 1:4; 2:10, 20;
3:11
Josh 13:19

**14:7**
Gen 16:14; 20:1
Num 13:26
Deut 1:4
2 Chr 20:2

**14:12**
Gen 11:27

**14:13**
Gen 10:16; 13:18;
39:14

**14:14**
Gen 12:5
Deut 34:1

**14:15**
Gen 15:2

**14:17**
2 Sam 18:18

**14:18**
Heb 5:6, 10; 7:1

**14:19**
Gen 27:25; 48:9
Mark 10:16

---

**14:4-16** Who was Kedorlaomer, and why was he important? In Abram's time, most cities had their own kings. Wars and rivalries among kings were common. A conquered city paid tribute to the victorious king. Nothing is known about Kedorlaomer except what we read in the Bible but apparently he was quite powerful. Five cities including Sodom had paid tribute to him for 12 years. The five cities formed an lliance and rebelled by withholding tribute. Kedorlaomer reated swiftly and reconquered them all. When he defeated Sodom, he captured Lot, his family, and his possessions. Abram, with only 318 men, chased Kedorlaomer's army and attacked him near Damascus. With God's help, he defeated them and recovered Lot, his family, and their possessions.

**14:12** Lot's greedy desire for the best of everything led him into sinful surroundings. His burning desire for possessions and success cost him his freedom and enjoyment. As a captive to Kedorlaomer, he faced torture, slavery, or death. In much the same way, we can be niced into doing things or going places we shouldn't. The prosperity we long for is captivating; it can both entice us and insnare us if our motives are not in line with God's desires.

**14:14-16** These incidents portray two of Abram's characteristics: (1) He had courage that came from God; facing a powerful foe, he attacked. (2) He was prepared; he had taken time to train his men for a potential conflict. We never know when we will be called upon to complete difficult tasks. Like Abram, we should prepare for those times and take courage from God when they come.

**14:14-16** When Abram learned that Lot was a captive, he immediately tried to rescue his nephew. It is easier and safer not to become involved. But with Lot in serious trouble, Abram acted at once. Sometimes we must get involved in a messy or painful situation in order to help others. We should be willing to act immediately when others need our help.

Mediterranean Sea

Damascus

Dan

Sea of Galilee

N

Jordan River

Jerusalem

Hebron•

Dead Sea

0   20 Mi.
0   20 Km.

Possible location of Sodom and Gomorrah

**LOT'S RESCUE**
Having conquered Sodom, Kedorlaomer left for his home country, taking many captives with him. Abram learned what had happened and chased Kedorlaomer past Dan and beyond Damascus. There he defeated the king and rescued the captives, among them Lot.

**14:18** Who was Melchizedek? He was obviously a God-fearing man, for his name means "king of righteousness," and king of Salem means "king of peace." He was a "priest of God Most

"Blessed be Abram by God Most High,
   Creator of heaven and earth.

14:20
Gen 9:26; 24:27
†Heb 7:1-2

20 And blessed be God Most High,
   who has helped you conquer your enemies."

Then Abram gave Melchizedek a tenth of all the goods he had recovered.

21 The king of Sodom told him, "Give back my people who were captured. But you may keep for yourself all the goods you have recovered."

14:22
Gen 1:1

14:23
2 Kgs 5:16

14:24
Gen 14:13

22 Abram replied, "I have solemnly promised the LORD, God Most High, Creator of heaven and earth, 23 that I will not take so much as a single thread or sandal thong from you. Otherwise you might say, 'I am the one who made Abram rich!' 24 All I'll accept is what these young men of mine have already eaten. But give a share of the goods to my allies—Aner, Eshcol, and Mamre."

---

**LOT**

Some people simply drift through life. Their choices, when they can muster the will to choose, tend to follow the course of least resistance. Lot, Abram's nephew, was such a person.

While still young, Lot lost his father. Although this must have been hard on him, he was not left without strong role models in his grandfather Terah and his uncle Abram, who raised him. Still, Lot did not develop their sense of purpose. Throughout his life he was so caught up in the present moment that he seemed incapable of seeing the consequences of his actions. It is hard to imagine what his life would have been like without Abram's careful attention and God's intervention.

By the time Lot drifted out of the picture, his life had taken an ugly turn. He had so blended into the sinful culture of his day that he did not want to leave it. His drifting finally took him in a very specific direction—destruction. Then his daughters committed incest with him.

Lot, however, is called "righteous" in the New Testament (2 Peter 2:7, 8). Ruth, a descendant of Moab, was an ancestor of Jesus, even though Moab was born as a result of Lot's incestuous relationship with one of his daughters. Lot's story gives hope to us that God forgives and often brings about positive circumstances from evil.

What is the direction of your life? Are you headed toward God or away from him? If you're a drifter, the choice for God may seem difficult, but it is the one choice that puts all other choices in a different light.

| | |
|---|---|
| **Strengths and accomplishments** | • He was a successful businessman<br>• Peter calls him a righteous man (2 Peter 2:7, 8) |
| **Weaknesses and mistakes** | • When faced with decisions, he tended to put off deciding, then chose the easiest course of action<br>• When given a choice, his first reaction was to think of himself |
| **Lesson from his life** | • God wants us to do more than drift through life; he wants us to be an influence for him |
| **Vital statistics** | • Where: Lived first in Ur of the Chaldeans, then moved to Canaan with Abram. Eventually he moved to the wicked city of Sodom<br>• Occupation: Wealthy sheep and cattle rancher; also a city official<br>• Relatives: Father: Haran. Adopted by Abram when his father died. The name of his wife, who turned into a pillar of salt, is not mentioned |
| **Key verse** | "When Lot still hesitated, the angels seized his hand and the hands of his wife and two daughters and rushed them to safety outside the city, for the LORD was merciful" (Genesis 19:16). |

Lot's story is told in Genesis 11—14, 19. He is also mentioned in Deuteronomy 2:9; Luke 17:28-32; 2 Peter 2:7, 8.

---

High" (Hebrews 7:1, 2). He recognized God as Creator of heaven and earth. What else is known about him? Four main theories have been suggested: (1) Melchizedek was a respected king of that region. Abram was simply showing him the respect he deserved. (2) The name Melchizedek may have been a standing title for all the kings of Salem. (3) Melchizedek was a type of Christ (Hebrews 7:3). A type is an Old Testament event or teaching that is so closely related to what Christ did that it illustrates a lesson about Christ. (4) Melchizedek was the appearance on earth of the preincarnate Christ in a temporary bodily form.

**14:20** Abram gave a tenth of the goods he recovered to Melchizedek. Even in some pagan religions, it was traditional to give a tenth of one's earnings to the gods. Abram followed accepted tradition; however, he refused to take any of the recovered goods from the king of Sodom. Even though this huge amount would significantly increase what he could have given to God, he chose to reject it for more important reasons—he didn't want the ungodly king of Sodom to say, "I have made Abram rich." Instead, Abram wanted him to say, "God has made Abram rich." In this case, accepting the gifts would have focused everyone's attention on Abram or the king of Sodom rather than on God, the giver of victory. When people look at us, they need to see what God has accomplished in our lives.

## 3. God promises a son to Abram

*The LORD's Covenant with Abram*

**15** Afterward the LORD spoke to Abram in a vision and said to him, "Do not be afraid, Abram, for I will protect you, and your reward will be great."

<sup></sup>²But Abram replied, "O Sovereign LORD, what good are all your blessings when I don't even have a son? Since I don't have a son, Eliezer of Damascus, a servant in my household, will inherit all my wealth. ³You have given me no children, so one of my servants will have to be my heir."

⁴Then the LORD said to him, "No, your servant will not be your heir, for you will have a son of your own to inherit everything I am giving you." ⁵Then the LORD brought Abram outside beneath the night sky and told him, "Look up into the heavens and count the stars if you can. Your descendants will be like that—too many to count!" ⁶And Abram believed the LORD, and the LORD declared him righteous because of his faith. ⁷Then the LORD told him, "I am the LORD who brought you out of Ur of the Chaldeans to give you this land."

⁸But Abram replied, "O Sovereign LORD, how can I be sure that you will give it to me?"

⁹Then the LORD told him, "Bring me a three-year-old heifer, a three-year-old female goat, a three-year-old ram, a turtledove, and a young pigeon." ¹⁰Abram took all these and killed them. He cut each one down the middle and laid the halves side by side. He did not, however, divide the birds in half. ¹¹Some vultures came down to eat the carcasses, but Abram chased them away. ¹²That evening, as the sun was going down, Abram fell into a deep sleep. He saw a terrifying vision of darkness and horror.

¹³Then the LORD told Abram, "You can be sure that your descendants will be strangers in a foreign land, and they will be oppressed as slaves for four hundred years. ¹⁴But I will punish the nation that enslaves them, and in the end they will come away with great wealth. ¹⁵(But you will die in peace, at a ripe old age.) ¹⁶After four generations your descendants will return here to this land, when the sin of the Amorites has run its course."

¹⁷As the sun went down and it became dark, Abram saw a smoking firepot and a flaming torch pass between the halves of the carcasses. ¹⁸So the LORD made a covenant with Abram that day and said, "I have given this land to your descendants, all the way from the border

**15:1**
Gen 21:17; 26:24
Deut 33:29
Ps 3:3

**15:4**
†Gal 4:28

**15:5**
Gen 12:2; 22:17;
32:13
†Rom 4:18

**15:6**
Ps 106:31
†Rom 4:3, 9, 22
†Gal 3:6

**15:7**
Gen 12:1; 13:17
Acts 7:2-4

**15:8**
Luke 1:18

**15:9**
Lev 1:14

**15:12**
Gen 2:21; 28:11

**15:13**
Exod 12:40
†Acts 7:6
Gal 3:17

**15:14**
Exod 6:5

**15:15**
Gen 25:8

**15:16**
Exod 12:40

**15:17**
Jer 34:18-19

**15:18**
Num 34:1-15
Deut 1:7-8

---

**15:1** Why would Abram be afraid? Perhaps he feared revenge from the kings he had just defeated (14:15). God gave him two good reasons for courage: (1) He promised to protect Abram, and (2) he promised a great reward to Abram. When you fear what lies ahead, remember that God will stay with you through difficult times and that he has promised you great blessings.

**15:2, 3** Eliezer was Abram's most trusted servant, acting as household administrator. According to custom, if Abram were to die without a son, his eldest servant would become his heir. Although Abram loved his servant, he wanted a son to carry on the family line.

**15:5** Abram wasn't promised wealth or fame; he already had that. Instead, God promised descendants like the stars in the sky or the grains of sand on the seashore (22:17), too numerous to count. To appreciate the vast number of stars scattered through the sky, you need to be, like Abram, away from any distractions. Or pick up a handful of sand and try to count the grains—it can't be done! Just when Abram was despairing of ever having an heir, God promised descendants too numerous to imagine. God's blessings are beyond our imagination!

**15:6** Although Abram had been demonstrating his faith through his actions, it was his belief in the Lord, not his actions, that made Abram right with God (Romans 4:1-5). We, too, can have a right relationship with God by trusting him. Our outward actions—church attendance, prayer, good deeds—will not by themselves make us right with God. A right relationship is based on faith—

the heartfelt inner confidence that God is who he says he is and does what he says he will do. Right actions will follow naturally as by-products.

**15:8** Abram was looking for confirmation and assurance that he was doing God's will. We also want assurance when we ask for guidance. But we can know for sure that what we are doing is right if we do what the Bible says. Abram didn't have the Bible—we do.

**15:13, 14** The book of Exodus tells the story of the enslavement and miraculous deliverance of Abram's descendants.

**15:16** The Amorites were one of the nations living in Canaan, the land God promised Abram. God knew the people would grow more wicked and would someday need to be punished. Part of that punishment would involve taking away their land and giving it to Abram's descendants. God in his mercy was giving the Amorites plenty of time to repent, but he already knew they would not. At the right time, they would have to be punished. Everything God does is true to his character. He is merciful, knows all, and acts justly—and his timing is perfect.

**15:17** Why did God send this strange vision to Abram? God's covenant with Abram was serious business. It represented an incredible promise from God and a huge responsibility for Abram. To confirm his promise, God gave Abram a sign—the smoking firepot and a flaming torch. The fire and smoke suggest God's holiness, his zeal for righteousness, and his judgment on all the nations. God took the initiative, gave the confirmation, and followed through on his promises. God's passing through the pieces was a visible assurance to Abram that the covenant God had made was real.

**15:19**
Num 24:21

of Egypt* to the great Euphrates River—¹⁹the land of the Kenites, Kenizzites, Kadmonites, ²⁰Hittites, Perizzites, Rephaites, ²¹Amorites, Canaanites, Girgashites, and Jebusites."

*The Birth of Ishmael*

**16:1**
Gen 11:30
Gal 4:24-25

**16:2**
Gen 30:3

**16:3**
Gen 12:4-5

**16** But Sarai, Abram's wife, had no children. So Sarai took her servant, an Egyptian woman named Hagar, ²and gave her to Abram so she could bear his children. "The LORD has kept me from having any children," Sarai said to Abram. "Go and sleep with my servant. Perhaps I can have children through her." And Abram agreed. ³So Sarai, Abram's wife, took Hagar the Egyptian servant and gave her to Abram as a wife. (This happened ten years after Abram first arrived in the land of Canaan.)

**15:18** Hebrew *the river of Egypt,* referring either to an eastern branch of the Nile River or to the brook of Egypt in the Sinai (see Num 34:5).

---

MELCHIZEDEK

Do you like a good mystery? History is full of them! They usually involve people. One of the most mysterious people in the Bible is the king of peace, Melchizedek. He appeared one day in the life of Abraham (then Abram) and was never heard from again. What happened that day, however, was to be remembered throughout history and eventually became a subject of a New Testament letter (Hebrews).

This meeting between Abram and Melchizedek was most unusual. Although the two men were strangers and foreigners to each other, they shared a most important characteristic: Both worshiped and served the one God who made heaven and earth. This was a great moment of triumph for Abram. He had just defeated an army and regained the freedom of a large group of captives. If there was any doubt in his mind about whose victory it was, Melchizedek set the record straight by reminding Abram, "And blessed be God Most High, who has helped you conquer your enemies" (Genesis 14:20). Abram recognized that this man worshiped the same God he did.

Melchizedek was one of a small group of God-honoring people throughout the Old Testament who came in contact with the Jews (Israelites) but were not Jews themselves. This indicates that the requirement to be a follower of God is not genetic but is based on faithfully obeying his teachings and recognizing his greatness.

Do you let God speak to you through other people? In evaluating others, do you consider God's impact on their lives? Are you aware of the similarities between yourself and others who worship God, even if their form of worship is quite different from yours? Do you know the God of the Bible well enough to know if you truly worship him? Allow Melchizedek, Abraham, David, and Jesus, along with many other persons in the Bible, to show you this great God, Creator of heaven and earth. He wants you to know how much he loves you; he wants you to know him personally.

| | |
|---|---|
| **Strengths and accomplishments** | • The first priest/king of Scripture—a leader with a heart tuned to God<br>• Good at encouraging others to serve God wholeheartedly<br>• A man whose character reflected his love for God<br>• A person in the Old Testament who reminds us of Jesus and who some believe really was Jesus |
| **Lesson from his life** | • Live for God and you're likely to be at the right place at the right time. Examine your heart. To whom or what is your greatest loyalty? If you can honestly answer *God,* you are living for him |
| **Vital statistics** | • Where: Ruled in Salem, site of the future Jerusalem<br>• Occupation: King of Salem and priest of God Most High |
| **Key verses** | "This Melchizedek was king of the city of Salem and also a priest of God Most High. When Abraham was returning home after winning a great battle against many kings, Melchizedek met him and blessed him. . . . Consider then how great this Melchizedek was. Even Abraham, the great patriarch of Israel, recognized how great Melchizedek was by giving him a tenth of what he had taken in battle" (Hebrews 7:1, 4). |

Melchizedek's story is told in Genesis 14:17-20. He is also mentioned in Psalm 110:4; Hebrews 5—7.

---

**16:1-3** Sarai gave Hagar to Abram as a substitute wife, a common practice of that time. A married woman who could not have children was shamed by her peers and was often required to give a female servant to her husband in order to produce heirs. The children born to the servant woman were considered the children of the wife. Abram was acting in line with the custom of the day, but his action showed a lack of faith that God would fulfill his promise.

**16:3** Sarai took matters into her own hands by giving Hagar to Abram. Like Abram she had trouble believing God's promise that

was apparently directed specifically toward Abram and Sarai. Out of this lack of faith came a series of problems. This invariably happens when we take over for God, trying to make his promise come true through efforts that are not in line with his specific directions. In this case, time was the greatest test of Abram and Sarai's willingness to let God work in their lives. Sometimes we too must simply wait. When we ask God for something and have to wait, it is a temptation to take matters into our own hands and interfere with God's plans.

⁴So Abram slept with Hagar, and she became pregnant. When Hagar knew she was pregnant, she began to treat her mistress Sarai with contempt. ⁵Then Sarai said to Abram, "It's all your fault! Now this servant of mine is pregnant, and she despises me, though I myself gave her the privilege of sleeping with you. The LORD will make you pay for doing this to me!*"

⁶Abram replied, "Since she is your servant, you may deal with her as you see fit." So Sarai treated her harshly, and Hagar ran away.

⁷The angel of the LORD found Hagar beside a desert spring along the road to Shur. ⁸The angel said to her, "Hagar, Sarai's servant, where have you come from, and where are you going?"

"I am running away from my mistress," she replied.

⁹Then the angel of the LORD said, "Return to your mistress and submit to her authority." ¹⁰The angel added, "I will give you more descendants than you can count." ¹¹And the angel also said, "You are now pregnant and will give birth to a son. You are to name him Ishmael,* for the LORD has heard about your misery. ¹²This son of yours will be a wild one—free and untamed as a wild donkey! He will be against everyone, and everyone will be against him. Yes, he will live at odds with the rest of his brothers."

¹³Thereafter, Hagar referred to the LORD, who had spoken to her, as "the God who sees me,"* for she said, "I have seen the One who sees me!" ¹⁴Later that well was named Beer-lahairoi,* and it can still be found between Kadesh and Bered.

¹⁵So Hagar gave Abram a son, and Abram named him Ishmael. ¹⁶Abram was eighty-six years old at that time.

### Abram Is Named Abraham

**17** When Abram was ninety-nine years old, the LORD appeared to him and said, "I am God Almighty; serve me faithfully and live a blameless life. ²I will make a covenant with you, by which I will guarantee to make you into a mighty nation." ³At this, Abram fell face down in the dust. Then God said to him, ⁴"This is my covenant with you: I will make you the father of not just one nation, but a multitude of nations! ⁵What's more, I am changing your name. It will no longer be Abram; now you will be known as Abraham,* for you will be the father of many nations. ⁶I will give you millions of descendants who will represent many nations. Kings will be among them!

**16:5** Hebrew *Let the LORD judge between you and me.*   **16:11** *Ishmael* means "God hears."   **16:13** Hebrew *El-roi.*   **16:14** *Beer-lahairoi* means "well of the Living One who sees me."   **17:5** *Abram* means "exalted father"; *Abraham* means "father of many."

**16:4**
Gen 16:15

**16:5**
Gen 31:53

**16:7**
Gen 21:17; 22:11, 15

**16:8**
Gen 3:9; 4:9

**16:9**
Gen 21:12
Eph 6:5
Titus 2:9

**16:10**
Gen 17:20

**16:11**
Gen 16:15
Exod 3:7-8

**16:12**
Job 39:5-8

**16:13**
Gen 32:30

**16:14**
Gen 14:7

**16:15**
Gen 21:9; 25:12

**16:16**
Gen 12:4; 16:3

**17:1**
Gen 12:7; 28:3; 35:11; 48:3
Deut 18:13
Matt 5:48

**17:2**
Gen 12:2; 15:18

**17:3**
Gen 17:17; 18:2

**17:5**
Neh 9:7
†Rom 4:17

**17:6**
Gen 35:11

**16:5** Although Sarai arranged for Hagar to have a child by Abram, she later blamed Abram for the results. It is often easier to strike out in frustration and accuse someone else than to admit an error and ask forgiveness. (Adam and Eve did the same thing in 3:12, 13.)

**16:6** Sarai was angry with Abram, but she took it out on Hagar, and her treatment was harsh enough to cause Hagar to run away. Anger, especially when it arises from our own shortcomings, can be dangerous.

**16:8** Hagar was running away from her mistress and her problem. The angel of the Lord gave her this advice: (1) to return and face Sarai, the cause of her problem, and (2) to submit to her. Hagar needed to work on her attitude toward Sarai, no matter how justified it may have been. Running away from our problems rarely solves them. It is wise to return to our problems, face them squarely, accept God's promise of help, correct our attitudes, and act as we should.

**16:13** We have watched three people make serious mistakes: (1) Sarai, who took matters into her own hands and gave her servant to Abram; (2) Abram, who went along with the plan but, when circumstances began to go wrong, refused to help solve the problem; and (3) Hagar, who ran away from the problem. In spite of this messy situation, God demonstrated his ability to work in all things for good (Romans 8:28). Sarai and Abram still received the son they so desperately wanted, and God solved Hagar's problem despite Abram's refusal to get involved. No problem is too complicated for God if you are willing to let him help you.

**17:1** The Lord told Abram, "I am God Almighty; serve me faithfully and live a blameless life." God has the same message for us today. We are to obey the Lord in every respect because he is God—that is reason enough. If you don't think the benefits of obedience are worth it, consider who God is—the only one with the power and ability to meet your every need.

**17:2-8** Why did God repeat his covenant to Abram? Twice before, he had mentioned this agreement (Genesis 12 and 15). Here, however, God was bringing it into focus and preparing to carry it out. He revealed to Abram several specific parts of his covenant: (1) God would give Abram many descendants; (2) many nations would descend from him; (3) God would maintain his covenant with Abram's descendants; (4) God would give Abram's descendants the land of Canaan.

**17:5** God changed Abram's name to Abraham ("father of many") shortly before the promised son was conceived. From this point on, the Bible calls him Abraham.

**17:5-14** God was making a covenant, or contract, between himself and Abraham. The terms were simple: Abraham would obey God and circumcise all the males in his household; God's part was to give Abraham heirs, property, power, and wealth. Most contracts are even trades: We give something and in turn receive something of equal value. But when we become part of God's covenant family, the blessings we receive far outweigh what we must give up.

**17:7**
Gen 15:18
Lev 11:45; 26:12
Ps 105:8-11
†Gal 3:16

7"I will continue this everlasting covenant between us, generation after generation. It will continue between me and your offspring* forever. And I will always be your God and the God of your descendants after you. 8Yes, I will give all this land of Canaan to you and to your offspring forever. And I will be their God.

### The Sign of Circumcision

**17:10**
John 7:22
Acts 7:8

**17:11**
Exod 12:48
Deut 10:16

**17:12**
Gen 21:4
Lev 12:3
Luke 1:59; 2:21

9"Your part of the agreement," God told Abraham, "is to obey the terms of the covenant. You and all your descendants have this continual responsibility. 10This is the covenant that you and your descendants must keep: Each male among you must be circumcised; 11the flesh of his foreskin must be cut off. This will be a sign that you and they have accepted this covenant. 12Every male child must be circumcised on the eighth day after his birth. This applies not only to members of your family, but also to the servants born

**17:7** Hebrew *seed;* also in 17:8.

---

## ISHMAEL

Have you ever wondered if you were born into the wrong family? We don't know much about how Ishmael viewed life, but that question must have haunted him at times. His life, his name, and his position were bound up in a conflict between two jealous women. Sarah (Sarai), impatient with God's timetable, had taken matters into her own hands, deciding to have a child through another woman. Hagar, servant that she was, submitted to being used this way. But her pregnancy gave birth to strong feelings of superiority toward Sarah. Into this tense atmosphere, Ishmael was born.

For 13 years Abraham thought Ishmael's birth had fulfilled God's promise. He was surprised to hear God say that the promised child would be Abraham and Sarah's very own. Sarah's pregnancy and Isaac's birth must have had a devastating impact on Ishmael. Until then he had been treated as a son and heir, but this late arrival made his future uncertain. During Isaac's weaning celebration, Sarah caught Ishmael teasing his half brother. As a result, Hagar and Ishmael were permanently expelled from Abraham's family.

Much of what happened throughout his life cannot be blamed on Ishmael. He was caught in a process much bigger than he was. However, his own actions showed that he had chosen to become part of the problem and not part of the solution. He chose to live under his circumstances rather than above them.

The choice he made is one we must all make. There are circumstances over which we have no control (heredity for instance), but there are others that we can control (decisions we make). At the heart of the matter is the sin-oriented nature we have all inherited. It can be partly controlled, although not overcome, by human effort. In the context of history, Ishmael's life represents the mess we make when we don't try to change the things we could change. The God of the Bible has offered a solution. His answer is not control but a changed life. To have a changed life, turn to God, trust him to forgive your sinful past, and begin to change your attitude toward him and others.

| | |
|---|---|
| **Strengths and accomplishments** | ▪ One of the first to experience the physical sign of God's covenant, circumcision<br>▪ Known for his ability as an archer and hunter<br>▪ Fathered 12 sons who became leaders of warrior tribes |
| **Weakness and mistake** | ▪ Failed to recognize the place of his half brother, Isaac, and mocked him |
| **Lesson from his life** | ▪ God's plans incorporate people's mistakes |
| **Vital statistics** | ▪ Where: Canaan and Egypt<br>▪ Occupation: Hunter, archer, warrior<br>▪ Relatives: Parents: Hagar and Abraham. Half brother: Isaac |
| **Key verses** | "Then God heard the boy's cries, and the angel of God called to Hagar from the sky, 'Hagar, what's wrong? Do not be afraid! God has heard the boy's cries from the place where you laid him. Go to him and comfort him, for I will make a great nation from his descendants' " (Genesis 21:17, 18) |

Ishmael's story is told in Genesis 16—17; 21:8-20; 25:12-18; 28:8, 9; 36:1-3. He is also mentioned in 1 Chronicles 1:28-31; Romans 9:7-9; Galatians 4:21-31.

---

**17:9, 10** Why did God require circumcision? (1) As a sign of obedience to him in all matters. (2) As a sign of belonging to his covenant people. Once circumcised, there was no turning back. The man would be identified as a Jew forever. (3) As a symbol of "cutting off" the old life of sin, purifying one's heart, and dedicating oneself to God. (4) Possibly as a health measure.

Circumcision more than any other practice separated God's people from their pagan neighbors. In Abraham's day, this was essential to develop the pure worship of the one true God.

in your household and the foreign-born servants whom you have purchased. 13All must be circumcised. Your bodies will thus bear the mark of my everlasting covenant. 14Anyone who refuses to be circumcised will be cut off from the covenant family for violating the covenant."

**17:14**
Exod 30:33
Lev 7:20

### Sarai Is Named Sarah

15Then God added, "Regarding Sarai, your wife—her name will no longer be Sarai; from now on you will call her Sarah.* 16And I will bless her and give you a son from her! Yes, I will bless her richly, and she will become the mother of many nations. Kings will be among her descendants!"

**17:15**
Gen 17:5

**17:16**
Gen 18:10

17Then Abraham bowed down to the ground, but he laughed to himself in disbelief. "How could I become a father at the age of one hundred?" he wondered. "Besides, Sarah is ninety; how could she have a baby?" 18And Abraham said to God, "Yes, may Ishmael enjoy your special blessing!"

**17:17**
Gen 17:3; 18:11-13

19But God replied, "Sarah, your wife, will bear you a son. You will name him Isaac,* and I will confirm my everlasting covenant with him and his descendants. 20As for Ishmael, I will bless him also, just as you have asked. I will cause him to multiply and become a great nation. Twelve princes will be among his descendants. 21But my covenant is with Isaac, who will be born to you and Sarah about this time next year."

**17:19**
Gen 21:2; 26:2-5

**17:20**
Gen 25:12-16

**17:21**
Gen 18:10, 14

22That ended the conversation, and God left Abraham. 23On that very day Abraham took his son Ishmael and every other male in his household and circumcised them, cutting off their foreskins, exactly as God had told him. 24Abraham was ninety-nine years old at that time, 25and Ishmael his son was thirteen. 26Both were circumcised the same day, 27along with all the other men and boys of the household, whether they were born there or bought as servants.

**17:22**
Gen 18:33; 35:13

**17:23**
Gen 14:14

**17:24**
Rom 4:11

**17:25**
Gen 16:16

## 4. Sodom and Gomorrah

### A Son Promised to Sarah

**18** The LORD appeared again to Abraham while he was camped near the oak grove belonging to Mamre. One day about noon, as Abraham was sitting at the entrance to his tent, 2he suddenly noticed three men standing nearby. He got up and ran to meet them, welcoming them by bowing low to the ground. 3"My lord," he said, "if it pleases you, stop here for a while. 4Rest in the shade of this tree while my servants get some water to wash your feet. 5Let me prepare some food to refresh you. Please stay awhile before continuing on your journey."

**18:1**
Gen 12:7; 13:18

**18:2**
Gen 32:24
Josh 5:13
Judg 13:6-11

**18:4**
Gen 19:2; 24:32

**18:5**
Judg 6:18-19;
13:15-16

"All right," they said. "Do as you have said."

6So Abraham ran back to the tent and said to Sarah, "Quick! Get three measures* of your best flour, and bake some bread." 7Then Abraham ran out to the herd and chose a fat calf and told a servant to hurry and butcher it. 8When the food was ready, he took some cheese curds and milk and the roasted meat, and he served it to the men. As they ate, Abraham waited on them there beneath the trees.

9"Where is Sarah, your wife?" they asked him.

"In the tent," Abraham replied.

10Then one of them said, "About this time next year I will return, and your wife Sarah will have a son."

**18:10**
†Rom 9:9

Now Sarah was listening to this conversation from the tent nearby. 11And since

**18:11**
Gen 17:17

**17:15** Sarah means "princess." **17:19** Isaac means "he laughs." **18:6** Hebrew 3 seahs, about 15 quarts or 18 liters.

---

**17:17-27** How could Abraham doubt God? It seemed incredible that he and Sarah in their advanced years could have a child. Abraham, the man God considered righteous because of his faith, had trouble believing God's promise to him. Despite his doubts, however, he followed God's commands (17:22-27). Even people of great faith may have doubts. When God seems to want the impossible and you begin to doubt his leading, be like Abraham. Focus on God's commitment to fulfill his promises to you, and then continue to obey.

**17:20** God did not forget Ishmael. Although he was not to be Abraham's heir, he would also be the father of a great nation.

Regardless of your circumstances, God has not forgotten you. Obey him and trust in his plan.

**18:2-5** Abraham was eager to show hospitality to these three visitors, as was Lot (19:2). In Abraham's day, a person's reputation was largely connected to his hospitality—the sharing of home and food. Even strangers were to be treated as highly honored guests. Meeting another's need for food or shelter was and still is one of the most immediate and practical ways to obey God. It is also a time-honored relationship builder. Hebrews 13:2 suggests that we, like Abraham, might actually entertain angels. This thought should be on our minds the next time we have the opportunity to meet a stranger's needs.

**18:12**
1 Pet 3:6

Abraham and Sarah were both very old, and Sarah was long past the age of having children, [12] she laughed silently to herself. "How could a worn-out woman like me have a baby?" she thought. "And when my master—my husband—is also so old?"

**18:14**
Gen 18:10
Jer 32:17, 27
†Rom 9:9

[13] Then the LORD said to Abraham, "Why did Sarah laugh? Why did she say, 'Can an old woman like me have a baby?' [14] Is anything too hard for the LORD? About a year from now, just as I told you, I will return, and Sarah will have a son." [15] Sarah was afraid, so she denied that she had laughed. But he said, "That is not true. You did laugh."

*Abraham Intercedes for Sodom*

**18:16**
Gen 18:22; 19:1

[16] Then the men got up from their meal and started on toward Sodom. Abraham went with them part of the way.

**18:18**
Gen 12:2-3
†Gal 3:18

[17] "Should I hide my plan from Abraham?" the LORD asked. [18] "For Abraham will become a great and mighty nation, and all the nations of the earth will be blessed through

---

We all know that there are consequences to any action we take. What we do can set into motion a series of events that may continue long after we're gone. Unfortunately, when we are making a decision, most of us think only of the immediate consequences. These are often misleading because they are short-lived.

Abraham had a choice to make. His decision was between setting out with his family and belongings for parts unknown or staying right where he was. He had to decide between the security of what he already had and the uncertainty of traveling under God's direction. All he had to go on was God's promise to guide and bless him. Abraham could hardly have been expected to visualize how much of the future was resting on his decision of whether to go or stay, but his obedience affected the history of the world. His decision to follow God set into motion the development of the nation that God would eventually use as his own when he visited earth himself. When Jesus Christ came to earth, God's promise was fulfilled; through Abraham the entire world was blessed.

You probably don't know the long-term effects of most decisions you make. But shouldn't the fact that there will be long-term results cause you to think carefully and seek God's guidance as you make choices and take action today?

| | |
|---|---|
| **Strengths and accomplishments** | • His faith pleased God<br>• Became the founder of the Jewish nation<br>• Was respected by others and was courageous in defending his family at any cost<br>• Was not only a caring father to his own family, but practiced hospitality to others<br>• Was a successful and wealthy rancher<br>• Usually avoided conflicts, but when they were unavoidable, he allowed his opponent to set the rules for settling the dispute |
| **Weakness and mistake** | • Under direct pressure, he distorted the truth |
| **Lessons from his life** | • God desires dependence, trust, and faith in him—not faith in our ability to please him<br>• God's plan from the beginning has been to make himself known to all people |
| **Vital statistics** | • Where: Born in Ur of the Chaldeans; spent most of his life in the land of Canaan<br>• Occupation: Wealthy livestock owner<br>• Relatives: Brothers: Nahor and Haran. Father: Terah. Wife: Sarah. Nephew: Lot. Sons: Ishmael and Isaac<br>• Contemporaries: Abimelech, Melchizedek |
| **Key verse** | "And Abram believed the LORD, and the LORD declared him righteous because of his faith" (Genesis 15:6). |

Abraham's story is told in Genesis 11—25. He is also mentioned in Exodus 2:24; Matthew 1:1, 2; Luke 3:34; Acts 7:2–8; Romans 4; Galatians 3; Hebrews 2, 6, 7, 11.

---

**18:14** "Is anything too hard for the LORD?" The obvious answer is, "Of course not!" This question reveals much about God. Make it a habit to insert your specific needs into the question. "Is this day in my life too hard for the Lord?" "Is this habit I'm trying to break too hard for him?" "Is the communication problem I'm having too hard for him?" Asking the question this way reminds you that God is personally involved in your life and nudges you to ask for his power to help you.

**18:15** Sarah lied because she was afraid of being discovered. Fear is the most common motive for lying. We are afraid that our inner thoughts and emotions will be exposed or our wrongdoings discovered. But lying causes greater complications than telling the truth and brings even more problems. If God can't be trusted with our innermost thoughts and fears, we are in greater trouble than we first imagined.

him. ¹⁹I have singled him out so that he will direct his sons and their families to keep the
way of the LORD and do what is right and just. Then I will do for him all that I have
promised." ²⁰So the LORD told Abraham, "I have heard that the people of Sodom and
Gomorrah are extremely evil, and that everything they do is wicked. ²¹I am going down
to see whether or not these reports are true. Then I will know."

²²The two other men went on toward Sodom, but the LORD remained with Abraham
for a while. ²³Abraham approached him and said, "Will you destroy both innocent and
guilty alike? ²⁴Suppose you find fifty innocent people there within the city—will you
still destroy it, and not spare it for their sakes? ²⁵Surely you wouldn't do such a thing,
destroying the innocent with the guilty. Why, you would be treating the innocent and the
guilty exactly the same! Surely you wouldn't do that! Should not the Judge of all the
earth do what is right?"

²⁶And the LORD replied, "If I find fifty innocent people in Sodom, I will spare the
entire city for their sake."

²⁷Then Abraham spoke again. "Since I have begun, let me go on and speak further to
my Lord, even though I am but dust and ashes. ²⁸Suppose there are only forty-five? Will
you destroy the city for lack of five?"

And the LORD said, "I will not destroy it if I find forty-five."

²⁹Then Abraham pressed his request further. "Suppose there are only forty?"

And the LORD replied, "I will not destroy it if there are forty."

³⁰"Please don't be angry, my Lord," Abraham pleaded. "Let me speak—suppose only
thirty are found?"

And the LORD replied, "I will not destroy it if there are thirty."

³¹Then Abraham said, "Since I have dared to speak to the Lord, let me continue—suppose there are only twenty?"

And the LORD said, "Then I will not destroy it for the sake of the twenty."

³²Finally, Abraham said, "Lord, please do not get angry; I will speak but once more!
Suppose only ten are found there?"

And the LORD said, "Then, for the sake of the ten, I will not destroy it."

³³The LORD went on his way when he had finished his conversation with Abraham,
and Abraham returned to his tent.

### Sodom and Gomorrah Destroyed

**19** That evening the two angels came to the entrance of the city of Sodom, and Lot
was sitting there as they arrived. When he saw them, he stood up to meet them.
Then he welcomed them and bowed low to the ground. ²"My lords," he said, "come to

**Cross-references (right margin):**

**18:19** Neh 9:7
**18:20** Gen 19:13
**18:21** Gen 11:5; Exod 3:8
**18:22** Gen 18:16; 19:1
**18:23** Exod 23:7
**18:25** Deut 1:16-17; 32:4; Ps 58:11
**18:27** Gen 2:7; Job 30:19; 42:6
**18:30** Exod 32:32
**18:33** Gen 17:22; 35:13
**19:1** Gen 18:2
**19:2** Gen 18:4

---

**18:20-33** Did Abraham change God's mind? Of course not.
The more likely answer is that God changed Abraham's mind.
Abraham knew that God is just and that he punishes sin, but he
may have wondered about God's mercy. Abraham seemed to
be probing God's mind to see how merciful he really was. He
left his conversation with God convinced that God was both
kind and fair. Our prayers won't change God's mind, but they
may change ours just as Abraham's prayer changed his. Prayer
helps us better understand the mind of God.

**18:20-33** Why did God let Abraham question his justice and intercede for a wicked city? Abraham knew that God must punish sin,
but he also knew from experience that God is merciful to sinners.
God knew there were not 10 innocent people in the city, but he
was merciful enough to allow Abraham to intercede. He was also
merciful enough to help Lot, Abraham's nephew, get out of Sodom
before it was destroyed. God does not take pleasure in destroying
the wicked, but he must punish sin. He is both just and merciful.
We should be thankful that God's mercy extends to us.

**18:21** God gave the men of Sodom a fair test. He was not
ignorant of the city's wicked practices, but in his fairness and
patience he gave the people of Sodom one last chance to
repent. God is still waiting, giving people the opportunity to
turn to him (2 Peter 3:9). Those who are wise will turn to him
before his patience wears out.

**18:25** Was God being unfair to the people of Sodom? Did he
really plan to destroy the innocent with the guilty? On the contrary, God's fairness stood out. (1) He agreed to spare the entire
city if only 10 innocent people lived there. (2) He showed great
mercy toward Lot, apparently the only man in the city who had
any kind of relationship with him (and even that was question-
able). (3) He showed great patience toward Lot, almost forcing
him to leave Sodom before it was destroyed. Remember God's
patience when you are tempted to think he is unfair. Even the
most godly people deserve his justice. We should be glad God
doesn't direct his justice toward us as he did toward Sodom.

**18:33** God showed Abraham that asking for anything is allowed,
with the understanding that God's answers come from God's perspective. They are not always in harmony with our expectations,
for only he knows the whole story. Are you missing God's answer
to a prayer because you haven't considered any possible answers
other than the one you expect?

**19:1** The entrance of the city was the meeting place for city
officials and other men to discuss current events and transact business. It was a place of authority and status where a person could
see and be seen. Evidently Lot held an important position in the
government or associated with those who did because the angels
found him at the city's entrance. Perhaps Lot's status in Sodom
was one reason he was so reluctant to leave (19:16, 18-22).

my home to wash your feet, and be my guests for the night. You may then get up in the morning as early as you like and be on your way again."

"Oh no," they said. "we'll just spend the night out here in the city square."

**19:3**
Gen 18:6-8

3But Lot insisted, so at last they went home with him. He set a great feast before them, complete with fresh bread made without yeast. After the meal, 4as they were preparing to retire for the night. all the men of Sodom, young and old, came from all over the city and surrounded the house. 5They shouted to Lot, "Where are the men who came to spend the night with you? Bring them out so we can have sex with them."

**19:4**
Gen 13:13; 18:20

**19:5**
Lev 18:22
Judg 19:22

6Lot stepped outside to talk to them, shutting the door behind him. 7"Please, my brothers," he begged, "don't do such a wicked thing. 8Look—I have two virgin daughters. Do with them as you wish, but leave these men alone, for they are under my protection."

**19:8**
Deut 23:17

9"Stand back!" they shouted. "Who do you think you are? We let you settle among us, and now you are trying to tell us what to do! We'll treat you far worse than those other men!" And they lunged at Lot and began breaking down the door. 10But the two angels

**19:9**
Exod 2:14

**19:10**
Gen 19:1

---

There probably isn't anything harder to do than wait whether we are expecting something good, something bad, or an unknown.

One way we often cope with a long wait (or even a short one) is to begin helping God get his plan into action. Sarah tried this approach. She was too old to expect to have a child of her own, so she thought God must have something else in mind. From Sarah's limited point of view, this could only be to give Abraham a son through another woman—a common practice in her day. The plan seemed harmless enough. Abraham would sleep with Sarah's servant, who would then give birth to a child. Sarah would take the child as her own. The plan worked beautifully—at first. But as you read about the events that followed, you will be struck by how often Sarah must have regretted the day she decided to push God's timetable ahead.

Another way we cope with a long wait is to gradually conclude that what we're waiting for is never going to happen. Sarah waited 90 years for a baby. When God told her she would finally have one of her own, she laughed, not so much from a lack of faith in what God could do, but from doubt about what he could do *through her.* When confronted about her laughter, she lied—as she had seen her husband do from time to time. She probably didn't want her true feelings to be known.

What parts of your life seem to be on hold right now? Do you understand that this may be part of God's plan for you? The Bible has more than enough clear direction to keep us busy while we're waiting for some particular part of life to move ahead.

| | |
|---|---|
| **Strengths and accomplishments** | • Was intensely loyal to her own child<br>• Became the mother of a nation and an ancestor of Jesus<br>• Was a woman of faith, the first woman listed in the Hall of Faith in Hebrews 11 |
| **Weaknesses and mistakes** | • Had trouble believing God's promises to her<br>• Attempted to work problems out on her own, without consulting God<br>• Tried to cover her faults by blaming others |
| **Lessons from her life** | • God responds to faith even in the midst of failure<br>• God is not bound by what usually happens; he can stretch the limits and cause unheard-of events to occur |
| **Vital statistics** | • Where: Married Abram in Ur of the Chaldeans, then moved with him to Canaan<br>• Occupation: Wife, mother, household manager<br>• Relatives: Father: Terah. Husband: Abraham. Half brothers: Nahor and Haran. Nephew: Lot. Son: Isaac |
| **Key verse** | "It was by faith that Sarah together with Abraham was able to have a child, even though they were too old and Sarah was barren. Abraham believed that God would keep his promise" (Hebrews 11:11). |

Sarah's story is told in Genesis 11—25. She is also mentioned in Isaiah 51:2; Romans 4:19; 9:9; Hebrews 11:11; 1 Peter 3:6.

---

**19:8** How could any father give his daughters to be ravished by a mob of perverts, just to protect two strangers? Possibly Lot was scheming to save both the girls and the visitors, hoping the girls' fiancés would rescue them or that the homosexual men would be disinterested in the girls and simply go away. Although it was the custom of the day to protect guests at any cost, this terrible suggestion reveals how deeply sin had been absorbed into Lot's life. He had become hardened to evil acts in an evil city. Whatever Lot's motives were, we see here an illustration of Sodom's terrible wickedness—a wickedness so great that God had to destroy the entire city.

reached out and pulled Lot in and bolted the door. [11]Then they blinded the men of Sodom so they couldn't find the doorway.

[12]"Do you have any other relatives here in the city?" the angels asked. "Get them out of this place—sons-in-law, sons, daughters, or anyone else. [13]For we will destroy the city completely. The stench of the place has reached the LORD, and he has sent us to destroy it."

[14]So Lot rushed out to tell his daughters' fiancés, "Quick, get out of the city! The LORD is going to destroy it." But the young men thought he was only joking.

[15]At dawn the next morning the angels became insistent. "Hurry," they said to Lot. "Take your wife and your two daughters who are here. Get out of here right now, or you will be caught in the destruction of the city."

[16]When Lot still hesitated, the angels seized his hand and the hands of his wife and two daughters and rushed them to safety outside the city, for the LORD was merciful. [17]"Run for your lives!" the angels warned. "Do not stop anywhere in the valley. And don't look back! Escape to the mountains, or you will die."

[18]"Oh no, my lords, please," Lot begged. [19]"You have been so kind to me and saved my life, and you have granted me such mercy. But I cannot go to the mountains. Disaster would catch up to me there, and I would soon die. [20]See, there is a small village nearby. Please let me go there instead; don't you see how small it is? Then my life will be saved."

[21]"All right," the angel said, "I will grant your request. I will not destroy that little village. [22]But hurry! For I can do nothing until you are there." From that time on, that village was known as Zoar.*

[23]The sun was rising as Lot reached the village. [24]Then the LORD rained down fire and burning sulfur from the heavens on Sodom and Gomorrah. [25]He utterly destroyed them, along with the other cities and villages of the plain, eliminating all life—people, plants, and animals alike. [26]But Lot's wife looked back as she was following along behind him, and she became a pillar of salt.

[27]The next morning Abraham was up early and hurried out to the place where he had stood in the LORD's presence. [28]He looked out across the plain to Sodom and Gomorrah and saw columns of smoke and fumes, as from a furnace, rising from the cities there. [29]But God had listened to Abraham's request and kept Lot safe, removing him from the disaster that engulfed the cities on the plain.

**19:22** Zoar means "little."

**19:11**
Deut 28:28-29
2 Kgs 6:18
Acts 13:11

**19:13**
Gen 18:20
1 Chr 21:15
Jude 1:7

**19:14**
Exod 9:21
Jer 5:12; 43:1-2

**19:17**
Gen 13:10; 19:26
Jer 48:6

**19:22**
Gen 13:10

**19:24**
Luke 17:29
Jude 1:7

**19:25**
Deut 29:23
Isa 13:19
Lam 4:6
2 Pet 2:6

**19:26**
Gen 19:17
Luke 17:32

**19:27**
Gen 18:22

**19:28**
Rev 9:2

**19:29**
Deut 7:8; 9:5
2 Pet 2:7-8

---

**19:13** God promised to spare Sodom if only 10 innocent people lived there (18:32). Obviously not even 10 could be found, because the angels arrived to destroy the city. Archaeological evidence points to an advanced civilization in this area during Abraham's day. Most researchers also confirm some kind of sudden and devastating destruction. It is now widely thought that the buried city lies beneath the waters of the southern end of the Dead Sea. The story of Sodom reveals that the people of Lot's day had to deal with the same kinds of repulsive sins the world faces today. We should follow Abraham's example of trusting God. His selfless faith contrasts with the self-gratifying people of Sodom.

**19:14** Lot had lived so long and was so contented among ungodly people that he was no longer a believable witness for God. He had allowed his environment to shape him, rather than he shaping his environment. Do those who know you see you as a witness for God, or are you just one of the crowd, blending in unnoticed? Lot had compromised to the point that he was almost useless to God. When he finally made a stand, nobody listened. Have you, too, become useless to God because you are too much like your environment? To make a difference, you must first decide to be different in your faith and your conduct.

**19:16** Lot hesitated, so the angel seized his hand and rushed him to safety. Lot did not want to abandon the wealth, position, and comfort he enjoyed in Sodom. It is easy to criticize Lot for being hypnotized by Sodom when the choice seems so clear to us. To be wiser than Lot, we must see that our hesitation to obey stems from the false attractions of our culture's pleasures.

**19:16-29** Notice how God's mercy toward Abraham extended to Lot and his family. Because Abraham pleaded for Lot, God was merciful and saved Lot from the fiery destruction of Sodom. A righteous person can often affect others for good. James says that the "earnest prayer of a righteous person has great power" (James 5:16). All Christians should follow Abraham's example and pray for others to be saved.

**19:24** In the story of Sodom and Gomorrah, we see two facets of God's character: his great patience (agreeing to spare a wicked city for 10 good people) and his fierce anger (destroying both cities). As we grow spiritually, we should find ourselves developing not only a deeper respect for God because of his anger toward sin but also a deeper love for God because of his patience when we sin.

**19:26** Lot's wife turned back to look at the smoldering city of Sodom. Clinging to the past, she was unwilling to turn completely away. Are you looking back longingly at sin while trying to move forward with God? You can't make progress with God as long as you are holding on to pieces of your old life. Jesus said it this way in Matthew 6:24: "No one can serve two masters."

### Lot and His Daughters

**19:30**
Gen 13:10

30Afterward Lot left Zoar because he was afraid of the people there, and he went to live in a cave in the mountains with his two daughters. 31One day the older daughter said to her sister. "There isn't a man anywhere in this entire area for us to marry. And our father will soon be too old to have children. 32Come, let's get him drunk with wine, and then we will sleep with him. That way we will preserve our family line through our father."

**19:33**
Gen 9:21

33So that night they got him drunk, and the older daughter went in and slept with her father. He was unaware of her lying down or getting up again.

34The next morning the older daughter said to her younger sister, "I slept with our father last night. Let's get him drunk with wine again tonight, and you go in and sleep

**ISAAC**

A name carries great authority. It sets you apart. It triggers memories. The sound of it calls you to attention anywhere.

Many Bible names accomplished even more. They were often descriptions of important facts about one's past and hopes for the future. The choice of the name *Isaac*, "he laughs," for Abraham and Sarah's son must have created a variety of feelings in them each time it was spoken. At times it must have recalled their shocked laughter at God's announcement that they would be parents in their old age. At other times, it must have brought back the joyful feelings of receiving their long-awaited answer to prayer for a child. Most important, it was a testimony to God's power in making his promise a reality.

In a family of forceful initiators, Isaac was the quiet, mind-my-own-business type unless he was specifically called on to take action. He was the protected only child from the time Sarah got rid of Ishmael until Abraham arranged his marriage to Rebekah.

In his own family Isaac had the patriarchal position, but Rebekah had the power. Rather than stand his ground, Isaac found it easier to compromise or lie to avoid confrontations.

In spite of these shortcomings, Isaac was part of God's plan. The model his father gave him included a great gift of faith in the one true God. God's promise to create a great nation through which he would bless the world was passed on by Isaac to his twin sons.

It is usually not hard to identify with Isaac in his weaknesses. But consider for a moment that God works through people in spite of their shortcomings and often through them. As you pray, put into words your desire to be available to God. You will discover that his willingness to use you is even greater than your desire to be used.

| | |
|---|---|
| **Strengths and accomplishments** | • He was the miracle child born to Sarah and Abraham when she was 90 years old and he was 100<br>• He was the first descendant in fulfillment of God's promise to Abraham<br>• He seems to have been a caring and consistent husband, at least until his sons were born<br>• He demonstrated great patience |
| **Weaknesses and mistakes** | • Under pressure he tended to lie<br>• In conflict he sought to avoid confrontation<br>• He played favorites between his sons and alienated his wife |
| **Lessons from his life** | • Patience often brings rewards<br>• Both God's plans and his promises are larger than people<br>• God keeps his promises! He remains faithful though we are often faithless<br>• Playing favorites is sure to bring family conflict |
| **Vital statistics** | • Where: Various places in the southern part of Palestine, including Beersheba (Genesis 26:23)<br>• Occupation: Wealthy livestock owner<br>• Relatives: Parents: Abraham and Sarah. Half brother: Ishmael. Wife: Rebekah. Sons: Jacob and Esau |
| **Key verse** | "But God replied, Sarah, your wife, will bear you a son. You will name him Isaac, and I will confirm my everlasting covenant with him and his descendants' " (Genesis 17:19). |

Isaac's story is told in Genesis 17:15—35:29. He is also mentioned in Romans 9:7-10; Hebrews 11:17-20; James 2:21.

---

**19:30-38** In this pitiful sequel to the story of the destruction of Sodom, we see two women compelled to preserve their family line. They were driven not by lust but by desperation—they feared they would never marry. Lot's tendency to compromise and refusal to act reached its peak. He should have found right partners for his daughters long before this; Abraham's family

wasn't far away. Now the two daughters stooped to incest, showing their acceptance of the morals of Sodom. We are most likely to sin when we are desperate for what we feel we must have.

**19:30-38** Why doesn't the Bible openly condemn these sisters for what they did? In many cases, the Bible does not judge people

with him. That way our family line will be preserved." ³⁵So that night they got him drunk again, and the younger daughter went in and slept with him. As before, he was unaware of her lying down or getting up again. ³⁶So both of Lot's daughters became pregnant by their father.

³⁷When the older daughter gave birth to a son, she named him Moab.* He became the ancestor of the nation now known as the Moabites. ³⁸When the younger daughter gave birth to a son, she named him Ben-ammi.* He became the ancestor of the nation now known as the Ammonites.

### Abraham Deceives Abimelech

**20** Now Abraham moved south to the Negev and settled for a while between Kadesh and Shur at a place called Gerar. ²Abraham told people there that his wife, Sarah, was his sister. So King Abimelech sent for her and had her brought to him at his palace.

³But one night God came to Abimelech in a dream and told him, "You are a dead man, for that woman you took is married."

⁴But Abimelech had not slept with her yet, so he said, "Lord, will you kill an innocent man? ⁵Abraham told me, 'She is my sister,' and she herself said, 'Yes, he is my brother.' I acted in complete innocence!"

⁶"Yes, I know you are innocent," God replied. "That is why I kept you from sinning against me; I did not let you touch her. ⁷Now return her to her husband, and he will pray for you, for he is a prophet. Then you will live. But if you don't return her to him, you can be sure that you and your entire household will die."

⁸Abimelech got up early the next morning and hastily called a meeting of all his servants. When he told them what had happened, great fear swept through the crowd. ⁹Then Abimelech called for Abraham. "What is this you have done to us?" he demanded. "What have I done to you that deserves treatment like this, making me and my kingdom guilty of this great sin? This kind of thing should not be done! ¹⁰Why have you done this to us?"

¹¹"Well," Abraham said, "I figured this to be a godless place. I thought, 'They will want my wife and will kill me to get her.' ¹²Besides, she is my sister—we both have the same father, though different mothers—and I married her. ¹³When God sent me to travel far from my father's home, I told her, 'Wherever we go, have the kindness to say that you are my sister.'"

¹⁴Then Abimelech took sheep and oxen and servants—both men and women—and gave them to Abraham, and he returned his wife, Sarah, to him. ¹⁵"Look over my kingdom, and choose a place where you would like to live," Abimelech told him. ¹⁶Then he turned to Sarah. "Look," he said, "I am giving your 'brother' a thousand pieces of silver* to compensate for any embarrassment I may have caused you. This will settle any claim against me in this matter."

**19:37** *Moab* sounds like a Hebrew term that means "from father." **19:38** *Ben-ammi* means "son of my people." **20:16** Hebrew *1,000 shekels of silver,* about 25 pounds or 11.4 kilograms in weight.

**19:37**
Gen 36:35
Exod 15:15
Num 21:29
Deut 2:9
Ruth 1:1

**19:38**
Num 21:24
Deut 2:19

**20:1**
Gen 14:7; 18:1;
26:1

**20:2**
Gen 12:13

**20:3**
Gen 28:12; 31:24;
37:5

**20:4**
Gen 18:23-25

**20:5**
Gen 12:19
1 Kgs 9:4
Pss 7:8; 26:6

**20:7**
1 Sam 7:5
Job 42:8

**20:9**
Gen 12:18

**20:11**
Gen 12:12; 42:18

**20:13**
Gen 12:1

**20:14**
Gen 12:16

**20:16**
Gen 23:15

---

for their actions. It simply reports the events. However, incest is clearly condemned in other parts of Scripture (Leviticus 18:6-18; 20:11, 12, 17, 19-21; Deuteronomy 22:30; 27:20-23; Ezekiel 22:11; 1 Corinthians 5:1). Perhaps the consequence of their action—Moab and Ammon became enemies of Israel—was God's way of judging their sin.

**19:37, 38** Moab and Ben-ammi were the products of incest. They became the fathers of two of Israel's greatest enemies, the Moabites and the Ammonites. These nations settled east of the Jordan River, and Israel never conquered them. Because of the family connection, Moses was forbidden to attack them (Deuteronomy 2:9). Ruth, great-grandmother of David and an ancestor of Jesus, was from Moab.

**20:2** Abraham had used this same trick before to protect himself (12:11-13). Although Abraham is one of our heroes of faith, he did not learn his lesson well enough the first time. In fact, by giving in to the temptation again, he risked turning a sinful act into a sinful pattern of lying whenever he suspected his life was in danger.

No matter how much we love God, certain temptations are especially difficult to resist. These are the vulnerable spots in our spiritual armor. As we struggle with these weaknesses, we can be encouraged to know that God is watching out for us just as he did for Abraham.

**20:6** Abimelech had unknowingly taken a married woman to be his wife and was about to commit adultery. But God somehow prevented him from touching Sarah and held him back from sinning. What mercy on God's part! How many times has God done the same for us, holding us back from sin in ways we can't even detect? We have no way of knowing—we just know from this story that he can. God works just as often in ways we can't see as in ways we can.

**20:11-13** Because Abraham mistakenly assumed that Abimelech was a wicked man, he made a quick decision to tell a half-truth. Abraham thought it would be more effective to deceive Abimelech than to trust God to work in the king's life. Don't assume that God will not work in a situation that has potential problems. You may not completely understand the situation, and God may intervene when you least expect it.

**20:17**
Num 12:13; 21:7

**20:18**
Gen 12:17

[17] Then Abraham prayed to God, and God healed Abimelech, his wife, and the other women of the household, so they could have children. [18] For the LORD had stricken all the women with infertility as a warning to Abimelech for having taken Abraham's wife.

## 5. Birth and near sacrifice of Isaac

### The Birth of Isaac

**21:2**
Gen 18:10
Gal 4:22
Heb 11:11

**21:4**
Gen 17:10, 12

**21:5**
Heb 6:15

**21:6**
Isa 54:1

**21:7**
Gen 18:13

**21** Then the LORD did exactly what he had promised. [2] Sarah became pregnant, and she gave a son to Abraham in his old age. It all happened at the time God had said it would. [3] And Abraham named his son Isaac.* [4] Eight days after Isaac was born, Abraham circumcised him as God had commanded. [5] Abraham was one hundred years old at the time.

[6] And Sarah declared, "God has brought me laughter! All who hear about this will laugh with me. [7] For who would have dreamed that I would ever have a baby? Yet I have given Abraham a son in his old age!"

### Hagar and Ishmael Sent Away

**21:8**
1 Sam 1:23

**21:9**
Gal 4:29

**21:10**
†Gal 4:30

**21:12**
†Rom 9:7
†Heb 11:18

**21:13**
Gen 16:10; 21:18;
25:12-18

**21:14**
Gen 16:1

**21:16**
Jer 6:26

[8] As time went by and Isaac grew and was weaned, Abraham gave a big party to celebrate the happy occasion. [9] But Sarah saw Ishmael—the son of Abraham and her Egyptian servant Hagar—making fun of Isaac. [10] So she turned to Abraham and demanded, "Get rid of that servant and her son. He is not going to share the family inheritance with my son, Isaac. I won't have it!"

[11] This upset Abraham very much because Ishmael was his son. [12] But God told Abraham, "Do not be upset over the boy and your servant wife. Do just as Sarah says, for Isaac is the son through whom your descendants will be counted. [13] But I will make a nation of the descendants of Hagar's son because he also is your son."

[14] So Abraham got up early the next morning, prepared food for the journey, and strapped a container of water to Hagar's shoulders. He sent her away with their son, and she walked out into the wilderness of Beersheba, wandering aimlessly. [15] When the water was gone, she left the boy in the shade of a bush. [16] Then she went and sat down by herself about a hundred yards* away. "I don't want to watch the boy die," she said, as she burst into tears.

**21:17**
Exod 3:7
Deut 26:7
Ps 6:8

**21:18**
Gen 26:24

**21:20**
Gen 28:15

**21:21**
Gen 25:18

[17] Then God heard the boy's cries, and the angel of God called to Hagar from the sky, "Hagar, what's wrong? Do not be afraid! God has heard the boy's cries from the place where you laid him. [18] Go to him and comfort him, for I will make a great nation from his descendants."

[19] Then God opened Hagar's eyes, and she saw a well. She immediately filled her water container and gave the boy a drink. [20] And God was with the boy as he grew up in the wilderness of Paran. He became an expert archer, [21] and his mother arranged a marriage for him with a young woman from Egypt.

### A Treaty with Abimelech

**21:22**
Gen 26:26

**21:23**
Gen 24:2

[22] About this time, Abimelech came with Phicol, his army commander, to visit Abraham. "It is clear that God helps you in everything you do," Abimelech said. [23] "Swear to me in God's

**21:3** *Isaac* means "he laughs." **21:16** Hebrew *a bowshot*.

---

**20:17, 18** Why did God punish Abimelech when he had no idea Sarah was married? (1) Even though Abimelech's intentions were good, as long as Sarah was living in his harem he was in danger of sinning. A person who eats a poisonous toadstool, thinking it's a harmless mushroom, no doubt has perfectly good intentions—but will still suffer. Sin is a poison that damages us and those around us, whatever our intentions. (2) The punishment, striking all the women of Abimelech's household with infertility, lasted only as long as Abimelech was in danger of sleeping with Sarah. It was meant to change the situation, not to harm Abimelech. (3) The punishment clearly showed that Abraham was in league with almighty God. This incident may have made Abimelech respect and fear Abraham's God.

**21:1-7** Who could believe that Abraham would have a son at 100 years of age—and live to raise him to adulthood? But

doing the impossible is everyday business for God. Our big problems won't seem so impossible if we let God handle them.

**21:7** After repeated promises, a visit by two angels, and the appearance of the Lord himself, Sarah finally cried out with surprise and joy at the birth of her son. Because of her doubt, worry, and fear, she had forfeited the peace she could have felt in God's wonderful promise to her. The way to bring peace to a troubled heart is to focus on God's promises. Trust him to do what he says.

**21:18** What happened to Ishmael, and who are his descendants? Ishmael became ruler of a large tribe or nation. The Ishmaelites were nomads living in the wilderness of Sinai and Paran, south of Israel. One of Ishmael's daughters married Esau, Ishmael's nephew (28:9). The Bible pictures the Ishmaelites as hostile to Israel and to God (Psalm 83:5-6).

name that you won't deceive me, my children, or my grandchildren. I have been loyal to you, so now swear that you will be loyal to me and to this country in which you are living."

²⁴Abraham replied, "All right, I swear to it!" ²⁵Then Abraham complained to Abimelech about a well that Abimelech's servants had taken violently from Abraham's servants.

²⁶"This is the first I've heard of it," Abimelech said. "And I have no idea who is responsible. Why didn't you say something about this before?" ²⁷Then Abraham gave sheep and oxen to Abimelech, and they made a treaty. ²⁸But when Abraham took seven additional ewe lambs and set them off by themselves, ²⁹Abimelech asked, "Why are you doing that?"

³⁰Abraham replied, "They are my gift to you as a public confirmation that I dug this well." ³¹So ever since, that place has been known as Beersheba—"well of the oath"— because that was where they had sworn an oath. ³²After making their covenant, Abimelech left with Phicol, the commander of his army, and they returned home to the land of the Philistines. ³³Then Abraham planted a tamarisk tree at Beersheba, and he worshiped the LORD, the Eternal God, at that place. ³⁴And Abraham lived in Philistine country for a long time.

### Abraham's Obedience Tested

**22** Later on God tested Abraham's faith and obedience. "Abraham!" God called. "Yes," he replied. "Here I am."

²"Take your son, your only son—yes, Isaac, whom you love so much—and go to the land of Moriah. Sacrifice him there as a burnt offering on one of the mountains, which I will point out to you."

³The next morning Abraham got up early. He saddled his donkey and took two of his servants with him, along with his son Isaac. Then he chopped wood to build a fire for a burnt offering and set out for the place where God had told him to go. ⁴On the third day of the journey, Abraham saw the place in the distance. ⁵"Stay here with the donkey," Abraham told the young men. "The boy and I will travel a little farther. We will worship there, and then we will come right back."

⁶Abraham placed the wood for the burnt offering on Isaac's shoulders, while he himself carried the knife and the fire. As the two of them went on together, ⁷Isaac said, "Father?"

**21:25**
Gen 26:15

**21:27**
Gen 26:31

**21:30**
Gen 31:44
**21:31**
Gen 21:14; 26:33
**21:33**
1 Sam 22:6; 31:13
Ps 90:2
Isa 9:6; 40:28

**22:1**
Exod 15:25; 16:4
Deut 8:2, 16
**22:2**
2 Chr 3:1
John 3:16

**22:6**
John 19:17
**22:7**
Gen 8:20
Exod 29:38-42
John 1:29, 36
Rev 13:8

---

**21:31** Beersheba, the southernmost city of Israel, lay on the edge of a vast desert that stretched as far as Egypt to the southwest and Mount Sinai to the south. The phrase "from Dan to Beersheba" was often used to describe the traditional boundaries of the Promised Land (2 Samuel 17:11). Beersheba's southern location and the presence of several wells in the area may explain why Abraham settled there. Beersheba was also the home of Isaac, Abraham's son.

**22:1** God tested Abraham, not to trip him and watch him fall, but to deepen his capacity to obey God and thus to develop his character. Just as fire refines ore to extract precious metals, God refines us through difficult circumstances. When we are tested, we can complain, or we can try to see how God is stretching us to develop our character.

**22:3** That morning Abraham began one of the greatest acts of obedience in recorded history. He traveled 50 miles to Mount Moriah near the site of Jerusalem. Over the years he had learned many tough lessons about the importance of obeying God. This time his obedience was prompt and complete. Obeying God is often a struggle because it may mean giving up something we truly want. We should not expect our obedience to God to be easy or to come naturally.

**22:6** We don't know how Abraham carried the fire. Perhaps he carried a live coal or a flint to start a fire.

**22:7, 8** Why did God ask Abraham to perform human sacrifice? Pagan nations practiced human sacrifice, but God condemned this as a terrible sin (Leviticus 20:1-5). God did not want Isaac to die, but he wanted Abraham to sacrifice Isaac in his heart so it

would be clear that Abraham loved God more than he loved his promised and long-awaited son. God was testing Abraham. The purpose of testing is to strengthen our character and deepen our commitment to God and his perfect timing. Through this difficult experience, Abraham strengthened his commitment to obey God. He also learned about God's ability to provide.

**ABRAHAM'S TRIP TO MOUNT MORIAH**
Abraham and Isaac traveled the 50 or 60 miles from Beersheba to Mount Moriah in about three days. This was a very difficult time for Abraham, who was on his way to sacrifice his beloved son, Isaac.

"Yes, my son," Abraham replied.

"We have the wood and the fire,' said the boy, "but where is the lamb for the sacrifice?"

8"God will provide a lamb, my son," Abraham answered. And they both went on together.

**22:9**
Heb 11:17-19
Jas 2:21

9When they arrived at the place where God had told Abraham to go, he built an altar and placed the wood on it. Then he tied Isaac up and laid him on the altar over the wood. 10And Abraham took the knife and lifted it up to kill his son as a sacrifice to the LORD.

**22:11**
Gen 16:7; 21:17

11At that moment the angel of the LORD shouted to him from heaven, "Abraham! Abraham!"

**22:12**
Heb 11:17

"Yes," he answered. "I'm listening.'

12"Lay down the knife," the angel said. "Do not hurt the boy in any way, for now I know that you truly fear God. You have not withheld even your beloved son from me."

**22:13**
Gen 8:20

**22:14**
Gen 22:7-8

13Then Abraham looked up and saw a ram caught by its horns in a bush. So he took the ram and sacrificed it as a burnt offering on the altar in place of his son. 14Abraham

---

Escape of some kind is usually the most tempting solution to our problems. In fact, it can become a habit. Hagar was a person who used that approach. When the going got tough, she usually got going—in the other direction.

However, it is worthwhile to note that the biggest challenges Hagar faced were brought on by *other* people's choices. Sarah chose her to bear Abraham's child, and Hagar probably had little to say in the matter.

It isn't hard to understand how Hagar's pregnancy caused her to look down on Sarah. But that brought on hard feelings, and Sarah consequently punished Hagar. This motivated her first escape. When she returned to the family and gave birth to Ishmael, Sarah's continued barrenness must have contributed to bitterness on both sides.

When Isaac was finally born, Sarah looked for any excuse to have Hagar and Ishmael sent away. She found it when she caught Ishmael teasing Isaac. In the wilderness, out of water and facing the death of her son, Hagar once again tried to escape. She walked away so she wouldn't have to watch her son die. Once again, God graciously intervened.

Have you noticed how patiently God operates to make our escape attempts fail? Have you begun to learn that escape is only a temporary solution? God's continual desire is for us to face our problems with his help. We experience his help most clearly in and through conflicts and difficulties, not away from them. Are there problems in your life for which you've been using the "Hagar solution"? Choose one of those problems, ask for God's help, and begin to face it today.

| Strength and accomplishment | • Mother of Abraham's first child, Ishmael, who became founder of the Arab nations |
|---|---|
| Weaknesses and mistakes | • When faced with problems, she tended to run away<br>• Her pregnancy brought out strong feelings of pride and arrogance |
| Lessons from her life | • God is faithful to his plan and promises, even when humans complicate the process<br>• God shows himself as one who knows us and wants to be known by us<br>• The New Testament uses Hagar as a symbol of those who would pursue favor with God by their own efforts, rather than by trusting in his mercy and forgiveness |
| Vital statistics | • Where: Canaan and Egypt<br>• Occupation: Servant, mother<br>• Relatives: Son: Ishmael |
| Key verse | "Then the angel of the LORD said, 'Return to your mistress and submit to her authority' " (Genesis 16:9). |

Hagar's story is told in Genesis 16—21. She is also mentioned in Galatians 4:24.

---

**22:12** It is difficult to let go of what we deeply love. What could be more proper than to love your only child? Yet when we do give to God what he asks, he returns to us far more than we could dream. The spiritual benefits of his blessings far outweigh our sacrifices. Have you withheld your love, your children, or your time from him? Trust him to provide (22:8).

**22:13** Notice the parallel between the ram offered on the altar as a substitute for Isaac and Christ offered on the cross as a substitute for us. Whereas God stopped Abraham from sacrificing his son, God did not spare his own Son, Jesus, from dying on the cross. If Jesus had lived, the rest of humankind would have died. God sent his only Son to die for us so that we can be spared from the eternal death we deserve and instead receive eternal life (John 3:16).

named the place "The LORD Will Provide."* This name has now become a proverb: "On the mountain of the LORD it will be provided."

¹⁵Then the angel of the LORD called again to Abraham from heaven, ¹⁶"This is what the LORD says: Because you have obeyed me and have not withheld even your beloved son, I swear by my own self that ¹⁷I will bless you richly. I will multiply your descendants into countless millions, like the stars of the sky and the sand on the seashore. They will conquer their enemies, ¹⁸and through your descendants,* all the nations of the earth will be blessed—all because you have obeyed me." ¹⁹Then they returned to Abraham's young men and traveled home again to Beersheba, where Abraham lived for quite some time.

²⁰Soon after this, Abraham heard that Milcah, his brother Nahor's wife, had borne Nahor eight sons. ²¹The oldest was named Uz, the next oldest was Buz, followed by Kemuel (the father of Aram), ²²Kesed, Hazo, Pildash, Jidlaph, and Bethuel. ²³Bethuel became the father of Rebekah. ²⁴In addition to his eight sons from Milcah, Nahor had four other children from his concubine Reumah. Their names were Tebah, Gaham, Tahash, and Maacah.

### The Burial of Sarah

**23** When Sarah was 127 years old, ²she died at Kiriath-arba (now called Hebron) in the land of Canaan. There Abraham mourned and wept for her. ³Then, leaving her body, he went to the Hittite elders and said, ⁴"Here I am, a stranger in a foreign land, with no place to bury my wife. Please let me have a piece of land for a burial plot."

⁵The Hittites replied to Abraham, ⁶"Certainly, for you are an honored prince among us. It will be a privilege to have you choose the finest of our tombs so you can bury her there."

⁷Then Abraham bowed low before them and said, ⁸"Since this is how you feel, be so kind as to ask Ephron son of Zohar ⁹to let me have the cave of Machpelah, down at the end of his field. I want to pay the full price, of course, whatever is publicly agreed upon, so I may have a permanent burial place for my family."

¹⁰Ephron was sitting there among the others, and he answered Abraham as the others listened, speaking publicly before all the elders of the town. ¹¹"No, sir," he said to Abraham, "please listen to me. I will give you the cave and the field. Here in the presence of my people, I give it to you. Go and bury your dead."

¹²Abraham bowed again to the people of the land, ¹³and he replied to Ephron as

**22:14** Hebrew *Yahweh Yir'eh.*   **22:18** Hebrew *seed.*

| | |
|---|---|
| **22:16** | †Heb 6:13-14 |
| **22:17** | Gen 12:2; 15:5; 26:4 †Heb 6:14 |
| **22:18** | †Acts 3:25 †Gal 3:8, 16 |
| **22:19** | Gen 21:14 |
| **22:20** | Gen 11:29 |
| **22:23** | Gen 24:15 |
| **23:2** | Josh 14:15 |
| **23:3** | Gen 10:15 |
| **23:4** | Lev 25:23 1 Chr 29:15 Ps 39:12 Heb 11:9 |
| **23:6** | Gen 14:14-16 |
| **23:8-9** | Gen 25:9 |
| **23:10** | Ruth 4:1, 11 |

**22:15-18** Abraham received abundant blessings because he did not hold back but obeyed God. First, God gave Abraham's descendants the ability to conquer their enemies. Second, God promised Abraham children and grandchildren who would in turn bless the whole earth. People's lives would be changed as a result of knowing of the faith of Abraham and his descendants. Most often we think of blessings as gifts to be enjoyed. But when God blesses us, his blessings are intended to overflow to others.

**23:1-4** In Abraham's day, death and burial were steeped in ritual and traditions. Failing to honor a dead person demonstrated the greatest possible lack of respect. An improper burial was the equivalent of a curse. Mourning was an essential part of the death ritual. Friends and relatives let out loud cries for the whole neighborhood to hear. Because there were no funeral homes or undertakers, these same friends and relatives helped prepare the body for burial, which usually took place on the same day because of the warm climate.

**23:4-6** Abraham was in a foreign land looking for a place to bury his wife. Strangers offered to help him because he was "an honored prince," and they respected him. Although Abraham had not established roots in the area, his reputation was above reproach. Those who invest their time and money in serving God often earn a pleasant return on their investment—a good reputation and the respect of others.

**23:10-16** The polite interchange between Abraham and Ephron was typical of bargaining at that time. Ephron graciously offered to give his land to Abraham at no charge; Abraham insisted on paying for it; Ephron politely mentioned the price

but said, in effect, that it wasn't important; Abraham paid the 400 shekels of silver. Both men knew what was going on as they went through the bargaining process. If Abraham had accepted the land as a gift when it was offered, he would have insulted Ephron, who then would have rescinded his offer. Many Middle Eastern shopkeepers still follow this ritual with their customers.

**CAVE OF MACHPELAH**
Sarah died in Hebron. Abraham bought the cave of Machpelah, near Hebron, as her burial place. Abraham was also buried there, as were his son and grandson, Isaac and Jacob.

Mediterranean Sea

Sea of Galilee

Jordan River

N

Jerusalem (Salem)

Hebron

Dead Sea

Cave of Machpelah

0   20 Mi.

0   20 Km.

everyone listened. "No, listen to me," he insisted. "I will buy it from you. Let me pay the full price for the field so I can bury my dead there."

14 "Well," Ephron answered, 15 "the land is worth four hundred pieces* of silver, but what is that between friends? Go ahead and bury your dead."

16 So Abraham paid Ephron the amount he had suggested, four hundred pieces of silver, as was publicly agreed. 17 He bought the plot of land belonging to Ephron at Machpelah, near Mamre. This included the field, the cave that was in it, and all the trees nearby. 18 They became Abraham's permanent possession by the agreement made in the presence of the Hittite elders at the city gate. 19 So Abraham buried Sarah there in Canaan, in the cave of Machpelah, near Mamre, which is at Hebron. 20 The field and the cave were sold to Abraham by the Hittites as a permanent burial place.

## 6. Isaac and Rebekah

**24** Abraham was now a very old man, and the LORD had blessed him in every way. 2 One day Abraham said to the man in charge of his household, who was his oldest servant, 3 "Swear* by the LORD, the God of heaven and earth, that you will not let my

23:15 Hebrew *400 shekels*: about 10 pounds or 4.6 kilograms in weight; also in 23:16.   24:3 Hebrew *Put your hand under my thigh, and I will make you swear.*

---

# REBEKAH

Some people are initiators. They help get the ball rolling. Rebekah would easily stand out in this group. Her life was characterized by initiative. When she saw a need, she took action, even though the action was not always right.

It was Rebekah's initiative that first caught the attention of Eliezer, the servant Abraham sent to find a wife for Isaac. It was common courtesy to give a drink to a stranger, but it took added character to also fetch water for ten thirsty camels. Later, after hearing the details of Eliezer's mission, Rebekah was immediately willing to be Isaac's bride.

Several later events help us see how initiative can be misdirected. Rebekah was aware that God's plan would be channeled through Jacob, not Esau (Genesis 25:23). So not only did Jacob become her favorite; she actually planned ways to ensure that he would over-shadow his older twin. Meanwhile, Isaac preferred Esau. This created a conflict between the couple. She felt justified in deceiving her husband when the time came to bless the sons, and her ingenious plan was carried out to perfection.

Most of the time we try to justify the things we choose to do. Often we attempt to add God's approval to our actions. While it is true that our actions will not spoil God's plan, it is also true that we are responsible for what we do and must always be cautious about our motives. When thinking about a course of action, are you simply seeking God's stamp of approval on something you've already decided to do? Or are you willing to set the plan aside if the principles and commands of God's Word are against the action? Initiative and action are admirable and right when they are controlled by God's wisdom.

| Strengths and accomplishments | • When confronted with a need, she took immediate action<br>• She was accomplishment oriented |
|---|---|
| Weaknesses and mistakes | • Her initiative was not always balanced by wisdom<br>• She favored one of her sons<br>• She deceived her husband |
| Lessons from her life | • Our actions must be guided by God's Word<br>• God makes use even of our mistakes in his plan<br>• Parental favoritism hurts a family |
| Vital statistics | • Where: Haran, Canaan<br>• Occupation: Wife, mother, household manager<br>• Relatives: Grandparents: Nahor and Milcah. Father: Bethuel. Husband: Isaac. Brother: Laban. Twin sons: Esau and Jacob |
| Key verses | "Isaac brought Rebekah into his mother's tent, and she became his wife. He loved her very much, and she was a special comfort to him after the death of his mother" (Genesis 24:67). "Isaac loved Esau in particular because of the wild game he brought home, but Rebekah favored Jacob" (Genesis 25:28). |

Rebekah's story is told in Genesis 24—27. She is also mentioned in Romans 9:10.

---

**23:16** Four hundred pieces of silver was a high price for the piece of property Abraham bought. The Hittites weren't thrilled about foreigners buying their property, so Abraham had little bargaining leverage.

Ephron asked an outrageous price. The custom of the day was to ask double the fair market value of the land, fully expecting the buyer to offer half the stated price. Abraham, however, did not bargain. He simply paid the initial price. He was not trying to take anything he didn't deserve. Even though God had promised the land to Abraham, he did not just take it away from Ephron.

son marry one of these local Canaanite women. ⁴Go instead to my homeland, to my relatives, and find a wife there for my son Isaac."

⁵The servant asked, "But suppose I can't find a young woman who will travel so far from home? May I then take Isaac there to live among your relatives?"

⁶"No!" Abraham warned. "Be careful never to take my son there. ⁷For the LORD, the God of heaven, who took me from my father's house and my native land, solemnly promised to give this land to my offspring.* He will send his angel ahead of you, and he will see to it that you find a young woman there to be my son's wife. ⁸If she is unwilling to come back with you, then you are free from this oath. But under no circumstances are you to take my son there."

⁹So the servant took a solemn oath* that he would follow Abraham's instructions. ¹⁰He loaded ten of Abraham's camels with gifts and set out, taking with him the best of everything his master owned. He traveled to Aram-naharaim* and went to the village where Abraham's brother Nahor had settled. ¹¹There the servant made the camels kneel down beside a well just outside the village. It was evening, and the women were coming out to draw water.

¹²"O LORD, God of my master," he prayed. "Give me success and show kindness to my master, Abraham. Help me to accomplish the purpose of my journey. ¹³See, here I am, standing beside this spring, and the young women of the village are coming out to draw water. ¹⁴This is my request. I will ask one of them for a drink. If she says, 'Yes, certainly, and I will water your camels, too!'—let her be the one you have appointed as Isaac's wife. By this I will know that you have shown kindness to my master."

¹⁵As he was still praying, a young woman named Rebekah arrived with a water jug on her shoulder. Her father was Bethuel, who was the son of Abraham's brother Nahor and his wife, Milcah. ¹⁶Now Rebekah was very beautiful, and she was a virgin; no man had ever slept with her. She went down to the spring, filled her jug, and came up again. ¹⁷Running over to her, the servant asked, "Please give me a drink."

¹⁸"Certainly, sir," she said, and she quickly lowered the jug for him to drink. ¹⁹When he had finished, she said, "I'll draw water for your camels, too, until they have had enough!" ²⁰So she quickly emptied the jug into the watering trough and ran down to the well again. She kept carrying water to the camels until they had finished drinking. ²¹The servant watched her in silence, wondering whether or not she was the one the LORD

**24:4** Gen 12:1
**24:5** Gen 24:39
**24:7** Gen 12:1, 7; 16:7; 22:11; Rom 4:13; †Gal 3:16
**24:10** Gen 11:29; Deut 23:4
**24:11** Gen 24:42
**24:12** Gen 24:27, 48
**24:14** Judg 6:17; 1 Sam 14:10
**24:15** Gen 22:20-24
**24:16** Gen 12:11; 29:17
**24:17** 1 Kgs 17:10; John 4:7
**24:19** Gen 24:14

**24:7** Hebrew *seed.* **24:9** Hebrew *put his hand under the thigh of Abraham his master and swore an oath.* **24:10** *Aram-naharaim* means "Aram of the two rivers," thought to have been located between the Euphrates and Balih Rivers in northwestern Mesopotamia.

**24:4** Abraham wanted Isaac to marry within the family. This was a common and acceptable practice at this time that had the added advantage of avoiding intermarriage with pagan neighbors. A son's wife was usually chosen by the parents. It was common for a woman to be married in her early teens, although Rebekah was probably older.

**24:6** Abraham wanted Isaac to stay in Canaan, but he didn't want him to marry one of the local girls. This contrasts with the way Hagar selected a wife for Ishmael in 21:21. To have Isaac stay and marry a woman from Canaan would have been easier. But Abraham wanted to obey God in the *who* as well as in the *where.* Make your obedience full and complete.

**24:11** The well, the chief source of water for an entire village, was usually located outside town along the main road. Many people had to walk a mile or more for their water. They could use only what they could carry home. Farmers and shepherds would come from nearby fields to draw water for their animals. The well was a good place to meet new friends or to chat with old ones. Rebekah would have visited the well twice daily to draw water for her family.

**24:12** Abraham's servant asked God for guidance in this very important task. Obviously Eliezer had learned much about faith and about God from his master. What are your family members, friends, and associates learning about God from watching you? Be like Abraham, setting an example of

dependent faith. And be like Eliezer, asking God for guidance before any venture.

**24:14** Was it right for Abraham's servant to ask God for such a specific sign? The sign he requested was only slightly out of the ordinary. The hospitality of the day required women at the well to offer water to weary travelers, but not to their animals. Eliezer was simply asking God to show him a woman with an attitude of service—someone who would go beyond the expected. An offer to water his camels would indicate that kind of attitude. Eliezer did not ask for a woman with good looks or wealth. He knew the importance of having the right heart, and he asked God to help him with his task.

**24:15, 16** Rebekah had physical beauty, but the servant was looking for a sign of inner beauty. Appearance is important to us, and we spend time and money improving it. But how much effort do we put into developing our inner beauty? Patience, kindness, and joy are the beauty treatments that help us become truly lovely—on the inside.

**24:18-21** Rebekah's servant spirit was clearly demonstrated as she willingly and quickly drew water for Eliezer and his camels. The pots used for carrying water were large and heavy. It took a lot of water to satisfy a thirsty camel—up to 25 gallons per camel after a week's travel. Seeing Rebekah go to work, Eliezer knew this was a woman with a heart for doing far more than the bare minimum. Do you have a servant spirit? When asked to help or when you see a need, go beyond the minimum.

intended him to meet. ²²Then at last, when the camels had finished drinking, he gave her a gold ring for her nose and two large gold bracelets* for her wrists.

²³"Whose daughter are you?" he asked. "Would your father have any room to put us up for the night?"

²⁴"My father is Bethuel," she replied. "My grandparents are Nahor and Milcah. ²⁵Yes, we have plenty of straw and food for the camels, and we have a room for guests."

²⁶The man fell down to the ground and worshiped the LORD. ²⁷"Praise be to the LORD, the God of my master, Abraham," he said. "The LORD has been so kind and faithful to Abraham, for he has led me straight to my master's relatives."

²⁸The young woman ran home to tell her family about all that had happened. ²⁹Now Rebekah had a brother named Laban. ³⁰When he saw the nose-ring and the bracelets on his sister's wrists, and when he heard her story, he rushed out to the spring, where the man was still standing beside his camels. Laban said to him, ³¹"Come and stay with us, you who are blessed by the LORD. Why do you stand here outside the village when we have a room all ready for you and a place prepared for the camels!"

³²So the man went home with Laban, and Laban unloaded the camels, gave him straw to bed them down, fed them, and provided water for the camel drivers to wash their feet. ³³Then supper was served. But Abraham's servant said, "I don't want to eat until I have told you why I have come."

"All right," Laban said, "tell us your mission."

³⁴"I am Abraham's servant," he explained. ³⁵"And the LORD has blessed my master richly; he has become a great man. The LORD has given him flocks of sheep and herds of cattle, a fortune in silver and gold, and many servants and camels and donkeys. ³⁶When Sarah, my master's wife, was very old, she gave birth to my master's son, and my master has given him everything he owns. ³⁷And my master made me swear that I would not let Isaac marry one of the local Canaanite women. ³⁸Instead, I was to come to his relatives here in this far-off land, to his father's home. I was told to bring back a young woman from here to marry his son.

³⁹"But suppose I can't find a young woman willing to come back with me?' I asked him. ⁴⁰'You will,' he told me, 'for the LORD, in whose presence I have walked, will send his angel with you and will make your mission successful. Yes, you must get a wife for my son from among my relatives, from my father's family. ⁴¹But if you go to my relatives and they refuse to let her come, you will be free from your oath.'

⁴²"So this afternoon when I came to the spring I prayed this prayer: 'O LORD, the God of my master, Abraham, if you are planning to make my mission a success, please guide me in a special way. ⁴³Here I am, standing beside this spring. I will say to some young woman who comes to draw water, "Please give me a drink of water!" ⁴⁴And she will

**24:22** Hebrew *a gold nose-ring weighing a half shekel* [0.2 ounces or 6 grams] *and two gold bracelets weighing 10 shekels* [4 ounces or 114 grams].

---

**ELIEZER: PROFILE OF A TRUE SERVANT**

Have you ever approached a responsibility with this kind of single-mindedness and careful planning, while ultimately depending on God?

| | |
|---|---|
| Accepted the challenge | 24:3, 9 |
| Examined alternatives | 24:5 |
| Promised to follow instructions | 24:9 |
| Made a plan | 24:12–14 |
| Submitted the plan to God | 24:12–14 |
| Prayed for guidance | 24:12–14 |
| Devised a strategy with room for God to operate | 24:12–14 |
| Waited | 24:21 |
| Watched closely | 24:21 |
| Accepted the answer thankfully | 24:26 |
| Explained the situation to concerned parties | 24:34–49 |
| Refused unnecessary delay | 24:56 |
| Followed through with entire plan | 24:66 |

---

**24:26, 27** As soon as Abraham's servant knew that God had answered his prayer, he prayed and thanked God for his goodness and guidance. God will also use and lead us if we are available like Eliezer. And our first response should be praise and thanksgiving that God would choose to work in and through us.

**24:42, 48** When Eliezer told his story to Laban, he spoke openly of God and his goodness. Often we do the opposite, afraid that we will be misunderstood or rejected or seen as too religious. Instead, we should share openly what God is doing for us.

reply, "Certainly! And I'll water your camels, too!" LORD, let her be the one you have selected to be the wife of my master's son.'

45"Before I had finished praying these words, I saw Rebekah coming along with her water jug on her shoulder. She went down to the spring and drew water and filled the jug. So I said to her, 'Please give me a drink.' 46She quickly lowered the jug from her shoulder so I could drink, and she said, 'Certainly, sir, and I will water your camels, too!' And she did. 47When I asked her whose daughter she was, she told me, 'My father is Bethuel, the son of Nahor and his wife, Milcah.' So I gave her the ring and the bracelets.

48"Then I bowed my head and worshiped the LORD. I praised the LORD, the God of my master, Abraham, because he had led me along the right path to find a wife from the family of my master's relatives. 49So tell me—will you or won't you show true kindness to my master? When you tell me, then I'll know what my next step should be, whether to move this way or that."

50Then Laban and Bethuel replied, "The LORD has obviously brought you here, so what can we say? 51Here is Rebekah; take her and go. Yes, let her be the wife of your master's son, as the LORD has directed."

52At this reply, Abraham's servant bowed to the ground and worshiped the LORD. 53Then he brought out silver and gold jewelry and lovely clothing for Rebekah. He also gave valuable presents to her mother and brother. 54Then they had supper, and the servant and the men with him stayed there overnight. But early the next morning, he said, "Send me back to my master."

55"But we want Rebekah to stay at least ten days," her brother and mother said. "Then she can go."

56But he said, "Don't hinder my return. The LORD has made my mission successful, and I want to report back to my master."

57"Well," they said, "we'll call Rebekah and ask her what she thinks." 58So they called Rebekah. "Are you willing to go with this man?" they asked her.

And she replied, "Yes, I will go."

59So they said good-bye to Rebekah and sent her away with Abraham's servant and his men. The woman who had been Rebekah's childhood nurse went along with her. 60They blessed her with this blessing as she parted:

"Our sister, may you become
   the mother of many millions!
May your descendants overcome
   all their enemies."

61Then Rebekah and her servants mounted the camels and left with Abraham's servant. 62Meanwhile, Isaac, whose home was in the Negev, had returned from Beer-lahairoi. 63One evening as he was taking a walk out in the fields, meditating, he looked up and saw the camels coming. 64When Rebekah looked up and saw Isaac, she quickly dismounted. 65"Who is that man walking through the fields to meet us?" she asked the servant.

And he replied, "It is my master." So Rebekah covered her face with her veil. 66Then the servant told Isaac the whole story.

67And Isaac brought Rebekah into his mother's tent, and she became his wife. He loved her very much, and she was a special comfort to him after the death of his mother.

## 7. Abraham dies

*The Death of Abraham*

**25** Now Abraham married again. Keturah was his new wife, 2and she bore him Zimran, Jokshan, Medan, Midian, Ishbak, and Shuah. 3Jokshan's two sons were Sheba and Dedan. Dedan's descendants were the Asshurites, Letushites, and Leummites. 4Midian's sons were Ephah, Epher, Hanoch, Abida, and Eldaah. These were all descendants of Abraham through Keturah.

Cross-references:
24:45 1 Sam 1:13
24:47 Gen 24:23-24
24:49 Gen 47:29
24:50 Ps 118:23
24:52 Gen 24:26
24:54 Gen 30:25
24:55 Judg 19:4
24:59 Gen 35:8
24:60 Gen 17:16; 22:17
24:62 Gen 16:14
24:63 Ps 119:15, 27, 48
24:67 Gen 23:1-2; 25:20; 29:18
25:1-4 1 Chr 1:32-33

---

**24:64, 65** When Rebekah learned that the man coming to greet them was Isaac, her husband-to-be, she followed two Oriental customs. She dismounted from her camel to show respect, and she placed a veil over her face as a bride.

**25:1-6** Abraham took another wife, Keturah, after Sarah died. Although the sons and grandson of Abraham and Keturah received many gifts from Abraham, all his property and authority went to Isaac, his principal heir.

**25:5**
Gen 24:35-36

**25:7**
Gen 12:4

**25:9-10**
Gen 23:17-18;
49:29; 50:13

**25:11**
Gen 12:2; 24:62

**25:12-16**
//1 Chr 1:29-31

**25:17**
Gen 25:8

⁵Abraham left everything he owned to his son Isaac. ⁶But before he died, he gave gifts to the sons of his concubines and sent them off to the east, away from Isaac.

⁷Abraham lived for 175 years, ⁸and he died at a ripe old age, joining his ancestors in death. ⁹His sons Isaac and Ishmael buried him in the cave of Machpelah, near Mamre, in the field of Ephron son of Zohar the Hittite. ¹⁰This was the field Abraham had purchased from the Hittites, where he had buried his wife Sarah. ¹¹After Abraham's death, God poured out rich blessings on Isaac, who settled near Beer-lahairoi in the Negev.

### Ishmael's Descendants

¹²This is the history of the descendants of Ishmael, the son of Abraham through Hagar, Sarah's Egyptian servant. ¹³Here is a list, by their names and clans, of Ishmael's descendants: The oldest was Nebaioth, followed by Kedar, Adbeel, Mibsam, ¹⁴Mishma, Dumah, Massa, ¹⁵Hadad, Tema, Jetur, Naphish, and Kedemah. ¹⁶These twelve sons of Ishmael became the founders of twelve tribes that bore their names, listed according to the places they settled and camped. ¹⁷Ishmael finally died at the age of 137 and joined

Common sense isn't all that common. In fact, the common thread in many decisions is that they don't make sense. Esau's life was filled with choices he must have regretted bitterly. He appears to have been a person who found it hard to consider consequences, reacting to the need of the moment without realizing what he was giving up to meet that need. Trading his birthright for a bowl of stew was the clearest example of this weakness. He also chose wives in direct opposition to his parents' wishes. He learned the hard way.

What are you willing to trade for the things you want? Do you find yourself, at times, willing to negotiate *anything* for what you feel you need *now?* Does your family, spouse, integrity, body, or soul get included in these deals? Do you sometimes feel that the important parts of life escaped while you were grabbing for something else?

If so, your initial response, like Esau's, may be deep anger. In itself that isn't wrong, as long as you direct the energy of that anger toward a solution and not toward yourself or others as the cause of the problem. Your greatest need is to find a focal point other than "what I need now." The only worthy focal point is God. A relationship with him will not only give an ultimate purpose to your life; it will also be a daily guideline for living. Meet him in the pages of the Bible.

| | |
|---|---|
| **Strengths and accomplishments** | • Ancestor of the Edomites<br>• Known for his archery skill<br>• Able to forgive after explosive anger |
| **Weaknesses and mistakes** | • When faced with important decisions, tended to choose according to the immediate need rather than the long-range effect<br>• Angered his parents by poor marriage choices |
| **Lessons from his life** | • God allows certain events in our lives to accomplish his overall purposes, but we are still responsible for our actions<br>• Consequences are important to consider<br>• It is possible to have great anger and yet not sin |
| **Vital statistics** | • Where: Canaan<br>• Occupation: Skillful hunter<br>• Relatives: Parents: Isaac and Rebekah. Brother: Jacob. Wives: Judith, Basemath, and Mahalath |
| **Key verses** | "Try to live in peace with everyone, and seek to live a clean and holy life, for those who are not holy will not see the Lord. Look after each other so that none of you will miss out on the special favor of God. Watch out that no bitter root of unbelief rises up among you, for whenever it springs up, many are corrupted by its poison. Make sure that no one is immoral or godless like Esau. He traded his birthright as the oldest son for a single meal. And afterward, when he wanted his father's blessing, he was rejected. It was too late for repentance, even though he wept bitter tears" (Hebrews 12:14–17). |

Esau's story is told in Genesis 25—36. He is also mentioned in Malachi 1:2, 3; Romans 9:13; Hebrews 12:16, 17.

**25:21** As Isaac pleaded with God for children, so the Bible encourages us to ask and even plead for our most personal and important requests. God wants to grant our requests, but he wants us to ask him. Even then, as Isaac learned, God may decide to withhold his answer for a while in order to (1) deepen our insight into what we really need, (2) broaden our appreciation for his answers, or (3) allow us to mature so we can use his gifts more wisely.

his ancestors in death. [18]Ishmael's descendants were scattered across the country from Havilah to Shur, which is east of Egypt in the direction of Asshur. The clans descended from Ishmael camped close to one another.*

**25:18**
Gen 16:12; 20:1

## E. THE STORY OF ISAAC (25:19—28:9)

Isaac inherited everything from his father, including God's promise to make his descendants into a great nation. As a boy, Isaac did not resist as his father prepared to sacrifice him, and as a man, he gladly accepted the wife that others chose for him. Through Isaac, we learn how to let God guide our life and place his will ahead of our own.

### 1. Jacob and Esau

[19]This is the history of the family of Isaac, the son of Abraham. [20]When Isaac was forty years old, he married Rebekah, the daughter of Bethuel the Aramean from Paddan-aram and the sister of Laban. [21]Isaac pleaded with the LORD to give Rebekah a child because she was childless. So the LORD answered Isaac's prayer, and his wife became pregnant with twins. [22]But the two children struggled with each other in her womb. So she went to ask the LORD about it. "Why is this happening to me?" she asked.

**25:21**
Gen 21:2

[23]And the LORD told her, "The sons in your womb will become two rival nations. One nation will be stronger than the other; the descendants of your older son will serve the descendants of your younger son."

**25:23**
Gen 17:2-4; 27:29;
48:19
Num 20:14
Deut 2:4, 8
†Rom 9:11-12

[24]And when the time came, the twins were born. [25]The first was very red at birth. He was covered with so much hair that one would think he was wearing a piece of clothing. So they called him Esau.* [26]Then the other twin was born with his hand grasping Esau's heel. So they called him Jacob.* Isaac was sixty years old when the twins were born.

**25:25**
Gen 27:11

**25:26**
Hos 12:3

*Esau Sells His Birthright*

[27]As the boys grew up, Esau became a skillful hunter, a man of the open fields, while Jacob was the kind of person who liked to stay at home. [28]Isaac loved Esau in particular because of the wild game he brought home, but Rebekah favored Jacob.

[29]One day when Jacob was cooking some stew, Esau arrived home exhausted and hungry from a hunt. [30]Esau said to Jacob, "I'm starved! Give me some of that red stew you've made." (This was how Esau got his other name, Edom—"Red.")

**25:30**
Gen 36:1, 8

[31]Jacob replied, "All right, but trade me your birthright for it."

**25:31**
Deut 21:16-17
1 Chr 5:1-2

[32]"Look, I'm dying of starvation!" said Esau. "What good is my birthright to me now?"

[33]So Jacob insisted, "Well then, swear to me right now that it is mine." So Esau swore an oath, thereby selling all his rights as the firstborn to his younger brother. [34]Then Jacob gave Esau some bread and lentil stew. Esau ate and drank and went on about his business, indifferent to the fact that he had given up his birthright.

**25:33**
Gen 27:36
Heb 12:16

### 2. Isaac and Abimelech

*Isaac Deceives Abimelech*

**26** Now a severe famine struck the land, as had happened before in Abraham's time. So Isaac moved to Gerar, where Abimelech, king of the Philistines, lived. [2]The LORD appeared to him there and said, "Do not go to Egypt. [3]Do as I say, and stay

**26:1**
Gen 12:10; 20:1-2

**26:2**
Gen 12:1, 7

25:18 The meaning of the Hebrew is uncertain.   25:25 *Esau* sounds like a Hebrew term that means "hair."
25:26 *Jacob* means "he grasps the heel"; this can also figuratively mean "he deceives."

---

**25:31** A birthright was a special honor given to the firstborn son. It included a double portion of the family inheritance along with the honor of one day becoming the family's leader. The oldest son could sell his birthright or give it away if he chose, but in so doing, he would lose both material goods and his leadership position. By trading his birthright, Esau showed complete disregard for the spiritual blessings that would have come his way if he had kept it.

**25:32, 33** Esau traded the lasting benefits of his birthright for the immediate pleasure of food. He acted on impulse, satisfying his immediate desires without pausing to consider the long-range consequences of what he was about to do. We can fall into the same trap. When we see something we want, our first impulse is to get it. At first we feel intensely satisfied and sometimes even powerful because we have obtained what we set out to get. But

immediate pleasure often loses sight of the future. We can avoid making Esau's mistake by comparing the short-term satisfaction with its long-range consequences before we act.

Esau exaggerated his hunger. "I'm dying of starvation!" he said. This thought made his choice much easier because if he was starving, what good was an inheritance anyway? The pressure of the moment distorted his perspective and made his decision seem urgent. We often experience similar pressures. For example, when we feel sexual pressure, a marriage vow may seem unimportant. We might feel such great pressure in one area that nothing else seems to matter and we lose our perspective. Getting through that short, pressure-filled moment is often the most difficult part of overcoming a temptation.

**26:1** The Philistine tribe would become one of Israel's fiercest enemies. The Philistines were one group of a number of

**26:3**
Gen 12:7; 15:15, 18

**26:4**
Gen 15:5; 22:17
Exod 32:13
†Acts 3:25
†Gal 3:8

here in this land. If you do, I will be with you and bless you. I will give all this land to you and your descendants, just as I solemnly promised Abraham, your father. ⁴I will cause your descendants to become as numerous as the stars, and I will give them all these lands. And through your descendants* all the nations of the earth will be blessed. ⁵I will do this because Abraham listened to me and obeyed all my requirements, commands, regulations, and laws."

**26:4** Hebrew *seed.*

---

Abraham, Isaac, and Jacob are among the most significant people in the Old Testament. It is important to realize that this significance is not based upon their personal characters, but upon the character of God. They were all men who earned the grudging respect and even fear of their peers: they were wealthy and powerful, and yet each was capable of lying, deceit, and selfishness. They were not the perfect heroes we might have expected; instead, they were just like us, trying to please God, but often falling short.

Jacob was the third link in God's plan to start a nation from Abraham. The success of that plan was more often in spite of than because of Jacob's life. Before Jacob was born, God promised that his plan would be worked out through Jacob and not his twin brother, Esau. Although Jacob's methods were not always respectable, his skill, determination, and patience have to be admired. As we follow him from birth to death, we are able to see God's work.

Jacob's life had four stages, each marked by a personal encounter with God. In the first stage, Jacob lived up to his name, which means "he grasps the heel" (figuratively, "he deceives"). He grabbed Esau's heel at birth, and by the time he fled from home, he had also grabbed his brother's birthright and blessing. During his flight, God first appeared to him. Not only did God confirm to Jacob his blessing, but he awakened in Jacob a personal knowledge of himself. In the second stage, Jacob experienced life from the other side, being manipulated and deceived by Laban. But there is a curious change: The Jacob of stage one would simply have left Laban, whereas the Jacob of stage two, after deciding to leave, waited six years for God's permission. In the third stage, Jacob was in a new role as grabber. This time, by the Jordan River, he grabbed on to God and wouldn't let go. He realized his dependence on the God who had continued to bless him. His relationship to God became essential to his life, and his name was changed to Israel, "he struggles with God." Jacob's last stage of life was to *be* grabbed—God achieved a firm hold on him. In responding to Joseph's invitation to come to Egypt, Jacob was clearly unwilling to make a move without God's approval.

Can you think of times when God has made himself known to you? Do you allow yourself to meet him as you study his Word? What difference have these experiences made in your life? Are you more like the young Jacob, forcing God to track you down in the desert of your own plans and mistakes? Or are you more like the older Jacob who presented his desires and plans before God for his approval before taking any action?

| | |
|---|---|
| **Strengths and accomplishments** | • Father of the 12 tribes of Israel<br>• Third in the Abrahamic line of God's plan<br>• Determined, willing to work long and hard for what he wanted<br>• Good businessman |
| **Weaknesses and mistakes** | • When faced with conflict, relied on his own resources rather than going to God for help<br>• Tended to accumulate wealth for its own sake |
| **Lessons from his life** | • Security does not lie in the accumulation of goods<br>• All human intentions and actions—for good or evil—are woven by God into his ongoing plan |
| **Vital statistics** | • Where: Canaan<br>• Occupation: Shepherd, livestock owner<br>• Relatives: Parents: Isaac and Rebekah. Brother: Esau. Father-in-law: Laban. Wives: Rachel and Leah. Twelve sons and one daughter are mentioned in the Bible |
| **Key verse** | "What's more, I will be with you, and I will protect you wherever you go. I will someday bring you safely back to this land. I will be with you constantly until I have finished giving you everything I have promised" (Genesis 28:15). |

Jacob's story is told in Genesis 25—50. He is also mentioned in Hosea 12:2–5; Matthew 1:2; 22:32; Acts 7:8–16; Romans 9:11–13; Hebrews 11:9, 20, 21.

---

migrating sea peoples from the Aegean Sea who settled in Palestine. They arrived by way of Crete and Cyprus and were used as mercenaries by Canaanite rulers. These people, living along the southwest coast, were few but ferocious in battle. Although friendly to Isaac, this small group was the forerunner of the nation that would plague Israel during the time of Joshua, the judges, and David. This King Abimelech was not the same Abimelech that Abraham encountered (chapters 20–21). *Abimelech* may have been a dynastic name of the Philistine rulers.

6So Isaac stayed in Gerar. 7And when the men there asked him about Rebekah, he said, "She is my sister." He was afraid to admit that she was his wife. He thought they would kill him to get her, because she was very beautiful. 8But some time later, Abimelech, king of the Philistines, looked out a window and saw Isaac fondling Rebekah.

9Abimelech called for Isaac and exclaimed, "She is obviously your wife! Why did you say she was your sister?"

"Because I was afraid someone would kill me to get her from me," Isaac replied.

10"How could you treat us this way!" Abimelech exclaimed. "Someone might have taken your wife and slept with her, and you would have made us guilty of great sin." 11Then Abimelech made a public proclamation: "Anyone who harms this man or his wife will die!"

### Conflict over Water Rights

12That year Isaac's crops were tremendous! He harvested a hundred times more grain than he planted, for the LORD blessed him. 13He became a rich man, and his wealth only continued to grow. 14He acquired large flocks of sheep and goats, great herds of cattle, and many servants. Soon the Philistines became jealous of him, 15and they filled up all of Isaac's wells with earth. These were the wells that had been dug by the servants of his father, Abraham.

16And Abimelech asked Isaac to leave the country. "Go somewhere else," he said, "for you have become too rich and powerful for us."

17So Isaac moved to the Gerar Valley and lived there instead. 18He reopened the wells his father had dug, which the Philistines had filled in after Abraham's death. Isaac renamed them, using the names Abraham had given them. 19His shepherds also dug in the Gerar Valley and found a gushing spring.

20But then the local shepherds came and claimed the spring. "This is our water," they said, and they argued over it with Isaac's herdsmen. So Isaac named the well "Argument,"* because they had argued about it with him. 21Isaac's men then dug another well, but again there was a fight over it. So Isaac named it "Opposition."* 22Abandoning that one, he dug another well, and the local people finally left him alone. So Isaac called it "Room Enough,"* for he said, "At last the LORD has made room for us, and we will be able to thrive."

26:20 Hebrew *Esek.*   26:21 Hebrew *Sitnah.*   26:22 Hebrew *Rehoboth.*

**Cross-references (margin):**

26:7 Gen 12:11-13; 20:2, 12

26:10 Gen 20:7-10

26:12 Gen 26:3

26:13 Gen 24:35; 25:5

26:15 Gen 21:25

26:16 Exod 1:9

26:19 John 4:10-11

26:22 Pss 4:1; 18:19 Isa 54:2

---

**26:7-11** Isaac was afraid that the men in Gerar would kill him to get his beautiful wife, Rebekah. So he lied, claiming that Rebekah was his sister. Where did he learn that trick? He may have known about the actions of his father, Abraham (see 12:10-13 and 20:1-5). Parents help shape the world's future by the way they shape their children's values. The first step toward helping children live right is for the parents to live right. Your actions are often copied by those closest to you. What kind of example are you setting for your children?

**26:12-16** God kept his promise to bless Isaac. The neighboring Philistines grew jealous because everything Isaac did seemed to go right. So they plugged his wells and tried to get rid of him. Jealousy is a dividing force strong enough to tear apart the mightiest of nations or the closest of friends. It forces you to separate yourself from what you were longing for in the first place. When you find yourself becoming jealous of others, try thanking God for their good fortune. Before striking out in anger, consider what you could lose—a friend, a job, a spouse?

**26:17, 18** The desolate Gerar area was located on the edge of a desert. Water was as precious as gold. If someone dug a well, he was staking a claim to the land. Some wells had locks to keep thieves from stealing the water. To fill in someone's well with dirt was an act of war; it was one of the most serious crimes in the land. Isaac had every right to fight back when the Philistines ruined his wells, and yet he chose to keep the peace. In the end, the Philistines respected him for his patience.

**26:17-22** Three times Isaac and his men dug new wells. When the first two disputes arose, Isaac moved on. Finally there was enough room for everyone. Rather than start a huge conflict, Isaac compromised for the sake of peace. Would you be willing to forsake an important position or valuable possession to keep peace? Ask God for the wisdom to know when to withdraw and when to stand and fight.

**ISAAC'S MOVE TO GERAR**
Isaac had settled near Beer-lahairoi ("the well of the Living One who sees me"), where his sons, Jacob and Esau, were born. A famine drove him to Gerar. But when he became wealthy, his jealous neighbors asked him to leave. From Gerar he moved to Beersheba.

Map labels: Mediterranean Sea; N; Sea of Galilee; Jordan River; Jerusalem (Salem); Hebron; Gerar; Dead Sea; Beersheba; Beer-lahairoi; 0   20 Mi.; 0   20 Km.

**26:23**
Gen 22:19

**26:24**
Gen 17:7; 22:17
Exod 3:6

**26:25**
Gen 12:7-8; 13:4

**26:26**
Gen 21:22

**26:27**
Gen 26:16

**26:28**
Gen 21:22-23

**26:30**
Gen 31:54

**26:31**
Gen 21:31

**26:33**
Gen 21:31

**26:34**
Gen 28:8

**26:35**
Gen 27:46

**27:1**
Gen 25:25; 48:10

**27:2**
Gen 47:29

**27:3**
Gen 25:27

**27:4**
Gen 24:60; 27:19;
48:9

**27:5-6**
Gen 25:27-28

**27:8**
Gen 27:13, 43

**27:11**
Gen 25:25

23 From there Isaac moved to Beersheba, 24 where the LORD appeared to him on the night of his arrival. "I am the God of your father, Abraham," he said. "Do not be afraid, for I am with you and will bless you. I will give you many descendants, and they will become a great nation. I will do this because of my promise to Abraham, my servant." 25 Then Isaac built an altar there and worshiped the LORD. He set up his camp at that place, and his servants dug a well.

*A Treaty with Abimelech*
26 One day Isaac had visitors from Gerar. King Abimelech arrived with his adviser, Ahuzzath, and also Phicol, his army commander. 27 "Why have you come?" Isaac asked them. "This is obviously no friendly visit, since you sent me from your land in a most unfriendly way."

28 They replied, "We can plainly see that the LORD is with you. So we decided we should have a treaty, a covenant between us. 29 Swear that you will not harm us, just as we did not harm you. We have always treated you well, and we sent you away from us in peace. And now look how the LORD has blessed you!"

30 So Isaac prepared a great feast for them, and they ate and drank in preparation for the treaty ceremony. 31 Early the next morning, they each took a solemn oath of nonaggression. Then Isaac sent them home again in peace. 32 That very day Isaac's servants came and told him about a well they had dug. "We've found water!" they said. 33 So Isaac named the well "Oath,"* and from that time to this, the town that grew up there has been called Beersheba—"well of the oath."

34 At the age of forty, Esau married a young woman named Judith, the daughter of Beeri the Hittite. He also married Basemath, the daughter of Elon the Hittite. 35 But Esau's wives made life miserable for Isaac and Rebekah.

## 3. Jacob gets Isaac's blessing

**27** When Isaac was old and almost blind, he called for Esau, his older son, and said, "My son?"

"Yes, Father?" Esau replied.

2 "I am an old man now," Isaac said, "and I expect every day to be my last. 3 Take your bow and a quiver full of arrows cut into the open country, and hunt some wild game for me. 4 Prepare it just the way I like it so it's savory and good, and bring it here for me to eat. Then I will pronounce the blessing that belongs to you, my firstborn son, before I die."

5 But Rebekah overheard the conversation. So when Esau left to hunt for the wild game, 6 she said to her son Jacob, "I overheard your father asking Esau 7 to prepare him a delicious meal of wild game. He wants to bless Esau in the LORD's presence before he dies. 8 Now, my son, do exactly as I tell you. 9 Go out to the flocks and bring me two fine young goats. I'll prepare your father's favorite dish from them. 10 Take the food to your father; then he can eat it and bless you instead of Esau before he dies."

11 "But Mother!" Jacob replied. "He won't be fooled that easily. Think how hairy Esau

**26:33** Hebrew *Shibah*, which can mean "oath" or "seven."

---

**26:26-31** With his enemies wanting to make a peace treaty, Isaac was quick to respond, turning the occasion into a celebration. We should be just as receptive to those who want to make peace with us. When God's influence in our lives attracts people—even enemies—we must take the opportunity to reach out to them with God's love.

**26:34, 35** Esau married pagan women, and this upset his parents greatly. Most parents can be a storehouse of good advice because they have a lifetime of insight into their children's character. You may not agree with everything your parents say, but at least talk with them and listen carefully. This will help avoid the hard feelings Esau experienced.

**27:5-10** When Rebekah learned that Isaac was preparing to bless Esau, she quickly devised a plan to trick him into blessing Jacob instead. Although God had already told her that Jacob would become the family leader (25:23), Rebekah took matters

into her own hands. She resorted to doing something wrong to try to bring about what God had already said would happen. For Rebekah, the end justified the means. No matter how good we think our goals are, we should not attempt to achieve them by doing what is wrong. Would God approve of the methods you are using to accomplish your goals?

**27:11, 12** How we react to a moral dilemma often exposes our real motives. Frequently we are more worried about getting caught than about doing what is right. Jacob did not seem concerned about the deceitfulness of his mother's plan; instead he was afraid of getting in trouble while carrying it out. If you are worried about getting caught, you are probably in a position that is less than honest. Let your fear of getting caught be a warning to do right. Jacob paid a huge price for carrying out this dishonest plan.

is and how smooth my skin is! 12 What if my father touches me? He'll see that I'm trying to trick him, and then he'll curse me instead of blessing me."

13 "Let the curse fall on me, dear son," said Rebekah. "Just do what I tell you. Go out and get the goats."

14 So Jacob followed his mother's instructions, bringing her the two goats. She took them and cooked a delicious meat dish, just the way Isaac liked it. 15 Then she took Esau's best clothes, which were there in the house, and dressed Jacob with them. 16 She made him a pair of gloves from the hairy skin of the young goats, and she fastened a strip of the goat's skin around his neck. 17 Then she gave him the meat dish, with its rich aroma, and some freshly baked bread. 18 Jacob carried the platter of food to his father and said, "My father?"

"Yes, my son," he answered. "Who is it—Esau or Jacob?"

19 Jacob replied, "It's Esau, your older son. I've done as you told me. Here is the wild game, cooked the way you like it. Sit up and eat it so you can give me your blessing."

20 Isaac asked, "How were you able to find it so quickly, my son?"

"Because the LORD your God put it in my path!" Jacob replied.

21 Then Isaac said to Jacob, "Come over here. I want to touch you to make sure you really are Esau." 22 So Jacob went over to his father, and Isaac touched him. "The voice is Jacob's, but the hands are Esau's," Isaac said to himself. 23 But he did not recognize Jacob because Jacob's hands felt hairy just like Esau's. So Isaac pronounced his blessing on Jacob. 24 "Are you really my son Esau?" he asked.

"Yes, of course," Jacob replied.

25 Then Isaac said, "Now, my son, bring me the meat. I will eat it, and then I will give you my blessing." So Jacob took the food over to his father, and Isaac ate it. He also drank the wine that Jacob served him. Then Isaac said, 26 "Come here and kiss me, my son."

27 So Jacob went over and kissed him. And when Isaac caught the smell of his clothes, he was finally convinced, and he blessed his son. He said, "The smell of my son is the good smell of the open fields that the LORD has blessed. 28 May God always give you plenty of dew for healthy crops and good harvests of grain and wine. 29 May many nations become your servants. May you be the master of your brothers. May all your mother's sons bow low before you. All who curse you are cursed, and all who bless you are blessed."

30 As soon as Isaac had blessed Jacob, and almost before Jacob had left his father, Esau returned from his hunting trip. 31 Esau prepared his father's favorite meat dish and brought it to him. Then he said, "I'm back, Father, and I have the wild game. Sit up and eat it so you can give me your blessing."

32 But Isaac asked him, "Who are you?"

"Why, it's me, of course!" he replied. "It's Esau, your older son."

33 Isaac began to tremble uncontrollably and said, "Then who was it that just served me wild game? I have already eaten it, and I blessed him with an irrevocable blessing before you came."

**27:12** Gen 9:25; 27:21-22

**27:13** Gen 27:8

**27:15** Gen 27:27

**27:19** Gen 27:31

**27:21** Gen 27:12

**27:23** Gen 27:16

**27:25** Gen 27:4

**27:27** Ps 65:10; Heb 11:20

**27:28** Deut 7:13; 33:13, 28; Zech 8:12

**27:29** Gen 9:25-27; 12:3; Isa 45:14

**27:31** Gen 27:4

**27:32** Gen 27:18

**27:33** Gen 27:35

---

**27:11-13** Jacob hesitated when he heard Rebekah's deceitful plan. Although he questioned it for the wrong reason (fear of getting caught), he protested and thus gave her one last chance to reconsider. But Rebekah had become so wrapped up in her plan that she no longer saw clearly what she was doing. Sin had trapped her and was degrading her character. Correcting yourself in the middle of doing wrong may bring hurt and disappointment, but it also will bring freedom from sin's control.

**27:24** Although Jacob got the blessing he wanted, deceiving his father cost him dearly. These are some of the consequences of that deceit: (1) He never saw his mother again; (2) his brother wanted to kill him; (3) he was deceived by his uncle, Laban; (4) his family became torn by strife; (5) Esau became the founder of an enemy nation; (6) he was exiled from his family for years. Ironically, Jacob would have received the birthright and blessing anyway (25:23). Imagine how different his life would have been had he and his mother waited for God to work his way, in his time!

**27:33** In ancient times, a person's word was binding (much like a written contract today), especially when it was a formal oath. This is why Isaac's blessing was irrevocable.

**27:33-37** Before the father died, he performed a ceremony of blessing, in which he officially handed over the birthright to the rightful heir. Although the firstborn son was entitled to the birthright, it was not actually his until the blessing was pronounced. Before the blessing was given, the father could take the birthright away from the oldest son and give it to a more deserving son. But after the blessing was given, the birthright could no longer be taken away. This is why fathers usually waited until late in life to pronounce the blessing. Although Jacob had been given the birthright by his older brother years before, he still needed his father's blessing to make it binding.

**27:34**
Heb 12:17

**27:35**
Gen 27:19

**27:36**
Gen 25:26

**27:37**
Gen 27:28-29

**27:38**
Heb 12:17

**27:39**
Heb 11:20

**27:40**
2 Kgs 8:20-22

**27:41**
Gen 32:3-11; 37:4

**27:43**
Gen 27:8

**27:44**
Gen 31:41

**27:46**
Gen 26:34-35

**28:1**
Gen 24:3

**28:2**
Gen 25:20

**28:3**
Gen 17:16; 35:11

**28:4**
Gen 12:1-3; 15:7;
35:11

**28:6**
Gen 28:1

**28:8**
Gen 26:35

**28:9**
Gen 36:2

34 When Esau understood, he let out a loud and bitter cry. "O my father, bless me, too!" he begged.

35 But Isaac said, "Your brother was here, and he tricked me. He has carried away your blessing."

36 Esau said bitterly, "No wonder his name is Jacob,* for he has deceived me twice, first taking my birthright and now stealing my blessing. Oh, haven't you saved even one blessing for me?"

37 Isaac said to Esau, "I have made Jacob your master and have declared that all his brothers will be his servants. I have guaranteed him an abundance of grain and wine— what is there left to give?"

38 Esau pleaded, "Not one blessing left for me? O my father, bless me, too!" Then Esau broke down and wept.

39 His father, Isaac, said to him, "You will live off the land and what it yields, 40 and you will live by your sword. You will serve your brother for a time, but then you will shake loose from him and be free."

### Jacob Flees to Paddan-Aram

41 Esau hated Jacob because he had stolen his blessing, and he said to himself, "My father will soon be dead and gone. Then I will kill Jacob."

42 But someone got wind of what Esau was planning and reported it to Rebekah. She sent for Jacob and told him, "Esau is threatening to kill you. 43 This is what you should do. Flee to your uncle Laban in Haran. 44 Stay there with him until your brother's fury is spent. 45 When he forgets what you have done, I will send for you. Why should I lose both of you in one day?"

46 Then Rebekah said to Isaac, "I'm sick and tired of these local Hittite women. I'd rather die than see Jacob marry one of them."

**28** So Isaac called for Jacob, blessed him, and said, "Do not marry any of these Canaanite women. 2 Instead, go at once to Paddan-aram, to the house of your grandfather Bethuel, and marry one of your uncle Laban's daughters. 3 May God Almighty bless you and give you many children. And may your descendants become a great assembly of nations! 4 May God pass on to you and your descendants the blessings he promised to Abraham. May you own this land where we now are foreigners, for God gave it to Abraham."

5 So Isaac sent Jacob away, and he went to Paddan-aram to stay with his uncle Laban, his mother's brother, the son of Bethuel the Aramean.

6 Esau heard that his father had blessed Jacob and sent him to Paddan-aram to find a wife, and that he had warned Jacob not to marry a Canaanite woman. 7 He also knew that Jacob had obeyed his parents and gone to Paddan-aram. 8 It was now very clear to Esau that his father despised the local Canaanite women. 9 So he visited his uncle Ishmael's family and married one of Ishmael's daughters, in addition to the wives he already had. His new wife's name was Mahalath. She was the sister of Nebaioth and the daughter of Ishmael, Abraham's son.

### F. THE STORY OF JACOB (28:10—36:43)

Jacob did everything, both right and wrong, with great zeal. He deceived his own brother, Esau, and his father Isaac. He wrestled with an angel and worked fourteen years to marry the woman he loved. Through Jacob we learn how a strong leader can also be a servant. We also see how wrong actions will always come back to haunt us.

**27:36** *Jacob* means "he grasps the heel"; this can also figuratively mean "he deceives."

---

**27:41** Esau was so angry at Jacob that he failed to see his own wrong in giving away the birthright in the first place. Jealous anger blinds us from seeing the benefits we have and makes us dwell on what we don't have.

**27:41** When Esau lost the valuable family blessing, his future suddenly changed. Reacting in anger, he decided to kill Jacob. When you lose something of great value, or if others conspire against you and succeed, anger is the first and most natural

reaction. But you can control your feelings by (1) recognizing your reaction for what it is, (2) praying for strength, and (3) asking God for help to see the opportunities that even your bad situation may provide.

**28:9** Ishmael was Isaac's half brother, the son of Abraham and Hagar, Sarah's maidservant (16:1-4, 15). After marrying two foreign girls (26:34), Esau hoped his marriage into Ishmael's family would please his parents, Isaac and Rebekah.

## 1. Jacob starts a family

### Jacob's Dream at Bethel

[10]Meanwhile, Jacob left Beersheba and traveled toward Haran. [11]At sundown he arrived at a good place to set up camp and stopped there for the night. Jacob found a stone for a pillow and lay down to sleep. [12]As he slept, he dreamed of a stairway that reached from earth to heaven. And he saw the angels of God going up and down on it.

[13]At the top of the stairway stood the LORD, and he said, "I am the LORD, the God of your grandfather Abraham and the God of your father, Isaac. The ground you are lying on belongs to you. I will give it to you and your descendants. [14]Your descendants will be as numerous as the dust of the earth! They will cover the land from east to west and from north to south. All the families of the earth will be blessed through you and your descendants.* [15]What's more, I will be with you, and I will protect you wherever you go. I will someday bring you safely back to this land. I will be with you constantly until I have finished giving you everything I have promised."

[16]Then Jacob woke up and said, "Surely the LORD is in this place, and I wasn't even aware of it." [17]He was afraid and said, "What an awesome place this is! It is none other than the house of God—the gateway to heaven!" [18]The next morning he got up very early. He took the stone he had used as a pillow and set it upright as a memorial pillar. Then he poured olive oil over it. [19]He named the place Bethel—"house of God"— though the name of the nearby village was Luz.

[20]Then Jacob made this vow: "If God will be with me and protect me on this journey and give me food and clothing, [21]and if he will bring me back safely to my father, then I will make the LORD my God. [22]This memorial pillar will become a place for worshiping God, and I will give God a tenth of everything he gives me."

### Jacob Arrives at Paddan-Aram

**29** Jacob hurried on, finally arriving in the land of the east. [2]He saw in the distance three flocks of sheep lying in an open field beside a well, waiting to be watered. But a heavy stone covered the mouth of the well. [3]It was the custom there to wait for all the flocks to arrive before removing the stone. After watering them, the stone would be rolled back over the mouth of the well. [4]Jacob went over to the shepherds and asked them, "Where do you live?"

"At Haran," they said.

[5]"Do you know a man there named Laban, the grandson of Nahor?"

"Yes, we do," they replied.

[6]"How is he?" Jacob asked.

"He's well and prosperous. Look, here comes his daughter Rachel with the sheep."

**28:14** Hebrew *seed.*

### Margin references

**28:10** Gen 26:23

**28:12** Gen 20:3; Num 12:6; †John 1:51

**28:14** Gen 12:2; 13:14; 22:17

**28:15** Gen 48:21; Deut 7:9; 31:6, 8

**28:17** Exod 3:5; Ps 68:35

**28:18** Gen 35:14

**28:19** Gen 12:8; 35:6; 48:3

**28:21** Exod 15:2

**28:22** Gen 14:20; 35:7; Deut 14:22

**29:1** Judg 6:3, 33

**29:2** Gen 24:10-11

**29:4** Gen 28:10

**29:5** Gen 11:29

**29:6** Exod 2:16

**JACOB'S TRIP TO HARAN** After deceiving Esau, Jacob ran for his life, traveling more than 400 miles to Haran, where an uncle, Laban, lived. In Haran, Jacob married and started a family.

**28:10-15** God's covenant promise to Abraham and Isaac was offered to Jacob as well. But it was not enough to be Abraham's grandson; Jacob had to establish his own personal relationship with God. God has no grandchildren; each of us must have a personal relationship with him. It is not enough to hear wonderful stories about Christians in your family. You need to become part of the story yourself (see Galatians 3:6, 7).

**28:19** Bethel was about ten miles north of Jerusalem and 60 miles north of Beersheba, where Jacob left his family. This was where Abraham made one of his first sacrifices to God when he entered the land. At first, Bethel became an important center for worship; later it was a center of idol worship. The prophet Hosea condemned its evil practices.

**28:20-22** Was Jacob trying to bargain with God? It is possible that he, in his ignorance of how to worship and serve God, treated God like a servant who would perform a service for a tip. More likely, Jacob was not bargaining but pledging his future to God. He may have been saying, in effect, "Because you have blessed me, I will follow you." Whether Jacob was bargaining or pledging, God blessed him. But God also had some difficult lessons for Jacob to learn.

⁷"Why don't you water the flocks so they can get back to grazing?" Jacob asked. "They'll be hungry if you stop so early in the day."

⁸"We don't roll away the stone and begin the watering until all the flocks and shepherds are here," they replied.

⁹As this conversation was going on, Rachel arrived with her father's sheep, for she was a shepherd. ¹⁰And because she was his cousin, the daughter of his mother's brother, and because the sheep were his uncle's, Jacob went over to the well and rolled away the stone and watered his uncle's flock. ¹¹Then Jacob kissed Rachel, and tears came to his eyes. ¹²He explained that he was her cousin on her father's side, her aunt Rebekah's son. So Rachel quickly ran and told her father, Laban.

¹³As soon as Laban heard about Jacob's arrival, he rushed out to meet him and greeted him warmly. Laban then brought him home, and Jacob told him his story. ¹⁴"Just think, my very own flesh and blood!" Laban exclaimed.

### Jacob Marries Leah and Rachel

After Jacob had been there about a month, ¹⁵Laban said to him, "You shouldn't work for me without pay just because we are relatives. How much do you want?"

¹⁶Now Laban had two daughters: Leah, who was the oldest, and her younger sister, Rachel. ¹⁷Leah had pretty eyes,* but Rachel was beautiful in every way, with a lovely face and shapely figure. ¹⁸Since Jacob was in love with Rachel, he told her father, "I'll work for you seven years if you'll give me Rachel, your younger daughter, as my wife."

¹⁹"Agreed!" Laban replied. "I'd rather give her to you than to someone outside the family."

²⁰So Jacob spent the next seven years working to pay for Rachel. But his love for her was so strong that it seemed to him but a few days. ²¹Finally, the time came for him to marry her. "I have fulfilled my contract," Jacob said to Laban. "Now give me my wife so we can be married."

29:17 Or *dull eyes.* The meaning of the Hebrew is uncertain.

**29:10**
Exod 2:17

**29:11**
Gen 33:4

**29:12**
Gen 28:5

**29:14**
Judg 9:2
2 Sam 5:1

**29:15**
Gen 30:28; 31:7, 41

**29:16**
Gen 29:25-26

**29:17**
Gen 12:11

**29:18**
Gen 24:67
Hos 12:12

**29:20**
Song 8:7

---

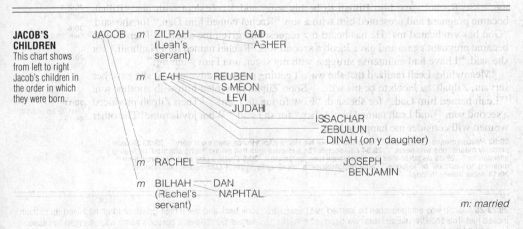

**JACOB'S CHILDREN**
This chart shows from left to right Jacob's children in the order in which they were born.

JACOB  m  ZILPAH —— GAD
             (Leah's ——— ASHER
             servant)

         m  LEAH —— REUBEN
                      SIMEON
                      LEVI
                      JUDAH
                      ISSACHAR
                      ZEBULUN
                      DINAH (only daughter)

         m  RACHEL —— JOSEPH
                        BENJAMIN

         m  BILHAH —— DAN
             (Rachel's    NAPHTALI
             servant)                          m: married

Jacob's many wives (two wives and two "substitute" wives) led to sad and bitter consequences among the children. Anger, resentment, and jealousy were common among Jacob's sons. It is interesting to note that the worst fighting and rivalry occurred between Leah's children and Rachel's children, and among the tribes that descended from them.

---

**29:18-27**  It was the custom of the day for a man to present a dowry, or substantial gift, to the family of his future wife. This was to compensate the family for the loss of the girl. Jacob's dowry was not a material possession, for he had none to offer. Instead, he agreed to work seven years for Laban. But there was another custom of the land that Laban did not tell Jacob. The older daughter had to be married first. By giving Jacob Leah and not Rachel, Laban tricked him into promising another seven years of hard work.

**29:20-28**  People often wonder if working a long time for something they desire is worth it. Jacob worked seven years to

marry Rachel. After being tricked, he agreed to work seven more years for her (although he did get to marry Rachel shortly after he married Leah)! The most important goals and desires are worth working and waiting for. Movies and television have created the illusion that people have to wait only about an hour to solve their problems or get what they want. Don't be trapped into thinking the same is true in real life. Patience is hardest when we need it the most, but it is the key to achieving our goals.

22 So Laban invited everyone in the neighborhood to celebrate with Jacob at a wedding feast. 23 That night, when it was dark, Laban took Leah to Jacob, and he slept with her. 24 And Laban gave Leah a servant, Zilpah, to be her maid.

25 But when Jacob woke up in the morning—it was Leah! "What sort of trick is this?" Jacob raged at Laban. "I worked seven years for Rachel. What do you mean by this trickery?"

26 "It's not our custom to marry off a younger daughter ahead of the firstborn," Laban replied. 27 "Wait until the bridal week is over, and you can have Rachel, too—that is, if you promise to work another seven years for me."

28 So Jacob agreed to work seven more years. A week after Jacob had married Leah, Laban gave him Rachel, too. 29 And Laban gave Rachel a servant, Bilhah, to be her maid. 30 So Jacob slept with Rachel, too, and he loved her more than Leah. He then stayed and worked the additional seven years.

### Jacob's Many Children

31 But because Leah was unloved, the LORD let her have a child, while Rachel was childless. 32 So Leah became pregnant and had a son. She named him Reuben,* for she said, "The LORD has noticed my misery, and now my husband will love me." 33 She soon became pregnant again and had another son. She named him Simeon,* for she said, "The LORD heard that I was unloved and has given me another son." 34 Again she became pregnant and had a son. She named him Levi,* for she said, "Surely now my husband will feel affection for me, since I have given him three sons!" 35 Once again she became pregnant and had a son. She named him Judah,* for she said, "Now I will praise the LORD!" And then she stopped having children.

**30** When Rachel saw that she wasn't having any children, she became jealous of her sister. "Give me children, or I'll die!" she exclaimed to Jacob.

2 Jacob flew into a rage. "Am I God?" he asked. "He is the only one able to give you children!"

3 Then Rachel told him, "Sleep with my servant, Bilhah, and she will bear children for me." 4 So Rachel gave him Bilhah to be his wife, and Jacob slept with her. 5 Bilhah became pregnant and presented him with a son. 6 Rachel named him Dan,* for she said, "God has vindicated me! He has heard my request and given me a son." 7 Then Bilhah became pregnant again and gave Jacob a second son. 8 Rachel named him Naphtali,* for she said, "I have had an intense struggle with my sister, and I am winning!"

9 Meanwhile, Leah realized that she wasn't getting pregnant anymore, so she gave her servant, Zilpah, to Jacob to be his wife. 10 Soon Zilpah presented him with another son. 11 Leah named him Gad,* for she said, "How fortunate I am!" 12 Then Zilpah produced a second son, 13 and Leah named him Asher,* for she said, "What joy is mine! The other women will consider me happy indeed!"

**29:22** Judg 14:10
**29:23** Gen 24:65; 38:14
**29:24** Gen 30:9
**29:25** Gen 12:18
**29:27** Judg 14:12
**29:29** Gen 30:3
**29:30** Gen 29:16
**29:31** Deut 21:15-17
**29:32** Gen 30:23; 37:21; 46:8
**29:33** Deut 21:15
**29:34** Gen 49:5
**29:35** Gen 49:8; Matt 1:2-3
**30:1** 1 Sam 1:5-6
**30:2** Gen 20:18; 29:31
**30:3-4** Gen 16:2-4
**30:6** Gen 30:23
**30:8** Gen 32:28
**30:11** Gen 35:26; 46:16; 49:19

**29:32** Reuben means "Look, a son!" It also sounds like the Hebrew for "He has seen my misery." **29:33** Simeon probably means "one who hears." **29:34** Levi sounds like a Hebrew term that means "being attached" or "feeling affection for." **29:35** Judah sounds like the Hebrew term for "praise." **30:6** Dan is a play on the Hebrew term meaning "to vindicate" or "to judge." **30:8** Naphtali means "my struggle." **30:11** Gad means "good fortune." **30:13** Asher means "happy."

---

**29:23-25** Jacob was enraged when he learned that Laban had tricked him. The deceiver of Esau was now deceived himself. How natural it is for us to become upset at an injustice done to us while closing our eyes to the injustices we do to others. Sin has a way of coming back to haunt us.

**29:28-30** Although Jacob was tricked by Laban, he kept his part of the bargain. There was more at stake than just Jacob's hurt. There was Rachel to think about, as well as God's plan for his life. When we are tricked by others, keeping our part of the bargain may still be wise. Nursing our wounds or plotting revenge makes us unable to see from God's perspective.

**29:32** Today parents usually give their children names that sound good or have sentimental appeal. But the Old Testament portrays a more dynamic use of names. Parents often chose names that reflected the situation at the time of the birth. They sometimes hoped their children would fulfill the meaning of the names given them. Later the parents could

look back and see if their grown children had lived up to their names. Sometimes a person's name was changed because his or her character and name did not match. This happened to Jacob ("he grasps the heel," figuratively, "he deceives"), whose name was changed to Israel ("one who struggles with God"). Jacob's character had changed to the point that he was no longer seen as a deceiver, but as a God-honoring man.

**30:3** Each of the three great patriarchs (Abraham, Isaac, and Jacob) had wives who had difficulty conceiving children. It is interesting to note how each man reacted to his wife's predicament. Abraham had relations with Sarah's servant in order to have his own child, thus introducing bitterness and jealousy into his family. Isaac, by contrast, prayed to God when his wife was barren. God eventually answered his prayers, and Rebekah had twin sons. Jacob, however, followed his grandfather's example and had children by his wives' servants, leading to sad and sometimes bitter consequences.

**30:14**
Song 7:13

**30:17**
Gen 25:21

**30:18**
Gen 49:14

**30:22**
1 Sam 1:19-20

¹⁴One day during the wheat harvest, Reuben found some mandrakes growing in a field and brought the roots to his mother, Leah. Rachel begged Leah to give some of them to her. ¹⁵But Leah angrily replied, "Wasn't it enough that you stole my husband? Now will you steal my son's mandrake roots, too?"

Rachel said, "I will let him sleep with you tonight in exchange for the mandrake roots." ¹⁶So that evening, as Jacob was coming home from the fields, Leah went out to meet him. "You must sleep with me tonight!" she said. "I have paid for you with some mandrake roots my son has found." So Jacob slept with her. ¹⁷And God answered her prayers. She became pregnant again and gave birth to her fifth son. ¹⁸She named him Issachar,* for she said, "God has rewarded me for giving my servant to my husband as a wife." ¹⁹Then she became pregnant again and had a sixth son. ²⁰She named him Zebulun,* for she said, "God has given me good gifts for my husband. Now he will honor me, for I have given him six sons." ²¹Later she gave birth to a daughter and named her Dinah.

²²Then God remembered Rachel's plight and answered her prayers by giving her a

**30:18** *Issachar* sounds like a Hebrew term that means "reward." **30:20** *Zebulun* probably means "honor."

## RACHEL

History seems to repeat itself here. Twice a town well at Haran was the site of significant events in one family's story. It was here that Rebekah met Eliezer, Abraham's servant, who had come to find a wife for Isaac. Some 40 years later, Rebekah's son Jacob returned the favor by serving his cousin Rachel and her sheep from the same well. The relationship that developed between them not only reminds us that romance is not a modern invention but also teaches us a few lessons about patience and love.

Jacob's love for Rachel was both patient and practical. Jacob had the patience to wait seven years for her, but he kept busy in the meantime. His commitment to Rachel kindled a strong loyalty within her. In fact, her loyalty to Jacob got out of hand and became self-destructive. She was frustrated by her barrenness and desperate to compete with her sister for Jacob's affection. She was trying to gain from Jacob what he had already given: devoted love.

Rachel's attempts to earn the unearnable are a picture of a much greater error we can make. Like her, we find ourselves trying somehow to earn love—God's love. But apart from his Word, we end up with one of two false ideas. Either we think we've been good enough to deserve his love or we recognize we aren't able to earn his love and assume that it cannot be ours. If the Bible makes no other point, it shouts this one: God loves us! His love had no beginning and is incredibly patient. All we need to do is respond, not try to earn what is freely offered. God has said in many ways, "I love you. I have demonstrated that love to you by all I've done for you. I have even sacrificed my Son, Jesus, to pay the price for what is unacceptable about you—your sin. Now, live because of my love. Respond to me; love me with your whole being; give yourself to me in thanksgiving, not as payment." Live life fully, in the freedom of knowing you are loved.

| | |
|---|---|
| **Strengths and accomplishments** | • She showed great loyalty to her family<br>• She gave birth to Joseph and Benjamin after being barren for many years |
| **Weaknesses and mistakes** | • Her envy and competitiveness marred her relationship with her sister, Leah<br>• She was capable of dishonesty when she took her loyalty too far<br>• She failed to recognize that Jacob's devotion was not dependent on her ability to have children |
| **Lessons from her life** | • Loyalty must be controlled by what is true and right<br>• Love is accepted, not earned |
| **Vital statistics** | • Where: Haran<br>• Occupation: Shepherdess, wife, mother, household manager<br>• Relatives: Father: Laban. Aunt: Rebekah. Sister: Leah. Husband: Jacob. Sons: Joseph and Benjamin |
| **Key verse** | "So Jacob spent the next seven years working to pay for Rachel. But his love for her was so strong that it seemed to him but a few days" (Genesis 29:20) |

Rachel's story is told in Genesis 29—35:20. She is also mentioned in Ruth 4:11.

**30:4-13** Rachel and Leah were locked in a cruel contest. In their race to have more children, they both gave their servants to Jacob as concubines. Jacob would have been wise to refuse even though this was an accepted custom of the day. The fact that a custom is socially acceptable does not mean it's wise or right. You will be spared much heartbreak if you look at the potential consequences, to you or others, of your actions. Are you doing anything now that might cause future problems?

**30:22-24** Eventually God answered Rachel's prayers and gave her a child of her own. In the meantime, however, she had given her servant to Jacob. Trusting God when nothing seems to happen is difficult. But it is harder still to live with the consequences of taking matters into our own hands. Resist the temptation to think God has forgotten you. Have patience and courage to wait for God to act.

9Then Jacob prayed, "O God of my grandfather Abraham and my father, Isaac— O LORD, you told me to return to my land and to my relatives, and you promised to treat me kindly. 10I am not worthy of all the faithfulness and unfailing love you have shown to me, your servant. When I left home, I owned nothing except a walking stick, and now my household fills two camps! 11O LORD, please rescue me from my brother, Esau. I am afraid that he is coming to kill me, along with my wives and children. 12But you promised to treat me kindly and to multiply my descendants until they become as numerous as the sands along the seashore—too many to count."

13Jacob stayed where he was for the night and prepared a present for Esau: 14two hundred female goats, twenty male goats, two hundred ewes, twenty rams, 15thirty female camels with their young, forty cows, ten bulls, twenty female donkeys, and ten male donkeys. 16He told his servants to lead them on ahead, each group of animals by itself, separated by a distance in between.

17He gave these instructions to the men leading the first group: "When you meet Esau, he will ask, 'Where are you going? Whose servants are you? Whose animals are these?' 18You should reply, 'These belong to your servant Jacob. They are a present for his master Esau! He is coming right behind us.'" 19Jacob gave the same instructions to each of the herdsmen and told them, "You are all to say the same thing to Esau when you see him. 20And be sure to say, 'Your servant Jacob is right behind us.'" Jacob's plan was to appease Esau with the presents before meeting him face to face. "Perhaps," Jacob hoped, "he will be friendly to us." 21So the presents were sent on ahead, and Jacob spent that night in the camp.

### Jacob Wrestles with God

22But during the night Jacob got up and sent his two wives, two concubines, and eleven sons across the Jabbok River. 23After they were on the other side, he sent over all his possessions. 24This left Jacob all alone in the camp, and a man came and wrestled with him until dawn. 25When the man saw that he couldn't win the match, he struck Jacob's hip and knocked it out of joint at the socket. 26Then the man said, "Let me go, for it is dawn."

But Jacob panted, "I will not let you go unless you bless me."

27"What is your name?" the man asked.

He replied, "Jacob."

28"Your name will no longer be Jacob," the man told him. "It is now Israel,* because you have struggled with both God and men and have won."

29"What is your name?" Jacob asked him.

"Why do you ask?" the man replied. Then he blessed Jacob there.

30Jacob named the place Peniel—"face of God"—for he said, "I have seen God face to face, yet my life has been spared." 31The sun rose as he left Peniel,* and he was limping because of his hip. 32That is why even today the people of Israel don't eat meat from near the hip, in memory of what happened that night.

### Jacob and Esau Make Peace

**33** Then, in the distance, Jacob saw Esau coming with his four hundred men. 2Jacob now arranged his family into a column, with his two concubines and their children at the front, Leah and her children next, and Rachel and Joseph last. 3Then Jacob went on ahead. As he approached his brother, he bowed low seven times before him. 4Then

32:28 *Israel* means "God struggles" or "one who struggles with God." 32:31 Hebrew *Penuel*, a variant name for Peniel.

**32:9** Gen 28:13-15; 31:13
**32:10** Gen 24:27
**32:11** Gen 27:41
**32:12** Gen 28:14
**32:18** Gen 32:13
**32:20** 1 Sam 25:19
**32:22** Deut 3:16; Josh 12:2
**32:24** Gen 18:2
**32:26** Hos 12:3-4
**32:28** Gen 35:10; 1 Kgs 18:31
**32:29** Exod 3:13; Judg 13:17
**32:30** Gen 16:13; Exod 24:10; 33:20; Num 12:8; Deut 5:24; 34:10; Judg 6:22; John 1:18
**33:1** Gen 32:6-7
**33:3** Gen 18:2; 42:6
**33:4** Gen 45:14-15

**32:9-12** How would you feel if you knew you were about to meet the person you had cheated out of his most precious possession? Jacob had taken Esau's birthright (25:33) and his blessing (27:27-40). Now he was about to meet this brother for the first time in 20 years, and he was frantic with fear. He collected his thoughts, however, and decided to pray. When we face a difficult conflict, we can run about frantically or we can pause to pray. Which approach will be more effective?

**32:26** Jacob continued this wrestling match all night just to be blessed. He was persistent. God encourages persistence in all areas of our lives, including the spiritual. Where in your spiritual life do you need more persistence? Strong character develops as you struggle through tough conditions.

**32:27-29** God gave many Bible people new names (Abraham, Sarah, Peter). Their new names were symbols of how God had changed their lives. Here we see how Jacob's character had changed. Jacob, the ambitious deceiver, had now become Israel, the one who struggles with God and overcomes.

**33:1-11** It is refreshing to see Esau's change of heart when the two brothers meet again. The bitterness over losing his birthright and blessing (27:36-41) seems gone. Instead, Esau was content with what he had. Jacob even exclaimed how great it was to see his brother obviously pleased with him (33:10).

**33:5**
Gen 48:9

Esau ran to meet him and embraced him affectionately and kissed him. Both of them were in tears.

5 Then Esau looked at the women and children and asked, "Who are these people with you?"

"These are the children God has graciously given to me," Jacob replied. 6 Then the concubines came forward with their children and bowed low before him. 7 Next Leah came with her children, and they bowed down. Finally, Rachel and Joseph came and made their bows.

**33:8**
Gen 32:14-16

**33:9**
Gen 27:39

8 "And what were all the flocks and herds I met as I came?" Esau asked.

Jacob replied, "They are gifts, my lord, to ensure your goodwill."

9 "Brother, I have plenty," Esau answered. "Keep what you have."

10 "No, please accept them," Jacob said, "for what a relief it is to see your friendly smile. It is like seeing the smile of God! 11 Please take my gifts, for God has been very generous to me. I have more than enough." Jacob continued to insist, so Esau finally accepted them.

12 "Well, let's be going," Esau said. "I will stay with you and lead the way."

**33:14**
Gen 32:3

13 But Jacob replied, "You can see, my lord, that some of the children are very young, and the flocks and herds have their young, too. If they are driven too hard, they may die. 14 So go on ahead of us. We will follow at our own pace and meet you at Seir."

15 "Well," Esau said, "at least let me leave some of my men to guide and protect you."

**33:17**
Judg 8:5, 14
Ps 60:6

"There is no reason for you to be so kind to me," Jacob insisted.

16 So Esau started back to Seir that same day. 17 Meanwhile, Jacob and his household traveled on to Succoth. There he built himself a house and made shelters for his flocks and herds. That is why the place was named Succoth.* 18 Then they arrived safely at Shechem, in Canaan, and they set up camp just outside the town. 19 Jacob bought the land he camped on from the family of Hamor, Shechem's father, for a hundred pieces of silver.* 20 And there he built an altar and called it El-Elohe-Israel.*

**33:18**
Gen 12:6; 25:20

**33:19**
Josh 24:32
John 4:5

**34:1**
Gen 30:21

**34:2**
Deut 21:14
2 Sam 13:14

### Revenge against Shechem

**34** One day Dinah, Leah's daughter, went to visit some of the young women who lived in the area. 2 But when the local prince, Shechem son of Hamor the Hivite, saw her, he took her and raped her. 3 But Shechem's love for Dinah was strong, and he

**33:17** *Succoth* means "shelters." **33:19** Hebrew *100 kesitahs;* the value or weight of the kesitah is no longer known. **33:20** *El-Elohe-Israel* means "God, the God of Israel."

---

Life can bring us some bad situations. We can feel cheated as Esau did, but we don't have to remain bitter. We can remove bitterness from our lives by honestly expressing our feelings to God, forgiving those who have wronged us, and being content with what we have.

**33:3** Bowing to the ground seven times was the sign of respect given to a king. Jacob was taking every precaution as he met Esau, hoping to dispel any thoughts of revenge.

**33:4** Esau greeted his brother, Jacob, with a great hug. Imagine how difficult this must have been for a man who once had actually plotted his brother's death (27:41). But time away from each other allowed the bitter wounds to heal. With the passing of time, each brother was able to see that their relationship was more important than their real estate.

**33:11** Why did Jacob send gifts ahead for Esau? In Bible times, gifts were given for several reasons. (1) This may have been a bribe. Gifts are still given to win someone over or buy his or her support. Esau may first have refused Jacob's gifts (33:9) because he didn't want or need a bribe. He had already forgiven Jacob, and he had ample wealth of his own. (2) This may have been an expression of affection. (3) It may have been the customary way of greeting someone before an important meeting. Such gifts were often related to a person's occupation. This explains why Jacob sent Esau, who was a herdsman, sheep, goats, and cattle.

**33:14-17** Why did Jacob imply that he was going to Seir but then stop at Succoth? We don't know the answer, but perhaps Jacob decided to stop there as they journeyed because Suc-

coth is a beautiful site on the eastern side of the Jordan River. Whatever the reason, Jacob and Esau parted in peace. But they still lived fairly close to each other until after their father's death (36:6-8).

**JACOB'S JOURNEY TO SHECHEM**

After a joyful reunion with his brother, Esau (who journeyed from Edom), Jacob set up camp in Succoth. Later he moved on to Shechem where his daughter, Dinah, was raped and two of his sons took revenge on the city.

tried to win her affection. ⁴He even spoke to his father about it. "Get this girl for me," he demanded. "I want to marry her."

**34:4**
Gen 21:21

⁵Word soon reached Jacob that his daughter had been defiled, but his sons were out in the fields herding cattle so he did nothing until they returned. ⁶Meanwhile, Hamor, Shechem's father, came out to discuss the matter with Jacob. ⁷He arrived just as Jacob's sons were coming in from the fields. They were shocked and furious that their sister had been raped. Shechem had done a disgraceful thing against Jacob's family,* a thing that should never have been done.

**34:7**
2 Sam 13:12

⁸Hamor told Jacob and his sons, "My son Shechem is truly in love with your daughter, and he longs for her to be his wife. Please let him marry her. ⁹We invite you to let your daughters marry our sons, and we will give our daughters as wives for your young men. ¹⁰And you may live among us; the land is open to you! Settle here and trade with us. You are free to acquire property among us."

**34:10**
Gen 33:19

¹¹Then Shechem addressed Dinah's father and brothers. "Please be kind to me, and let me have her as my wife," he begged. "I will give whatever you require. ¹²No matter what dowry or gift you demand, I will pay it—only give me the girl as my wife."

**34:12**
Exod 22:16

¹³But Dinah's brothers deceived Shechem and Hamor because of what Shechem had done to their sister. ¹⁴They said to them, "We couldn't possibly allow this, because you aren't circumcised. It would be a disgrace for her to marry a man like you! ¹⁵But here is a solution. If every man among you will be circumcised like we are, ¹⁶we will intermarry with you and live here and unite with you to become one people. ¹⁷Otherwise we will take her and be on our way."

**34:13**
Gen 27:36

**34:14**
Gen 17:14

¹⁸Hamor and Shechem gladly agreed, ¹⁹and Shechem lost no time in acting on this request, for he wanted Dinah desperately. Shechem was a highly respected member of his family, ²⁰and he appeared with his father before the town leaders to present this proposal. ²¹"Those men are our friends," they said. "Let's invite them to live here among us and ply their trade. For the land is large enough to hold them, and we can intermarry with them. ²²But they will consider staying here only on one condition. Every one of us men must be circumcised, just as they are. ²³But if we do this, all their flocks and possessions will become ours. Come, let's agree to this so they will settle here among us."

**34:19**
Gen 29:20

**34:20**
Gen 18:1

**34:22**
Gen 34:15

²⁴So all the men agreed and were circumcised. ²⁵But three days later, when their wounds were still sore, two of Dinah's brothers, Simeon and Levi, took their swords, entered the town without opposition, and slaughtered every man there, ²⁶including Hamor and Shechem. They rescued Dinah from Shechem's house and returned to their camp. ²⁷Then all of Jacob's sons plundered the town because their sister had been defiled there. ²⁸They seized all the flocks and herds and donkeys—everything they could lay their hands on, both inside the town and outside in the fields. ²⁹They also took all the women and children and wealth of every kind.

**34:24**
Gen 28:15

**34:25**
Gen 49:5-7
Josh 5:8

**34:28**
Gen 43:18

³⁰Afterward Jacob said to Levi and Simeon, "You have made me stink among all the people of this land—among all the Canaanites and Perizzites. We are so few that they will come and crush us. We will all be killed!"

**34:30**
Gen 13:7; 49:5-7
Exod 5:21
2 Sam 10:6
1 Chr 16:19

³¹"Should he treat our sister like a prostitute?" they retorted angrily.

**34:7** Hebrew *in Israel.*

---

**34:1-4** Shechem may have been a victim of "love at first sight," but his actions were impulsive and evil. Not only did he sin against Dinah; he sinned against the entire family (34:6, 7). The consequences of his deed were severe both for his family and for Jacob's (34:25-31). Even Shechem's declared love for Dinah could not excuse the evil he did by raping her. Don't allow sexual passion to boil over into evil actions. Passion must be controlled.

**34:25-31** Why did Simeon and Levi take such harsh action against the city of Shechem? Jacob's family saw themselves as set apart from others. God wanted them to remain separate from their pagan neighbors. But the brothers wrongly thought that being set apart also meant being better. This arrogant attitude led to the terrible slaughter of innocent people.

**34:27-29** When Shechem raped Dinah, the consequences were far greater than he could have imagined. Dinah's brothers were outraged and took revenge. Pain, deceit, and murder followed. Sexual sin is devastating because its consequences are so far-reaching.

**34:30, 31** In seeking revenge against Shechem, Simeon and Levi lied, stole, and murdered. Their desire for justice was right, but their ways of achieving it were wrong. Because of their sin, their father cursed them with his dying breath (49:5-7). Generations later, their descendants lost the part of the Promised Land allotted to them. When tempted to return evil for evil, leave revenge to God and spare yourself the dreadful consequences of sin.

## Jacob's Return to Bethel

**35:1**
Gen 12:8; 28:19

**35** God said to Jacob, "Now move on to Bethel and settle there. Build an altar there to worship me—the God who appeared to you when you fled from your brother, Esau."

**35:2**
Gen 31:19

**35:3**
Gen 28:15-22

2 So Jacob told everyone in his household, "Destroy your idols, wash yourselves, and put on clean clothing. 3 We are now going to Bethel, where I will build an altar to the God who answered my prayers when I was in distress. He has stayed with me wherever I have gone."

**35:4**
Exod 32:3
Judg 8:24
Hos 2:13

**35:5**
Exod 15:16

**35:6**
Gen 28:19

**35:7**
Gen 28:19

4 So they gave Jacob all their idols and their earrings, and he buried them beneath the tree near Shechem. 5 When they set out again, terror from God came over the people in all the towns of that area, and no one attacked them. 6 Finally, they arrived at Luz (now called Bethel) in Canaan. 7 Jacob built an altar there and named it El-bethel,* because God had appeared to him there at Bethel when he was fleeing from Esau.

**35:8**
Gen 24:59

8 Soon after this, Rebekah's old nurse, Deborah, died. She was buried beneath the oak tree in the valley below Bethel. Ever since, the tree has been called the "Oak of Weeping."*

**35:9**
Gen 28:13

**35:10**
Gen 32:28

**35:11**
Gen 12:2; 17:1, 6

**35:12**
Gen 13:15; 28:13

**35:13**
Judg 6:21; 13:20

9 God appeared to Jacob once again when he arrived at Bethel after traveling from Paddan-aram. God blessed him 10 and said, "Your name is no longer Jacob; you will now be called Israel."* 11 Then God said, "I am God Almighty. Multiply and fill the earth! Become a great nation, even many nations. Kings will be among your descendants! 12 And I will pass on to you the land I gave to Abraham and Isaac. Yes, I will give it to you and your descendants." 13 Then God went up from the place where he had spoken to Jacob.

**35:14**
Gen 28:18-19

14 Jacob set up a stone pillar to mark the place where God had spoken to him. He then poured wine over it as an offering to God and anointed the pillar with olive oil. 15 Jacob called the place Bethel—"house of God"—because God had spoken to him there.

## The Deaths of Rachel and Isaac

**35:16**
Ruth 4:11

**35:17**
Gen 30:22-24

**35:18**
Gen 49:27

16 Leaving Bethel, they traveled on toward Ephrath (that is, Bethlehem). But Rachel's pains of childbirth began while they were still some distance away. 17 After a very hard delivery, the midwife finally exclaimed, "Don't be afraid—you have another son!" 18 Rachel was about to die, but with her last breath she named him Ben-oni; the baby's

**35:7** El-bethel means "the God of Bethel." **35:8** Hebrew Allon-bacuth. **35:10** Jacob means "he grasps the heel"; this can also figuratively mean "he deceives"; Israel means 'God struggles" or "one who struggles with God."

---

**35:2** Why did the people have these idols? Idols were sometimes seen more as good luck charms than as gods. Some Israelites, even though they worshiped God, had idols in their homes, just as some Christians today own good luck trinkets. Jacob believed that idols should have no place in his household. He wanted nothing to divert his family's spiritual focus.

Jacob ordered his household to get rid of their idols. Unless we remove idols from our lives, they can ruin our faith. What idols do we have? An idol is anything we put before God. Idols don't have to be physical objects; they can be thoughts or desires. Like Jacob, we should get rid of anything that could stand between us and God.

**35:4** Why did the people give Jacob their earrings? Jewelry, in itself was not evil, but in Jacob's day earrings were often worn as good luck charms to ward off evil. The people in his family had to cleanse themselves of all pagan influences, including reminders of foreign gods.

**35:10** God reminded Jacob of his new name, Israel, which meant "one who struggles with God." Although Jacob's life was littered with difficulties and trials, his new name was a tribute to his desire to stay close to God despite life's disappointments.

Many people believe that Christianity should offer a problem-free life. Consequently, as life gets tough, they draw back disappointed. Instead, they should determine to prevail with God through life's storms. Problems and difficulties are painful but inevitable; you might as well see them as opportunities for growth. You can't prevail with God unless you have troubles to prevail over.

**35:13, 14** This oil used to anoint the pillar was olive oil of the finest grade of purity. It was expensive, so using it showed the high value placed on the anointed object. Jacob was showing the greatest respect for the place where he met with God.

**JACOB'S JOURNEY BACK TO HEBRON**
After Jacob's sons Simeon and Levi destroyed Shechem, God told Jacob to move to Bethel, where God reminded him that his name had been changed to Israel. He then traveled to Hebron, but along the way, his dear wife Rachel died near Ephrath (Bethlehem)

father, however, called him Benjamin.* ¹⁹So Rachel died and was buried on the way to
Ephrath (that is, Bethlehem). ²⁰Jacob set up a stone monument over her grave, and it can
be seen there to this day.

²¹Jacob* then traveled on and camped beyond the tower of Eder. ²²While he was there,
Reuben slept with Bilhah, his father's concubine, and someone told Jacob about it.

These are the names of the twelve sons of Jacob:

²³The sons of Leah were Reuben (Jacob's oldest son), Simeon, Levi, Judah, Issachar,
and Zebulun.

²⁴The sons of Rachel were Joseph and Benjamin.

²⁵The sons of Bilhah, Rachel's servant, were Dan and Naphtali.

²⁶The sons of Zilpah, Leah's servant, were Gad and Asher.

These were the sons born to Jacob at Paddan-aram.

²⁷So Jacob came home to his father Isaac in Mamre, which is near Kiriath-arba (now
called Hebron), where Abraham had also lived. ²⁸Isaac lived for 180 years, ²⁹and he died
at a ripe old age, joining his ancestors in death. Then his sons, Esau and Jacob, buried him.

### Descendants of Esau

**36** This is the history of the descendants of Esau (also known as Edom). ²Esau
married two young women from Canaan: Adah, the daughter of Elon the Hittite;
and Oholibamah, the daughter of Anah and granddaughter of Zibeon the Hivite. ³He also
married his cousin Basemath, who was the daughter of Ishmael and the sister of
Nebaioth. ⁴Esau and Adah had a son named Eliphaz. Esau and Basemath had a son
named Reuel. ⁵Esau and Oholibamah had sons named Jeush, Jalam, and Korah. All these
sons were born to Esau in the land of Canaan.

⁶Then Esau took his wives, children, household servants, cattle, and flocks—all the
wealth he had gained in the land of Canaan—and moved away from his brother, Jacob.
⁷There was not enough land to support them both because of all their cattle and livestock.
⁸So Esau (also known as Edom) settled in the hill country of Seir.

⁹This is a list of Esau's descendants, the Edomites, who lived in the hill country of Seir.

¹⁰Among Esau's sons were Eliphaz, the son of Esau's wife Adah; and Reuel, the son
of Esau's wife Basemath.

¹¹The sons of Eliphaz were Teman, Omar, Zepho, Gatam, and Kenaz. ¹²Eliphaz had
another son named Amalek, born to Timna, his concubine. These were all
grandchildren of Esau's wife Adah.

¹³The sons of Reuel were Nahath, Zerah, Shammah, and Mizzah. These were all
grandchildren of Esau's wife Basemath.

¹⁴Esau also had sons through Oholibamah, the daughter of Anah and granddaughter
of Zibeon. Their names were Jeush, Jalam, and Korah.

¹⁵Esau's children and grandchildren became the leaders of different clans.

The sons of Esau's oldest son, Eliphaz, became the leaders of the clans of Teman,
Omar, Zepho, Kenaz, ¹⁶Korah, Gatam, and Amalek. These clans in the land of
Edom were descended from Eliphaz, the son of Esau and Adah.

**35:18** *Ben-oni* means "son of my sorrow"; *Benjamin* means "son of my right hand."   **35:21** Hebrew *Israel;* also in 35:22a.

**Cross-references (right margin):**

**35:19**
Gen 48:7

**35:22**
Gen 49:4
Lev 18:8
1 Chr 5:1

**35:23-26**
//1 Chr 2:1-2

**35:23**
Gen 29:31-35;
30:18-20

**35:24**
Gen 30:24

**35:25**
Gen 30:5-8

**35:26**
Gen 30:10-13

**35:27**
Gen 13:18; 23:2

**35:28**
Gen 25:7-8, 20

**36:1**
Gen 25:30

**36:2**
Gen 26:34
1 Chr 1:40

**36:3**
Gen 25:13

**36:4**
1 Chr 1:35

**36:5**
Gen 36:18

**36:7**
Gen 13:6

**36:8**
Gen 14:6; 25:30

**36:9**
Gen 36:43

**36:10-14**
//1 Chr 1:35-37

---

**35:22** Reuben's sin was costly, although not right away. As the oldest son, he stood to receive a double portion of the family inheritance and a place of leadership among his people. Reuben may have thought he got away with his sin. No more is mentioned of it until Jacob, on his deathbed, assembled his family for the final blessing. Suddenly Jacob took away Reuben's double portion and gave it to someone else. The reason? "You slept with one of my wives; you dishonored me in my own bed" (49:4).

Sin's consequences can plague us long after the sin is committed. When we do something wrong, we may think we can escape unnoticed, only to discover later that the sin has been quietly breeding serious consequences.

**36:9** The Edomites were descendants of Esau who lived south and east of the Dead Sea. The country featured rugged mountains and desolate wilderness. Several major roads led through Edom because it was rich in natural resources. During the Exodus, God told Israel to leave the Edomites alone (Deuteronomy 2:4, 5) because they were "relatives." But Edom refused to let them enter the land, and later they became bitter enemies of King David. The nations of Edom and Israel shared the same ancestor, Isaac, and the same border. Israel looked down on the Edomites because they intermarried with the Canaanites.

17 The sons of Esau's son Reuel became the leaders of the clans of Nahath, Zerah, Shammah, and Mizzah. These clans in the land of Edom were descended from Reuel, the son of Esau and Basemath.

18 The sons of Esau and his wife Oholibamah became the leaders of the clans of Jeush, Jalam, and Korah. These are the clans descended from Esau's wife Oholibamah, the daughter of Anah.

**36:19**
1 Chr 1:35

19 These are all the clans descended from Esau (also known as Edom).

*Original Peoples of Edom*

**36:20-28**
//1 Chr 1:38-42

**36:20**
Gen 14:6
Deut 2:12, 22

20 These are the names of the tribes that descended from Seir the Horite, one of the families native to the land of Seir: Lotan, Shobal, Zibeon, Anah, 21 Dishon, Ezer, and Dishan. These were the Horite clans, the descendants of Seir, who lived in the land of Edom.

22 The sons of Lotan were Hori and Heman. Lotan's sister was named Timna.
23 The sons of Shobal were Alvan, Manahath, Ebal, Shepho, and Onam.
24 The sons of Zibeon were Aiah and Anah. This is the Anah who discovered the hot springs in the wilderness while he was grazing his father's donkeys.

**36:25**
Gen 36:2, 5, 14, 18
1 Chr 1:41

25 The son of Anah was Dishon, and Oholibamah was his daughter.

**36:27**
1 Chr 1:38, 42

26 The sons of Dishon* were Hemdan, Eshban, Ithran, and Keran.
27 The sons of Ezer were Bilhan, Zaavan, and Akan.
28 The sons of Dishan were Uz and Aran.

**36:29-30**
Gen 36:20

29 So the leaders of the Horite clans were Lotan, Shobal, Zibeon, Anah, 30 Dishon, Ezer, and Dishan. The Horite clans are named after their clan leaders, who lived in the land of Seir.

**36:26** Hebrew *Dishan*, a variant name for Dishon; compare 36:21, 28.

## JOSEPH

As a youngster, Joseph was overconfident. His natural self-assurance, increased by being Jacob's favorite son and by knowing of God's designs on his life, was unbearable to his ten older brothers, who eventually conspired against him. But this self-assurance, molded by pain and combined with a personal knowledge of God, allowed him to survive and prosper where most would have failed. He added quiet wisdom to his confidence and won the hearts of everyone he met—Potiphar, the chief jailer, other prisoners, the king, and after many years, even those ten brothers.

Perhaps you can identify with one or more of these hardships Joseph experienced: He was betrayed and deserted by his family, exposed to sexual temptation, and punished for doing the right thing; he endured a long imprisonment and was forgotten by those he helped. As you read his story, note what Joseph did in each case. His positive response transformed each setback into a step forward. He didn't spend much time asking why. His approach was "What shall I do now?" Those who met Joseph were aware that wherever he went and whatever he did, God was with him. When you're facing a setback, the beginning of a Joseph-like attitude is to acknowledge that God is with you. There is nothing like his presence to shed new light on a dark situation.

| | |
|---|---|
| **Strengths and accomplishments** | • Rose in power from slave to ruler of Egypt<br>• Was known for his personal integrity<br>• Was a man of spiritual sensitivity<br>• Prepared a nation to survive a famine |
| **Weakness and mistake** | • His youthful pride caused friction with his brothers |
| **Lessons from his life** | • What matters is not so much the events or circumstances of life, but your response to them<br>• With God's help, any situation can be used for good, even when others intend it for evil |
| **Vital statistics** | • Where: Canaan, Egypt<br>• Occupation: Shepherd, slave, convict, ruler<br>• Relatives: Parents: Jacob and Rachel. Eleven brothers and one sister. Wife: Asenath. Sons: Manasseh and Ephraim |
| **Key verse** | "As they discussed who should be appointed for the job, Pharaoh said, 'Who could do it better than Joseph? For he is a man who is obviously filled with the spirit of God'" (Genesis 41:38). |

Joseph's story is told in Genesis 30—50. He is also mentioned in Hebrews 11:22.

### Rulers of Edom

31 These are the kings who ruled in Edom before there were kings in Israel*:

**36:31-43**
//1 Chr 1:43-54

32 Bela son of Beor, who ruled from his city of Dinhabah.

33 When Bela died, Jobab son of Zerah from Bozrah became king.

34 When Jobab died, Husham from the land of the Temanites became king.

35 When Husham died, Hadad son of Bedad became king and ruled from the city of Avith. He was the one who destroyed the Midianite army in the land of Moab.

36 When Hadad died, Samlah from the city of Masrekah became king.

37 When Samlah died, Shaul from the city of Rehoboth on the Euphrates River* became king.

38 When Shaul died, Baal-hanan son of Acbor became king.

39 When Baal-hanan died, Hadad* became king and ruled from the city of Pau. Hadad's wife was Mehetabel, the daughter of Matred and granddaughter of Me-zahab.

40 These are the leaders of the clans of Esau, who lived in the places named for them: Timna, Alvah, Jetheth, 41 Oholibamah, Elah, Pinon, 42 Kenaz, Teman, Mibzar, 43 Magdiel, and Iram. These are the names of the clans of Esau, the ancestor of the Edomites, each clan giving its name to the area it occupied.

## G. THE STORY OF JOSEPH (37:1—50:26)

Joseph, one of Jacob's 12 sons, was obviously the favorite. Hated by his brothers for this, Joseph was sold to slave traders only to emerge as ruler of all Egypt. Through Joseph, we learn how suffering, no matter how unfair, develops strong character and deep wisdom.

## 1. Joseph is sold into slavery

### Joseph's Dreams

**37** So Jacob settled again in the land of Canaan, where his father had lived. 2 This is the history of Jacob's family. When Joseph was seventeen years old, he often tended his father's flocks with his half brothers, the sons of his father's wives Bilhah and Zilpah. But Joseph reported to his father some of the bad things his brothers were doing. 3 Now Jacob* loved Joseph more than any of his other children because Joseph had been born to him in his old age. So one day he gave Joseph a special gift—a beautiful robe.* 4 But his brothers hated Joseph because of their father's partiality. They couldn't say a kind word to him.

5 One night Joseph had a dream and promptly reported the details to his brothers, causing them to hate him even more. 6 "Listen to this dream," he announced. 7 "We were out in the field tying up bundles of grain. My bundle stood up, and then your bundles all gathered around and bowed low before it!"

8 "So you are going to be our king, are you?" his brothers taunted. And they hated him all the more for his dream and what he had said.

9 Then Joseph had another dream and told his brothers about it. "Listen to this dream," he said. "The sun, moon, and eleven stars bowed low before me!"

10 This time he told his father as well as his brothers, and his father rebuked him. "What do you mean?" his father asked. "Will your mother, your brothers, and I actually

**37:1**
Gen 17:8; 28:4

**37:2**
Gen 35:22-26;
41:46

**37:3**
Gen 37:23, 32;
44:20

**37:4**
Gen 27:41

**37:5**
Gen 28:12
Num 12:6
Dan 2:1

**37:7**
Gen 42:6, 9; 43:26

**37:8**
Deut 33:16

**37:10**
Gen 27:29

**36:31** Or *before an Israelite king ruled over them.*    **36:37** Hebrew *the river.*    **36:39** As in some Hebrew manuscripts, Samaritan Pentateuch, and Syriac version (see also 1 Chr 1:50); most Hebrew manuscripts read *Hadar.*    **37:3a** Hebrew *Israel;* also in 37:13.    **37:3b** Traditionally rendered *a coat of many colors.* The exact meaning of the Hebrew is uncertain.

---

**37:3** In Joseph's day, everyone had a robe or cloak. Robes were used to warm oneself, to bundle up belongings for a trip, to wrap babies, to sit on, or even to serve as security for a loan. Most robes were knee length, short sleeved, and plain. In contrast, Joseph's robe was probably of the kind worn by royalty—long sleeved, ankle length, and colorful. The robe became a symbol of Jacob's favoritism toward Joseph, and it aggravated the already strained relations between Joseph and his brothers. Favoritism in families may be unavoidable, but its divisive effects should be minimized. Parents may not be able to change their feelings toward a favorite child, but they can change their actions toward the others.

**37:6-11** Joseph's brothers were already angry over the possibility of being ruled by their little brother. Joseph then fueled the fire with his immature attitude and boastful manner. No one enjoys a braggart. Joseph learned his lesson the hard way. His angry brothers sold him into slavery to get rid of him. After several years of hardship, Joseph learned an important lesson: Because our talents and knowledge come from God, it is more appropriate to thank him for them than to brag about them. Later Joseph gives God the credit (41:16).

**37:11**
Luke 2:19, 51
Acts 7:9

come and bow before you?" 11 But while his brothers were jealous of Joseph, his father gave it some thought and wondered what it all meant.

**37:13**
Gen 33:19

12 Soon after this, Joseph's brothers went to pasture their father's flocks at Shechem. 13 When they had been gone for some time, Jacob said to Joseph, "Your brothers are over at Shechem with the flocks. I'm going to send you to them."

"I'm ready to go," Joseph replied.

**37:14**
Gen 35:27

14 "Go and see how your brothers and the flocks are getting along," Jacob said. "Then come back and bring me word." So Jacob sent him on his way, and Joseph traveled to Shechem from his home in the valley of Hebron.

15 When he arrived there, a man noticed him wandering around the countryside. "What are you looking for?" he asked.

16 "For my brothers and their flocks," Joseph replied. "Have you seen them?"

**37:17**
2 Kgs 6:13

17 "Yes," the man told him, "but they are no longer here. I heard your brothers say they were going to Dothan." So Joseph followed his brothers to Dothan and found them there.

### Joseph Sold into Slavery

**37:20**
Gen 37:33

**37:21**
Gen 42:22

**37:22**
Gen 37:29

18 When Joseph's brothers saw him coming, they recognized him in the distance and made plans to kill him. 19 "Here comes that dreamer!" they exclaimed. 20 "Come on, let's kill him and throw him into a deep pit. We can tell our father that a wild animal has eaten him. Then we'll see what becomes of all his dreams!"

21 But Reuben came to Joseph's rescue. "Let's not kill him," he said. 22 "Why should

---

## REUBEN

Parents are usually the best judges of their children's character. Jacob summarized the personality of his son Reuben by comparing him to water. Except when frozen, water has no stable shape of its own. It always shapes itself to its container or environment. Reuben usually had good intentions, but he seemed unable to stand against a crowd. His instability made him hard to trust. He had both private and public values, but these contradicted each other. He went along with his brothers in their action against Joseph while hoping to counteract the evil in private. The plan failed. Compromise has a way of destroying convictions. Without convictions, lack of direction will destroy life. Reuben's sleeping with one of his father's wives showed how little he had left of the integrity he had displayed earlier in life.

How consistent are your public and private lives? We may want to think they are separate, but we can't deny that they affect each other. What convictions are present in your life at all times? How closely does Jacob's description of his son—"unruly as the waves of the sea"—describe your life?

| | |
|---|---|
| **Strengths and accomplishments** | • Saved Joseph's life by talking the other brothers out of murder<br>• Showed intense love for his father by offering his own sons as a guarantee that Benjamin's life would be safe |
| **Weaknesses and mistakes** | • Gave in quickly to group pressure<br>• Did not directly protect Joseph from his brothers, although as oldest son he had the authority to do so<br>• Slept with one of his father's wives |
| **Lessons from his life** | • Public and private integrity must be the same, or one will destroy the other<br>• Punishment for sin may not be immediate, but it is certain |
| **Vital statistics** | • Where: Canaan, Egypt<br>• Occupation: Shepherd<br>• Relatives: Parents: Jacob and Leah. Eleven brothers, one sister |
| **Key verses** | "Reuben, you are my oldest son, the child of my vigorous youth. You are first on the list in rank and honor. But you are as unruly as the waves of the sea, and you will be first no longer. For you slept with one of my wives; you dishonored me in my own bed" (Genesis 49:3, 4). |

Reuben's story is told in Genesis 29—50.

---

**37:19, 20** Could jealousy ever make you feel like killing someone? Before saying, "Of course not," look at what happened in this story. Ten men were willing to kill their younger brother over a robe and a few reported dreams. Their deep jealousy had grown into ugly rage, completely blinding them to what was right. Jealousy can be difficult to recognize because our reasons for it seem to make sense. But left unchecked, jealousy grows quickly and leads to serious sins. The longer you cultivate jealous feelings, the harder it is to uproot them. The time to deal with jealousy is when you notice yourself keeping score of what others have.

we shed his blood? Let's just throw him alive into this pit here. That way he will die without our having to touch him." Reuben was secretly planning to help Joseph escape, and then he would bring him back to his father.

23 So when Joseph arrived, they pulled off his beautiful robe 24 and threw him into the pit. This pit was normally used to store water, but it was empty at the time. 25 Then, just as they were sitting down to eat, they noticed a caravan of camels in the distance coming toward them. It was a group of Ishmaelite traders taking spices, balm, and myrrh from Gilead to Egypt.

26 Judah said to the others, "What can we gain by killing our brother? That would just give us a guilty conscience. 27 Let's sell Joseph to those Ishmaelite traders. Let's not be responsible for his death; after all, he is our brother!" And his brothers agreed. 28 So when the traders* came by, his brothers pulled Joseph out of the pit and sold him for twenty pieces* of silver, and the Ishmaelite traders took him along to Egypt.

29 Some time later, Reuben returned to get Joseph out of the pit. When he discovered that Joseph was missing, he tore his clothes in anguish and frustration. 30 Then he went back to his brothers and lamented, "The boy is gone! What can I do now?"

31 Then Joseph's brothers killed a goat and dipped the robe in its blood. 32 They took the beautiful robe to their father and asked him to identify it. "We found this in the field," they told him. "It's Joseph's robe, isn't it?"

33 Their father recognized it at once. "Yes," he said, "it is my son's robe. A wild animal has attacked and eaten him. Surely Joseph has been torn in pieces!" 34 Then Jacob tore his clothes and put on sackcloth. He mourned deeply for his son for many days. 35 His family all tried to comfort him, but it was no use. "I will die in mourning for my son," he would say, and then begin to weep.

36 Meanwhile, in Egypt, the traders sold Joseph to Potiphar, an officer of Pharaoh, the king of Egypt. Potiphar was captain of the palace guard.

**37:23**
Gen 37:3

**37:24**
Jer 38:6; 41:7

**37:25**
Gen 31:21; 37:28
Jer 8:22; 46:11

**37:28**
Gen 39:1; 45:4-5
Lev 27:5
Judg 8:22-24
Acts 7:9

**37:29**
Gen 37:34; 44:13
Num 14:6

**37:30**
Gen 42:13, 36

**37:32**
Luke 15:30

**37:33**
Gen 37:20; 44:28

**37:34**
Gen 37:29

**37:35**
Gen 44:29
2 Sam 12:17
Ps 77:2

**37:36**
Gen 39:1; 40:3

**37:28a** Hebrew *Midianites;* also in 37:36.   **37:28b** Hebrew *20 shekels,* about 8 ounces or 228 grams in weight.

---

**37:26, 27** The brothers were worried about bearing the guilt of Joseph's death. Judah suggested an option that was not right but would leave them guiltless of murder. Sometimes we jump at a solution because it is the lesser of two evils, but it still is not the right action to take. When someone proposes a seemingly workable solution, first ask, "Is it right?"

**37:28** Although Joseph's brothers didn't kill him outright, they wouldn't expect him to survive for long as a slave. They were quite willing to let cruel slave traders do their dirty work for them. Joseph faced a 30-day journey through the desert, probably chained and on foot. He would be treated like baggage and, once in Egypt, would be sold as a piece of merchandise. His brothers thought they would never see him again. But God was in control of Joseph's life.

**37:29, 30** Reuben returned to the pit to find Joseph, but his little brother was gone. His first response, in effect, was "What is going to happen to me?" rather than "What is going to happen to Joseph?" In a tough situation, are you usually concerned first about yourself? Consider the person most affected by the problem, and you will be more likely to find a solution for it.

**37:31-35** To cover their evil action, Jacob's sons deceived their father into thinking Joseph was dead. Jacob himself had deceived others many times (including his own father; 27:35). Now, though blessed by God, he still had to face the consequences of his sins. God may not have punished Jacob immediately for his deceit, but the consequences came nevertheless and stayed with him for the rest of his life.

**37:34** Tearing one's clothes and wearing sackcloth were signs of mourning, much like wearing black today.

**37:36** Imagine the culture shock Joseph experienced upon arriving in Egypt. Joseph had lived as a nomad, traveling the countryside with his family, caring for sheep. Suddenly he was thrust into the world's most advanced civilization with great pyramids, beautiful homes, sophisticated people, and a new language. While Joseph saw Egypt's skill and intelligence at their best, he also saw the Egyptians' spiritual blindness. They worshiped countless gods related to every aspect of life.

**JOSEPH GOES TO MEET HIS BROTHERS**
Jacob asked Joseph to go find his brothers, who were grazing their flocks near Shechem. When Joseph arrived, he learned that his brothers had gone on to Dothan, which lay along a major trade route to Egypt. There the jealous brothers sold Joseph as a slave to a group of Ishmaelite traders on their way to Egypt.

## 2. Judah and Tamar

**38** About this time, Judah left home and moved to Adullam, where he visited a man named Hirah. ²There he met a Canaanite woman, the daughter of Shua, and he married her. ³She became pregnant and had a son, and Judah named the boy Er. ⁴Then Judah's wife had another son, and she named him Onan. ⁵And when she had a third son, she named him Shelah. At the time of Shelah's birth, they were living at Kezib.

⁶When his oldest son, Er, grew up, Judah arranged his marriage to a young woman named Tamar. ⁷But Er was a wicked man in the LORD's sight, so the LORD took his life. ⁸Then Judah said to Er's brother Onan, "You must marry Tamar, as our law requires of the brother of a man who has died. Her first son from you will be your brother's heir."

⁹But Onan was not willing to have a child who would not be his own heir. So whenever he had intercourse with Tamar, he spilled the semen on the ground to keep her from having a baby who would belong to his brother. ¹⁰But the LORD considered it a wicked thing for Onan to deny a child to his dead brother. So the LORD took Onan's life, too.

¹¹Then Judah told Tamar, his daughter-in-law, not to marry again at that time but to return to her parents' home. She was to remain a widow until his youngest son, Shelah, was old enough to marry her. (But Judah didn't really intend to do this because he was afraid Shelah would also die, like his two brothers.) So Tamar went home to her parents.

¹²In the course of time Judah's wife died. After the time of mourning was over, Judah and his friend Hirah the Adullamite went to Timnah to supervise the shearing of his sheep. ¹³Someone told Tamar that her father-in-law had left for the sheep-shearing at Timnah. ¹⁴Tamar was aware that Shelah had grown up, but they had not called her to come and marry him. So she changed out of her widow's clothing and covered herself with a veil to disguise herself. Then she sat beside the road at the entrance to the village of Enaim, which is on the way to Timnah. ¹⁵Judah noticed her as he went by and thought she was a prostitute, since her face was veiled. ¹⁶So he stopped and propositioned her to sleep with him, not realizing that she was his own daughter-in-law.

"How much will you pay me?" Tamar asked.

¹⁷"I'll send you a young goat from my flock," Judah promised.

---

**WOMEN
IN JESUS'
FAMILY TREE**

| | | |
|---|---|---|
| Tamar | Canaanite | Genesis 38:1-30 |
| Rahab | Canaanite | Joshua 6:22-25 |
| Ruth | Moabite | Ruth 4:13-22 |
| Bathsheba | Israelite | 2 Samuel 12:24, 25 |

---

**38:1ff** This chapter vividly contrasts the immoral character of Judah with the moral character of Joseph. Judah's lack of integrity resulted in family strife and deception. In chapter 39, we see how Joseph's integrity and wise choices reflect his godly character. His faithfulness was rewarded with blessings greater than he could imagine, both for himself and for his family.

**38:8-10** This law about marrying a widow in the family is explained in Deuteronomy 25:5-10. Its purpose was to ensure that a childless widow would have a son who would receive her late husband's inheritance and who, in turn, would care for her. Because Judah's son (Tamar's husband) had no children, there was no family line through which the inheritance and the blessing of the covenant could continue. God killed Onan because he refused to fulfill his obligation to his brother and to Tamar.

**38:15-23** Why does this story seem to take a light view of prostitution? Prostitutes were common in pagan cultures such as Canaan. Public prostitutes served Canaanite goddesses and were common elements of the religious cults. Fornication was encouraged to improve fertility in crops and flocks. They were more highly respected than private prostitutes who were sometimes punished when caught. Tamar was driven to seduce Judah because of her intense desire to have children and be the matriarch of Judah's line; Judah was driven by his lust. Neither case was justified.

**38:15-24** Why was Judah so open about his relations with a prostitute, yet ready to execute his daughter-in-law for being one? To understand this apparent contradiction, we must understand the place of women in Canaan. A woman's most important function was bearing children, who would perpetuate the family line. To ensure that children belonged to the husband, the bride was expected to be a virgin, and the wife was expected to have relations only with him. If a wife committed adultery, she could be executed. Some women, however, did not belong to families. They might be shrine prostitutes supported by offerings or common prostitutes supported by the men who used their services. Their children were nobody's heirs, and men who hired them adulterated nobody's bloodlines.

Judah saw no harm in hiring a prostitute for a night; after all, he was more than willing to pay. He was ready to execute Tamar, however, because if she was pregnant as a result of prostitution, his grandchild would not be part of his family line. Apparently the question of sexual morality never entered Judah's mind; his concern was for keeping his inheritance in the family. Ironically, it was Tamar, not Judah, who acted to provide him with legal heirs. By seducing him, she acted more in the spirit of the law than he did when he refused to send his third son to her.

This story in no way implies that God winks at prostitution. Throughout Scripture, prostitution is condemned as a serious sin. If the story has a moral, it is that faithfulness to family obligations is important. Incidentally, Judah and Tamar are direct ancestors of Jesus Christ (see Matthew 1:1-6).

"What pledge will you give me so I can be sure you will send it?" she asked. [18]"Well, what do you want?" he inquired.

She replied, "I want your identification seal, your cord, and the walking stick you are carrying." So Judah gave these items to her. She then let him sleep with her, and she became pregnant. [19]Afterward she went home, took off her veil, and put on her widow's clothing as usual.

[20]Judah asked his friend Hirah the Adullamite to take the young goat back to her and to pick up the pledges he had given her, but Hirah couldn't find her. [21]So he asked the men who lived there, "Where can I find the prostitute* who was sitting beside the road at the entrance to the village?"

"We've never had a prostitute here," they replied. [22]So Hirah returned to Judah and told him that he couldn't find her anywhere and that the men of the village had claimed they didn't have a prostitute there.

[23]"Then let her keep the pledges!" Judah exclaimed. "We tried our best to send her the goat. We'd be the laughingstock of the village if we went back again."

[24]About three months later, word reached Judah that Tamar, his daughter-in-law, was pregnant as a result of prostitution. "Bring her out and burn her!" Judah shouted.

[25]But as they were taking her out to kill her, she sent this message to her father-in-law: "The man who owns this identification seal and walking stick is the father of my child. Do you recognize them?"

[26]Judah admitted that they were his and said, "She is more in the right than I am, because I didn't keep my promise to let her marry my son Shelah." But Judah never slept with Tamar again.

[27]In due season the time of Tamar's delivery arrived, and she had twin sons. [28]As they were being born, one of them reached out his hand, and the midwife tied a scarlet thread around the wrist of the child who appeared first, saying, "This one came out first." [29]But then he drew back his hand, and the other baby was actually the first to be born. "What!" the midwife exclaimed. "How did you break out first?" And ever after, he was called Perez.* [30]Then the baby with the scarlet thread on his wrist was born, and he was named Zerah.*

**38:18**
Gen 41:42
Hos 4:11

**38:24**
Lev 20:10; 21:9

**38:26**
1 Sam 24:17

**38:27**
Gen 25:24

**38:29**
Gen 46:12
Num 26:20-21
Ruth 4:12
1 Chr 2:4
Matt 1:3
Luke 3:33

## 3. Joseph is thrown into prison
*Joseph in Potiphar's House*

**39** Now when Joseph arrived in Egypt with the Ishmaelite traders, he was purchased by Potiphar, a member of the personal staff of Pharaoh, the king of Egypt. Potiphar was the captain of the palace guard.

[2]The LORD was with Joseph and blessed him greatly as he served in the home of his Egyptian master. [3]Potiphar noticed this and realized that the LORD was with Joseph, giving him success in everything he did. [4]So Joseph naturally became quite a favorite

**39:1**
Gen 37:25

**39:2**
Acts 7:9

**39:4**
Gen 40:4
Prov 22:29

**38:21** Hebrew *shrine prostitute;* also in 38:21b, 22.   **38:29** *Perez* means "breaking out."   **38:30** *Zerah* means "scarlet" or "brightness."

---

**38:18** A seal was a form of identification used to authenticate legal documents. Usually a unique design carved in stone and worn on a ring or necklace inseparable from its owner, the seal was used by the wealthy and powerful to mark clay or wax. Because Tamar had Judah's seal, she could prove beyond a doubt that he had been with her.

**38:24-26** When Tamar revealed she was pregnant, Judah, who unknowingly had gotten her pregnant, moved to have her killed. Judah had concealed his own sin, yet he came down harshly on Tamar. Often the sins we try to cover up are the ones that anger us most when we see them in others. If you become indignant at the sins of others, you may have a similar tendency to sin that you don't wish to face. When we admit our sins and ask God to forgive us, forgiving others becomes easier.

**39:1** The date of Joseph's arrival in Egypt is debatable. Many believe he arrived during the period of the Hyksos rulers, foreigners who came from the region of Canaan. They invaded Egypt and controlled the land for almost 150 years. If Joseph arrived during their rule, it is easy to see why he was rapidly promoted

up the royal ladder. Because the Hyksos were foreigners themselves, they would not hold this brilliant young foreigner's ancestry against him.

**39:1** *Pharaoh* was the general name for all the kings of Egypt. It was a title like "king" or "president" used to address the country's leader. The pharaohs in Genesis and Exodus were different men.

**39:1** Ancient Egypt was a land of great contrasts. People were either rich beyond measure or poverty stricken. There wasn't much middle ground. Joseph found himself serving Potiphar, an extremely rich officer in Pharaoh's service. Rich families like Potiphar's had elaborate homes two or three stories tall with beautiful gardens and balconies. They enjoyed live entertainment at home as they chose delicious fruit from expensive bowls. They surrounded themselves with alabaster vases, paintings, beautiful rugs, and hand-carved chairs. Dinner was served on golden tableware, and the rooms were lighted with gold lampstands. Servants, like Joseph, worked on the first floor, while the family occupied the upper stories.

**39:5**
Deut 28:3-4, 11

**39:6**
Gen 29:17
1 Sam 16:12, 18
Acts 7:20

**39:7**
Prov 7:15-20

**39:8**
Gen 39:5
Prov 6:23-24

**39:10**
1 Thes 5:22

**39:12**
Prov 7:13
2 Tim 2:22

**39:17**
Exod 20:16; 23:1
Ps 55:3

**39:20**
Gen 40:1-3, 15;
41:10
Ps 105:18

**39:21**
Ps 105:19
Acts 7:9

**39:23**
Gen 39:3

**40:1**
Neh 1:11

**40:4**
Gen 37:36; 39:4

**40:5**
Gen 20:3; 41:11

with him. Potiphar soon put Joseph in charge of his entire household and entrusted him with all his business dealings. 5From the day Joseph was put in charge, the LORD began to bless Potiphar for Joseph's sake. All his household affairs began to run smoothly, and his crops and livestock flourished. 6So Potiphar gave Joseph complete administrative responsibility over everything he owned. With Joseph there, he didn't have a worry in the world, except to decide what he wanted to eat!

Now Joseph was a very handsome and well-built young man. 7And about this time, Potiphar's wife began to desire him and invited him to sleep with her. 8But Joseph refused. "Look," he told her, "my master trusts me with everything in his entire household. 9No one here has more authority than I do! He has held back nothing from me except you, because you are his wife. How could I ever do such a wicked thing? It would be a great sin against God."

10She kept putting pressure on him day after day, but he refused to sleep with her, and he kept out of her way as much as possible. 11One day, however, no one else was around when he was doing his work inside the house. 12She came and grabbed him by his shirt, demanding, "Sleep with me." Joseph tore himself away, but as he did, his shirt came off. She was left holding it as he ran from the house.

13When she saw that she had his shirt and that he had fled, 14she began screaming. Soon all the men around the place came running. "My husband has brought this Hebrew slave here to insult us!" she sobbed. "He tried to rape me, but I screamed. 15When he heard my loud cries, he ran and left his shirt behind with me."

16She kept the shirt with her, and when her husband came home that night, 17she told him her story. "That Hebrew slave you've had around here tried to make a fool of me," she said. 18"I was saved only by my screams. He ran out, leaving his shirt behind!"

### Joseph Put in Prison

19After hearing his wife's story, Potiphar was furious! 20He took Joseph and threw him into the prison where the king's prisoners were held. 21But the LORD was with Joseph there, too, and he granted Joseph favor with the chief jailer. 22Before long, the jailer put Joseph in charge of all the other prisoners and over everything that happened in the prison. 23The chief jailer had no more worries after that, because Joseph took care of everything. The LORD was with him, making everything run smoothly and successfully.

### Joseph Interprets Two Dreams

**40** Some time later, Pharaoh's chief cup-bearer and chief baker offended him. 2Pharaoh became very angry with these officials, 3and he put them in the prison where Joseph was, in the palace of Potiphar, the captain of the guard. 4They remained in prison for quite some time, and Potiphar assigned Joseph to take care of them.

5One night the cup-bearer and the baker each had a dream, and each dream had its own meaning. 6The next morning Joseph noticed the dejected look on their faces. 7"Why do you look so worried today?" he asked.

---

**39:9** Potiphar's wife failed to seduce Joseph, who resisted this temptation by saying it would be a sin against God. Joseph didn't say, "I'd be hurting you," or "I'd be sinning against Potiphar," or "I'd be sinning against myself." Under pressure, such excuses are easily rationalized away. Remember that sexual sin is not just between two consenting adults. It is an act of disobedience against God.

**39:10-15** Joseph avoided Potiphar's wife as much as possible. He refused her advances and finally *ran* from her. Sometimes merely trying to avoid temptation is not enough. We must turn and run, especially when the temptations seem very strong, as is often the case in sexual temptations.

**39:20** Prisons were grim places with vile conditions. They were used to house forced laborers or, like Joseph, the accused who were awaiting trial. Prisoners were guilty until proven innocent, and there was no right to a speedy trial. Many prisoners never made it to court, because trials were held at the whim of the ruler. Joseph was in prison a long time before he appeared before Pharaoh, and then he was called out to interpret a dream, not to stand trial.

**39:21-23** As a prisoner and slave, Joseph could have seen his situation as hopeless. Instead, he did his best with each small task given him. His diligence and positive attitude were soon noticed by the warden, who promoted him to prison administrator. Are you facing a seemingly hopeless predicament? At work, at home, or at school, follow Joseph's example by taking each small task and doing your best. Remember how God turned Joseph's situation around. He will see your efforts and can reverse even overwhelming odds.

**40:1-3** The cup-bearer and the chief baker were two of the most trusted men in Pharaoh's kingdom. The baker was in charge of making the Pharaoh's food, and the cup-bearer tasted all of his food and drink before giving it to him, in case any of it was contaminated or poisoned. These trusted men must have been suspected of a serious wrong, perhaps of conspiring against Pharaoh. Later the cup-bearer was released and the baker executed.

8And they replied, "We both had dreams last night, but there is no one here to tell us what they mean."

"Interpreting dreams is God's business," Joseph replied. "Tell me what you saw."

9The cup-bearer told his dream first. "In my dream," he said, "I saw a vine in front of me. 10It had three branches that began to bud and blossom, and soon there were clusters of ripe grapes. 11I was holding Pharaoh's wine cup in my hand, so I took the grapes and squeezed the juice into it. Then I placed the cup in Pharaoh's hand."

12"I know what the dream means," Joseph said. "The three branches mean three days. 13Within three days Pharaoh will take you out of prison and return you to your position as his chief cup-bearer. 14And please have some pity on me when you are back in his favor. Mention me to Pharaoh, and ask him to let me out of here. 15For I was kidnapped from my homeland, the land of the Hebrews, and now I'm here in jail, but I did nothing to deserve it."

16When the chief baker saw that the first dream had such a good meaning, he told his dream to Joseph, too. "In my dream," he said, "there were three baskets of pastries on my head. 17In the top basket were all kinds of bakery goods for Pharaoh, but the birds came and ate them."

18"I'll tell you what it means," Joseph told him. "The three baskets mean three days. 19Three days from now Pharaoh will cut off your head and impale your body on a pole. Then birds will come and peck away at your flesh."

20Pharaoh's birthday came three days later, and he gave a banquet for all his officials and household staff. He sent for his chief cup-bearer and chief baker, and they were brought to him from the prison. 21He then restored the chief cup-bearer to his former position, 22but he sentenced the chief baker to be impaled on a pole, just as Joseph had predicted. 23Pharaoh's cup-bearer, however, promptly forgot all about Joseph, never giving him another thought.

## 4. Joseph is placed in charge of Egypt
### Pharaoh's Dreams

**41** Two years later, Pharaoh dreamed that he was standing on the bank of the Nile River. 2In his dream, seven fat, healthy-looking cows suddenly came up out of the river and began grazing along its bank. 3Then seven other cows came up from the river, but these were very ugly and gaunt. These cows went over and stood beside the fat cows. 4Then the thin, ugly cows ate the fat ones! At this point in the dream, Pharaoh woke up.

5Soon he fell asleep again and had a second dream. This time he saw seven heads of grain on one stalk, with every kernel well formed and plump. 6Then suddenly, seven more heads appeared on the stalk, but these were shriveled and withered by the east wind. 7And these thin heads swallowed up the seven plump, well-formed heads! Then Pharaoh woke up again and realized it was a dream.

8The next morning, as he thought about it, Pharaoh became very concerned as to what the dreams might mean. So he called for all the magicians and wise men of Egypt and told them about his dreams, but not one of them could suggest what they meant. 9Then the king's cup-bearer spoke up. "Today I have been reminded of my failure," he said. 10"Some time ago, you were angry with the chief baker and me, and you imprisoned us in the palace of the captain of the guard. 11One night the chief baker and I each had a dream, and each dream had a meaning. 12We told the dreams to a young Hebrew man who was a servant of the captain of the guard. He told us what each of our dreams meant,

**40:8**
Gen 41:15-16
Dan 2:27-28

**40:12**
Gen 41:12
**40:13**
Gen 40:19-20
**40:14**
1 Sam 20:14
**40:15**
Gen 37:26-28;
39:20

**40:18**
Gen 40:12
**40:19**
Deut 21:22-23
**40:20**
2 Kgs 25:27
Jer 52:31
**40:22**
Gen 40:19
**40:23**
Gen 40:14

**41:2**
Isa 19:6-7

**41:5**
2 Kgs 4:42
**41:6**
Ezek 19:12

**41:8**
Exod 7:11-12
Dan 2:1-3; 4:5
**41:9**
Gen 40:14
**41:10**
Gen 40:2
**41:11**
Gen 40:5
**41:12**
Gen 40:12

---

**40:8** When the subject of dreams came up, Joseph focused everyone's attention on God. Rather than using the situation to make himself look good, he turned it into a powerful witness for the Lord. One secret of effective witnessing is to recognize opportunities to relate God to the other person's experience. When the opportunity arises, we must have the courage to speak, as Joseph did.

**40:23** When Pharaoh's cup-bearer was freed from prison, he forgot about Joseph, even though he had Joseph to thank for his freedom. It was two full years before Joseph had another opportunity to be freed (41:1). Yet Joseph's faith was deep,

and he would be ready when the next chance came. When we feel passed by, overlooked, or forgotten, we shouldn't be surprised that people are often ungrateful. In similar situations, trust God as Joseph did. More opportunities may be waiting.

**41:8** Magicians and wise men were common in the palaces of ancient rulers. Their job description included studying sacred arts and sciences, reading the stars, interpreting dreams, predicting the future, and performing magic. These men had power (see Exodus 7:11, 12), but their power was satanic. They were unable to interpret Pharaoh's dream, but God had revealed it to Joseph in prison.

**41:13**
Gen 40:22

**41:14**
Ps 105:20

**41:15**
Dan 2:25

**41:16**
Gen 40:8

**41:17**
Gen 41:1

**41:27**
2 Kgs 8:1

**41:29**
Gen 41:47

**41:30**
Gen 47:13

**41:33**
Gen 41:39

**41:36**
Gen 47:14

**41:38**
Dan 4:8, 18; 5:11, 14

**41:39**
Gen 41:33

**41:40**
Gen 39:9
Acts 7:10

¹³and everything happened just as he said it would. I was restored to my position as cup-bearer, and the chief baker was executed and impaled on a pole."

¹⁴Pharaoh sent for Joseph at once, and he was brought hastily from the dungeon. After a quick shave and change of clothes, he went in and stood in Pharaoh's presence. ¹⁵"I had a dream last night," Pharaoh told him, "and none of these men can tell me what it means. But I have heard that you can interpret dreams, and that is why I have called for you."

¹⁶"It is beyond my power to do this," Joseph replied. "But God will tell you what it means and will set you at ease."

¹⁷So Pharaoh told him the dream. "I was standing on the bank of the Nile River," he said. ¹⁸"Suddenly, seven fat, healthy-looking cows came up out of the river and began grazing along its bank. ¹⁹But then seven other cows came up from the river. They were very thin and gaunt—in fact, I've never seen such ugly animals in all the land of Egypt. ²⁰These thin, ugly cows ate up the seven fat ones that had come out of the river first, ²¹but afterward they were still as ugly and gaunt as before! Then I woke up.

²²"A little later I had another dream. This time there were seven heads of grain on one stalk, and all seven heads were plump and full. ²³Then out of the same stalk came seven withered heads, shriveled by the east wind. ²⁴And the withered heads swallowed up the plump ones! I told these dreams to my magicians, but not one of them could tell me what they mean."

²⁵"Both dreams mean the same thing," Joseph told Pharaoh. "God was telling you what he is about to do. ²⁶The seven fat cows and the seven plump heads of grain both represent seven years of prosperity. ²⁷The seven thin, ugly cows and the seven withered heads of grain represent seven years of famine. ²⁸This will happen just as I have described it, for God has shown you what he is about to do. ²⁹The next seven years will be a period of great prosperity throughout the land of Egypt. ³⁰But afterward there will be seven years of famine so great that all the prosperity will be forgotten and wiped out. Famine will destroy the land. ³¹This famine will be so terrible that even the memory of the good years will be erased. ³²As for having the dream twice, it means that the matter has been decreed by God and that he will make these events happen soon.

³³"My suggestion is that you find the wisest man in Egypt and put him in charge of a nationwide program. ³⁴Let Pharaoh appoint officials over the land, and let them collect one-fifth of all the crops during the seven good years. ³⁵Have them gather all the food and grain of these good years into the royal storehouses, and store it away so there will be food in the cities. ³⁶That way there will be enough to eat when the seven years of famine come. Otherwise disaster will surely strike the land, and all the people will die."

*Joseph Made Ruler of Egypt*

³⁷Joseph's suggestions were well received by Pharaoh and his advisers. ³⁸As they discussed who should be appointed for the job, Pharaoh said, "Who could do it better than Joseph? For he is a man who is obviously filled with the spirit of God." ³⁹Turning to Joseph, Pharaoh said, "Since God has revealed the meaning of the dreams to you, you are the wisest man in the land! ⁴⁰I hereby appoint you to direct this project. You

**41:14** Our most important opportunities may come when we least expect them. Joseph was brought hastily from the dungeon and pushed before Pharaoh. Did he have time to prepare? Yes and no. He had no warning that he would be suddenly pulled from prison and questioned by the king. Yet Joseph was ready for almost anything because of his right relationship with God. It was not Joseph's knowledge of dreams that helped him interpret their meaning. It was his knowledge of God. Be ready for opportunities by getting to know more about God. Then you will be ready to call on him when opportunities come your way.

**41:16** Joseph made sure that he gave the credit to God. We should be careful to do the same. To take the honor for ourselves is a form of stealing God's honor. Don't be silent when you know you should be giving glory and credit to God.

**41:28-36** After interpreting Pharaoh's dream, Joseph gave the king a survival plan for the next 14 years. The only way to prevent starvation was through careful planning; without a famine plan Egypt would have turned from prosperity to ruin.

Many find detailed planning boring and unnecessary. But planning is a responsibility, not an option. Joseph was able to save a nation by translating God's plan for Egypt into practical actions (implementation). We must take time to translate God's plan for us into practical actions, too.

**41:38** Pharaoh recognized that Joseph was a man "filled with the spirit of God." You probably won't get to interpret dreams for a king, but those who know you should be able to see God in you, through your kind words, merciful acts, and wise advice. Do your relatives, neighbors, and co-workers see you as a person in whom the Spirit of God lives?

**41:39, 40** Joseph rose quickly to the top, from prison walls to Pharaoh's palace. His training for this important position involved being first a slave and then a prisoner. In each situation he learned the importance of serving God and others. Whatever your situation, no matter how undesirable, consider it part of your training program for serving God.

will manage my household and organize all my people. Only I will have a rank higher than yours."

⁴¹And Pharaoh said to Joseph, "I hereby put you in charge of the entire land of Egypt." ⁴²Then Pharaoh placed his own signet ring on Joseph's finger as a symbol of his authority. He dressed him in beautiful clothing and placed the royal gold chain about his neck. ⁴³Pharaoh also gave Joseph the chariot of his second-in-command, and wherever he went the command was shouted, "Kneel down!" So Joseph was put in charge of all Egypt. ⁴⁴And Pharaoh said to Joseph, "I am the king, but no one will move a hand or a foot in the entire land of Egypt without your approval."

⁴⁵Pharaoh renamed him Zaphenath-paneah* and gave him a wife—a young woman named Asenath, the daughter of Potiphera, priest of Heliopolis.* So Joseph took charge of the entire land of Egypt. ⁴⁶He was thirty years old when he entered the service of Pharaoh, the king of Egypt. And when Joseph left Pharaoh's presence, he made a tour of inspection throughout the land.

⁴⁷And sure enough, for the next seven years there were bumper crops everywhere. ⁴⁸During those years, Joseph took a portion of all the crops grown in Egypt and stored them for the government in nearby cities. ⁴⁹After seven years, the granaries were filled to overflowing. There was so much grain, like sand on the seashore, that the people could not keep track of the amount.

⁵⁰During this time, before the arrival of the first of the famine years, two sons were born to Joseph and his wife, Asenath, the daughter of Potiphera, priest of Heliopolis. ⁵¹Joseph named his older son Manasseh,* for he said, "God has made me forget all my troubles and the family of my father." ⁵²Joseph named his second son Ephraim,* for he said, "God has made me fruitful in this land of my suffering."

⁵³At last the seven years of plenty came to an end. ⁵⁴Then the seven years of famine began, just as Joseph had predicted. There were crop failures in all the surrounding countries, too, but in Egypt there was plenty of grain in the storehouses. ⁵⁵Throughout the land of Egypt the people began to starve. They pleaded with Pharaoh for food, and he told them, "Go to Joseph and do whatever he tells you." ⁵⁶So with severe famine everywhere in the land, Joseph opened up the storehouses and sold grain to the Egyptians. ⁵⁷And people from surrounding lands also came to Egypt to buy grain from Joseph because the famine was severe throughout the world.

## 5. Joseph and his brothers meet in Egypt
### Joseph's Brothers Go to Egypt

**42** When Jacob heard that there was grain available in Egypt, he said to his sons, "Why are you standing around looking at one another? ²I have heard there is grain in Egypt. Go down and buy some for us before we all starve to death." ³So Joseph's ten older brothers went down to Egypt to buy grain. ⁴Jacob wouldn't let Joseph's younger brother, Benjamin, go with them, however, for fear some harm

41:45a *Zaphenath-paneah* probably means "God speaks and lives." 41:45b Hebrew *of On;* also in 41:50. 41:51 *Manasseh* sounds like a Hebrew term that means "causing to forget." 41:52 *Ephraim* sounds like a Hebrew term that means "fruitful."

**41:41** Esth 8:2 / Dan 6:3
**41:42** Esth 3:10; 6:8
**41:44** Gen 45:8 / Ps 105:22
**41:45** Ezek 30:17
**41:46** Gen 37:2
**41:51** Gen 48:1 / Deut 33:17
**41:52** Gen 17:6
**41:54** Gen 41:30 / Ps 105:16 / Acts 7:11
**41:55** Gen 41:41
**41:57** Gen 42:5; 47:15 / Ps 105:16
**42:1** Acts 7:12
**42:2** Gen 43:2, 4
**42:3** Gen 43:20
**42:4** Gen 35:24

---

**41:45** Pharaoh may have been trying to make Joseph more acceptable by giving him an Egyptian name and wife. He probably wanted to (1) play down the fact that Joseph was a nomadic shepherd, an occupation disliked by the Egyptians, (2) make Joseph's name easier for Egyptians to pronounce and remember, and (3) show how highly he was honored by giving him the daughter of a prominent Egyptian official.

**41:46** Joseph was 30 years old when he became second-in-command in Egypt. He was 17 when he was sold into slavery by is brothers. Thus he spent 13 years as an Egyptian slave and in prison.

**41:54** Famine was a catastrophe in ancient times, just as it still is in many parts of the world today. Almost perfect conditions were needed to produce good crops because there were no chemical fertilizers or pesticides. Any variances in rainfall or insect activity could cause crop failure and great hunger because the people relied almost exclusively on their own crops for food. Lack of storage, refrigeration, or transportation turned a moderate famine into a desperate situation. The famine Joseph prepared for was severe. Without God's intervention, the Egyptian nation would have crumbled.

**42:1, 2** Why was grain so valuable in those days? As a food source it was universal and used in nearly everything eaten. It could be dried and stored much longer than any vegetables, milk products, or meat. It was so important that it was even used as money.

**42:4** Jacob was especially fond of Benjamin because he was Joseph's only full brother and—as far as Jacob knew—the only surviving son of his beloved wife, Rachel. Benjamin was Jacob's youngest son and a child of his old age.

**42:5**
Gen 41:57
Acts 7:11

**42:6**
Ps 105:16-21

**42:7**
Gen 42:30

**42:8**
Gen 37:2

**42:9**
Gen 42:16, 30-34

**42:10**
Gen 37:6-9

**42:11**
Gen 42:19, 31-34

**42:13**
Gen 37:30-33;
44:20; 46:31

**42:14**
Gen 42:9

**42:17**
Gen 40:4

**42:18**
Gen 20:11
Lev 25:43

**42:20**
Gen 42:34; 43:15

**42:21**
Gen 37:23-28;
45:3-5

**42:22**
Gen 9:6; 37:21-22

**42:24**
Gen 43:14, 23

**42:25**
Gen 44:1

**42:28**
Gen 43:23

might come to him. 5 So Jacob's* sons arrived in Egypt along with others to buy food, for the famine had reached Canaan as well.

6 Since Joseph was governor of all Egypt and in charge of the sale of the grain, it was to him that his brothers came. They bowed low before him, with their faces to the ground. 7 Joseph recognized them instantly, but he pretended to be a stranger. "Where are you from?" he demanded roughly.

"From the land of Canaan," they replied. "We have come to buy grain."

8 Joseph's brothers didn't recognize him, but Joseph recognized them. 9 And he remembered the dreams he had had many years before. He said to them, "You are spies! You have come to see how vulnerable our land has become."

10 "No, my lord!" they exclaimed. "We have come to buy food. 11 We are all brothers and honest men, sir! We are not spies!"

12 "Yes, you are!" he insisted. "You have come to discover how vulnerable the famine has made us."

13 "Sir," they said, "there are twelve of us brothers, and our father is in the land of Canaan. Our youngest brother is there with our father, and one of our brothers is no longer with us."

14 But Joseph insisted, "As I said, you are spies! 15 This is how I will test your story. I swear by the life of Pharaoh that you will not leave Egypt unless your youngest brother comes here. 16 One of you go and get your brother! I'll keep the rest of you here, bound in prison. Then we'll find out whether or not your story is true. If it turns out that you don't have a younger brother, then I'll know you are spies."

17 So he put them all in prison for three days. 18 On the third day Joseph said to them, "I am a God-fearing man. If you do as I say, you will live. 19 We'll see how honorable you really are. Only one of you will remain in the prison. The rest of you may go on home with grain for your families. 20 But bring your youngest brother back to me. In this way, I will know whether or not you are telling me the truth. If you are, I will spare you." To this they agreed.

21 Speaking among themselves, they said, "This has all happened because of what we did to Joseph long ago. We saw his terror and anguish and heard his pleadings, but we wouldn't listen. That's why this trouble has come upon us."

22 "Didn't I tell you not to do it?" Reuben asked. "But you wouldn't listen. And now we are going to die because we murdered him."

23 Of course, they didn't know that Joseph understood them as he was standing there, for he had been speaking to them through an interpreter. 24 Now he left the room and found a place where he could weep. Returning, he talked some more with them. He then chose Simeon from among them and had him tied up right before their eyes.

25 Joseph then ordered his servants to fill the men's sacks with grain, but he also gave secret instructions to return each brother's payment at the top of his sack. He also gave them provisions for their journey. 26 So they loaded up their donkeys with the grain and started for home.

27 But when they stopped for the night and one of them opened his sack to get some grain to feed the donkeys, he found his money in the sack. 28 "Look!" he exclaimed to his brothers. "My money is here in my sack!" They were filled with terror and said to each other, "What has God done to us?" 29 So they came to their father, Jacob, in the land of Canaan and told him all that had happened.

**42:5** Hebrew *Israel's.*

---

**42:7** Joseph could have revealed his identity to his brothers at once. But Joseph's last memory of them was of staring in horror at their faces as slave traders carried him away. Were his brothers still evil and treacherous, or had they changed over the years? Joseph decided to put them through a few tests to find out.

**42:8, 9** Joseph remembered his dreams about his brothers bowing down to him (37:6-9). Those dreams were coming true! As a young boy, Joseph was boastful about his dreams. As a man, he no longer flaunted his superior status. He did not feel

the need to say, "I told you so." It was not yet time to reveal his identity, so he kept quiet. Sometimes it is best for us to remain quiet, even when we would like to have the last word.

**42:15** Joseph was testing his brothers to make sure they had not been as cruel to Benjamin as they had been to him. Benjamin was his only full brother, and he wanted to see him face to face.

**42:22** Reuben couldn't resist saying, "I told you so." He thought they were being punished by God for what they had done to Joseph. Selling Joseph into slavery amounted to murder in their minds, for they did not expect him to have survived.

<sup>30</sup>"The man who is ruler over the land spoke very roughly to us," they told him. "He took us for spies. <sup>31</sup>But we said, 'We are honest men, not spies. <sup>32</sup>We are twelve brothers, sons of one father; one brother has disappeared, and the youngest is with our father in the land of Canaan.' <sup>33</sup>Then the man, the ruler of the land, told us, 'This is the way I will find out if you are honest men. Leave one of your brothers here with me, and take grain for your families and go on home. <sup>34</sup>But bring your youngest brother back to me. Then I will know that you are honest men and not spies. If you prove to be what you say, then I will give you back your brother, and you may come as often as you like to buy grain.'"

<sup>35</sup>As they emptied out the sacks, there at the top of each one was the bag of money paid for the grain. Terror gripped them, as it did their father. <sup>36</sup>Jacob exclaimed, "You have deprived me of my children! Joseph has disappeared, Simeon is gone, and now you want to take Benjamin, too. Everything is going against me!"

<sup>37</sup>Then Reuben said to his father, "You may kill my two sons if I don't bring Benjamin back to you. I'll be responsible for him."

<sup>38</sup>But Jacob replied, "My son will not go down with you, for his brother Joseph is dead, and he alone is left of his mother's children. If anything should happen to him, you would bring my gray head down to the grave in deep sorrow."

### The Brothers Return to Egypt

**43** But there was no relief from the terrible famine throughout the land. <sup>2</sup>When the grain they had brought from Egypt was almost gone, Jacob said to his sons, "Go again and buy us a little food."

<sup>3</sup>But Judah said, "The man wasn't joking when he warned that we couldn't see him again unless Benjamin came along. <sup>4</sup>If you let him come with us, we will go down and buy some food. <sup>5</sup>But if you don't let Benjamin go, we may as well stay at home. Remember that the man said, 'You won't be allowed to come and see me unless your brother is with you.'"

<sup>6</sup>"Why did you ever tell him you had another brother?" Jacob* moaned. "Why did you have to treat me with such cruelty?"

<sup>7</sup>"But the man specifically asked us about our family," they replied. "He wanted to know whether our father was still living, and he asked us if we had another brother so we told him. How could we have known he would say, 'Bring me your brother'?"

<sup>8</sup>Judah said to his father, "Send the boy with me, and we will be on our way. Otherwise we will all die of starvation—and not only we, but you and our little ones. <sup>9</sup>I personally guarantee his safety. If I don't bring him back to you, then let me bear the blame forever. <sup>10</sup>For we could have gone and returned twice by this time if you had let him come without delay."

<sup>11</sup>So their father, Jacob, finally said to them, "If it can't be avoided, then at least do this. Fill your bags with the best products of the land. Take them to the man as gifts—balm, honey, spices, myrrh, pistachio nuts, and almonds. <sup>12</sup>Take double the money that you found in your sacks, as it was probably someone's mistake. <sup>13</sup>Then take your brother and go back to the man. <sup>14</sup>May God Almighty give you mercy as you go

**43:6** Hebrew *Israel;* also in 43:11.

**42:30** Gen 42:7
**42:31** Gen 42:11
**42:32** Gen 42:13
**42:34** Gen 34:10
**42:35** Gen 43:12, 15, 18
**42:36** Gen 43:14; 44:20-22
**42:37** Gen 43:9; 44:32
**42:38** Gen 37:35; 44:29, 34
**43:1** Gen 41:56-57
**43:2** Gen 42:25
**43:3** Gen 42:15; 44:23
**43:7** Gen 42:13; 43:27
**43:8** Gen 42:2
**43:9** Gen 42:37 Phlm 1:18-19
**43:11** Gen 32:13; 37:25
**43:12** Gen 42:25, 35
**43:13** Gen 43:3
**43:14** Gen 42:24 Ps 106:46

**43:1** Jacob and his sons had no relief from the famine. They could not see God's overall plan of sending them to Egypt to be reunited with Joseph and fed from Egypt's storehouses. If you are praying for relief from suffering or pressure and God is not bringing it as quickly as you would like, remember that God may be leading you to special treasures.

**43:9** Judah accepted full responsibility for Benjamin's safety. He did not know what that might mean for him, but he was determined to do his duty. In the end it was Judah's stirring words that caused Joseph to break down with emotion and reveal himself to his brothers (44:18-34). Accepting responsibilities is difficult, but it builds character and confidence, earns others' respect, and motivates us to complete our work. When you have been given

an assignment to complete or a responsibility to fulfill, commit yourself to seeing it through.

**43:11** These gifts of balm, honey, spices, myrrh, pistachio nuts, and almonds were highly valuable specialty items not common in Egypt. Because of the famine, they were even more rare.

**43:12** Joseph's brothers arrived home from Egypt only to find in their grain sacks the money they had used to pay for the grain (42:35). Some months later, when it was time to return to Egypt for more food, Jacob instructed them to take extra money so they could pay for the previous purchase as well as for additional grain. Jacob did not try to get away with anything. He was a man of integrity who paid for what he bought, whether he had to or not. We should follow his example and guard our integrity. A reputation for honesty is worth far more than the money we might gain by compromising it.

before the man, that he might release Simeon and return Benjamin. And if I must bear the anguish of their deaths, then so be it."

**43:16**
Gen 44:1

15 So they took Benjamin and the gifts and double the money and hurried to Egypt, where they presented themselves to Joseph. 16 When Joseph saw that Benjamin was with them, he said to the manager of his household, "These men will eat with me this noon. Take them inside and prepare a big feast." 17 So the man did as he was told and took them to Joseph's palace.

**43:18**
Gen 42:28, 35

18 They were badly frightened when they saw where they were being taken. "It's because of the money returned to us in our sacks," they said. "He plans to pretend that we stole it. Then he will seize us as slaves and take our donkeys."

### A Feast at Joseph's Palace

19 As the brothers arrived at the entrance to the palace, they went over to the man in charge of Joseph's household. 20 They said to him, "Sir, after our first trip to Egypt to buy food, 21 as we were returning home we stopped for the night and opened our sacks. The money we had used to pay for the grain was there in our sacks. Here it is; we have brought it back again. 22 We also have additional money to buy more grain. We have no idea how the money got into our sacks."

**43:21**
Gen 42:25, 35;
43:12

**43:22**
Gen 42:28

**43:23**
Gen 42:24

23 "Relax. Don't worry about it," the household manager told them. "Your God, the God of your ancestors, must have put it there. We collected your money all right." Then he released Simeon and brought him out to them.

**43:24**
Gen 18:4; 24:32

24 The brothers were then led into the palace and given water to wash their feet and food for their donkeys. 25 They were told they would be eating there, so they prepared their gifts for Joseph's arrival at noon.

**43:27**
Gen 43:7; 45:3

26 When Joseph came, they gave him their gifts and bowed low before him. 27 He asked them how they had been getting along, and then he said, "How is your father—the old man you spoke about? Is he still alive?"

**43:28**
Exod 18:7

28 "Yes," they replied. "He is alive and well." Then they bowed again before him.

**43:29**
Num 6:25
Ps 67:1

29 Looking at his brother Benjamin, Joseph asked, "Is this your youngest brother, the one you told me about? May God be gracious to you, my son." 30 Then Joseph made a hasty exit because he was overcome with emotion for his brother and wanted to cry. Going into his private room, he wept there. 31 Then he washed his face and came out, keeping himself under control. "Bring on the food!" he ordered.

**43:30**
Gen 42:24; 45:2,
14-15; 46:29

**43:31**
Gen 45:1

32 Joseph ate by himself, and his brothers were served at a separate table. The Egyptians sat at their own table because Egyptians despise Hebrews and refuse to eat with them. 33 Joseph told each of his brothers where to sit, and to their amazement, he seated them in the order of their ages, from oldest to youngest. 34 Their food was served to them from Joseph's own table. He gave the largest serving to Benjamin—five times as much as to any of the others. So they all feasted and drank freely with him.

**43:32**
Gen 46:34
Exod 8:26

**43:33**
Gen 44:12

### Joseph's Silver Cup

**44:1**
Gen 42:25; 43:16

**44** When his brothers were ready to leave, Joseph gave these instructions to the man in charge of his household: "Fill each of their sacks with as much grain as they can carry, and put each man's money back into his sack. 2 Then put my personal silver cup at the top of the youngest brother's sack, along with his grain money." So the household manager did as he was told.

3 The brothers were up at dawn and set out on their journey with their loaded donkeys.

**44:4**
Prov 17:13

4 But when they were barely out of the city, Joseph said to his household manager, "Chase after them and stop them. Ask them, 'Why have you repaid an act of kindness with such

---

**43:23** How did the money get into the sacks? Most likely, Joseph instructed his household manager to replace the money and then explain it with this response. Note that the household manager credited their God, not some Egyptian deity.

**43:32** Joseph ate by himself because he was following the laws of the Egyptians' caste system. Egyptians considered themselves highly intelligent and sophisticated. They looked upon shepherds and nomads as uncultured and even vulgar. As a Hebrew, Joseph could not eat with Egyptians even though he outranked them. As foreigners and shepherds,

his brothers were lower in rank than any Egyptian citizens, so they had to eat separately, too.

**44:2** Joseph's silver cup was a symbol of his authority. It was thought to have supernatural powers, and to steal it was a serious crime. Such goblets were used for predicting the future. A person poured water into the cup and interpreted the reflections, ripples, and bubbles. Joseph wouldn't have needed his cup since God told him everything he needed to know about the future.

evil? ⁵What do you mean by stealing my master's personal silver drinking cup, which he uses to predict the future? What a wicked thing you have done!'"

⁶So the man caught up with them and spoke to them in the way he had been instructed. ⁷"What are you talking about?" the brothers responded. "What kind of people do you think we are, that you accuse us of such a terrible thing? ⁸Didn't we bring back the money we found in our sacks? Why would we steal silver or gold from your master's house? ⁹If you find his cup with any one of us, let that one die. And all the rest of us will be your master's slaves forever."

¹⁰"Fair enough," the man replied, "except that only the one who stole it will be a slave. The rest of you may go free."

¹¹They quickly took their sacks from the backs of their donkeys and opened them. ¹²Joseph's servant began searching the oldest brother's sack, going on down the line to the youngest. The cup was found in Benjamin's sack! ¹³At this, they tore their clothing in despair, loaded the donkeys again, and returned to the city. ¹⁴Joseph was still at home when Judah and his brothers arrived, and they fell to the ground before him.

¹⁵"What were you trying to do?" Joseph demanded. "Didn't you know that a man such as I would know who stole it?"

¹⁶And Judah said, "Oh, my lord, what can we say to you? How can we plead? How can we prove our innocence? God is punishing us for our sins. My lord, we have all returned to be your slaves—we and our brother who had your cup in his sack."

¹⁷"No," Joseph said. "Only the man who stole the cup will be my slave. The rest of you may go home to your father."

### Judah Speaks for His Brothers

¹⁸Then Judah stepped forward and said, "My lord, let me say just this one word to you. Be patient with me for a moment, for I know you could have me killed in an instant, as though you were Pharaoh himself.

¹⁹"You asked us, my lord, if we had a father or a brother. ²⁰We said, 'Yes, we have a father, an old man, and a child of his old age, his youngest son. His brother is dead, and he alone is left of his mother's children, and his father loves him very much.' ²¹And you said to us, 'Bring him here so I can see him.' ²²But we said to you, 'My lord, the boy cannot leave his father, for his father would die.' ²³But you told us, 'You may not see me again unless your youngest brother is with you.' ²⁴So we returned to our father and told him what you had said. ²⁵And when he said, 'Go back again and buy us a little food,' ²⁶we replied, 'We can't unless you let our youngest brother go with us. We won't be allowed to see the man in charge of the grain unless our youngest brother is with us.' ²⁷Then my father said to us, 'You know that my wife had two sons, ²⁸and that one of them went away and never returned—doubtless torn to pieces by some wild animal. I have never seen him since. ²⁹If you take away his brother from me, too, and any harm comes to him, you would bring my gray head down to the grave in deep sorrow.'

³⁰"And now, my lord, I cannot go back to my father without the boy. Our father's life is bound up in the boy's life. ³¹When he sees that the boy is not with us, our father will die. We will be responsible for bringing his gray head down to the grave in sorrow. ³²My

**44:5**
Gen 30:27
Lev 19:26
Deut 18:10-14

**44:8**
Gen 43:21

**44:9**
Gen 31:32

**44:12**
Gen 44:2

**44:13**
Gen 37:29, 34

**44:15**
Gen 44:5

**44:16**
Gen 42:11; 43:18

**44:18**
Gen 37:7-8

**44:19**
Gen 42:11; 43:7

**44:21**
Gen 42:11, 15

**44:23**
Gen 43:3

**44:24**
Gen 42:29-34

**44:25**
Gen 42:2

**44:26**
Gen 43:5

**44:27**
Gen 46:19

**44:28**
Gen 37:33

**44:29**
Gen 42:38

**44:30**
1 Sam 18:1

**44:32**
Gen 43:9

---

**44:13** Tearing clothes was an expression of deep sorrow, a customary manner of showing grief. The brothers were terrified that Benjamin might be harmed.

**44:16-34** When Judah was younger, he showed no regard for his brother Joseph or his father, Jacob. First he convinced his brothers to sell Joseph as a slave (37:27); then he joined his brothers in lying to his father about Joseph's fate (37:32). But what a change had taken place in Judah! The man who sold one favored little brother into slavery now offered to become a slave himself to save another favored little brother. He was so concerned for his father and younger brother that he was willing to die for them. When you are ready to give up hope on yourself or others, remember that God can work a complete change in even the most selfish personality.

**44:18-34** Judah finally could take no more and stepped forward to plead their case. This was risky because Joseph could have had him killed. But Judah courageously defended himself and his brothers and pled for mercy. And he offered to put himself in Benjamin's place. There are times when we should be silent, but there are also times when we should speak up, even if there could be serious repercussions. When faced with a situation that needs a strong voice and courageous action, remember Judah and speak up.

**44:32, 33** Judah had promised Jacob that he would guarantee young Benjamin's safety (43:9). Now Judah had a chance to keep that promise. Becoming a slave was a terrible fate, but Judah was determined to keep his word to his father. He showed great courage in carrying out his promise. Accepting a responsibility means carrying it out with determination and courage, regardless of the personal sacrifice.

lord, I made a pledge to my father that I would take care of the boy. I told him, 'If I don't bring him back to you, I will bear the blame forever.' 33Please, my lord, let me stay here as a slave instead of the boy, and let the boy return with his brothers. 34For how can I return to my father if the boy is not with me? I cannot bear to see what this would do to him."

### Joseph Reveals His Identity

**45:1**
Gen 43:31
Acts 7:13

**45** Joseph could stand it no longer. "Out, all of you!" he cried out to his attendants. He wanted to be alone with his brothers when he told them who he was. 2Then he broke down and wept aloud. His sobs could be heard throughout the palace, and the news was quickly carried to Pharaoh's palace.

**45:3**
Gen 43:7

**45:4**
Gen 37:28

3"I am Joseph!" he said to his brothers. "Is my father still alive?" But his brothers were speechless! They were stunned to realize that Joseph was standing there in front of them. 4"Come over here," he said. So they came closer. And he said again, "I am

---

## JUDAH

People who are leaders stand out. They don't necessarily look or act a certain way until the need for their action is apparent. Among their skills are outspokenness, decisiveness, action, and control. These skills can be used for great good or great evil. Jacob's fourth son, Judah, was a natural leader. The events of his life provided many opportunities to exercise those skills. Unfortunately Judah's decisions were often shaped more by the pressures of the moment than by a conscious desire to cooperate with God's plan. But when he did recognize his mistakes, he was willing to admit them. His experience with Tamar and the final confrontation with Joseph are both examples of Judah's willingness to bear the blame when confronted. It was one of the qualities he passed on to his descendant David.

Whether or not we have Judah's natural leadership qualities, we share with him a tendency to be blind toward our own sin. Too often, however, we don't share his willingness to admit mistakes. From Judah we can learn that it is not wise to wait until our errors force us to admit to wrongdoing. It is far better to admit our mistakes openly, to shoulder the blame, and to seek forgiveness.

| | |
|---|---|
| **Strengths and accomplishments** | • Was a natural leader—outspoken and decisive<br>• Thought clearly and took action in high-pressure situations<br>• Was willing to stand by his word and put himself on the line when necessary<br>• Was the fourth son of 12, through whom God would eventually bring David and Jesus, the Messiah |
| **Weaknesses and mistakes** | • Suggested to his brothers they sell Joseph into slavery<br>• Failed to keep his promise to his daughter-in-law, Tamar |
| **Lessons from his life** | • God is in control, far beyond the immediate situation<br>• Procrastination often makes matters worse<br>• Judah's offer to substitute his life for Benjamin's is a picture of what his descendant Jesus would do for all people |
| **Vital statistics** | • Where: Canaan and Egypt<br>• Occupation: Shepherd<br>• Relatives: Parents: Jacob and Leah. Wife: The daughter of Shua (1 Chronicles 2:3). Daughter-in-law: Tamar. Eleven brothers, at least one sister, and at least five sons |
| **Key verses** | "Judah, your brothers will praise you. You will defeat your enemies. All your relatives will bow before you. Judah is a young lion that has finished eating its prey. Like a lion he crouches and lies down; like a lioness—who will dare to rouse him? The scepter will not depart from Judah, nor the ruler's staff from his descendants, until the coming of the one to whom it belongs, the one whom all nations will obey" (Genesis 49:8-10). |

Judah's story is told in Genesis 29:35—50:26. He is also mentioned in 1 Chronicles 2—4.

---

**44:33** Joseph wanted to see if his brothers' attitudes had changed for the better, so he tested the way they treated each other. Judah, the brother who had stepped forward with the plan to sell Joseph (37:27), now stepped forward to take Benjamin's punishment so that Benjamin could return to their father. This courageous act convinced Joseph that his brothers had dramatically changed for the better.

**45:4-8** Although Joseph's brothers had wanted to get rid of him, God used even their evil actions to fulfill his ultimate plan. He sent Joseph ahead to preserve their lives, save Egypt, and prepare the way for the beginning of the nation of Israel. God is sovereign. His plans are not dictated by human actions. When others intend evil toward you, remember that they are only God's tools. As Joseph said to his brothers, "God turned into good what you meant for evil. He brought me to the high position I have today so I could save the lives of many people" (50:20).

Joseph, your brother whom you sold into Egypt. [5]But don't be angry with yourselves that you did this to me, for God did it. He sent me here ahead of you to preserve your lives. [6]These two years of famine will grow to seven, during which there will be neither plowing nor harvest. [7]God has sent me here to keep you and your families alive so that you will become a great nation. [8]Yes, it was God who sent me here, not you! And he has made me a counselor to Pharaoh—manager of his entire household and ruler over all Egypt.

[9]"Hurry, return to my father and tell him, 'This is what your son Joseph says: God has made me master over all the land of Egypt. Come down to me right away! [10]You will live in the land of Goshen so you can be near me with all your children and grand-children, your flocks and herds, and all that you have. [11]I will take care of you there, for there are still five years of famine ahead of us. Otherwise you and your household will come to utter poverty.'"

[12]Then Joseph said, "You can see for yourselves, and so can my brother Benjamin, that I really am Joseph! [13]Tell my father how I am honored here in Egypt. Tell him about everything you have seen, and bring him to me quickly." [14]Weeping with joy, he embraced Benjamin, and Benjamin also began to weep. [15]Then Joseph kissed each of his brothers and wept over them, and then they began talking freely with him.

### Pharaoh Invites Jacob to Egypt

[16]The news soon reached Pharaoh: "Joseph's brothers have come!" Pharaoh was very happy to hear this and so were his officials.

[17]Pharaoh said to Joseph, "Tell your brothers to load their pack animals and return quickly to their homes in Canaan. [18]Tell them to bring your father and all of their families, and to come here to Egypt to live. Tell them, 'Pharaoh will assign to you the very best territory in the land of Egypt. You will live off the fat of the land!' [19]And tell your brothers to take wagons from Egypt to carry their wives and little ones and to bring your father here. [20]Don't worry about your belongings, for the best of all the land of Egypt is yours."

[21]So the sons of Jacob* did as they were told. Joseph gave them wagons, as Pharaoh had commanded, and he supplied them with provisions for the journey. [22]And he gave each of them new clothes—but to Benjamin he gave five changes of clothes and three hundred pieces* of silver! [23]He sent his father ten donkeys loaded with the good things of Egypt, and ten donkeys loaded with grain and all kinds of other food to be eaten on his journey. [24]So he sent his brothers off, and as they left, he called after them, "Don't quarrel along the way!" [25]And they left Egypt and returned to their father, Jacob, in the land of Canaan.

[26]"Joseph is still alive!" they told him. "And he is ruler over all the land of Egypt!" Jacob was stunned at the news—he couldn't believe it. [27]But when they had given him Joseph's messages, and when he saw the wagons loaded with the food sent by Joseph, his spirit revived.

[28]Then Jacob said, "It must be true! My son Joseph is alive! I will go and see him before I die."

## 6. Jacob's family moves to Egypt

### Jacob's Journey to Egypt

**46** So Jacob* set out for Egypt with all his possessions. And when he came to Beersheba, he offered sacrifices to the God of his father, Isaac. [2]During the night God spoke to him in a vision. "Jacob! Jacob!" he called.

**45:21** Hebrew *Israel;* also in 45:28.　**45:22** Hebrew *300 shekels,* about 7.5 pounds or 3.4 kilograms in weight. **46:1** Hebrew *Israel;* also in 46:30.

**45:5** Gen 50:20

**45:6** Gen 41:30

**45:8** Gen 41:41 Judg 17:10

**45:9** Acts 7:14

**45:10** Gen 46:28, 34

**45:11** Gen 47:12

**45:13** Acts 7:14

**45:14** Gen 45:2

**45:16** Acts 7:13

**45:17** Gen 42:26

**45:18** Gen 27:28

**45:19** Gen 45:27; 46:5

**45:20** Gen 46:6

**45:22** Gen 24:53 2 Kgs 5:5

**45:23** Gen 43:11

**45:24** Gen 42:21-22

**45:26** Gen 37:31-35

**45:27** Gen 45:19

**45:28** Gen 44:28

**46:1** Gen 21:14; 26:24; 28:13; 31:42

**46:2** Gen 22:11; 31:11 Num 12:6

---

**45:17-20** Joseph was rejected, kidnapped, enslaved, and imprisoned. Although his brothers had been unfaithful to him, he graciously forgave them and shared his prosperity. Joseph demonstrated how God forgives us and showers us with good-ness even though we have sinned against him. The same for-giveness and blessings are ours if we ask for them.

**45:26, 27** Jacob needed some evidence before he could believe the incredible news that Joseph was alive. Similarly, Thomas refused to believe that Jesus had risen from the dead until he could see and touch him (John 20:25). It is hard to change what you believe without all the facts—or sometimes even with the facts. Good news can be hard to believe. Don't ever give up hope that God has a wonderful future in store for you.

**46:3**
Gen 17:1; 26:2

**46:4**
Gen 28:13;
Exod 3:8

**46:5**
Gen 45:19

**46:6**
Num 20:15
Deut 26:5
Acts 7:15

**46:8**
Gen 29:32; 35:26

**46:9**
1 Chr 5:3

**46:10**
1 Chr 4:24

**46:11**
1 Chr 6:16

**46:12**
1 Chr 2:3

**46:13**
1 Chr 7:1

**46:14**
Gen 30:20

**46:15**
Gen 30:21

**46:16**
Gen 30:11
Num 26:15

**46:17**
Gen 30:13

**46:19**
Gen 44:27

**46:20**
Gen 41:45, 50-52

"Here I am," Jacob replied.

³"I am God," the voice said, "the God of your father. Do not be afraid to go down to Egypt, for I will see to it that you become a great nation there. ⁴I will go with you down to Egypt, and I will bring your descendants back again. But you will die in Egypt with Joseph at your side."

⁵So Jacob left Beersheba, and his sons brought him to Egypt. They carried their little ones and wives in the wagons Pharaoh had provided for them. ⁶They brought their livestock, too, and all the belongings they had acquired in the land of Canaan. Jacob and his entire family arrived in Egypt—sons and daughters, grandsons and grand-daughters—all his descendants.

⁸These are the names of the Israelites, the descendants of Jacob, who went with him to Egypt:

Reuben was Jacob's oldest son. ⁹The sons of Reuben were Hanoch, Pallu, Hezron, and Carmi.

¹⁰The sons of Simeon were Jemuel, Jamin, Ohad, Jakin, Zohar, and Shaul. (Shaul's mother was a Canaanite woman.)

¹¹The sons of Levi were Gershon, Kohath, and Merari.

¹²The sons of Judah were Er, Onan, Shelah, Perez, and Zerah. (But Er and Onan had died in the land of Canaan.) The sons of Perez were Hezron and Hamul.

¹³The sons of Issachar were Tola, Puah,* Jashub,* and Shimron.

¹⁴The sons of Zebulun were Sered, Elon, and Jahleel.

¹⁵These are the sons of Jacob who were born to Leah in Paddan-aram, along with their sister, Dinah. In all, Jacob's descendants through Leah numbered thirty-three.

¹⁶The sons of Gad were Zephon,* Haggi, Shuni, Ezbon, Eri, Arodi, and Areli.

¹⁷The sons of Asher were Imnah, Ishvah, Ishvi, and Beriah. Their sister was named Serah. Beriah's sons were Heber and Malkiel.

¹⁸These sixteen were descendants of Jacob through Zilpah, the servant given to Leah by her father, Laban.

¹⁹The sons of Jacob's wife Rachel were Joseph and Benjamin.

²⁰Joseph's sons, born in the land of Egypt, were Manasseh and Ephraim. Their mother was Asenath, daughter of Potiphera, priest of Heliopolis.*

**46:13a** As in Syriac version and Samaritan Pentateuch (see also 1 Chr 7:1); Hebrew reads *Puvah*.   **46:13b** As in some Greek manuscripts and Samaritan Pentateuch (see also Num 26:24; 1 Chr 7:1); Hebrew reads *iob*.   **46:16** As in Greek version and Samaritan Pentateuch (see also Num 26:15) Hebrew reads *Ziphion*.   **46:20** Hebrew *of On*.

---

**JACOB MOVES TO EGYPT**

After hearing the joyful news that Joseph was alive, Jacob packed up and moved his family to Egypt. Stopping first in Beersheba, Jacob offered sacrifices and received assurance from God that Egypt was where he should go. Jacob and his family settled in the region of Goshen, in the northeastern part of Egypt.

**46:3, 4** The Israelites did become a great nation and Jacob's descendants eventually returned to Canaan. The book of Exodus recounts the story of Israel's slavery in Egypt for 400 years (fulfilling God's words to Abraham in 15:13-16), and the book of Joshua gives an exciting account of the Israelites entering and conquering Canaan, the Promised Land.

**46:3, 4** God told Jacob to leave his home and travel to a strange and faraway land. But God reassured him by promising to go with him and take care of him. When new situations or surroundings frighten you, recognize that experiencing fear is normal. To be paralyzed by fear, however, is an indication that you question God's ability to take care of you.

**46:4** Jacob never returned to Canaan, but God promised that his descendants would return. That Jacob would die in Egypt with Joseph at his side was God's promise to Jacob that he would never know the bitterness of being lonely again.

²¹Benjamin's sons were Bela, Beker, Ashbel, Gera, Naaman, Ehi, Rosh, Muppim, Huppim, and Ard.

²²These fourteen were the descendants of Jacob and his wife Rachel.

²³The son of Dan was Hushim.
²⁴The sons of Naphtali were Jahzeel, Guni, Jezer, and Shillem.

²⁵These seven were the descendants of Jacob through Bilhah, the servant given to Rachel by her father, Laban.

²⁶So the total number of Jacob's direct descendants who went with him to Egypt, not counting his sons' wives, was sixty-six. ²⁷Joseph also had two sons* who had been born in Egypt. So altogether, there were seventy* members of Jacob's family in the land of Egypt.

### Jacob's Family Arrives in Goshen

²⁸Jacob sent Judah on ahead to meet Joseph and get directions to the land of Goshen. And when they all arrived there, ²⁹Joseph prepared his chariot and traveled to Goshen to meet his father. As soon as Joseph arrived, he embraced his father and wept on his shoulder for a long time. ³⁰Then Jacob said to Joseph, "Now let me die, for I have seen you with my own eyes and know you are still alive."

³¹And Joseph said to his brothers and to all their households, "I'll go and tell Pharaoh that you have all come from the land of Canaan to join me. ³²And I will tell him, 'These men are shepherds and livestock breeders. They have brought with them their flocks and herds and everything they own.' ³³So when Pharaoh calls for you and asks you about your occupation, ³⁴tell him, 'We have been livestock breeders from our youth, as our ancestors have been for many generations.' When you tell him this, he will let you live here in the land of Goshen, for shepherds are despised in the land of Egypt."

### Jacob Blesses Pharaoh

**47** So Joseph went to see Pharaoh and said, "My father and my brothers are here from Canaan. They came with all their flocks and herds and possessions, and they are now in the land of Goshen."

²Joseph took five of his brothers with him and presented them to Pharaoh. ³Pharaoh asked them, "What is your occupation?"

And they replied, "We are shepherds like our ancestors. ⁴We have come to live here in Egypt, for there is no pasture for our flocks in Canaan. The famine is very severe there. We request permission to live in the land of Goshen."

⁵And Pharaoh said to Joseph, "Now that your family has joined you here, ⁶choose any place you like for them to live. Give them the best land of Egypt—the land of Goshen will be fine. And if any of them have special skills, put them in charge of my livestock, too."

⁷Then Joseph brought his father, Jacob, and presented him to Pharaoh, and Jacob blessed Pharaoh. ⁸"How old are you?" Pharaoh asked him.

⁹Jacob replied, "I have lived for 130 hard years, but I am still not nearly as old as many of my ancestors." ¹⁰Then Jacob blessed Pharaoh again before he left.

¹¹So Joseph assigned the best land of Egypt—the land of Rameses—to his father and brothers, just as Pharaoh had commanded. ¹²And Joseph furnished food to his father and brothers in amounts appropriate to the number of their dependents.

**46:27a** Greek version reads *nine sons,* probably including Joseph's grandsons through Ephraim and Manasseh (see 1 Chr 7:14-20).   **46:27b** Greek version reads *seventy-five;* see note on Exod 1:5.

---

**46:31-34** Jacob moved his whole family to Egypt, but they wanted to live apart from the Egyptians. To ensure this, Joseph told them to let Pharaoh know they were shepherds. Although Pharaoh may have been sympathetic to shepherds (for he was probably descended from the nomadic Hyksos line), the Egyptian culture would not willingly accept shepherds among them. The strategy worked, and Jacob's family was able to benefit from Pharaoh's generosity as well as from the Egyptians' prejudice.

**47:1-6** The faithfulness of Joseph affected his entire family. When he was in the pit and in prison, Joseph must have wondered about his future. Instead of despairing, he faithfully obeyed God and did what was right. Here we see one of the exciting results. We may not always see the effects of our faith, but we can be sure that God will honor faithfulness.

**46:21**
Num 26:38-41
1 Chr 7:6-12

**46:22**
Gen 35:24

**46:23**
Gen 30:6
Num 26:42

**46:24**
Gen 30:8

**46:25**
Gen 35:2

**46:27**
Exod 1:5
Deut 10:22
Acts 7:14

**46:28**
Gen 43:3; 45:10

**46:29**
Gen 45:14-15

**46:30**
Gen 44:28

**46:31**
Gen 47:1

**46:32**
Gen 37:2; 47:3

**46:33**
Gen 47:3

**46:34**
Gen 13:7; 26:20; 37:2

**47:1**
Gen 46:31

**47:2**
Gen 43:15

**47:3**
Gen 46:32-33

**47:4**
Gen 46:34

**47:6**
Gen 45:18
Exod 18:21, 25

**47:7**
Gen 47:10
2 Sam 14:22
1 Kgs 8:66

**47:10**
Gen 14:19

**47:11**
Exod 1:11; 12:37

**47:12**
Gen 45:11

*Joseph's Leadership in the Famine*

**47:13**
Gen 41:30
Acts 7:11

**47:14**
Gen 41:56

**47:15**
Gen 47:18-19

[13] Meanwhile, the famine became worse and worse, and the crops continued to fail throughout Egypt and Canaan. [14] Joseph collected all the money in Egypt and Canaan in exchange for grain, and he brought the money to Pharaoh's treasure-house. [15] When the people of Egypt and Canaan ran out of money, they came to Joseph crying again for food. "Our money is gone," they said, "but give us bread. Why should we die?"

**47:17**
Exod 14:9

[16] "Well, then," Joseph replied, "since your money is gone, give me your livestock. I will give you food in exchange." [17] So they gave their livestock to Joseph in exchange for food. Soon all the horses, flocks, herds, and donkeys of Egypt were in Pharaoh's possession. But at least they were able to purchase food for that year.

**47:19**
Neh 5:2
Job 2:4
Lam 1:11

[18] The next year they came again and said, "Our money is gone, and our livestock are yours. We have nothing left but our bodies and land. [19] Why should we die before your very eyes? Buy us and our land in exchange for food; we will then become servants to Pharaoh. Just give us grain so that our lives may be saved and so the land will not become empty and desolate."

**47:22**
Deut 14:28-29

[20] So Joseph bought all the land of Egypt for Pharaoh. All the Egyptians sold him their fields because the famine was so severe, and their land then belonged to Pharaoh. [21] Thus, all the people of Egypt became servants to Pharaoh.* [22] The only land he didn't buy was that belonging to the priests, for they were assigned food from Pharaoh and didn't need to sell their land.

**47:24**
Gen 41:34

**47:25**
Gen 32:5

**47:26**
Gen 47:22

[23] Then Joseph said to the people, "See, I have bought you and your land for Pharaoh. I will provide you with seed, so you can plant the fields. [24] Then when you harvest it, a fifth of your crop will belong to Pharaoh. Keep four-fifths for yourselves, and use it to plant the next year's crop and to feed yourselves, your households, and your little ones."

[25] "You have saved our lives!" they exclaimed. "May it please you, sir, to let us be Pharaoh's servants." [26] Joseph then made it a law throughout the land of Egypt—and it is still the law—that Pharaoh should receive one-fifth of all the crops grown on his land. But since Pharaoh had not taken over the priests' land, they were exempt from this payment.

### 7. Jacob and Joseph die in Egypt

**47:27**
Exod 1:7

**47:29**
Gen 24:2;
50:24-25

**47:30**
Gen 23:17-20;
25:9; 49:29
Acts 7:15-16

**47:31**
Heb 11:21

[27] So the people of Israel settled in the land of Goshen in Egypt. And before long, they began to prosper there, and their population grew rapidly. [28] Jacob lived for seventeen years after his arrival in Egypt, so he was 147 years old when he died. [29] As the time of his death drew near, he called for his son Joseph and said to him, "If you are pleased with me, swear most solemnly that you will honor this, my last request: Do not bury me in Egypt. [30] When I am dead, take me out of Egypt and bury me beside my ancestors." So Joseph promised that he would. [31] "Swear that you will do it," Jacob insisted. So Joseph gave his oath, and Jacob* bowed in worship as he leaned on his staff.*

*Jacob Blesses Manasseh and Ephraim*

**48:1**
Gen 41:51-52
Heb 11:21

**48** One day not long after this, word came to Joseph that his father was failing rapidly. So Joseph went to visit him, and he took with him his two sons, Manasseh and Ephraim. [2] When Jacob heard that Joseph had arrived, he gathered his strength and sat up in bed to greet him.

**48:3**
Gen 28:13-19;
35:9-12

**48:5**
Gen 29:32-33

**48:7**
Gen 35:19

[3] Jacob said to Joseph, "God Almighty appeared to me at Luz in the land of Canaan and blessed me. [4] He said to me, 'I will make you a multitude of nations, and I will give this land of Canaan to you and your descendants as an everlasting possession.' [5] Now I am adopting as my own sons these two boys of yours, Ephraim and Manasseh, who were born here in the land of Egypt before I arrived. They will inherit from me just as Reuben and Simeon will. [6] But the children born to you in the future will be your own. The land they inherit will be within the territories of Ephraim and Manasseh. [7] As I was returning

**47:21** As in Greek version and Samaritan Pentateuch; Hebrew reads *He moved the people into the towns throughout the land of Egypt.* **47:31a** Hebrew *israel.* **47:31b** As in Greek version; Hebrew reads *bowed in worship at the head of his bed.*

**47:29-31** Jacob had Joseph promise to bury him in his homeland. Few things were written in this culture, so a person's word then carried as much force as a written contract today. People today seem to find it easy to say, "I didn't mean that." God's people, however, are to speak the truth and live the truth. Let your words be as binding as a written contract.

from Paddan, Rachel died in the land of Canaan. We were still on the way, just a short distance from Ephrath (that is, Bethlehem). So with great sorrow I buried her there beside the road to Ephrath."

8Then Jacob* looked over at the two boys. "Are these your sons?" he asked.

9"Yes," Joseph told him, "these are the sons God has given me here in Egypt." And Jacob said, "Bring them over to me, and I will bless them."

10Now Jacob was half blind because of his age and could hardly see. So Joseph brought the boys close to him, and Jacob kissed and embraced them. 11Then Jacob said to Joseph, "I never thought I would see you again, but now God has let me see your children, too."

12Joseph took the boys from their grandfather's knees, and he bowed low to him. 13Then he positioned the boys so Ephraim was at Jacob's left hand and Manasseh was at his right hand. 14But Jacob crossed his arms as he reached out to lay his hands on the boys' heads. So his right hand was on the head of Ephraim, the younger boy, and his left hand was on the head of Manasseh, the older.

15Then he blessed Joseph and said, "May God, the God before whom my grandfather Abraham and my father, Isaac, walked, the God who has been my shepherd all my life, 16and the angel who has kept me from all harm—may he bless these boys. May they preserve my name and the names of my grandfather Abraham and my father, Isaac. And may they become a mighty nation."

17But Joseph was upset when he saw that his father had laid his right hand on Ephraim's head. So he lifted it to place it on Manasseh's head instead. 18"No, Father," he said, "this one over here is older. Put your right hand on his head."

19But his father refused. "I know what I'm doing, my son," he said. "Manasseh, too, will become a great people, but his younger brother will become even greater. His descendants will become a multitude of nations!" 20So Jacob blessed the boys that day with this blessing: "The people of Israel will use your names to bless each other. They will say, 'May God make you as prosperous as Ephraim and Manasseh.'" In this way, Jacob put Ephraim ahead of Manasseh.

21Then Jacob said to Joseph, "I am about to die, but God will be with you and will bring you again to Canaan, the land of your ancestors. 22And I give you an extra portion* beyond what I have given your brothers—the portion that I took from the Amorites with my sword and bow."

### Jacob Blesses His Sons

**49** Then Jacob called together all his sons and said, "Gather around me, and I will tell you what is going to happen to you in the days to come.

2 "Come and listen, O sons of Jacob;
   listen to Israel, your father.

**48:8** Hebrew *Israel;* also in 48:10, 11, 13, 14, 21.    **48:22** Or *give you the ridge of land.* The meaning of the Hebrew is uncertain.

**Cross-references (margin):**
- 48:9 Gen 33:5
- 48:10 Gen 27:1
- 48:11 Gen 44:28
- 48:12 Gen 33:3; 42:6
- 48:14 Gen 41:51-52
- 48:15 Gen 17:1; 49:24
- 48:16 Gen 22:11; 28:13-15; 31:11; †Heb 11:21
- 48:19 Gen 28:14; 46:3
- 48:20 Ruth 4:11
- 48:21 Gen 28:15; 46:4; 50:24
- 48:22 Josh 24:32; John 4:5
- 49:1 Num 24:14

---

**48:8-20** Jacob gave Ephraim, instead of his older brother Manasseh, the greater blessing. When Joseph objected, Jacob refused to listen because God had told him that Ephraim would become greater. God often works in unexpected ways. When he chooses people to fulfill his plans, he always goes deeper than appearance, tradition, or position. He sometimes surprises us by choosing the less obvious person, at least by human reasoning. God can use you to carry out his plans, even if you don't think you have all the qualifications.

**48:11** When Joseph became a slave, Jacob thought he was dead and wept in despair (37:34). But eventually God's plan allowed Jacob to regain not only his son but his grandchildren as well. Circumstances are never so bad that they are beyond God's help. Jacob regained his son. Job got a new family (Job 42:10-17). Mary regained her brother, Lazarus (John 11:1-44). We need never despair because we belong to a loving God. We never know what good he will bring out of a seemingly hopeless situation.

**48:15** Jacob spoke of God as his shepherd throughout his life. In his old age, he could clearly see his dependence upon God. This marks a total attitude change from that of his scheming and dishonest youth. To develop an attitude like Jacob's, let God shepherd you as you trust in his provision and care. When you realize that all good things come from God, you can quit trying to grab them for yourself.

**48:20-22** Jacob was giving these young boys land occupied by the Philistines and Canaanites. His gift became reality when the tribes of Ephraim and Manasseh occupied the east and west sides of the Jordan River (Joshua 16).

**49:3-28** Jacob blessed each of his sons and then made a prediction about each one's future. The way the men had lived played an important part in Jacob's blessing and prophecy. Our past also affects our present and future. By sunrise tomorrow, our actions of today will have become part of the past. Yet they will already have begun to shape the future. What actions can you choose or avoid that will positively shape your future?

**49:3**
Num 26:5
Deut 21:17
Pss 78:51; 105:36

3 "Reuben, you are my oldest son,
    the child of my vigorous youth.
    You are first on the list in rank and honor.

**49:4**
Gen 35:22
Deut 27:20

4 But you are as unruly as the waves of the sea,
    and you will be first no longer.
    For you slept with one of my wives;
    you dishonored me in my own bed.

**49:5**
Gen 29:33-34;
34:25-30

5 "Simeon and Levi are two of a kind—
    men of violence.

**49:6**
Gen 34:26

6 O my soul, stay away from them.
    May I never be a party to their wicked plans.
    For in their anger they murdered men,
    and they crippled oxen just for sport.

**49:7**
Josh 19:1, 9;
21:1-42

7 Cursed be their anger, for it is fierce;
    cursed be their wrath, for it is cruel.
    Therefore, I will scatter their descendants
    throughout the nation of Israel.

**49:8**
1 Chr 5:2
Heb 7:14

8 "Judah, your brothers will praise you.
    You will defeat your enemies.
    All your relatives will bow before you.

**49:9**
Num 24:9
Mic 5:8

9 Judah is a young lion
    that has finished eating its prey.
    Like a lion he crouches and lies down;
    like a lioness—who will dare to rouse him?

---

**PARALLELS BETWEEN JOSEPH AND JESUS**
Genesis 37—50

| Joseph | Parallels | Jesus |
|---|---|---|
| 37:3 | Their fathers loved them dearly | Matthew 3:17 |
| 37:2 | Shepherds of their fathers' sheep | John 10:11, 27 |
| 37:13, 14 | Sent by father to brothers | Hebrews 2:11 |
| 37:4 | Hated by brothers | John 7:5 |
| 37:20 | Others plotted to harm them | John 11:53 |
| 39:7 | Tempted | Matthew 4:1 |
| 37:25 | Taken to Egypt | Matthew 2:14, 15 |
| 37:23 | Robes taken from them | John 19:23 |
| 37:28 | Sold for the price of a slave | Matthew 26:15 |
| 39:20 | Bound in chains | Matthew 27:2 |
| 39:16–18 | Falsely accused | Matthew 26:59, 60 |
| 40:2, 3 | Placed with two other prisoners, one who was saved and the other lost | Luke 23:32 |
| 41:46 | Both 30 years old at the beginning of public recognition | Luke 3:23 |
| 41:41 | Exalted after suffering | Philippians 2:9–11 |
| 45:1–15 | Forgave those who wronged them | Luke 23:34 |
| 45:7 | Saved their nation | Matthew 1:21 |
| 50:20 | What people did to hurt them God turned to good | 1 Corinthians 2:7, 8 |

---

**49:4** The oldest son was supposed to receive a double inheritance, but Reuben lost his special honor. Unstable and untrustworthy, especially in his younger days, he had gone so far as to sleep with one of his father's concubines. Jacob could not give the birthright blessing to such a dishonorable son.

**49:8-12** Why was Judah—known for selling Joseph into slavery and trying to defraud his daughter-in-law—so greatly blessed? God had chosen Judah to be the ancestor of Israel's line of kings (that is the meaning of "the scepter will not depart from Judah"). This may have been due to Judah's dramatic change of character (44:33, 34) Judah's line would produce the promised Messiah, Jesus.

10 The scepter will not depart from Judah,
　　nor the ruler's staff from his descendants,
　until the coming of the one to whom it belongs,*
　　the one whom all nations will obey.
11 He ties his foal to a grapevine,
　　the colt of his donkey to a choice vine.
　He washes his clothes in wine
　　because his harvest is so plentiful.
12 His eyes are darker than wine,
　　and his teeth are whiter than milk.

13 "Zebulun will settle on the shores of the sea
　　and will be a harbor for ships;
　　his borders will extend to Sidon.

14 "Issachar is a strong beast of burden,
　　resting among the sheepfolds.*
15 When he sees how good the countryside is,
　　how pleasant the land,
　he will bend his shoulder to the task
　　and submit to forced labor.

16 "Dan will govern his people
　　like any other tribe in Israel.
17 He will be a snake beside the road,
　　a poisonous viper along the path,
　that bites the horse's heels
　　so the rider is thrown off.
18 I trust in you for salvation, O LORD!

19 "Gad will be plundered by marauding bands,
　　but he will turn and plunder them.

20 "Asher will produce rich foods,
　　food fit for kings.

21 "Naphtali is a deer let loose,
　　producing magnificent fawns.

22 "Joseph is a fruitful tree,
　　a fruitful tree beside a fountain.
　　His branches reach over the wall.
23 He has been attacked by archers,
　　who shot at him and harassed him.
24 But his bow remained strong,
　　and his arms were strengthened

**49:10**
Num 24:17
Pss 2:6-9; 60:7

**49:11**
Deut 8:7-8
2 Kgs 18:32

**49:13**
Deut 33:18-19

**49:14**
Judg 5:16
Ps 68:13

**49:15**
Josh 19:17-23

**49:16**
Deut 33:22
Judg 18:26-27

**49:19**
Deut 33:20

**49:20**
Deut 33:24-25

**49:21**
Deut 33:23

**49:22**
Deut 33:13-17

**49:23**
Gen 37:24

**49:24**
Ps 132:2, 5
Isa 41:10; 49:26

**49:10** Or *until tribute is brought to him and the peoples obey;* traditionally rendered *until Shiloh comes.* **49:14** Or *saddlebags,* or *hearths.*

---

**49:10** "Until the coming of the one to whom it belongs" may also be translated, "until Shiloh comes." What is *Shiloh?* The meaning of this difficult passage is disputed. *Shiloh* may be another name for the Messiah, because its literal meaning is "sent." *Shiloh* might also refer to the Tabernacle set up at the city of Shiloh (Joshua 18:1).

**49:18** In the middle of his prophecy to Dan, Jacob exclaimed, "I trust in you for salvation, O LORD!" He was emphasizing to Dan that he would be a strong leader only if his trust was in God, not in his natural strength or ability. Those who are strong, attractive, or talented often find it easier to trust in themselves than in God who gave them their gifts. Remember to thank God for what you are and have so your trust does not become misplaced.

**49:22** Joseph was indeed fruitful, with some heroic descendants. Among them were Joshua, who would lead the Israelites into the Promised Land (Joshua 1:10, 11); and Deborah, Gideon, and Jephthah, judges of Israel (Judges 4:4; 6:11, 12; 11:11).

**49:23, 24** These verses celebrate the times God rescued Joseph when his enemies attacked him. So often we struggle by ourselves, forgetting that God is able to help us fight our battles, whether they are against men with weapons or against spiritual forces. Joseph was able to draw closer to God as adversity mounted. To trust God to rescue you shows great faith. Can you trust him when injury or persecution is directed at you? Such spiritual battles require teamwork between courageous, faithful people and a mighty God.

by the Mighty One of Jacob,
the Shepherd, the Rock of Israel.
25 May the God of your ancestors help you;
may the Almighty bless you
with the blessings of the heavens above,
blessings of the earth beneath,
and blessings of the breasts and womb.
26 May the blessings of your ancestors
be greater than the blessings of the eternal mountains,
reaching to the utmost bounds of the everlasting hills.
These blessings will fall on the head of Joseph,
who is a prince among his brothers.

27 "Benjamin is a wolf that prowls.
He devours his enemies in the morning,
and in the evening he divides the plunder."

28 These are the twelve tribes of Israel, and these are the blessings with which Jacob*
blessed his twelve sons. Each received a blessing that was appropriate to him.

*Jacob's Death and Burial*

29 Then Jacob told them. "Soon I will die. Bury me with my father and grandfather in
the cave in Ephron's field. 30 This is the cave in the field of Machpelah, near Mamre
in Canaan, which Abraham bought from Ephron the Hittite for a permanent burial
place. 31 There Abraham and his wife Sarah are buried. There Isaac and his wife,
Rebekah, are buried. And there I buried Leah. 32 It is the cave that my grandfather
Abraham bought from the Hittites." 33 Then when Jacob had finished this charge to
his sons, he lay back in the bed, breathed his last, and died.

**50** Joseph threw himself on his father and wept over him and kissed him. 2 Then
Joseph told his morticians to embalm the body. 3 The embalming process took
forty days, and there was a period of national mourning for seventy days. 4 When the
period of mourning was over, Joseph approached Pharaoh's advisers and asked them
to speak to Pharaoh on his behalf. 5 He told them, "Tell Pharaoh that my father made
me swear an oath. He said to me, 'I am about to die; take my body back to the land of
Canaan, and bury me in our family's burial cave.' Now I need to go and bury my
father. After his burial is complete, I will return without delay."

**49:25** Gen 28:13

**49:26** Deut 33:15-16

**49:27** Deut 33:12

**49:29** Gen 23:16-20; 25:8-9

**49:31** Gen 23:19; 25:9; 35:29

**49:33** Gen 25:8 Acts 7:15

**50:1** Gen 46:4

**50:2** Gen 50:26

**50:3** Num 20:29 Deut 34:8

**50:5** Gen 47:29-31

**49:28** Hebrew *Israel.*

| **JACOB'S SONS AND THEIR NOTABLE DESCENDANTS** Jacob's 12 sons were the ancestors of the 12 tribes of Israel. The entire nation of Israel came from these men. | | |
|---|---|---|
| REUBEN | none | |
| SIMEON | none | |
| LEVI | Aaron, Moses, Eli | John the Baptist |
| JUDAH | David, Jesus | |
| DAN | Samson | |
| NAPHTALI | Barak, Elijah (?) | |
| GAD | Jephthah (?) | |
| ASHER | none | |
| ISSACHAR | none | |
| ZEBULUN | none | |
| JOSEPH | Joshua, Gideon, Samuel | |
| BENJAMIN | Saul, Esther, Paul | |

**50:1-11** When Jacob died at the age of 147, Joseph wept and mourned for months. When someone close to us dies, we need a long period of time to work through our grief. Crying and sharing our feelings with others helps us recover and go on with life. Allow yourself and others the freedom to grieve over the loss of a loved one, and give yourself time enough to complete your grieving process.

**50:2, 3** Embalming was typical for Egyptians but unusual for nomadic shepherds. Believing that the dead went to the next world in their physical bodies, the Egyptians embalmed bodies

to preserve them so they could function in the world to come. Jacob's family allowed him to be embalmed as a sign of courtesy and respect to the Egyptians.

**50:5** Joseph had proven himself trustworthy as Pharaoh's adviser. Because of his good record, Pharaoh had little doubt that he would return to Egypt as promised after burying his father in Canaan. Privileges and freedom often result when we have demonstrated our trustworthiness. Since trust must be built gradually over time, take every opportunity to prove your reliability even in minor matters.

⁶Pharaoh agreed to Joseph's request. "Go and bury your father, as you promised," he said. ⁷So Joseph went, with a great number of Pharaoh's counselors and advisers—all the senior officers of Egypt. ⁸Joseph also took his brothers and the entire household of Jacob. But they left their little children and flocks and herds in the land of Goshen. ⁹So a great number of chariots, cavalry, and people accompanied Joseph.

¹⁰When they arrived at the threshing floor of Atad, near the Jordan River, they held a very great and solemn funeral, with a seven-day period of mourning for Joseph's father. ¹¹The local residents, the Canaanites, renamed the place Abel-miz-raim,* for they said, "This is a place of very deep mourning for these Egyptians." ¹²So Jacob's sons did as he had commanded them. ¹³They carried his body to the land of Canaan and buried it there in the cave of Machpelah. This is the cave that Abraham had bought for a permanent burial place in the field of Ephron the Hittite, near Mamre.

### Joseph Reassures His Brothers

¹⁴Then Joseph returned to Egypt with his brothers and all who had accompanied him to his father's funeral. ¹⁵But now that their father was dead, Joseph's brothers became afraid. "Now Joseph will pay us back for all the evil we did to him," they said. ¹⁶So they sent this message to Joseph: "Before your father died, he instructed us ¹⁷to say to you: 'Forgive your brothers for the great evil they did to you.' So we, the servants of the God of your father, beg you to forgive us." When Joseph received the message, he broke down and wept. ¹⁸Then his brothers came and bowed low before him. "We are your slaves," they said.

¹⁹But Joseph told them, "Don't be afraid of me. Am I God, to judge and punish you? ²⁰As far as I am concerned, God turned into good what you meant for evil. He brought me to the high position I have today so I could save the lives of many people. ²¹No, don't be afraid. Indeed, I myself will take care of you and your families." And he spoke very kindly to them, reassuring them.

### The Death of Joseph

²²So Joseph and his brothers and their families continued to live in Egypt. Joseph was 110 years old when he died. ²³He lived to see three generations of descendants of his son Ephraim and the children of Manasseh's son Makir, who were treated as if they were his own.

²⁴"Soon I will die," Joseph told his brothers, "but God will surely come for you, to lead you out of this land of Egypt. He will bring you back to the land he vowed to give to the descendants of Abraham, Isaac, and Jacob."

**50:11** *Abel-mizraim* means "mourning of the Egyptians."

50:8
Gen 45:10
50:9
Gen 41:43

50:12
Gen 49:29
50:13
Gen 23:16-18

50:15
Gen 42:21-22
50:16
Gen 49:29
50:17
Gen 45:5, 7
Matt 6:14
Luke 6:27
Rom 12:19
50:18
Gen 37:7-10
50:19
Gen 30:2
50:20
Gen 37:26-27
50:21
Gen 45:11

50:24
Gen 13:15; 28:13

---

**50:12, 13** Abraham had purchased the cave in the field of Machpelah as a burial place for his wife Sarah (23:1-9). It was to be a burial place for his entire family. Jacob was Abraham's grandson, and Jacob's sons returned to Canaan to bury him in this cave along with Abraham and Isaac. Their desire to be buried in this cave expressed their faith in God's promise to give their descendants the land of Canaan.

**50:15-21** Now that Jacob (or Israel) was dead, the brothers feared revenge from Joseph. Could he really have forgiven them for selling him into slavery? But to their surprise, Joseph not only forgave them but reassured them, offering to care for them and their families. Joseph's forgiveness was complete. He demonstrated how God graciously accepts us even though we don't deserve it. Because God forgives us even when we have ignored or rejected him, we should graciously forgive others.

**50:20** God brought good from the brothers' evil deed, Potiphar's wife's false accusation, the cup-bearer's neglect, and seven years of famine. The experiences in Joseph's life taught him that God brings good from evil for those who

trust him. Do you trust God enough to wait patiently for him to bring good out of bad situations? You can trust him because, as Joseph learned, God can overrule people's evil intentions to bring about his intended results.

**50:24** Joseph was ready to die. He had no doubts that God would keep his promise and one day bring the Israelites back to their homeland. What a tremendous example! The secret of that kind of faith is a lifetime of trusting God. Your faith is like a muscle—it grows with exercise, gaining strength over time. After a lifetime of exercising trust, your faith can be as strong as Joseph's. Then at your death, you can be confident that God will fulfill all his promises to you and to all those faithful to him who may live after you.

**50:24** This verse sets the stage for what would begin to happen in Exodus and come to completion in Joshua. God was going to make Jacob's family into a great nation, lead them out of Egypt, and bring them into the land he had promised them. The nation would rely heavily on this promise, and Joseph emphasized his belief that God would do what he had promised.

**50:25**
Exod 13:19
Josh 24:32
Heb 11:22
**50:26**
Exod 1:6

<sup>25</sup>Then Joseph made the sons of Israel swear an oath, and he said, "When God comes to lead us back to Canaan, you must take my body back with you." <sup>26</sup>So Joseph died at the age of 110. They embalmed him, and his body was placed in a coffin in Egypt.

---

**50:26** The book of Genesis gives us rich descriptions of the lives of many great men and women who walked with God. They sometimes succeeded and often failed. Yet we learn much by reading the biographies of these people. Where did they get their motivation and courage? They got it by realizing God was with them despite their inadequacies. Knowing this should encourage us to be faithful to God, to rely on him for guidance, and to utilize the potential he has given us.

# EXODUS

## VITAL STATISTICS

**PURPOSE:**
To record the events of Israel's
deliverance from Egypt and
development as a nation

**AUTHOR:**
Moses

**DATE WRITTEN:**
1450–1410 B.C., approximately
the same as Genesis

**WHERE WRITTEN:**
In the wilderness during Israel's
wanderings, somewhere in the
Sinai peninsula

**SETTING:**
Egypt. God's people, once
highly favored in the land, are
now slaves. God is about to set
them free.

**KEY VERSES:**
"Then the LORD told him, 'You
can be sure I have seen the
misery of my people in Egypt.
I have heard their cries for
deliverance from their harsh
slave drivers. Yes, I am aware
of their suffering. . . . Now go,
for I am sending you to Pharaoh.
You will lead my people, the
Israelites, out of Egypt'"
(3:7, 10).

**KEY PEOPLE:**
Moses, Miriam, Pharaoh,
Pharaoh's daughter, Jethro,
Aaron, Joshua, Bezalel

**KEY PLACES:**
Egypt, Goshen, Nile River,
Midian, Red Sea, Sinai penin-
sula, Mount Sinai

**SPECIAL FEATURES:**
Exodus relates more miracles
than any other Old Testament
book and is noted for containing
the Ten Commandments

GET UP . . . leave . . . take off—these words
are good ones for those trapped or enslaved.
Some resist their marching orders, however,
preferring present surroundings to a new, unknown environment. It's not easy to trade the
comfortable security of the known for an uncertain future. But what if God gives the order to
move? Will we follow his lead? Exodus describes a series of God's calls and the responses
of his people.

Four hundred years had passed since Joseph
moved his family to Egypt. These descendants of Abraham had now
grown to over two million strong. To Egypt's new pharaoh, these
Hebrews were foreigners, and their numbers were frightening. Pharaoh
decided to make them slaves so they wouldn't upset his balance of
power. As it turned out, that was his biggest mistake, for God then came
to the rescue of his people.

Through a series of strange events, a Hebrew boy named Moses
became a prince in Pharaoh's palace and then an outcast in a wilderness
land. God visited Moses in the mysterious flames of a burning bush, and
after some discussion, Moses agreed to return to Egypt to lead God's
people out of slavery. Pharaoh was confronted, and through a cycle of
plagues and promises made and broken, Israel was torn from his grasp.

It was no easy task to mobilize this mass of humanity, but they
marched out of Egypt, through the Red Sea, and into the wilderness
behind Moses and the pillars of cloud and fire. Despite continual
evidence of God's love and power, the people complained and began to
yearn for their days in Egypt. God provided for their physical and
spiritual needs with food and a place to worship, but he also judged their
disobedience and unbelief. Then in the dramatic Sinai meeting with
Moses, God gave his laws for right living.

God led Moses and the nation of Israel, and he wants to lead us as
well. Is he preparing you, like Moses, for a specific task? He will be
with you; obey and follow. Is he delivering you from an enemy or a
temptation? Trust him, and do what he says. Have you heard his clear
moral directions? Read, study, and obey his Word. Is he calling you to
true worship? Discover God's presence in your life, in your home, and
in the body of assembled believers. Exodus is the exciting story of
God's guidance. Read with the determination to follow God wherever
he leads.

XXXXXXXXXXXX EXODUS

| Moses born 1526 (1350) | | Exodus from Egypt 1446 (1280) | Ten Command- ments given 1445 (1279) | Israel enters Canaan 1406 (1240) | Judges begin to rule 1375 (1220) |
|---|---|---|---|---|---|

## THE BLUEPRINT

**A. ISRAEL IN EGYPT (1:1—12:30)**
1. Slavery in Egypt
2. God chooses Moses
3. God sends Moses to Pharaoh
4. Plagues strike Egypt
5. The Passover

When the Israelites were enslaved in Egypt, God heard their cries and rescued them. We can be confident that God still hears the cries of his people. Just as he delivered the Israelites from their captors, he delivers us from sin, death, and evil.

**B. ISRAEL IN THE WILDERNESS (12:31—18:27)**
1. The Exodus
2. Crossing the sea
3. Complaining in the wilderness

After crossing the Red Sea, the Israelites became quarrelsome and discontent. Like the Israelites, we find it easy to complain and be dissatisfied. Christians still have struggles, but we should never allow difficulties and unpleasant circumstances to turn us away from trusting God.

**C. ISRAEL AT SINAI (19:1—40:38)**
1. Giving the law
2. Tabernacle instructions
3. Breaking the law
4. Tabernacle construction

God revealed his law to the Israelites at Sinai. Through the law, they learned more about what God is like and how he expected his people to live. The law is still instructional for us, for it exposes our sin and shows us God's standard for living.

## MEGATHEMES

| THEME | EXPLANATION | IMPORTANCE |
|---|---|---|
| Slavery | During the Israelites 400-year stay in the land of Egypt, they became enslaved to the Egyptians. Pharaoh, the king of Egypt, oppressed them cruelly. They prayed to God for deliverance from this situation. | Like the Israelites, we need both human and divine leadership to escape from the slavery of sin. After their escape, the memory of slavery helped the Israelites learn to treat others generously. We need to stand against those who oppress others. |
| Rescue/ Redemption | God rescued Israel through the leader Moses and through mighty miracles. The Passover celebration was an annual reminder of their escape from slavery. | God delivers us from the slavery of sin. Jesus Christ celebrated the Passover with his disciples at the Last Supper and then went on to rescue us from sin by dying in our place. |
| Guidance | God guided Israel out of Egypt by using the plagues, Moses' heroic courage, the miracle of the Red Sea, and the Ten Commandments. God is a trustworthy guide. | Although God is all-powerful and can do miracles, he normally leads us by wise leadership and team effort. His Word gives us the wisdom to make daily decisions and govern our lives. |
| Ten Commandments | God's law system had three parts. The Ten Commandments were the first part, containing the absolutes of spiritual and moral life. The civil law was the second part giving the people rules to manage their lives. The ceremonial law was the third part, showing them patterns for building the Tabernacle and for regular worship. | God was teaching Israel the importance of choice and responsibility. When they obeyed the conditions of the law, he blessed them; if they forgot or disobeyed, he punished them or allowed calamities to come. Many great countries of the world base their laws on the moral system set up in the book of Exodus. God's moral law is valid today. |
| The Nation | God founded the nation of Israel to be the source of truth and salvation to all the world. His relationship to his people was loving yet firm. The Israelites had no army, schools, governors, mayors, or police when they left Egypt. God had to instruct them in their constitutional laws and daily practices. He showed them how to worship and how to have national holidays. | Israel's newly formed nation had all the behavioral characteristics of Christians today. We are often disorganized, sometimes rebellious, and sometimes victorious. God's Person and Word are still our only guides. If our churches reflect his leadership, they will be effective in serving him. |

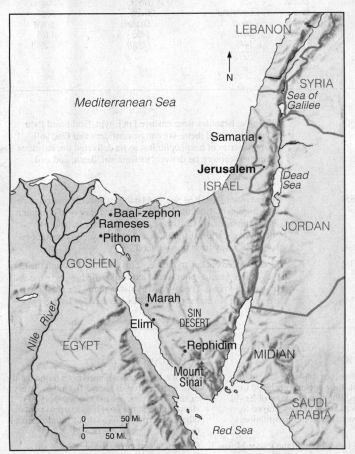

Modern names and boundaries are shown in gray.

spokesmen to Pharaoh, God worked a series of dramatic miracles in the land of Egypt to convince Pharaoh to let the Hebrews go (5:1—12:33). When finally freed, the entire nation set out with the riches of Egypt (12:34–36). One of their first stops was at Baal-zephon (14:2), where Pharaoh, who had changed his mind, chased the Hebrews and trapped them against the sea. But God parted the waters and led the people through the sea on dry land. When Pharaoh's army tried to pursue, the waters collapsed around them, and they were drowned (14:5–31).

**6 Marah** Moses now led the people southward. The long trek across the desert brought hot tempers and parched throats for this mass of people. At Marah, the water they found was bitter, but God sweetened it (15:22–25).

**7 Elim** As they continued their journey, the Hebrews (now called Israelites) came to Elim, an oasis with 12 springs (15:27).

**8 Sin Desert** Leaving Elim, the people headed into the Sin Desert. Here the people became hungry, so God provided them with manna that came from heaven and covered the ground each morning (16:1, 13–15). The people ate this manna until they entered the Promised Land.

**9 Rephidim** Moses led the people to Rephidim where they found no water. But God miraculously provided water from a rock (17:1, 5, 6). Here the Israelites encountered their first test in battle: the Amalekites attacked and were defeated (17:9–13). Moses' father-in-law, Jethro, then arrived on the scene with some sound advice on delegating responsibilities (18).

**10 Mount Sinai** God had previously appeared to Moses on this mountain and commissioned him to lead Israel (3:1–10). Now Moses returned with the people God had asked him to lead. For almost a year the people camped at the foot of Mount Sinai. During this time God gave them his Ten Commandments as well as other laws for right living. He also provided the blueprint for building the Tabernacle (19—40).

God was forging a holy nation, prepared to live for and serve him alone.

**1 Goshen** This area was given to Jacob and his family when they moved to Egypt (Genesis 47:5, 6). It became the Hebrews' homeland for 400 years and remained separate from the main Egyptian centers, for Egyptian culture looked down upon shepherds and nomads. As the years passed, Jacob's family grew into a large nation (1:7).

**2, 3 Pithom and Rameses** During the Israelites' stay in the land of Egypt, a pharaoh came to the throne who had no respect for these descendants of Joseph and feared their large numbers. He forced them into slavery in order to oppress and subdue them. Out of their slave labor, the supply cities of Pithom and Rameses were built (1:11).

**4 Midian** Moses, an Egyptian prince who was born a Hebrew, killed an Egyptian and fled for his life to Midian. Here he became a shepherd and married a woman named Zipporah. It was while he was here that God commissioned him for the job of leading the Hebrew people out of Egypt (2:15—4:31).

**5 Baal-zephon** Slavery was not to last because God planned to deliver his people. After choosing Moses and Aaron to be his

## A. ISRAEL IN EGYPT (1:1—12:30)

Joseph brought his family to Egypt and protected them there. But after Joseph's death, as they multiplied into a nation, they were forced into slavery. God then prepared Moses to free his people from slavery and lead them out of Egypt. To help Moses, God unleashed ten plagues upon the land. After the tenth plague, Pharaoh let the people go. On the night before the great Exodus, God's new nation celebrated the Passover. Just as God delivered Israel from Egypt, he delivers us from sin, death, and evil.

## 1. Slavery in Egypt

**1:1**
Gen 46:8-27

**1:5**
Gen 46:26

**1:6**
Gen 50:26
Acts 7:15-16

**1:7**
Gen 12:2; 35:11;
46:3; 47:27; 48:4
†Acts 7:17

**1:8**
Acts 7:18-19

**1:9**
Ps 105:25

**1:10**
Ps 105:24-25
Acts 7:17-19

**1:11**
Exod 2:11; 3:7

**1:14**
Exod 2:23

**1:16**
Acts 7:19

**1** These are the sons of Jacob* who went with their father to Egypt, each with his family: 2Reuben, Simeon, Levi, Judah, 3Issachar, Zebulun, Benjamin, 4Dan, Naphtali, Gad, and Asher. 5Joseph was already down in Egypt. In all, Jacob had seventy* direct descendants.

6In time, Joseph and each of his brothers died, ending that generation. 7But their descendants had many children and grandchildren. In fact, they multiplied so quickly that they soon filled the land. 8Then a new king came to the throne of Egypt who knew nothing about Joseph or what he had done. 9He told his people, "These Israelites are becoming a threat to us because there are so many of them. 10We must find a way to put an end to this. If we don't and if war breaks out, they will join our enemies and fight against us. Then they will escape from the country."

11So the Egyptians made the Israelites their slaves and put brutal slave drivers over them, hoping to wear them down under heavy burdens. They forced them to build the cities of Pithom and Rameses as supply centers for the king. 12But the more the Egyptians oppressed them, the more quickly the Israelites multiplied! The Egyptians soon became alarmed 13and decided to make their slavery more bitter still. 14They were ruthless with the Israelites, forcing them to make bricks and mortar and to work long hours in the fields.

15Then Pharaoh, the king of Egypt, gave this order to the Hebrew midwives, Shiphrah and Puah. 16"When you help the Hebrew women give birth, kill all the boys as soon as they are born. Allow only the baby girls to live." 17But because the midwives feared God, they refused to obey the king and allowed the boys to live, too.

**1:1** Hebrew *Israel.*   **1:5** Dead Sea Scrolls and Greek version read *seventy-five;* see notes on Gen 46:27.

---

**1:1** The children of Israel, or Israelites, were the descendants of Jacob, whose name was changed to Israel after he wrestled with the angel (see Genesis 32:24-30). Jacob's family had moved to Egypt at the invitation of Joseph, one of Jacob's sons who had become a great ruler under Pharaoh. Jacob's family grew into a large nation. But as foreigners and newcomers, their lives were quite different from the Egyptians. The Hebrews worshiped one God; the Egyptians worshiped many gods. The Hebrews were wanderers; the Egyptians had a deeply rooted culture. The Hebrews were shepherds; the Egyptians were builders. The Hebrews were also physically separated from the Egyptians: They lived in Goshen, north of the great Egyptian cultural centers.

**1:9, 10** Pharaoh was afraid the Israelites were becoming so numerous that they would organize and threaten his kingdom, so he made them slaves and oppressed them to kill their spirit and stop their growth. Slavery was an ancient practice used by almost all nations to employ conquered people and other captives. Most likely, the great pyramids of Egypt were built with slave labor. Although Israel was not a conquered nation, the people were foreigners and thus lacked the rights of native Egyptians.

**1:11** There were levels of slavery in Egypt. Some slaves worked long hours in mud pits while others were skilled carpenters, jewelers, and craftsmen. Regardless of their skill or level, all slaves were watched closely by ruthless slave drivers, supervisors whose assignment was to keep the slaves working as fast as possible. They were specialists at making a slave's life miserable.

**1:11** Ancient records indicate that these cities were built in 1290 B.C., which is why some scholars believe the Exodus occurred early in the 13th century. Looking at other evidence, however, other scholars believe the Hebrews left Egypt in 1446 B.C. How could they build two cities 150 years after they left? These scholars suggest that Rameses II, the pharaoh in 1290 B.C., did not build the cities of Pithom and Rameses. Instead, he renamed two cities that actually had been built 150 years previously. It was a common practice for an Egyptian ruler to make improvements on a city and then take credit for building it, thus wiping out all records of previous founders. Also see the second note on 13:17, 18.

**1:12** The Egyptians tried to wear down the Hebrew people by forcing them into slavery and mistreating them. Instead, the Hebrews multiplied and grew stronger. When we are burdened or mistreated, we may feel defeated. But our burdens can make us stronger and develop qualities in us that will prepare us for the future. We cannot be overcomers without troubles to overcome. Be true to God in the hard times because even the worst situations can make us better people.

**1:15-17** Shiphrah and Puah may have been supervisors over the midwives, or else these two were given special mention. Hebrew midwives helped women give birth and cared for the baby until the mother was stronger. When Pharaoh ordered the midwives to kill the Hebrew baby boys, he was asking the wrong group of people. Midwives were committed to helping babies be born, not to killing them. These women showed great courage and love for God by risking their lives to disobey Pharaoh's command.

**1:17-21** Against Pharaoh's orders, the midwives spared the Hebrew babies. Their faith in God gave them the courage to take a stand for what they knew was right. In this situation, disobeying the authority was proper. God does not expect us to obey those in authority when they ask us to disobey him or his Word. The Bible is filled with examples of those who were willing to sacrifice their very lives in order to obey God or save others. Esther and Mordecai (Esther 3:2; 4:13-16) and Shadrach, Meshach, and Abednego (Daniel 3:16-18) are some of the people who took a

¹⁸Then the king called for the midwives. "Why have you done this?" he demanded. "Why have you allowed the boys to live?"

¹⁹"Sir," they told him, "the Hebrew women are very strong. They have their babies so quickly that we cannot get there in time! They are not slow in giving birth like Egyptian women."

²⁰So God blessed the midwives, and the Israelites continued to multiply, growing more and more powerful. ²¹And because the midwives feared God, he gave them families of their own.

²²Then Pharaoh gave this order to all his people: "Throw all the newborn Israelite boys into the Nile River. But you may spare the baby girls."

## 2. God chooses Moses

*The Birth of Moses*

**2** During this time, a man and woman from the tribe of Levi got married. ²The woman became pregnant and gave birth to a son. She saw what a beautiful baby he was and kept him hidden for three months. ³But when she could no longer hide him, she got a little basket made of papyrus reeds and waterproofed it with tar and pitch. She put the baby in the basket and laid it among the reeds along the edge of the Nile River. ⁴The baby's sister then stood at a distance, watching to see what would happen to him.

⁵Soon after this, one of Pharaoh's daughters came down to bathe in the river, and her servant girls walked along the riverbank. When the princess saw the little basket among the reeds, she told one of her servant girls to get it for her. ⁶As the princess opened it, she found the baby boy. His helpless cries touched her heart. "He must be one of the Hebrew children," she said.

⁷Then the baby's sister approached the princess. "Should I go and find one of the Hebrew women to nurse the baby for you?" she asked.

⁸"Yes, do!" the princess replied. So the girl rushed home and called the baby's mother.

⁹"Take this child home and nurse him for me," the princess told her. "I will pay you for your help." So the baby's mother took her baby home and nursed him.

**1:19**
Josh 2:4-6
2 Sam 17:20

**1:20**
Exod 1:12

**1:22**
Acts 7:19

**2:1**
Exod 6:20
Num 26:59

**2:2**
Acts 7:20
Heb 11:23

**2:3**
Gen 6:14
Isa 18:2

**2:4**
Exod 15:20
Num 26:59

**2:5**
Exod 7:15; 8:20
Acts 7:21

---

bold stand for what was right. Whole nations can be caught up in immorality (racial hatred, slavery, prison cruelty); thus following the majority or the authority is not always right. Whenever we are ordered to disobey God's Word, we must "obey God rather than human authority" (Acts 5:29).

**1:19-21** Did God bless the Hebrew midwives for lying to Pharaoh? God blessed them not because they lied, but because they saved the lives of innocent children. This doesn't mean that a lie was necessarily the best way to answer Pharaoh. The midwives were blessed, however, for not violating the higher law of God that forbids the senseless slaughter of innocent lives.

**2:1, 2** Although a name is not mentioned yet, the baby in this story was Moses. Moses' mother and father were named Jochebed and Amram. His brother was Aaron and his sister, Miriam.

**2:3** This tiny boat made of papyrus reeds was fashioned by a woman who knew what she was doing. Egyptian riverboats were made with these same reeds and waterproofed with tar. The reeds, which grew as tall as 16 feet, could be gathered in swampy areas along the Nile. Thus a small basket hidden among the reeds would be well insulated from the weather and difficult to see.

**2:3ff** Moses' mother knew how wrong it would be to destroy her child. But there was little she could do to change Pharaoh's new law. Her only alternative was to hide the child and later place him in a tiny papyrus basket on the river. God used her courageous act to place her son, the Hebrew of his choice, in the house of Pharaoh. Do you sometimes feel surrounded by evil and frustrated by how little you can do about it? When faced with evil, look for ways to act against it. Then trust God to use your effort, however small it seems, in his war against evil.

**2:5** Who was Pharaoh's daughter? There are two popular explanations. (1) Some think that Hatshepsut was the woman who pulled Moses from the river. Her husband was Pharaoh Thutmose II. (This would match the earlier Exodus date.) Apparently Hatshepsut could not have children, so Thutmose had a son by another woman, and this son became heir to the throne. Hatshepsut would have considered Moses a gift from the gods because now she had her own son who would be the legal heir to the throne. (2) Some think the princess who rescued baby Moses was the daughter of Rameses II, an especially cruel Pharaoh who would have made life miserable for the Hebrew slaves. (This would match the later Exodus date.)

**2:7, 8** Miriam, the baby's sister, saw that Pharaoh's daughter had discovered Moses. Quickly she took the initiative to suggest a nurse (her mother) who might care for the baby. The Bible doesn't say if Miriam was afraid to approach the Egyptian princess or if the princess was suspicious of the Hebrew girl. But Miriam did approach her, and the princess bought the services of Miriam and her mother. Their family was reunited. Special opportunities may come our way unexpectedly. Don't let the fear of what might happen cause you to miss an opportunity. Be alert for the opportunities God gives you, and take full advantage of them.

**2:9** Moses' mother was reunited with her baby! God used her courageous act of saving and hiding her baby to begin his plan to rescue his people from Egypt. God doesn't need much from us to accomplish his plan for our lives. Focusing on our human predicament may paralyze us because the situation may appear humanly impossible. But concentrating on God and his power will help us see the way out. Right now you may feel unable to see through your troubles. Focus instead on God, and trust him for the way out. That is all he needs to begin his work in you.

**2:10**
1 Sam 1:20
2 Sam 22:17

<sup>10</sup>Later, when he was older, the child's mother brought him back to the princess, who adopted him as her son. The princess named him Moses,* for she said, "I drew him out of the water."

### Moses Escapes to Midian

**2:11**
Acts 7:23-24
Heb 11:24-26

<sup>11</sup>Many years later, when Moses had grown up, he went out to visit his people, the Israelites, and he saw how hard they were forced to work. During his visit, he saw an Egyptian beating one of the Hebrew slaves. <sup>12</sup>After looking around to make sure no one was watching, Moses killed the Egyptian and buried him in the sand.

**2:12**
Acts 7:24

**2:13**
Acts 7:26-28

<sup>13</sup>The next day, as Moses was out visiting his people again, he saw two Hebrew men fighting. "What are you doing, hitting your neighbor like that?" Moses said to the one in the wrong.

**2:14**
†Acts 7:27, 35

<sup>14</sup>"Who do you think you are?" the man replied. "Who appointed you to be our prince and judge? Do you plan to kill me as you killed that Egyptian yesterday?"

Moses was badly frightened because he realized that everyone knew what he had done. <sup>15</sup>And sure enough, when Pharaoh heard about it, he gave orders to have Moses arrested and killed. But Moses fled from Pharaoh and escaped to the land of Midian.

**2:15**
Acts 7:29

**2:16**
Gen 24:11
Exod 3:1; 18:1

When Moses arrived in Midian, he sat down beside a well. <sup>16</sup>Now it happened that the priest of Midian had seven daughters who came regularly to this well to draw water and fill the water troughs for their father's flocks. <sup>17</sup>But other shepherds would often come and chase the girls and their flocks away. This time, however, Moses came to their aid, rescuing the girls from the shepherds. Then he helped them draw water for their flocks.

**2:17**
Gen 29:10

**2:18**
Num 10:29

<sup>18</sup>When the girls returned to Reuel, their father, he asked, "How did you get the flocks watered so quickly today?"

<sup>19</sup>"An Egyptian rescued us from the shepherds," they told him. "And then he drew water for us and watered our flocks."

**2:20**
Gen 18:5

**2:21**
Exod 4:25; 18:2
Acts 7:29

<sup>20</sup>"Well, where is he then?" their father asked. "Did you just leave him there? Go and invite him home for a meal!"

<sup>21</sup>Moses was happy to accept the invitation, and he settled down to live with them. In time, Reuel gave Moses one of his daughters, Zipporah, to be his wife. <sup>22</sup>Later they had a baby boy, and Moses named him Gershom * for he said, "I have been a stranger in a foreign land."

**2:22**
Gen 23:4
Heb 11:13

**2:10** *Moses* sounds like a Hebrew term that means "to draw out." **2:22** *Gershom* sounds like a Hebrew term that means "a stranger there."

---

**2:12-14** Moses tried to make sure no one was watching before he killed the Egyptian. But as it turned out, someone did see, and Moses had to flee the country. Sometimes we mistakenly think we can get away with doing wrong if no one sees or catches us. Sooner or later, however, doing wrong will catch up with us as it did with Moses. Even if we are not caught in this life, we will still have to face God and his evaluation of our actions.

**2:15** To escape punishment for killing the Egyptian, Moses ran away to Midian. He became a stranger in a strange land separated from his home and family. It took many years after this incident for Moses to be ready to serve God. But he trusted God instead of fearing the king (Hebrews 11:27). We may feel abandoned or isolated because of something we have done. But though we feel afraid and separated, we should not give up. Moses didn't. He trusted God to deliver him, no matter how dark his past or bleak his future.

**2:17** How did Moses handle these shepherds so easily? As an Egyptian prince, Moses would have been well trained in the Egyptian military, the most advanced army in the world. Even a large group of shepherds would have been no match for the sophisticated fighting techniques of this trained warrior.

**2:18** Reuel is also called Jethro in 3:1.

**2:23-25** God's rescue doesn't always come the moment we want it. God had promised to bring the Hebrew slaves out of Egypt (Genesis 15:16; 46:3, 4). The people had waited a long time for that promise to be kept, but God rescued them when

he knew the right time had come. God knows the best time to act. When you feel that God has forgotten you in your troubles, remember that God has a time schedule we can't see.

**MOSES FLEES TO MIDIAN**
After murdering an Egyptian, Moses escaped into Midian. There he married Zipporah and became a shepherd.

23 Years passed, and the king of Egypt died. But the Israelites still groaned beneath their burden of slavery. They cried out for help, and their pleas for deliverance rose up to God. 24 God heard their cries and remembered his covenant promise to Abraham, Isaac, and Jacob. 25 He looked down on the Israelites and felt deep concern for their welfare.

### Moses and the Burning Bush

**3** One day Moses was tending the flock of his father-in-law, Jethro,* the priest of Midian, and he went deep into the wilderness near Sinai,* the mountain of God. 2 Suddenly, the angel of the LORD appeared to him as a blazing fire in a bush. Moses was amazed because the bush was engulfed in flames, but it didn't burn up. 3 "Amazing!" Moses said to himself. "Why isn't that bush burning up? I must go over to see this."

4 When the LORD saw that he had caught Moses' attention, God called to him from the bush, "Moses! Moses!"

"Here I am!" Moses replied.

5 "Do not come any closer," God told him. "Take off your sandals, for you are standing on holy ground." 6 Then he said, "I am the God of your ancestors—the God of Abraham, the God of Isaac, and the God of Jacob." When Moses heard this, he hid his face in his hands because he was afraid to look at God.

7 Then the LORD told him, "You can be sure I have seen the misery of my people in Egypt. I have heard their cries for deliverance from their harsh slave drivers. Yes, I am aware of their suffering. 8 So I have come to rescue them from the Egyptians and lead them out of Egypt into their own good and spacious land. It is a land flowing with milk and honey—the land where the Canaanites, Hittites, Amorites, Perizzites, Hivites, and Jebusites live. 9 The cries of the people of Israel have reached me, and I have seen how the Egyptians have oppressed them with heavy tasks. 10 Now go, for I am sending you to Pharaoh. You will lead my people, the Israelites, out of Egypt."

11 "But who am I to appear before Pharaoh?" Moses asked God. "How can you expect me to lead the Israelites out of Egypt?"

12 Then God told him, "I will be with you. And this will serve as proof that I have sent you: When you have brought the Israelites out of Egypt, you will return here to worship God at this very mountain."

13 But Moses protested, "If I go to the people of Israel and tell them, 'The God of your

**2:23**
Exod 6:5, 9
Acts 7:34

**2:24**
Gen 22:16-18;
26:2-3; 28:13
Ps 105:10, 42

**3:2**
†Acts 7:30

**3:3**
†Acts 7:31

**3:5**
Gen 28:17
Josh 5:15
†Acts 7:33

**3:6**
†Matt 22:32
†Mark 12:26
†Luke 20:37
†Acts 3:13; 7:32

**3:7**
†Acts 7:34

**3:8**
Gen 15:18-19;
46:4; 50:24
Exod 3:17
Deut 6:3; 8:7-9;
11:9; 26:9

**3:10**
†Acts 7:34

**3:11**
Exod 4:10; 6:12

**3:12**
Exod 4:12; 19:2
†Acts 7:7

**3:13**
Exod 15:3

**3:1a** Moses' father-in-law went by two names, Jethro and Reuel.   **3:1b** Hebrew *Horeb,* another name for Sinai.

---

**3:1** What a contrast between Moses' life as an Egyptian prince and his life as a Midianite shepherd! As a prince he had everything done for him; he was the famous son of an Egyptian princess. As a shepherd he had to do everything for himself; he was holding the very job he had been taught to despise (Genesis 43:32; 46:33, 34), and he lived as an unknown foreigner. What a humbling experience this must have been for Moses! But God was preparing him for leadership. Living the life of a shepherd and nomad, Moses learned about the ways of the people he would be leading and also about life in the wilderness. Moses couldn't appreciate this lesson, but God was getting him ready to free Israel from Pharaoh's grasp.

**3:1** Mount Sinai is the place where God would give the people his revealed law (3:12).

**3:2** God spoke to Moses from an unexpected source: a burning bush. When Moses saw it, he went to investigate. God may use unexpected sources when communicating to us too, whether people, thoughts, or experiences. Be willing to investigate, and be open to God's surprises.

**3:2-4** Moses saw a burning bush and spoke with God. Many people in the Bible experienced God in visible (not necessarily human) form. Abraham saw the smoking firepot and blazing torch (Genesis 15:17); Jacob wrestled with a man (Genesis 32:24-29). When the slaves were freed from Egypt, God led them by pillars of cloud and fire (13:17-22). God made such appearances to encourage his new nation, to guide them, and to prove the reliability of his verbal message.

**3:5, 6** At God's command, Moses removed his sandals and covered his face. Taking off his shoes was an act of reverence, conveying his own unworthiness before God. God is our friend, but he is also our sovereign Lord. To approach him frivolously shows a lack of respect and sincerity. When you come to God in worship, do you approach him casually, or do you come as though you were an invited guest before a king? If necessary, adjust your attitude so it is suitable for approaching a holy God.

**3:8** This "land flowing with milk and honey" is the land of Israel and Jordan today. This was a poetic word picture expressing the beauty and productivity of the Promised Land.

**3:10ff** Moses made excuses because he felt inadequate for the job God asked him to do. It was natural for him to feel that way. He *was* inadequate all by himself. But God wasn't asking Moses to work alone. He offered other resources to help (God himself, Aaron, and the ability to do miracles). God often calls us to do tasks that seem too difficult, but he doesn't ask us to do them alone. God offers us his resources, just as he did to Moses. We should not hide behind our inadequacies, as Moses did, but look beyond ourselves to the great resources available. Then we can allow God to use our unique contributions.

**3:13-15** The Egyptians had many gods by many different names. Moses wanted to know God's name so the Hebrew people would know exactly who had sent him to them. God called himself I AM, a name describing his eternal power and unchangeable character. In a world where values, morals, and laws change constantly, we can find stability and security in our

ancestors has sent me to you,' they won't believe me. They will ask, 'Which god are you talking about? What is his name?' Then what should I tell them?"

<sup>14</sup>God replied, "I AM THE ONE WHO ALWAYS IS.* Just tell them, 'I AM has sent me to you.'" <sup>15</sup>God also said, "Tell them, 'The LORD,* the God of your ancestors—the God of Abraham, the God of Isaac, and the God of Jacob—has sent me to you.' This will be my name forever; it has always been my name, and it will be used throughout all generations.

<sup>16</sup>"Now go and call together all the leaders of Israel. Tell them, 'The LORD, the God of your ancestors—the God of Abraham, Isaac, and Jacob—appeared to me in a burning bush. He said, "You can be sure that I am watching over you and have seen what is happening to you in Egypt. <sup>17</sup>I promise to rescue you from the oppression of the Egyptians. I will lead you to the land now occupied by the Canaanites, Hittites, Amorites, Perizzites, Hivites, and Jebusites—a land flowing with milk and honey."'

<sup>18</sup>"The leaders of the people of Israel will accept your message. Then all of you must go straight to the king of Egypt and tell him, 'The LORD, the God of the Hebrews, has met with us. Let us go on a three-day journey into the wilderness to offer sacrifices to the LORD our God.'

<sup>19</sup>"But I know that the king of Egypt will not let you go except under heavy pressure. <sup>20</sup>So I will reach out and strike at the heart of Egypt with all kinds of miracles. Then at last he will let you go. <sup>21</sup>And I will see to it that the Egyptians treat you well. They will load you down with gifts so you will not leave empty-handed. <sup>22</sup>The Israelite women will ask for silver and gold jewelry and fine clothing from their Egyptian neighbors and their neighbors' guests. With this clothing, you will dress your sons and daughters. In this way, you will plunder the Egyptians!"

### Signs of the LORD's Power

**4** But Moses protested again, "Look, they won't believe me! They won't do what I tell them. They'll just say, 'The LORD never appeared to you.'"

<sup>2</sup>Then the LORD asked him, "What do you have there in your hand?"

"A shepherd's staff," Moses replied.

<sup>3</sup>"Throw it down on the ground," the LORD told him. So Moses threw it down, and it became a snake! Moses was terrified, so he turned and ran away.

<sup>4</sup>Then the LORD told him, "Take hold of its tail." So Moses reached out and grabbed it, and it became a shepherd's staff again.

<sup>5</sup>"Perform this sign, and they will believe you," the LORD told him. "Then they will

**Marginal references:**

**3:14** Exod 6:3; John 8:58; Rev 1:8; 4:8

**3:15** Pss 72:17; 102:12; 135:13; †Acts 3:13

**3:16** Exod 4:29

**3:17** Exod 3:8; Josh 24:11

**3:18** Exod 4:23; 5:1, 3; Num 23:4, 16

**3:19** Exod 5:2; 6:1; 7:4

**3:20** Exod 11:1; 12:31-33; Neh 9:10; Acts 7:36

**3:21** Exod 11:3

**3:22** Exod 11:2; 12:35

**4:1** Exod 3:15-16, 18

**4:3** Exod 7:8-12, 15

**4:5** Exod 4:31; 19:9

---

**3:14** Or *I AM WHO I AM*, or *I WILL BE WHAT I WILL BE*.   **3:15** Hebrew *Yahweh*; traditionally rendered *Jehovah*.

---

unchanging God. The God who appeared to Moses is the same God who can live in us today. Hebrews 13:8 says God is the same "yesterday, today, and forever." Because God's nature is stable and trustworthy, we are free to follow and enjoy him rather than spend our time trying to figure him out.

**3:14, 15** God reminded Moses of his covenant promises to Abraham (Genesis 12:1-3; 15; 17), Isaac (Genesis 26:2-5), and Jacob (Genesis 28:13-15), and used the name I AM to show his unchanging nature. What God promised to the great patriarchs hundreds of years earlier he would fulfill through Moses.

**3:16, 17** God told Moses to tell the people what he saw and heard at the burning bush. Our God is a God who acts and speaks. One of the most convincing ways to tell others about him is to describe what he has done and how he has spoken to his people. If you are trying to explain God to others, talk about what he has done for you, for people you know, or for people whose stories are told in the Bible.

**3:18-20** The leaders of Israel would accept God's message, and the leaders of Egypt would reject it. God knew what both reactions would be before they happened. This is more than good psychology—God knows the future. Any believer can trust his or her future to God because God already knows what is going to happen.

**3:22** The jewelry and clothing were not merely borrowed—they were asked for and easily received. The Egyptians were so glad to see the Israelites go that they sent them out with gifts. These items were used later in building the Tabernacle (35:5, 22). The promise of being able to plunder the Egyptians seemed impossible to Moses at this time.

**4:1** Moses' reluctance and fear were caused by overanticipation. He was worried about how the people might respond to him. We often build up events in our minds and then panic over what might go wrong. God does not ask us to go where he has not provided the means to help. Where he leads, trusting him to supply courage, confidence, and resources at the right moment.

**4:2-4** A shepherd's staff was commonly a three- to six-foot wooden rod with a curved hook at the top. The shepherd used it for walking, guiding his sheep, killing snakes, and many other tasks. Still, it was just a stick. But God used the simple shepherd's staff Moses carried as a sign to teach him an important lesson. God sometimes takes joy in using ordinary things for extraordinary purposes. What are the ordinary things in your life—your voice, a pen, a hammer, a broom, a musical instrument? While it is easy to assume God can use only special skills, you must not hinder his use of the everyday contributions you can make. Little did Moses imagine the power his simple staff would wield when it became the staff of God.

realize that the LORD, the God of their ancestors—the God of Abraham, the God of Isaac, and the God of Jacob—really has appeared to you."

6 Then the LORD said to Moses, "Put your hand inside your robe." Moses did so, and when he took it out again, his hand was white as snow with leprosy.* 7 "Now put your hand back into your robe again," the LORD said. Moses did, and when he took it out this time, it was as healthy as the rest of his body.

8 "If they do not believe the first miraculous sign, they will believe the second," the LORD said. 9 "And if they do not believe you even after these two signs, then take some water from the Nile River and pour it out on the dry ground. When you do, it will turn into blood."

10 But Moses pleaded with the LORD, "O Lord, I'm just not a good speaker. I never have been, and I'm not now, even after you have spoken to me. I'm clumsy with words."

11 "Who makes mouths?" the LORD asked him. "Who makes people so they can speak or not speak, hear or not hear, see or not see? Is it not I, the LORD? 12 Now go, and do as I have told you. I will help you speak well, and I will tell you what to say."

13 But Moses again pleaded, "Lord, please! Send someone else."

14 Then the LORD became angry with Moses. "All right," he said. "What about your brother, Aaron the Levite? He is a good speaker. And look! He is on his way to meet you now. And when he sees you, he will be very glad. 15 You will talk to him, giving him the words to say. I will help both of you to speak clearly, and I will tell you what to do. 16 Aaron will be your spokesman to the people, and you will be as God to him, telling him what to say. 17 And be sure to take your shepherd's staff along so you can perform the miraculous signs I have shown you."

### Moses Returns to Egypt

18 Then Moses went back home and talked it over with Jethro, his father-in-law. "With your permission," Moses said, "I would like to go back to Egypt to visit my family. I don't even know whether they are still alive."

"Go with my blessing," Jethro replied.

19 Before Moses left Midian, the LORD said to him, "Do not be afraid to return to Egypt, for all those who wanted to kill you are dead."

20 So Moses took his wife and sons, put them on a donkey, and headed back to the land of Egypt. In his hand he carried the staff of God.

**4:6** Or *with a contagious skin disease.* The Hebrew word used here can describe various skin diseases.

**4:6**
Num 12:10
2 Kgs 5:27

**4:7**
2 Kgs 5:14
Matt 8:3
Luke 17:12-14

**4:9**
Exod 7:17-21

**4:10**
Exod 3:11
Jer 1:6

**4:11**
Ps 94:9
Matt 11:5

**4:12**
Deut 18:15, 18
Matt 10:19-20
Mark 13:11

**4:14**
Exod 4:27

**4:15**
Isa 51:16
Jer 1:9

**4:16**
Exod 7:1; 18:19-20

**4:17**
Exod 14:16; 17:9

**4:19**
Exod 2:15, 23

**4:20**
Exod 18:3
Acts 7:29

---

**4:6, 7** This contagious skin disease was leprosy, one of the most feared diseases of this time. There was no cure, and a great deal of suffering preceded eventual death. Through this experience, Moses learned that God could cause or cure any kind of problem. He saw that God indeed had all power and was commissioning him to exercise that power to lead the Hebrews out of Egypt.

**4:10-13** Moses pleaded with God to let him out of his mission. After all, he was not a good speaker and would probably embarrass both himself and God. But God looked at Moses' problem quite differently. All Moses needed was some help, and who better than God could help him say and do the right things. God made his mouth and would give him the words to say. It is easy for us to focus on our weaknesses, but if God asks us to do something, then he will help us get the job done. If the job involves some of our weak areas, then we can trust that he will provide words, strength, courage, and ability where needed.

**4:14** God finally agreed to let Aaron speak for Moses. Moses' feelings of inadequacy were so strong that he could not trust even God's ability to help him. Moses had to deal with his deep sense of inadequacy many times. When we face difficult or frightening situations, we must be willing to let God help us.

**4:16** The phrase "you will be as God to him" means that Moses would tell Aaron what to say as God was telling him.

**4:17-20** Moses clung tightly to the shepherd's staff as he left for Egypt to face the greatest challenge of his life. The staff was his assurance of God's presence and power. When feeling uncertain,

some people need something to stabilize and reassure them. For assurance when facing great trials, God has given promises from his Word and examples from great heroes of faith. Any Christian may cling tightly to these.

**MOSES RETURNS TO EGYPT**
God appeared to Moses in a mysterious burning bush on Mount Sinai. Later Aaron met Moses at the mountain, and together they returned to Egypt, a 200-mile trip.

**4:21**
Exod 7:3, 13; 9:12
Deut 2:30
John 12:40

**4:22**
Isa 63:16; 64:8
Jer 31:9
Hos 11:1
Rom 9:4

**4:23**
Exod 5:1; 6:11;
7:16

**4:24**
Num 22:22
1 Chr 21:16

**4:25-26**
Josh 5:2-3

**4:27**
Exod 4:14

**4:28**
Exod 4:16

**4:29**
Exod 3:16

**4:30**
Exod 4:15

**4:31**
Exod 3:18; 12:27

²¹ Then the LORD reminded him, "When you arrive back in Egypt, go to Pharaoh and perform the miracles I have empowered you to do. But I will make him stubborn so he will not let the people go. ²² Then you will tell him, 'This is what the LORD says: Israel is my firstborn son. ²³ I commanded you to let him go, so he could worship me. But since you have refused, be warned! I will kill your firstborn son!'"

²⁴ On the journey, when Moses and his family had stopped for the night, the LORD confronted Moses* and was about to kill him. ²⁵ But Zipporah, his wife, took a flint knife and circumcised her son. She threw the foreskin at Moses' feet and said, "What a blood-smeared bridegroom you are to me!" ²⁶ (When she called Moses a "blood-smeared bridegroom," she was referring to the circumcision.) After that, the LORD left him alone.

²⁷ Now the LORD had said to Aaron, "Go out into the wilderness to meet Moses." So Aaron traveled to the mountain of God, where he found Moses and greeted him warmly. ²⁸ Moses then told Aaron everything the LORD had commanded them to do and say. And he told him about the miraculous signs they were to perform.

²⁹ So Moses and Aaron returned to Egypt and called the leaders of Israel to a meeting. ³⁰ Aaron told them everything the LORD had told Moses, and Moses performed the miraculous signs as they watched. ³¹ The leaders were soon convinced that the LORD had sent Moses and Aaron. And when they realized that the LORD had seen their misery and was deeply concerned for them, they all bowed their heads and worshiped.

### 3. God sends Moses to Pharaoh
*Moses and Aaron Speak to Pharaoh*

**5:1**
Exod 3:18; 4:23

**5** After this presentation to Israel's leaders, Moses and Aaron went to see Pharaoh. They told him, "This is what the LORD, the God of Israel, says: 'Let my people go, for they must go out into the wilderness to hold a religious festival in my honor.'"

**5:2**
Exod 3:19
Job 21:15

² "Is that so?" retorted Pharaoh. "And who is the LORD that I should listen to him and let Israel go? I don't know the LORD, and I will not let Israel go."

**5:3**
Exod 3:18
Deut 28:21

³ But Aaron and Moses persisted. "The God of the Hebrews has met with us," they declared. "Let us take a three-day trip into the wilderness so we can offer sacrifices to the LORD our God. If we don't, we will surely die by disease or the sword."

**5:4-5**
Exod 1:11

⁴ "Who do you think you are," Pharaoh shouted, "distracting the people from their tasks? Get back to work! ⁵ Look, there are many people here in Egypt, and you are stopping them from doing their work."

**4:24** Or *confronted Moses' son*; Hebrew reads *confronted him.*

---

**4:24-26** God was about to kill Moses because Moses had not circumcised his son. Why hadn't Moses done this? Remember that Moses had spent half his life in Pharaoh's palace and half his life in the Midianite wilderness. He might not have been too familiar with God's laws, especially since all the requirements of God's covenant with Israel (Genesis 17) had not been actively carried out for over 400 years. In addition, Moses' wife, due to her Midianite background, may have opposed circumcision. But Moses could not effectively serve as deliverer of God's people until he had fulfilled the conditions of God's covenant, and one of those conditions was circumcision. Before they could go any farther, Moses and his family had to follow God's commands completely. Under Old Testament law, failing to circumcise your son was to remove yourself and your family from God's blessings. Moses learned that disobeying God was even more dangerous than tangling with an Egyptian pharaoh.

**4:25, 26** Why did Zipporah perform the circumcision? It may have been Zipporah who, as a Midianite unfamiliar with the circumcision requirement, had persuaded Moses not to circumcise their son. If she prevented the action, now she would have to perform it. It is also possible that Moses became ill as a result of permitting disobedience, and so Zipporah had to perform the circumcision herself to save both her husband and son. This would not have made her happy—hence, her unflattering comment to Moses.

**5:1, 2** Pharaoh was familiar with many gods (Egypt was filled with them), but he had never heard of the God of Israel. Pharaoh assumed that the God of the Hebrew slaves couldn't be very powerful. At first, Pharaoh was not at all worried about Moses' message, for he had not yet seen any evidence of the Lord's power.

**5:3** Pharaoh would not listen to Moses and Aaron because he did not know or respect God. People who do not know God may not listen to his Word or his messengers. Like Moses and Aaron, we need to persist. When others reject you or your faith, don't be surprised or discouraged. Continue to tell them about God, trusting him to open minds and soften stubborn hearts.

**5:4-9** Moses and Aaron took their message to Pharaoh just as God directed. The unhappy result was harder work and more oppression for the Hebrews. Sometimes hardship comes as a result of obeying God. Are you following God but still suffering—or suffering even worse than before? If your life is miserable, don't assume you have fallen out of God's favor. You may be suffering for doing good in an evil world.

*Making Bricks without Straw*

⁶That same day Pharaoh sent this order to the slave drivers and foremen he had set over the people of Israel: ⁷"Do not supply the people with any more straw for making bricks. Let them get it themselves! ⁸But don't reduce their production quotas by a single brick. They obviously don't have enough to do. If they did, they wouldn't be talking about going into the wilderness to offer sacrifices to their God. ⁹Load them down with more work. Make them sweat! That will teach them to listen to these liars!"

¹⁰So the slave drivers and foremen informed the people: "Pharaoh has ordered us not to provide straw for you. ¹¹Go and get it yourselves! Find it wherever you can. But you must produce just as many bricks as before!" ¹²So the people scattered throughout the land in search of straw.

¹³The slave drivers were brutal. "Meet your daily quota of bricks, just as you did before!" they demanded. ¹⁴Then they whipped the Israelite foremen in charge of the work crews. "Why haven't you met your quotas either yesterday or today?" they demanded.

¹⁵So the Israelite foremen went to Pharaoh and pleaded with him. "Please don't treat us like this," they begged. ¹⁶"We are given no straw, but we are still told to make as many bricks as before. We are beaten for something that isn't our fault! It is the fault of your slave drivers for making such unreasonable demands."

¹⁷But Pharaoh replied, "You're just lazy! You obviously don't have enough to do. If you did, you wouldn't be saying, 'Let us go, so we can offer sacrifices to the LORD.' ¹⁸Now, get back to work! No straw will be given to you, but you must still deliver the regular quota of bricks."

¹⁹Since Pharaoh would not let up on his demands, the Israelite foremen could see that they were in serious trouble. ²⁰As they left Pharaoh's court, they met Moses and Aaron, who were waiting outside for them. ²¹The foremen said to them, "May the LORD judge you for getting us into this terrible situation with Pharaoh* and his officials. You have given them an excuse to kill us!"

²²So Moses went back to the LORD and protested, "Why have you mistreated your own people like this, Lord? Why did you send me? ²³Since I gave Pharaoh your message, he has been even more brutal to your people. You have not even begun to rescue them!"

*Promises of Deliverance*

**6** "Now you will see what I will do to Pharaoh," the LORD told Moses. "When he feels my powerful hand upon him, he will let the people go. In fact, he will be so anxious to get rid of them that he will force them to leave his land!"

²And God continued, "I am the LORD. ³I appeared to Abraham, to Isaac, and to Jacob as God Almighty,* though I did not reveal my name, the LORD,* to them. ⁴And I entered into a solemn covenant with them. Under its terms, I swore to give them the land of Canaan, where they were living. ⁵You can be sure that I have heard the groans of the people of Israel, who are now slaves to the Egyptians. I have remembered my covenant with them.

⁶"Therefore, say to the Israelites: 'I am the LORD, and I will free you from your

**5:21** Hebrew *for making us a stench in the nostrils of Pharaoh.*   **6:3a** Hebrew *El Shaddai.*   **6:3b** Hebrew *Yahweh;* traditionally rendered *Jehovah.*

| | |
|---|---|
| **5:6** Exod 3:7; 5:10, 14 | |
| **5:7** Gen 11:13 | |
| **5:14** Isa 10:24 | |
| **5:17** Exod 5:8 | |
| **5:21** Gen 16:5; 34:30 | |
| **5:22** Num 11:11 Jer 4:10 | |
| **5:23** Exod 3:8 | |
| **6:1** Exod 3:19-20; 11:1; 12:31 | |
| **6:3** Gen 17:1 Ps 83:18 Isa 52:6 | |
| **6:4** Gen 15:18 | |
| **6:5** Exod 2:23-24 | |
| **6:6** Exod 3:17; 13:3, 14 Deut 6:12; 26:8 | |

**5:7, 8** Mixing straw with mud made bricks stronger and more durable. Pharaoh had supplied the slaves with straw, but now he made them find their own straw and keep up their production quota as well.

**5:15-21** The foremen were caught in the middle. First they tried to get the people to produce the same amount; then they complained to Pharaoh; finally they turned on Moses. Perhaps you have felt caught in the middle at work, or in relationships in your family or church. Complaining or turning on the leadership does not solve the problem. In the case of these supervisors, God had a larger purpose in mind, just as he might have in your situation. So rather than turning on the leadership when you feel pressured by both sides, turn to God to see what else he might be doing in this situation.

**5:22, 23** Pharaoh had just increased the Hebrews' workload, and Moses protested that God had not rescued his people. Moses expected faster results and fewer problems. When God is at work, suffering, setbacks, and hardship may still occur. In James 1:2-4, we are encouraged to be happy when difficulties come our way. Problems develop our patience and character by teaching us to (1) trust God to do what is best for us, (2) look for ways to honor God in our present situation, (3) remember that God will not abandon us, and (4) watch for God's plan for us.

**6:6** Small problems need only small answers. But when we face great problems, God has an opportunity to exercise his great power. As the Hebrews' troubles grew steadily worse, God planned to intervene with his mighty power and perform great miracles to deliver them. How big are your problems? Big problems put you in a perfect position to watch God give big answers.

slavery in Egypt. I will redeem you with mighty power and great acts of judgment. ⁷I will make you my own special people, and I will be your God. And you will know that I am the LORD your God who has rescued you from your slavery in Egypt. ⁸I will bring you into the land I swore to give to Abraham, Isaac, and Jacob. It will be your very own property. I am the LORD!'"

⁹So Moses told the people what the LORD had said, but they wouldn't listen anymore. They had become too discouraged by the increasing burden of their slavery.

¹⁰Then the LORD said to Moses. ¹¹"Go back to Pharaoh, and tell him to let the people of Israel leave Egypt."

¹²"But LORD!" Moses objected. "My own people won't listen to me anymore. How can I expect Pharaoh to listen? I'm no orator!"

¹³But the LORD ordered Moses and Aaron to return to Pharaoh, king of Egypt, and to demand that he let the people of Israel leave Egypt.

### The Ancestors of Moses and Aaron

¹⁴These are the ancestors of clans from some of Israel's tribes:

The descendants of Reuben, Israel's eldest son, included Hanoch, Pallu, Hezron, and Carmi. Their descendants became the clans of Reuben.

¹⁵The descendants of Simeon included Jemuel, Jamin, Ohad, Jakin, Zohar, and Shaul (whose mother was a Canaanite). Their descendants became the clans of Simeon.

¹⁶These are the descendants of Levi, listed according to their family groups. In the first generation were Gershon, Kohath, and Merari. (Levi, their father, lived to be 137 years old.)

¹⁷ The descendants of Gershon included Libni and Shimei, each of whom is the ancestor of a clan

¹⁸ The descendants of Kohath included Amram, Izhar, Hebron, and Uzziel. (Kohath lived to be 133 years old.)

¹⁹ The descendants of Merari included Mahli and Mushi.

These are the clans of the Levites, listed according to their genealogies.

²⁰Amram married his father's sister Jochebed, and she bore him Aaron and Moses. (Amram lived to be 137 years old.)

²¹ The descendants of Izhar included Korah, Nepheg, and Zicri.

²² The descendants of Uzziel included Mishael, Elzaphan, and Sithri.

²³Aaron married Elisheba, the daughter of Amminadab and sister of Nahshon, and she bore him Nadab, Abihu, Eleazar, and Ithamar.

²⁴ The descendants of Korah included Assir, Elkanah, and Abiasaph. Their descendants became the clans of Korah.

²⁵Eleazar son of Aaron married one of the daughters of Putiel, and she bore him Phinehas.

**6:7**
Exod 16:12
Deut 4:20
Isa 60:16

**6:8**
Num 14:30
Josh 24:13

**6:11**
Exod 5:1; 7:2

**6:12**
Exod 4:10; 6:30

**6:14**
Gen 46:9
Num 26:5-11

**6:15**
Gen 46:10

**6:16**
Gen 46:11
Num 3:17
1 Chr 6:1, 16-19

**6:17**
Num 3:18-20
1 Chr 6:17

**6:18**
Num 3:25-30
1 Chr 6:2, 18

**6:19**
1 Chr 6:19

**6:20**
Exod 2:1-2
Num 26:59

**6:21**
Num 16:1

**6:22**
Lev 10:4

**6:23**
Ruth 4:19-20

**6:24**
1 Chr 6:22-23, 37

**6:25**
Num 25:7, 11
Josh 24:33

---

**6:6-8** God's promises in these verses were fulfilled to the letter when the Hebrews left Egypt. He freed them from slavery, became their God, and accepted them as his people. Then he led them toward the land he had promised. When the Hebrews were rescued from slavery, they portrayed the drama of salvation for all of us. When God redeems us from sin, he delivers us accepts us, and becomes our God. Then he leads us to a new life as we follow him.

**6:9-12** When Moses gave God's message to the people, they were too discouraged to listen. The Hebrews didn't want to hear any more about God and his promises because the last time they listened to Moses, all they got was more work and greater suffering. Sometimes a clear message from God is followed by a period when no change in the situation is apparent. During that time, seeming setbacks may turn people away from wanting to hear more about God. If you are a leader, don't give up. Keep bringing people God's message as Moses did. By focusing on God, who must be obeyed, rather than on the results to be achieved, good leaders see beyond temporary setbacks and reversals.

**6:10-12** Think how hard it must have been for Moses to bring God's message to Pharaoh when his own people had trouble believing it. Eventually the Hebrews believed that God had sent Moses, but for a time he must have felt very alone. Moses obeyed God, however, and what a difference it made! When the chances for success appear slim, remember that anyone can obey God when the task is easy and everyone is behind it. Only those with persistent faith can obey when the task seems impossible.

**6:14-25** This genealogy or family tree was placed here to identify more firmly Moses and Aaron. Genealogies were used to establish credentials and authority as well as outlining the history of a family.

**6:26** To bring the Israelites out of Egypt by their divisions means that they would be brought out in tribes, clans, or family groups.

These are the ancestors of the Levite clans, listed according to their family groups.

26 The Aaron and Moses named in this list are the same Aaron and Moses to whom the LORD said, "Lead all the people of Israel out of the land of Egypt, division by division." 27 They are the ones who went to Pharaoh to ask permission to lead the people from the land of Egypt.

28 At that time, the LORD had said to them, 29 "I am the LORD! Give Pharaoh the message I have given you." 30 This is the same Moses who had argued with the LORD, saying, "I can't do it! I'm no orator. Why should Pharaoh listen to me?"

**6:26** Exod 6:13

**6:29** Exod 6:2, 6, 8; 7:2

**6:30** Exod 4:10; 6:12

### Aaron's Staff Becomes a Snake

**7** Then the LORD said to Moses, "Pay close attention to this. I will make you seem like God to Pharaoh. Your brother, Aaron, will be your prophet; he will speak for you. 2 Tell Aaron everything I say to you and have him announce it to Pharaoh. He will demand that the people of Israel be allowed to leave Egypt. 3 But I will cause Pharaoh to be stubborn so I can multiply my miraculous signs and wonders in the land of Egypt. 4 Even then Pharaoh will refuse to listen to you. So I will crush Egypt with a series of disasters, after which I will lead the forces of Israel out with great acts of judgment. 5 When I show the Egyptians my power and force them to let the Israelites go, they will realize that I am the LORD."

6 So Moses and Aaron did just as the LORD had commanded them. 7 Moses was eighty years old, and Aaron was eighty-three at the time they made their demands to Pharaoh.

8 Then the LORD said to Moses and Aaron, 9 "Pharaoh will demand that you show him a miracle to prove that God has sent you. When he makes this demand, say to Aaron, 'Throw down your shepherd's staff,' and it will become a snake."

10 So Moses and Aaron went to see Pharaoh, and they performed the miracle just as the LORD had told them. Aaron threw down his staff before Pharaoh and his court, and it became a snake. 11 Then Pharaoh called in his wise men and magicians, and they did the same thing with their secret arts. 12 Their staffs became snakes, too! But then Aaron's snake swallowed up their snakes. 13 Pharaoh's heart, however, remained hard and stubborn. He still refused to listen, just as the LORD had predicted.

**7:1** Exod 4:16

**7:3** Exod 4:21

**7:4** Exod 11:9

**7:5** Exod 8:19

**7:7** Deut 34:7 Acts 7:23, 30

**7:9** Exod 4:3 Isa 7:11

**7:11** Gen 41:8 Exod 8:7, 18 2 Tim 3:8-9

**7:13** Exod 4:21

## 4. Plagues strike Egypt

### A Plague of Blood

14 Then the LORD said to Moses, "Pharaoh is very stubborn, and he continues to refuse to let the people go. 15 So go to Pharaoh in the morning as he goes down to the river. Stand on the riverbank and meet him there. Be sure to take along the shepherd's staff that turned into a snake. 16 Say to him, 'The LORD, the God of the Hebrews, has sent me to say, "Let my people go, so they can worship me in the wilderness." Until now, you have refused to listen to him. 17 Now the LORD says, "You are going to find out that I am the LORD." Look! I will hit the water of the Nile with this staff, and the river will turn to blood. 18 The fish in it will die, and the river will stink. The Egyptians will not be able to drink any water from the Nile.'"

19 Then the LORD said to Moses: "Tell Aaron to point his staff toward the waters of Egypt—all its rivers, canals, marshes, and reservoirs. Everywhere in Egypt the water

**7:14** Exod 8:15

**7:15** Exod 2:5; 8:20

**7:16** Exod 4:23

**7:17** Rev 11:6; 16:4

**7:19** Exod 14:21

---

**7:1** God made Moses "like God to Pharaoh"—in other words, a powerful person who deserved to be listened to. Pharaoh himself was considered a god, so he recognized Moses as one of his peers. His refusal to give in to Moses shows, however, that he did not feel inferior to Moses.

**7:11** How were these wise men and magicians able to duplicate Moses' miracles? Some of their feats involved trickery or illusion, and some may have used satanic power since worshiping gods of the underworld was part of their religion. Ironically, whenever they duplicated one of Moses' plagues, it only made matters worse. If the magicians had been as powerful as God, they would have reversed the plagues, not added to them.

**7:12** God performed a miracle by turning Aaron's staff into a snake, and Pharaoh's magicians did the same through trickery

or sorcery. Although miracles can help us believe, it is dangerous to rely on them alone. Satan can imitate some parts of God's work and lead people astray. Pharaoh focused on the miracle rather than the message. We can avoid this error by letting the Word of God be the basis of our faith. No miracle from God would endorse any message that is contrary to the teachings of his Word.

**7:17** God dramatically turned the waters of the Nile into blood to show Pharaoh who he was. Do you sometimes wish for miraculous signs so you can be sure about God? God has given you the miracle of eternal life through your faith in him, something Pharaoh never obtained. This is a quiet miracle and, though less evident right now, just as extraordinary as water turned to blood. The desire for spectacular signs may cause us to ignore the more subtle miracles God is working every day.

will turn into blood, even the water stored in wooden bowls and stone pots in the people's homes."

**7:20**
Pss 78:44; 105:29

20 So Moses and Aaron did just as the LORD had commanded them. As Pharaoh and all of his officials watched, Aaron raised his staff and hit the water of the Nile. Suddenly, the whole river turned to blood! 21 The fish in the river died, and the water became so foul that the Egyptians couldn't drink it. There was blood everywhere throughout the land of Egypt.

**7:22**
Exod 8:7

22 But again the magicians of Egypt used their secret arts, and they, too, turned water into blood. So Pharaoh's heart remained hard and stubborn. He refused to listen to Moses and Aaron, just as the LORD had predicted. 23 Pharaoh returned to his palace and put the whole thing out of his mind. 24 Then the Egyptians dug wells along the riverbank to get drinking water, for they couldn't drink from the river. 25 An entire week passed from the time the LORD turned the water of the Nile to blood.

## A Plague of Frogs

**8:1**
Exod 5:1

**8** Then the LORD said to Moses, "Go to Pharaoh once again and tell him, 'This is what the LORD says: Let my people go, so they can worship me.

**8:2**
Ps 105:30

2 If you refuse, then listen carefully to this: I will send vast hordes of frogs across your entire land from one border to the other. 3 The Nile River will swarm with them. They will come up out of the river and into your houses, even into your bedrooms and onto your beds! Every home in Egypt will be filled with them. They will fill even your ovens and your kneading bowls. 4 You and your people will be overwhelmed by frogs!'"

**8:5**
Exod 7:9-20
**8:6**
Pss 78:45; 105:30
**8:7**
Exod 7:11

5 Then the LORD said to Moses, "Tell Aaron to point his shepherd's staff toward all the rivers, canals, and marshes of Egypt so there will be frogs in every corner of the land." 6 Aaron did so, and frogs covered the whole land of Egypt! 7 But the magicians were able to do the same thing with their secret arts. They, too, caused frogs to come up on the land.

**8:8**
Exod 9:28; 10:10

8 Then Pharaoh summoned Moses and Aaron and begged, "Plead with the LORD to take the frogs away from me and my people. I will let the people go, so they can offer sacrifices to the LORD."

9 "You set the time!" Moses replied. "Tell me when you want me to pray for you, your officials, and your people. I will pray that you and your houses will be rid of the frogs. Then only the frogs in the Nile River will remain alive."

**8:10**
Exod 9:14; 15:11
Deut 4:35
Isa 46:9

10 "Do it tomorrow," Pharaoh said.

"All right," Moses replied, "it will be as you have said. Then you will know that no one is as powerful as the LORD our God. 11 All the frogs will be destroyed, except those in the river."

**8:12**
Exod 8:30; 9:33;
10:18

12 So Moses and Aaron left Pharaoh, and Moses pleaded with the LORD about the frogs he had sent. 13 And the LORD did as Moses had promised. The frogs in the houses, the courtyards, and the fields all died.

**8:15**
Exod 7:14
Eccl 8:11

14 They were piled into great heaps, and a terrible stench filled the land. 15 But when Pharaoh saw that the frogs were gone, he hardened his heart. He refused to listen to Moses and Aaron, just as the LORD had predicted.

## A Plague of Gnats

**8:16**
Exod 4:2

16 So the LORD said to Moses, "Tell Aaron to strike the dust with his staff. The dust will turn into swarms of gnats throughout the land of Egypt." 17 So Moses and Aaron did just

**8:17**
Ps 105:31

as the LORD had commanded them. Suddenly, gnats infested the entire land, covering the Egyptians and their animals. All the dust in the land of Egypt turned into gnats.

---

**7:20** Egypt was a large country, but most of the population lived along the banks of the Nile River. This 3,000-mile waterway was truly a river of life for the Egyptians. It made life possible in a land that was mostly desert by providing water for drinking, farming, bathing, and fishing. Egyptian society was a ribbon of civilization lining the banks of this life source, rarely reaching very far into the surrounding desert. Without the Nile's water Egypt could not have existed. Imagine Pharaoh's dismay when Moses turned this sacred river to blood!

**8:3ff** Moses predicted that every house in Egypt would be infested with frogs. The poor of Egypt lived in small, mud-brick houses of one or two rooms with palm-trunk roofs. The homes of the rich, however, were often two or three stories high, sur-rounded by landscaped gardens and enclosed by a high wall. Servants lived and worked on the first floor while the family occupied the upper floors. Thus, if the frogs got into the royal bedrooms, they had infiltrated even the upper floors. No place in Egypt would be safe from them.

**8:15** After repeated warnings, Pharaoh still refused to obey God. He hardened his heart every time there was a break in the plagues. His stubborn disobedience brought suffering upon himself and his entire country. While persistence is good, stubbornness is usually self-centered. Stubbornness toward God is always disobedience. Avoid disobedience because the consequences may spill onto others.

[18] Pharaoh's magicians tried to do the same thing with their secret arts, but this time they failed. And the gnats covered all the people and animals.

[19] "This is the finger of God!" the magicians exclaimed to Pharaoh. But Pharaoh's heart remained hard and stubborn. He wouldn't listen to them, just as the LORD had predicted.

### A Plague of Flies

[20] Next the LORD told Moses, "Get up early in the morning and meet Pharaoh as he goes down to the river. Say to him, 'This is what the LORD says: Let my people go, so they can worship me. [21] If you refuse, I will send swarms of flies throughout Egypt. Your homes will be filled with them, and the ground will be covered with them. [22] But it will be very different in the land of Goshen, where the Israelites live. No flies will be found there. Then you will know that I am the LORD and that I have power even in the heart of your land. [23] I will make a clear distinction between your people and my people. This miraculous sign will happen tomorrow.'"

[24] And the LORD did just as he had said. There were terrible swarms of flies in Pharaoh's palace and in every home in Egypt. The whole country was thrown into chaos by the flies.

[25] Pharaoh hastily called for Moses and Aaron. "All right! Go ahead and offer sacrifices to your God," he said. "But do it here in this land. Don't go out into the wilderness."

[26] But Moses replied, "That won't do! The Egyptians would detest the sacrifices that we offer to the LORD our God. If we offer them here where they can see us, they will be sure to stone us. [27] We must take a three-day trip into the wilderness to offer sacrifices to the LORD our God, just as he has commanded us."

[28] "All right, go ahead," Pharaoh replied. "I will let you go to offer sacrifices to the LORD your God in the wilderness. But don't go too far away. Now hurry, and pray for me."

[29] "As soon as I go," Moses said, "I will ask the LORD to cause the swarms of flies to disappear from you and all your people. But I am warning you, don't change your mind again and refuse to let the people go to sacrifice to the LORD."

[30] So Moses left Pharaoh and asked the LORD to remove all the flies. [31] And the LORD did as Moses asked and caused the swarms to disappear. Not a single fly remained in the land! [32] But Pharaoh hardened his heart again and refused to let the people go.

### A Plague against Livestock

**9** "Go back to Pharaoh," the LORD commanded Moses. "Tell him, 'This is what the LORD, the God of the Hebrews, says: Let my people go, so they can worship me. [2] If you continue to oppress them and refuse to let them go, [3] the LORD will send a deadly plague to destroy your horses, donkeys, camels, cattle, and sheep. [4] But the LORD will again make a distinction between the property of the Israelites and that of the Egyptians. Not a single one of Israel's livestock will die!'"

[5] The LORD announced that he would send the plague the very next day, [6] and he did it, just as he had said. The next morning all the livestock of the Egyptians began to die, but the Israelites didn't lose a single animal from their flocks and herds. [7] Pharaoh sent officials to see whether it was true that none of the Israelites' animals were dead. But even after he found it to be true, his heart remained stubborn. He still refused to let the people go.

**8:18** Exod 7:11; 9:11
**8:19** Exod 7:5; 1 Sam 6:9
**8:20** Exod 7:15
**8:22** Exod 9:4; 10:23
**8:24** Pss 78:45; 105:31
**8:25** Exod 8:8; 10:8
**8:27** Exod 3:18
**8:28** Exod 8:8
**8:30** Exod 8:12
**8:32** Exod 8:8, 15
**9:1** Exod 8:1; 10:3
**9:3** Exod 7:4
**9:4** Exod 8:23; 9:26
**9:7** Exod 7:14; 8:32

---

**8:19** Some people think, "If only I could see a miracle, I could believe in God." God gave Pharaoh just such an opportunity. When gnats infested Egypt, even the magicians agreed that this was God's work ("the finger of God")—but still Pharaoh refused to believe. He was stubborn, and stubbornness can blind a person to the truth. When you rid yourself of stubbornness, you may be surprised by abundant evidence of God's work in your life.

**8:25-29** Pharaoh wanted a compromise. He would allow the Hebrews to sacrifice, but only if they would do it nearby. God's requirement, however, was firm: The Hebrews had to leave Egypt. Sometimes people urge believers to compromise and give only partial obedience to God's commands. But commit-ment and obedience to God cannot be negotiated. When it comes to obeying God, half measures won't do.

**8:26** The Israelites would be sacrificing animals that the Egyptians regarded as sacred, and this would be offensive to them. Moses was concerned about a violent reaction to sacrificing these animals near the Egyptians.

**9:1** This was the fifth time God sent Moses back to Pharaoh with the demand "Let my people go!" By this time, Moses may have been tired and discouraged, but he continued to obey. Is there a difficult conflict you must face again and again? Don't give up when you know what is right to do. As Moses discovered, persistence is rewarded.

### A Plague of Boils

**9:9**
Lev 13:18
Rev 16:2

8 Then the LORD said to Moses and Aaron, "Take soot from a furnace, and have Moses toss it into the sky while Pharaoh watches. 9 It will spread like fine dust over the whole land of Egypt, causing boils to break out on people and animals alike."

10 So they gathered soot from a furnace and went to see Pharaoh. As Pharaoh watched, Moses tossed the soot into the air, and terrible boils broke out on the people and animals throughout Egypt.

**9:11**
Exod 8:18

11 Even the magicians were unable to stand before Moses, because the boils had broken out on them, too.

**9:12**
Exod 4:21

12 But the LORD made Pharaoh even more stubborn, and he refused to listen, just as the LORD had predicted.

### A Plague of Hail

**9:13**
Exod 8:20

13 Then the LORD said to Moses, "Get up early in the morning. Go to Pharaoh and tell him, 'The LORD, the God of the Hebrews, says: Let my people go, so they can worship

**9:14**
Exod 8:10; 15:11

me. 14 If you don't, I will send a plague that will really speak to you and your officials and all the Egyptian people. I will prove to you that there is no other God like me in all the earth. 15 I could have killed you all by now. I could have attacked you with a plague that would have wiped you from the face of the earth.

**9:16**
Exod 14:4, 17
†Rom 9:17

16 But I have let you live for this reason—that you might see my power and that my fame might spread throughout the earth. 17 But you are still lording it over my people, and you refuse to

**THE PLAGUES**

| Reference | Plague | What Happened | Result |
|---|---|---|---|
| 7:14–24 | Blood | Fish die, the river smells, the people are without water | Pharaoh's magicians duplicate the miracle by "secret arts," and Pharaoh is unmoved |
| 8:1–15 | Frogs | Frogs come up from the water and completely cover the land | Again Pharaoh's magicians duplicate the miracle by sorcery, and Pharaoh is unmoved |
| 8:16–19 | Gnats | All the dust of Egypt becomes a massive swarm of gnats | Magicians are unable to duplicate this; they say it is the "finger of God," but Pharaoh's heart remains hard |
| 8:20–32 | Flies | Swarms of flies cover the land | Pharaoh promises to let the Hebrews go but then hardens his heart and refuses |
| 9:1–7 | Livestock | All the Egyptian livestock die—but none of Israel's is even sick | Pharaoh still refuses to let the people go |
| 9:8–12 | Boils | Horrible boils break out on everyone in Egypt | Magicians cannot respond because they are struck down with boils as well—Pharaoh refuses to listen |
| 9:13–35 | Hail | Hailstorms kill all the slaves and animals left out or unprotected and strip or destroy almost every plant | Pharaoh admits his sin but then changes his mind and refuses to let Israel go |
| 10:1–20 | Locusts | Locusts cover Egypt and eat everything left after the hail | Everyone advises Pharaoh to let the Hebrews go, but God hardens Pharaoh's heart and he refuses |
| 10:21–29 | Darkness | Total darkness covers Egypt for three days so no one can even move—except the Hebrews, who have light as usual | Pharaoh again promises to let Israel go but again changes his mind |
| 11:1—12:33 | Death of Firstborn | The firstborn of all the people and cattle of Egypt die—but Israel is spared | Pharaoh and the Egyptians urge Israel to leave quickly; after they are gone, Pharaoh again changes his mind and chases after them |

**9:12** God gave Pharaoh many opportunities to heed Moses' warnings. But finally God seemed to say, "All right, Pharaoh, have it your way," and Pharaoh's heart became permanently hardened. Did God intentionally harden Pharaoh's heart and overrule his free will? No, he simply confirmed that Pharaoh freely chose a life of resisting God. Similarly, after a lifetime of resisting God, you may find it impossible to turn to him. Don't wait until just the *right* time before turning to God. Do it now while you still have the chance. If you continually ignore God's voice, eventually you will be unable to hear it at all.

let them go. ¹⁸ So tomorrow at this time I will send a hailstorm worse than any in all of Egypt's history. ¹⁹ Quick! Order your livestock and servants to come in from the fields. Every person or animal left outside will die beneath the hail.'"

²⁰ Some of Pharaoh's officials believed what the LORD said. They immediately brought their livestock and servants in from the fields. ²¹ But those who had no respect for the word of the LORD left them out in the open.

²² Then the LORD said to Moses, "Lift your hand toward the sky, and cause the hail to fall throughout Egypt, on the people, the animals, and the crops."

²³ So Moses lifted his staff toward the sky, and the LORD sent thunder and hail, and lightning struck the earth. The LORD sent a tremendous hailstorm against all the land of Egypt. ²⁴ Never in all the history of Egypt had there been a storm like that, with such severe hail and continuous lightning. ²⁵ It left all of Egypt in ruins. Everything left in the fields was destroyed—people, animals, and crops alike. Even all the trees were destroyed. ²⁶ The only spot in all Egypt without hail that day was the land of Goshen, where the people of Israel lived.

²⁷ Then Pharaoh urgently sent for Moses and Aaron. "I finally admit my fault," he confessed. "The LORD is right, and my people and I are wrong. ²⁸ Please beg the LORD to end this terrifying thunder and hail. I will let you go at once."

²⁹ "All right," Moses replied. "As soon as I leave the city, I will lift my hands and pray to the LORD. Then the thunder and hail will stop. This will prove to you that the earth belongs to the LORD. ³⁰ But as for you and your officials, I know that you still do not fear the LORD God as you should."

³¹ All the flax and barley were destroyed because the barley was ripe and the flax was in bloom. ³² But the wheat and the spelt were not destroyed because they had not yet sprouted from the ground.

³³ So Moses left Pharaoh and went out of the city. As he lifted his hands to the LORD, all at once the thunder and hail stopped, and the downpour ceased. ³⁴ When Pharaoh saw this, he and his officials sinned yet again by stubbornly refusing to do as they had promised. ³⁵ Pharaoh refused to let the people leave, just as the LORD had predicted.

## A Plague of Locusts

**10** Then the LORD said to Moses, "Return to Pharaoh and again make your demands. I have made him and his officials stubborn so I can continue to display my power by performing miraculous signs among them. ² You will be able to tell wonderful stories to your children and grandchildren about the marvelous things I am doing among the Egyptians to prove that I am the LORD."

³ So Moses and Aaron went to Pharaoh and said, "This is what the LORD, the God of the Hebrews, says: How long will you refuse to submit to me? Let my people go, so they can worship me. ⁴ If you refuse, watch out! For tomorrow I will cover the whole country with locusts. ⁵ There will be so many that you won't be able to see the ground. They will devour everything that escaped the hailstorm, including all the trees in the fields. ⁶ They will overrun your palaces and the homes of your officials and all the houses of Egypt. Never in the history of Egypt has there been a plague like this one!" And with that, Moses turned and walked out.

⁷ The court officials now came to Pharaoh and appealed to him. "How long will you let these disasters go on? Please let the Israelites go to serve the LORD their God! Don't you realize that Egypt lies in ruins?"

⁸ So Moses and Aaron were brought back to Pharaoh. "All right, go and serve the LORD your God," he said. "But tell me, just whom do you want to take along?"

**9:18**
Exod 9:23, 24

**9:20**
Prov 13:13

**9:22**
Rev 16:21

**9:23**
Gen 19:24
Josh 10:11
Ps 78:47
Rev 8:7; 16:21

**9:25**
Ps 105:32

**9:26**
Exod 8:22; 10:23

**9:27**
2 Chr 12:6
Ps 129:4

**9:28**
Exod 8:8; 10:16-17

**9:29**
Ps 24:1
1 Cor 10:26

**9:30**
Exod 8:29

**9:35**
Exod 4:21

**10:1**
Exod 4:21; 7:14

**10:2**
Exod 13:8, 14
Deut 4:9
Ps 44:1

**10:3**
Exod 4:23

**10:4**
Rev 9:3

**10:5**
Exod 9:32
Joel 1:4; 2:25

**10:7**
Exod 7:5

**10:8**
Exod 8:8, 25

---

**9:20, 21** If all the Egyptian livestock were killed in the earlier plague (9:6), how could the slaves of Pharaoh put their cattle inside? The answer is probably that the earlier plague killed all the animals in the fields (9:3) but not those in the shelters.

**9:27-34** After promising to let the Hebrews go, Pharaoh immediately broke his promise and brought even more trouble upon the land. His actions reveal that his repentance was not real. We do damage to ourselves and to others if we pretend to change but don't mean it.

**10:2** God told Moses that his miraculous experiences with Pharaoh should be retold to his descendants. What stories Moses had to tell! Living out one of the greatest dramas in biblical history, he witnessed events few people would ever see. It is important to tell our children about God's work in our past and to help them see what he is doing right now. What are the turning points in your life where God intervened? What is God doing for you now? Your stories will form the foundations of your children's belief in God.

**10:9**
Exod 12:37

**10:10**
Gen 50:8
Exod 12:31

**10:11**
Exod 10:28

**10:12**
Exod 7:19

**10:13**
Pss 78:46; 105:34

**10:14**
Joel 1:4, 7; 2:1-11

**10:15**
Exod 10:5
Ps 105:35

**10:16**
Exod 8:8; 9:27

**10:17**
Exod 8:8, 29
1 Sam 15:25

**10:18**
Exod 8:30

**10:20**
Exod 4:21; 11:10

**10:21**
Deut 28:29

**10:22**
Ps 105:28

**10:23**
Exod 8:22

**10:24**
Exod 8:8, 10

**10:26**
Exod 10:9

**10:27**
Exod 4:21; 14:4

**10:28**
Exod 10:11

**10:29**
Heb 11:27

**11:1**
Exod 12:31, 33, 39

**11:2**
Exod 3:22;
12:35-36

**11:3**
Exod 3:21; 12:36
Deut 34:10-12

9"Young and old, all of us will go,' Moses replied. "We will take our sons and daughters and our flocks and herds. We must all join together in a festival to the LORD."

10Pharaoh retorted, "The LORD will certainly need to be with you if you try to take your little ones along I can see through your wicked intentions. 11Never! Only the men may go and serve the LORD, for that is what you requested." And Pharaoh threw them out of the palace.

12Then the LORD said to Moses, "Raise your hand over the land of Egypt to bring on the locusts. Let them cover the land and eat all the crops still left after the hailstorm."

13So Moses raised his staff, and the LORD caused an east wind to blow all that day and through the night. When morning arrived, the east wind had brought the locusts. 14And the locusts swarmed over the land of Egypt from border to border. It was the worst locust plague in Egyptian history, and there has never again been one like it. 15For the locusts covered the surface of the whole country, making the ground look black. They ate all the plants and all the fruit on the trees that had survived the hailstorm. Not one green thing remained, neither tree nor plant, throughout the land of Egypt.

16Pharaoh quickly sent for Moses and Aaron. "I confess my sin against the LORD your God and against you," he said to them. 17"Forgive my sin only this once, and plead with the LORD your God to take away this terrible plague."

18So Moses left Pharaoh and pleaded with the LORD. 19The LORD responded by sending a strong west wind that blew the locusts out into the Red Sea.* Not a single locust remained in all the land of Egypt. 20But the LORD made Pharaoh stubborn once again, and he did not let the people go

### A Plague of Darkness

21Then the LORD said to Moses, "Lift your hand toward heaven, and a deep and terrifying darkness will descend on the land of Egypt." 22So Moses lifted his hand toward heaven, and there was deep darkness over the entire land for three days. 23During all that time the people scarcely moved, for they could not see. But there was light as usual where the people of Israel lived

24Then Pharaoh called for Moses. "Go and worship the LORD," he said. "But let your flocks and herds stay here. You can even take your children with you."

25"No," Moses said, "we must take our flocks and herds for sacrifices and burnt offerings to the LORD our God. 26All our property must go with us; not a hoof can be left behind. We will have to choose our sacrifices for the LORD our God from among these animals. And we won't know which sacrifices he will require until we get there."

27So the LORD hardened Pharaoh's heart once more, and he would not let them go. 28"Get out of here!" Pharaoh shouted at Moses. "Don't ever let me see you again! The day you do, you will die!"

29"Very well," Moses replied. "I will never see you again."

### Death for Egypt's Firstborn

**11** Then the LORD said to Moses, "I will send just one more disaster on Pharaoh and the land of Egypt. After that, Pharaoh will let you go. In fact, he will be so anxious to get rid of you that he will practically force you to leave the country. 2Tell all the Israelite men and women to ask their Egyptian neighbors for articles of silver and gold." 3(Now the LORD had caused the Egyptians to look favorably on the people of Israel,

**10:19** Hebrew *sea of reeds.*

---

**10:22** As each gloomy plague descended upon the land, the Egyptian people realized how powerless their own gods were to stop it. Hapi, the god of the Nile River, could not prevent the waters from turning to blood (7:20). Hathor, the crafty cow-goddess, was helpless as Egyptian livestock died in droves (9:6). Amon-Re, the sun-god and chief of the Egyptian gods, could not stop an eerie darkness from covering the land for three full days (10:21, 22). The Egyptian gods were (1) nonpersonal, centering around images like the sun or the river; (2) numerous; (3) nonexclusive. By contrast, the God of the

Hebrews was (1) a living personal Being, (2) the only true God, and (3) the only God who should be worshiped. God was proving to both the Hebrews and the Egyptians that he alone is the living and all-powerful God.

**10:27, 28** Why was Pharaoh so reluctant to let the people go? The Hebrews were Egypt's free labor—the builders of their great cities. As Egypt's leader, Pharaoh would not easily let such a great resource go.

and Moses was considered a very great man in the land of Egypt. He was respected by Pharaoh's officials and the Egyptian people alike.)

⁴So Moses announced to Pharaoh, "This is what the LORD says: About midnight I will pass through Egypt. ⁵All the firstborn sons will die in every family in Egypt, from the oldest son of Pharaoh, who sits on the throne, to the oldest son of his lowliest slave. Even the firstborn of the animals will die. ⁶Then a loud wail will be heard throughout the land of Egypt; there has never been such wailing before, and there never will be again. ⁷But among the Israelites it will be so peaceful that not even a dog will bark. Then you will know that the LORD makes a distinction between the Egyptians and the Israelites. ⁸All the officials of Egypt will come running to me, bowing low. 'Please leave!' they will beg. 'Hurry! And take all your followers with you.' Only then will I go!" Then, burning with anger, Moses left Pharaoh's presence.

⁹Now the LORD had told Moses, "Pharaoh will not listen to you. But this will give me the opportunity to do even more mighty miracles in the land of Egypt." ¹⁰Although Moses and Aaron did these miracles in Pharaoh's presence, the LORD hardened his heart so he wouldn't let the Israelites leave the country.

## 5. The Passover

**12** Now the LORD gave the following instructions to Moses and Aaron while they were still in the land of Egypt: ²"From now on, this month will be the first month of the year for you. ³Announce to the whole community that on the tenth day of this month each family must choose a lamb or a young goat for a sacrifice. ⁴If a family is too small to eat an entire lamb, let them share the lamb with another family in the neighborhood. Whether or not they share in this way depends on the size of each family and how much they can eat. ⁵This animal must be a one-year-old male, either a sheep or a goat, with no physical defects.

⁶"Take special care of these lambs until the evening of the fourteenth day of this first month. Then each family in the community must slaughter its lamb. ⁷They are to take some of the lamb's blood and smear it on the top and sides of the doorframe of the house where the lamb will be eaten. ⁸That evening everyone must eat roast lamb with bitter

**11:4**
Exod 12:29

**11:5**
Exod 12:12, 29
Pss 78:51; 105:36;
135:8; 136:10

**11:6**
Exod 12:30
Amos 5:17

**11:7**
Exod 8:22

**11:8**
Exod 12:31-33
Heb 11:27

**11:9**
Exod 7:3-4

**11:10**
Exod 4:21
Rom 2:5; 9:17

**12:2**
Exod 13:4; 23:15;
34:18
Deut 16:1

**12:3**
Mark 14:12
1 Cor 5:7

**12:6**
Lev 23:5
Num 9:3
Deut 16:4, 6

**12:7**
Exod 12:22

**12:8**
Exod 34:25
Num 9:11-12
Deut 16:7

**11:7** Moses told Pharaoh that God made a distinction between Egypt and Israel. At this time the distinction was very clear in God's mind: He knew the Hebrews would become his chosen people. The distinction was taking shape in Moses' mind also. But the Hebrews still saw the distinction only in terms of slave and free. Later, when they were in the wilderness, God would teach them the laws, principles, and values that would make them distinct as his people. Remember that God sees us in terms of what we will become and not just what we are right now.

**11:9, 10** You may wonder how Pharaoh could be so foolish as to see God's miraculous power and still not listen to Moses. But Pharaoh had his mind made up long before the plagues began. He couldn't believe that someone was greater than he. This stubborn unbelief led to a heart so hard that even a major catastrophe couldn't soften it. Finally, it took the greatest of all calamities, the loss of his son, to force him to recognize God's authority. But even then he wanted God to leave, not to rule his country. We must not wait for great calamities to drive us to God but must open our hearts and minds to his direction now.

**11:10** Did God really harden Pharaoh's heart and force him to do wrong? Before the 10 plagues began, Moses and Aaron announced what God would do if Pharaoh didn't let the people go. But their message only made Pharaoh stubborn—he was hardening his own heart. In so doing, he defied both God and his messengers. Through the first six plagues, Pharaoh's heart grew even more stubborn. After the sixth plague, God passed judgment. Sooner or later, evil people will be punished for their sins. When it became evident that Pharaoh wouldn't change, God confirmed Pharaoh's prideful decision and set the painful consequences of his actions in motion. God didn't force Pharaoh to reject him; rather, he gave him every opportunity to

change his mind. In Ezekiel 33:11, God says, "I take no pleasure in the death of wicked people."

**12:1-3** Certain holidays were instituted by God himself. Passover was a holiday designed to celebrate Israel's deliverance from Egypt and to remind the people of what God had done. Holidays can be important today, too, as annual reminders of what God has done for us. Develop traditions in your family to highlight the religious significance of certain holidays. These serve as reminders to the older people and learning experiences for the younger ones.

**12:3ff** For the Israelites to be spared from the plague of death, a lamb with no defects had to be killed and its blood placed on the doorframes of each home. What was the significance of the lamb? In killing the lamb, the Israelites shed innocent blood. The lamb was a sacrifice, a substitute for the person who would have died in the plague. From this point on, the Hebrew people would clearly understand that for them to be spared from death, an innocent life had to be sacrificed in their place.

**12:6-11** The festival of Passover was to be an annual holiday in honor of the night when the Lord "passed over" the homes of the Israelites. The Hebrews followed God's instructions by smearing the blood of a lamb on the doorframes of their homes. That night the firstborn son of every family that did not have blood on the doorframes was killed. The lamb had to be killed in order to get the blood that would protect them. (This foreshadowed the blood of Christ, the Lamb of God, who gave his blood for the sins of all people.) Inside their homes, the Israelites ate a meal of roast lamb, bitter herbs, and bread made without yeast. Unleavened bread could be made quickly because the dough did not have to rise. Thus, they could leave at any time. Bitter herbs signified the bitterness of slavery.

**12:10**
Exod 23:18; 34:25

**12:11**
Num 28:16

**12:12**
Exod 11:4-5
Num 33:4

**12:13**
Heb 11:28

**12:14-20**
//Lev 23:4-8
//Num 28:16-25
//Deut 16:1-8

**12:15**
Exod 23:15; 34:18
Lev 23:5-6
Deut 16:3

**12:16**
Lev 23:7-8

**12:17**
Exod 13:3

herbs and bread made without yeast. 9 The meat must never be eaten raw or boiled; roast it all, including the head, legs, and internal organs. Do not leave any of it until the next day. Whatever is not eaten that night must be burned before morning.

11 "Wear your traveling clothes as you eat this meal, as though prepared for a long journey. Wear your sandals, and carry your walking sticks in your hands. Eat the food quickly, for this is the LORD's Passover. 12 On that night I will pass through the land of Egypt and kill all the firstborn sons and firstborn male animals in the land of Egypt. I will execute judgment against all the gods of Egypt, for I am the LORD! 13 The blood you have smeared on your doorposts will serve as a sign. When I see the blood, I will pass over you. This plague of death will not touch you when I strike the land of Egypt.

14 "You must remember this day forever. Each year you will celebrate it as a special festival to the LORD. 15 For seven days, you may eat only bread made without yeast. On the very first day you must remove every trace of yeast from your homes. Anyone who eats bread made with yeast at any time during the seven days of the festival will be cut off from the community of Israel. 16 On the first day of the festival, and again on the seventh day, all the people must gather for a time of special worship. No work of any kind may be done on these days except in the preparation of food.

17 "Celebrate this Festival of Unleavened Bread, for it will remind you that I brought

---

**THE HEBREW CALENDAR**
A Hebrew month began in the middle of a month on our calendar today. Crops are planted in November and December and harvested in March and April.

| Month | | Today's Calendar | Bible Reference | Israel's Holidays |
|---|---|---|---|---|
| 1 | Nisan (Abib) | March–April | Exodus 13:4; 23:15; 34:18; Deuteronomy 16:1 | Passover (Leviticus 23:5) Unleavened Bread (Leviticus 23:6) Firstfruits (Leviticus 23:10) |
| 2 | Iyyar (Ziv) | April–May | 1 Kings 6:1, 37 | Second Passover (Numbers 9:10, 11) |
| 3 | Sivan | May–June | Esther 8:9 | Pentecost (Harvest) (Leviticus 23:16) |
| 4 | Tammuz | June–July | | |
| 5 | Ab | July–August | | |
| 6 | Elul | August–September | Nehemiah 6:15 | |
| 7 | Tishri (Ethanim) | September–October | 1 Kings 8:2 | Trumpets (Numbers 29:1; Leviticus 23:24) Day of Atonement (Leviticus 23:27) Shelters (Leviticus 23:34) |
| 8 | Marcheshvan (Bul) | October–November | 1 Kings 6:38 | |
| 9 | Kislev | November–December | Nehemiah 1:1 | Dedication (John 10:22) |
| 10 | Tebeth | December–January | Esther 2:16 | |
| 11 | Shebat | January–February | Zechariah 1:7 | Purim (Esther 9:24–32) |
| 12 | Adar | February–March | Esther 3:7 | |

---

**12:11** Eating the Passover feast while dressed for travel was a sign of the Hebrews' faith. Although they were not yet free, they were to prepare themselves, for God had said he would lead them out of Egypt. Their preparation was an act of faith. Preparing ourselves for the fulfillment of God's promises, however unlikely they may seem, demonstrates our faith.

**12:17, 23** Passover became an annual remembrance of how God delivered the Hebrews from Egypt. Each year the people would pause to remember the day when the Destroyer (God's

angel of death) passed over their homes. They gave thanks to God for saving them from death and bringing them out of a land of slavery and sin. Believers today have experienced a day of deliverance as well—the day we were delivered from spiritual death and slavery to sin. The Lord's Supper is our Passover remembrance of our new life and freedom from sin. The next time struggles and trials come, remember how God has delivered you in the past and focus on his promise of new life with him.

your forces out of the land of Egypt on this very day. This festival will be a permanent regulation for you, to be kept from generation to generation. [18]Only bread without yeast may be eaten from the evening of the fourteenth day of the month until the evening of the twenty-first day of the month. [19]During those seven days, there must be no trace of yeast in your homes. Anyone who eats anything made with yeast during this week will be cut off from the community of Israel. These same regulations apply to the foreigners living with you, as if they had been born among you. [20]I repeat, during those days you must not eat anything made with yeast. Wherever you live, eat only bread that has no yeast in it."

[21]Then Moses called for the leaders of Israel and said, "Tell each of your families to slaughter the lamb they have set apart for the Passover. [22]Drain each lamb's blood into a basin. Then take a cluster of hyssop branches and dip it into the lamb's blood. Strike the hyssop against the top and sides of the doorframe, staining it with the blood. And remember, no one is allowed to leave the house until morning. [23]For the LORD will pass through the land and strike down the Egyptians. But when he sees the blood on the top and sides of the doorframe, the LORD will pass over your home. He will not permit the Destroyer to enter and strike down your firstborn.

[24]"Remember, these instructions are permanent and must be observed by you and your descendants forever. [25]When you arrive in the land the LORD has promised to give you, you will continue to celebrate this festival. [26]Then your children will ask, 'What does all this mean? What is this ceremony about?' [27]And you will reply, 'It is the celebration of the LORD's Passover, for he passed over the homes of the Israelites in Egypt. And though he killed the Egyptians, he spared our families and did not destroy us.'" Then all the people bowed their heads and worshiped.

[28]So the people of Israel did just as the LORD had commanded through Moses and Aaron. [29]And at midnight the LORD killed all the firstborn sons in the land of Egypt, from the firstborn son of Pharaoh, who sat on the throne, to the firstborn son of the captive in the dungeon. Even the firstborn of their livestock were killed. [30]Pharaoh and his officials and all the people of Egypt woke up during the night, and loud wailing was heard throughout the land of Egypt. There was not a single house where someone had not died.

**12:18**
Lev 23:5-8
Num 28:16-25

**12:19**
Exod 12:15

**12:21**
Mark 14:12-16
Heb 11:28

**12:22**
Lev 14:4, 6
Num 19:18
Ps 51:7
Heb 11:28

**12:23**
Exod 12:12
Isa 37:36

**12:24**
Exod 13:4-5, 10

**12:25**
Exod 3:17

**12:26**
Exod 10:2;
13:14-15

**12:27**
Exod 4:31

**12:29**
Exod 4:23; 11:4
Pss 78:51; 105:36

**12:30**
Exod 11:6

## B. ISRAEL IN THE WILDERNESS (12:31—18:27)

As Egypt buried its dead, the Hebrew slaves left the country, a free people at last. Pharaoh made one last attempt to bring them back, but the people escaped when God miraculously parted the waters of the Red Sea. But on the other side, the people soon became dissatisfied and complained bitterly to Moses and Aaron about their trek through the wilderness. Through these experiences of the Hebrews, we learn that the Christian life is not always trouble-free. We still have struggles and often complain bitterly to God about conditions in our lives.

### 1. The Exodus

[31]Pharaoh sent for Moses and Aaron during the night. "Leave us!" he cried. "Go away, all of you! Go and serve the LORD as you have requested. [32]Take your flocks and herds, and be gone. Go, but give me a blessing as you leave." [33]All the Egyptians urged the people of Israel to get out of the land as quickly as possible, for they thought, "We will all die!"

**12:31**
Exod 8:8, 25

**12:33**
Exod 10:7; 11:1

---

**12:29, 30** Every firstborn child of the Egyptians died, but the Israelite children were spared because the blood of the lamb had been smeared on their doorframes. So begins the story of redemption, the central theme of the Bible.

*Redemption* means "to buy back" or "to save from captivity by paying a ransom." One way to buy back a slave was to offer an equivalent or superior slave in exchange. That is the way God chose to buy us back—he offered his Son in exchange for us.

In Old Testament times, God accepted symbolic offerings. Jesus had not yet been sacrificed, so God accepted the life of an animal in place of the life of the sinner. When Jesus came, he substituted his perfect life for our sinful lives, taking the penalty for sin that we deserve. Thus he redeemed us from the power of sin

and restored us to God. Jesus' sacrifice made animal sacrifice no longer necessary.

We must recognize that if we want to be freed from the deadly consequences of our sins, a tremendous price must be paid. But we don't have to pay it. Jesus Christ, our substitute, has already redeemed us by his death on the cross. Our part is to trust him and accept his gift of eternal life. Our sins have been paid for, and the way has been cleared for us to begin a relationship with God (Titus 2:14; Hebrews 9:13-15, 23-26).

**12:34** A kneading bowl was a large bowl made of wood, bronze, or pottery and used for kneading dough. Bread was made by mixing water and flour in the bowl with a small piece of leavened dough saved from the previous day's batch. Bread was the primary food in the Hebrews' diet, and thus it was vital to bring the bowl along. It could be easily carried on the shoulder.

could travel whether it was day or night. 22And the LORD did not remove the pillar of cloud or pillar of fire from their sight.

**14:2**
Num 33:7-8

**14:4**
Exod 4:21; 7:5
Rom 9:17, 22-23

**14** Then the LORD gave these instructions to Moses: 2"Tell the people to march toward Pi-hahiroth between Migdol and the sea. Camp there along the shore, opposite Baal-zephon. 3Then Pharaoh will think, 'These Israelites are confused. They are trapped between the wilderness and the sea!' 4And once again I will harden Pharaoh's

## MOSES

Some people can't stay out of trouble. When conflict breaks out, they always manage to be nearby. Reaction is their favorite action. This was Moses. He seemed drawn to what needed to be righted. Throughout his life, he was at his finest and his worst responding to the conflicts around him. Even the burning bush experience was an illustration of his character. Having spotted the fire and seen that the bush did not burn, he had to investigate. Whether jumping into a fight to defend a Hebrew slave or trying to referee a struggle between two kinsmen, when Moses saw conflict, he reacted.

Over the years, however, an amazing thing happened to Moses' character. He didn't stop reacting, but rather learned to react correctly. The kaleidoscopic action of each day of leading two million people in the wilderness was more than enough challenge for Moses' reacting ability. Much of the time he served as a buffer between God and the people. At one moment he had to respond to God's anger at the people's stubbornness and forgetfulness. At another moment he had to react to the people's bickering and complaining. At still another moment he had to react to their unjustified attacks on his character.

Leadership often involves reaction. If we want to react with instincts consistent with God's will, we must develop habits of obedience to God. Consistent obedience to God is best developed in times of less stress. Then when stress comes, our natural reaction will be to obey God.

In our age of lowering moral standards, we find it almost impossible to believe that God would punish Moses for the one time he disobeyed outright. What we fail to see, however, is that God did not reject Moses; Moses simply disqualified himself to enter the Promised Land. Personal greatness does not make a person immune to error or its consequences.

In Moses we see an outstanding personality shaped by God. But we must not misunderstand what God did. He did not change who or what Moses was; he did not give Moses new abilities and strengths. Instead, he took Moses' characteristics and molded them until they were suited to his purposes. Does knowing this make a difference in your understanding of God's purpose in your life? He is trying to take what he created in the first place and use it for its intended purposes. The next time you talk with God don't ask, "What should I change into?" but "How should I use my own abilities and strengths to do your will?"

| | |
|---|---|
| **Strengths and accomplishments** | • Egyptian education; wilderness training<br>• Greatest Jewish leader; set the Exodus in motion<br>• Prophet and lawgiver; recorder of the Ten Commandments<br>• Author of the Pentateuch |
| **Weaknesses and mistakes** | • Failed to enter the Promised Land because of disobedience to God<br>• Did not always recognize and use the talents of others |
| **Lessons from his life** | • God prepares, then uses. His timetable is life-sized<br>• God does his greatest work through frail people |
| **Vital statistics** | • Where: Egypt, Midian, wilderness of Sinai<br>• Occupations: Prince, shepherd, leader of the Israelites<br>• Relatives: Sister: Miriam. Brother: Aaron. Wife: Zipporah. Sons: Gershom and Eliezer |
| **Key verses** | "It was by faith that Moses, when he grew up, refused to be treated as the son of Pharaoh's daughter. He chose to share the oppression of God's people instead of enjoying the fleeting pleasures of sin" (Hebrews 11:24, 25). |

Moses' story is told in the books of Exodus through Deuteronomy. He is also mentioned in Acts 7:20–44; Hebrews 11:23–29.

**13:21, 22** God gave the Hebrews a pillar of cloud and a pillar of fire so they would know day and night that God was with them on their journey to the Promised Land. What has God given us so that we can have the same assurance? The Bible—something the Israelites did not have. Look to God's Word for reassurance of his presence. As the Hebrews looked to the pillars of cloud and fire, we can look to God's Word day and night to know he is with us, helping us on our journey.

**13:21, 22** The pillars of fire and cloud were examples of *theophany*—God appearing in a physical form. In this form, God lighted Israel's path, protected them from their enemies, provided reassurance, controlled their movements, and inspired the burning zeal that Israel should have for their God.

heart, and he will chase after you. I have planned this so I will receive great glory at the expense of Pharaoh and his armies. After this, the Egyptians will know that I am the LORD!" So the Israelites camped there as they were told.

### The Egyptians Pursue Israel

5When word reached the king of Egypt that the Israelites were not planning to return to Egypt after three days, Pharaoh and his officials changed their minds. "What have we done, letting all these slaves get away?" they asked. 6So Pharaoh called out his troops and led the chase in his chariot. 7He took with him six hundred of Egypt's best chariots, along with the rest of the chariots of Egypt, each with a commander. 8The LORD continued to strengthen Pharaoh's resolve, and he chased after the people of Israel who had escaped so defiantly. 9All the forces in Pharaoh's army—all his horses, chariots, and charioteers—were used in the chase. The Egyptians caught up with the people of Israel as they were camped beside the shore near Pi-hahiroth, across from Baal-zephon.

10As Pharaoh and his army approached, the people of Israel could see them in the distance, marching toward them. The people began to panic, and they cried out to the LORD for help.

11Then they turned against Moses and complained, "Why did you bring us out here to die in the wilderness? Weren't there enough graves for us in Egypt? Why did you make us leave? 12Didn't we tell you to leave us alone while we were still in Egypt? Our Egyptian slavery was far better than dying out here in the wilderness!"

13But Moses told the people, "Don't be afraid. Just stand where you are and watch the LORD rescue you. The Egyptians that you see today will never be seen again. 14The LORD himself will fight for you. You won't have to lift a finger in your defense!"

### Escape through the Red Sea

15Then the LORD said to Moses, "Why are you crying out to me? Tell the people to get moving! 16Use your shepherd's staff—hold it out over the water, and a path will open up before you through the sea. Then all the people of Israel will walk through on dry ground. 17Yet I will harden the hearts of the Egyptians, and they will follow the Israelites into the sea. Then I will receive great glory at the expense of Pharaoh and his armies, chariots, and charioteers. 18When I am finished with Pharaoh and his army, all Egypt will know that I am the LORD!"

19Then the angel of God, who had been leading the people of Israel, moved to a position behind them, and the pillar of cloud also moved around behind them. 20The cloud settled between the Israelite and Egyptian camps. As night came, the pillar of cloud turned into a pillar of fire, lighting the Israelite camp. But the cloud became darkness to the Egyptians, and they couldn't find the Israelites.

21Then Moses raised his hand over the sea, and the LORD opened up a path through

**14:5**
Ps 105:25

**14:7**
Exod 15:4

**14:8**
Num 33:3
Acts 13:17

**14:9**
Exod 14:2; 15:9
Josh 24:6

**14:10**
Josh 24:7
Neh 9:9

**14:11**
Exod 5:21; 15:24
Ps 106:7-8

**14:13**
Gen 15:1
Exod 14:30; 15:2

**14:14**
Exod 15:3
Deut 1:30; 3:22
Isa 30:15

**14:15**
Josh 7:10

**14:16**
Exod 4:17, 20
Num 20:8-9, 11

**14:18**
Exod 14:25

**14:19**
Exod 13:21-22

**14:21**
Exod 7:19
Pss 106:9; 114:3, 5
Isa 63:12-13

---

**14:6-9** Six hundred Egyptian war chariots were bearing down on the helpless Israelites, who were trapped between the mountains and the sea. The war chariots each carried two people— one to drive and one to fight. These chariots were made of a wood or leather cab placed over two wheels, and they were pulled by horses. These were the armored tanks of Bible times. But even their power was no match for God, who destroyed both the chariots and their soldiers.

**14:10, 11** Trapped against the sea, the Israelites faced the Egyptian army sweeping in for the kill. The Israelites thought they were doomed. After watching God's powerful hand deliver them from Egypt, their only response was fear, whining, and despair. Where was their trust in God? Israel had to learn from repeated experience that God was able to provide for them. God has preserved these examples in the Bible so that we can learn to trust him the first time. By focusing on God's faithfulness in the past, we can face crises with confidence rather than with fear and complaining.

**14:11, 12** This is the first instance of grumbling and complain-

ing by the Israelites. Their lack of faith in God is startling. Yet how often do we find ourselves doing the same thing—complaining over inconveniences or discomforts? The Israelites were about to learn some tough lessons. Had they trusted God, they would have been spared much grief.

**14:13, 14** The people were hostile and despairing, but Moses encouraged them to watch the wonderful way God would rescue them. Moses had a positive attitude! When it looked as if they were trapped, Moses called upon God to intervene. We may not be chased by an army, but we may still feel trapped. Instead of giving in to despair, we should adopt Moses' attitude to "stand where you are and watch the LORD rescue you."

**14:15** The Lord told Moses to stop praying and get moving! Prayer must have a vital place in our lives, but there is also a place for action. Sometimes we know what to do, but we pray for more guidance as an excuse to postpone doing it. If we know what we should do, then it is time to get moving.

**14:21** There was no apparent way of escape, but the Lord opened up a dry path through the sea. Sometimes we find our-

**14:22**
Exod 15:19
Neh 9:11
Pss 66:6; 78:13
Heb 11:29

**14:24**
Exod 13:21

**14:26**
Exod 14:16

**14:27**
Exod 15:1, 7
Deut 11:4
Heb 11:29

**14:28**
Exod 15:19
Neh 9:11
Pss 78:53; 106:11

**14:29**
Ps 66:6
Isa 11:15

**14:30**
Pss 106:8
Isa 63:8, 11

**14:31**
Exod 4:31; 19:9
Ps 106:12

**15:1**
Ps 106:12
Isa 12:5; 42:10-12
Jer 51:21
Rev 15:3

**15:2**
Exod 3:15-16
Deut 10:21
2 Sam 22:47
Ps 18:1
Isa 12:2

**15:3**
Exod 14:14
Pss 24:8; 83:18

**15:4**
Exod 14:6-7, 17, 28

**15:5**
Exod 14:28
Neh 9:11

**15:6**
Exod 3:20
Ps 118:15-16

the water with a strong east wind. The wind blew all that night, turning the seabed into dry land. 22 So the people of Israel walked through the sea on dry ground, with walls of water on each side! 23 Then the Egyptians—all of Pharaoh's horses, chariots, and charioteers—followed them across the bottom of the sea. 24 But early in the morning, the LORD looked down on the Egyptian army from the pillar of fire and cloud, and he threw them into confusion. 25 Their chariot wheels began to come off, making their chariots impossible to drive. "Let's get out of here!" the Egyptians shouted. "The LORD is fighting for Israel against us!"

26 When all the Israelites were on the other side, the LORD said to Moses, "Raise your hand over the sea again. Then the waters will rush back over the Egyptian chariots and charioteers." 27 So as the sun began to rise, Moses raised his hand over the sea. The water roared back into its usual place, and the LORD swept the terrified Egyptians into the surging currents. 28 The waters covered all the chariots and charioteers—the entire army of Pharaoh. Of all the Egyptians who had chased the Israelites into the sea, not a single one survived.

29 The people of Israel had walked through the middle of the sea on dry land, as the water stood up like a wall on both sides. 30 This was how the LORD rescued Israel from the Egyptians that day. And the Israelites could see the bodies of the Egyptians washed up on the shore. 31 When the people of Israel saw the mighty power that the LORD had displayed against the Egyptians, they feared the LORD and put their faith in him and his servant Moses.

### A Song of Deliverance

**15** Then Moses and the people of Israel sang this song to the LORD:

"I will sing to the LORD, for he has triumphed gloriously;
　　he has thrown both horse and rider into the sea.

2 The LORD is my strength and my song;
　　he has become my victory.
He is my God, and I will praise him;
　　he is my father's God, and I will exalt him!

3 The LORD is a warrior;
　　yes, the LORD is his name!

4 Pharaoh's chariots and armies,
　　he has thrown into the sea.
The very best of Pharaoh's officers
　　have been drowned in the Red Sea.*

5 The deep waters have covered them;
　　they sank to the bottom like a stone.

6 "Your right hand, O LORD,
　　is glorious in power.

**15:4** Hebrew *sea cf reeds;* also in 15:22.

---

selves caught in a problem and see no way out. Don't panic; God can open up a way.

**14:21, 22** Some scholars believe the Israelites did not cross the main body of the Red Sea but one of the shallow lakes or marshes north of it that dry up at certain times of the year, or perhaps it was a smaller branch of the Red Sea where the water would have been shallow enough to wade across. But the Bible clearly states that the Lord "opened up a path through the water with a strong east wind . . . turning the sea bed into dry land" (14:21; see also Joshua 3:15, 16; and 2 Kings 2:13, 14). Also, the water was deep enough to cover the chariots (14:28). The God who created the earth and water performed a mighty miracle at exactly the right time to demonstrate his great power and love for his people.

**14:27, 28** No evidence of this great Exodus has been discovered in Egyptian historical records. This was because it was a common practice for Egyptian pharaohs not to record their

defeats. They even went so far as to take existing records and delete the names of traitors and political adversaries. Pharaoh would have been especially anxious not to record that his great army was destroyed chasing a band of runaway slaves. Since either the Egyptians failed to record the Exodus or the record has not yet been found, it is impossible to place a precise date on the event.

**15:1ff** Music played an important part in Israel's worship and celebration. Singing was an expression of love and thanks, and it was a creative way to pass down oral traditions. Some say this song of Moses is the oldest recorded song in the world. It was a festive epic poem celebrating God's victory, lifting the hearts and voices of the people outward and upward. After having been delivered from great danger, they sang with joy! Psalms and hymns can be great ways to express relief, praise, and thanks when you have been through trouble.

Your right hand, O LORD,
    dashes the enemy to pieces.
7 In the greatness of your majesty,
    you overthrew those who rose against you.
Your anger flashed forth;
    it consumed them as fire burns straw.
8 At the blast of your breath, the waters piled up!
    The surging waters stood straight like a wall;
    in the middle of the sea the waters became hard.

9 "The enemy said, 'I will chase them,
    catch up with them, and destroy them.
I will divide the plunder,
    avenging myself against them.
I will unsheath my sword;
    my power will destroy them.'
10 But with a blast of your breath,
    the sea covered them.
They sank like lead
    in the mighty waters.

11 "Who else among the gods is like you, O LORD?
    Who is glorious in holiness like you—
so awesome in splendor,
    performing such wonders?
12 You raised up your hand,
    and the earth swallowed our enemies.

13 "With unfailing love you will lead
    this people whom you have ransomed.
You will guide them in your strength
    to the place where your holiness dwells.
14 The nations will hear and tremble;
    anguish will grip the people of Philistia.
15 The leaders of Edom will be terrified;
    the nobles of Moab will tremble.
All the people of Canaan will melt with fear;
16     terror and dread will overcome them.
Because of your great power,
    they will be silent like a stone,
until your people pass by, O LORD,
until the people whom you purchased pass by.
17 You will bring them in and plant them on your own mountain—
    the place you have made as your home, O LORD,
    the sanctuary, O Lord, that your hands have made.
18 The LORD will reign forever and ever!"

19 When Pharaoh's horses, chariots, and charioteers rushed into the sea, the LORD brought the water crashing down on them. But the people of Israel had walked through on dry land!

20 Then Miriam the prophet, Aaron's sister, took a tambourine and led all the women in rhythm and dance. 21 And Miriam sang this song:

"I will sing to the LORD, for he has triumphed gloriously;
    he has thrown both horse and rider into the sea."

**15:7** Exod 9:16; 14:24; Ps 78:49-50

**15:8** Exod 14:22, 29; Ps 78:13

**15:9** Exod 14:5-9

**15:10** Exod 14:27-28

**15:11** Exod 8:10; Deut 3:24; 1 Sam 2:2; 2 Sam 7:22; Pss 22:23; 72:18; Isa 6:3; Rev 4:8

**15:12** Exod 15:6

**15:13** Neh 9:12; Ps 77:15, 20

**15:14** Deut 2:25; Hab 3:7

**15:15** Num 22:3; Deut 2:4; Josh 2:11; 5:1

**15:17** Exod 23:20; 32:34; Pss 2:6; 78:54, 68; Isa 5:2; Jer 2:21

**15:18** Pss 10:16; 29:10; Isa 57:15

**15:19** Exod 14:22, 28

**15:20** Exod 2:4; Num 26:59; 1 Sam 18:6; Pss 30:11; 150:4

**15:21** Exod 15:1

---

**15:20** Miriam was called a prophet not only because she received revelations from God (Numbers 12:1, 2; Micah 6:4) but also because of her musical skill. Prophecy and music were often closely related in the Bible (1 Samuel 10:5; 1 Chronicles 25:1).

## 3. Complaining in the wilderness

### Bitter Water at Marah

**15:22**
Num 33:8
Pss 77:20; 78:52

22 Then Moses led the people of Israel away from the Red Sea, and they moved out into the Shur Desert. They traveled in this desert for three days without water.

**15:23**
Num 33:8
Ruth 1:20

23 When they came to Marah, they finally found water. But the people couldn't drink it because it was bitter. (That is why the place was called Marah, which means "bitter.")

**15:24**
Exod 14:11
Ps 106:13

24 Then the people turned against Moses. "What are we going to drink?" they demanded.

**15:25**
Exod 14:10; 16:4

25 So Moses cried out to the LORD for help, and the LORD showed him a branch. Moses took the branch and threw it into the water. This made the water good to drink.

**15:26**
Exod 19:5-6
Deut 7:15
Ps 103:3

It was there at Marah that the LORD laid before them the following conditions to test their faithfulness to him: 26 "If you will listen carefully to the voice of the LORD your God and do what is right in his sight, obeying his commands and laws, then I will not make you suffer the diseases I sent on the Egyptians; for I am the LORD who heals you."

**15:27**
Num 33:9

27 After leaving Marah, they came to Elim, where there were twelve springs and seventy palm trees. They camped there beside the springs.

---

| FAMOUS SONGS IN THE BIBLE | Where | Purpose of Song |
|---|---|---|
| | Exodus 15:1–21 | Moses' song of deliverance and praise after God led Israel out of Egypt and saved them by parting the Red Sea; Miriam joined in the singing, too |
| | Numbers 21:17 | Israel's song of praise to God for giving them water in the wilderness |
| | Deuteronomy 32:1–43 | Moses' song of Israel's history with thanksgiving and praise as the Hebrews were about to enter the Promised Land |
| | Judges 5:2–31 | Deborah and Barak's song of praise thanking God for Israel's victory over King Jabin's army at Mount Tabor |
| | 2 Samuel 22:2–51 | David's song of thanks and praise to God for rescuing him from Saul and his other enemies |
| | Song of Songs | Solomon's song of love celebrating the union of husband and wife |
| | Isaiah 26:1 | Isaiah's prophetic song about how the redeemed will sing in the new Jerusalem |
| | Ezra 3:11 | Israel's song of praise at the completion of the Temple's foundation |
| | Luke 1:46–55 | Mary's song of praise to God for the conception of Jesus |
| | Luke 1:68–79 | Zechariah's song of praise for the birth of his son |
| | Acts 16:25 | Paul and Silas sang hymns in prison |
| | Revelation 5:9, 10 | The "new song" of the 24 elders acclaiming Christ as worthy to break the seven seals of God's scroll |
| | Revelation 14:3 | The song of the 144,000 redeemed from the earth |
| | Revelation 15:3, 4 | The song of all the redeemed in praise of the Lamb who redeemed them |

---

**15:23, 27** The waters of Marah are contrasted with the springs of Elim. Marah stood for the unbelieving, grumbling attitude of the people who would not trust God. Elim stands for God's bountiful provision. How easy it is to grumble and complain too quickly, only to be embarrassed by God's help!

**15:26** God promised that if the people obeyed him, they would be free from the diseases that plagued the Egyptians. Little did they know that many of the moral laws he later gave them were designed to keep them free from sickness. For

example, following God's law against prostitution would keep them free of venereal disease. God's laws for us are often designed to keep us from harm. Men and women are complex beings. Our physical, emotional, and spiritual lives are intertwined. Modern medicine is now acknowledging what these laws assumed. If we want God to care for us, we need to submit to his directions for living.

*Manna and Quail from Heaven*

**16** Then they left Elim and journeyed into the Sin* Desert, between Elim and Mount Sinai. They arrived there a month after leaving Egypt.* ²There, too, the whole community of Israel spoke bitterly against Moses and Aaron.

³"Oh, that we were back in Egypt," they moaned. "It would have been better if the LORD had killed us there! At least there we had plenty to eat. But now you have brought us into this desert to starve us to death."

⁴Then the LORD said to Moses, "Look, I'm going to rain down food from heaven for you. The people can go out each day and pick up as much food as they need for that day. I will test them in this to see whether they will follow my instructions. ⁵Tell them to pick up twice as much as usual on the sixth day of each week."

⁶Then Moses and Aaron called a meeting of all the people of Israel and told them, "In the evening you will realize that it was the LORD who brought you out of the land of Egypt. ⁷In the morning you will see the glorious presence of the LORD. He has heard your complaints, which are against the LORD and not against us. ⁸The LORD will give you meat to eat in the evening and bread in the morning, for he has heard all your complaints against him. Yes, your complaints are against the LORD, not against us."

⁹Then Moses said to Aaron, "Say this to the entire community of Israel: 'Come into the LORD's presence, and hear his reply to your complaints.'" ¹⁰And as Aaron spoke to the people, they looked out toward the desert. Within the guiding cloud, they could see the awesome glory of the LORD.

¹¹And the LORD said to Moses, ¹²"I have heard the people's complaints. Now tell them, 'In the evening you will have meat to eat, and in the morning you will be filled with bread. Then you will know that I am the LORD your God.'"

¹³That evening vast numbers of quail arrived and covered the camp. The next morning the desert all around the camp was wet with dew. ¹⁴When the dew disappeared later in the morning, thin flakes, white like frost, covered the ground. ¹⁵The Israelites were puzzled when they saw it. "What is it?" they asked.

And Moses told them, "It is the food the LORD has given you. ¹⁶The LORD says that each household should gather as much as it needs. Pick up two quarts* for each person."

¹⁷So the people of Israel went out and gathered this food—some getting more, and some getting less. ¹⁸By gathering two quarts for each person, everyone had just enough. Those who gathered a lot had nothing left over, and those who gathered only a little had enough. Each family had just what it needed.

¹⁹Then Moses told them, "Do not keep any of it overnight." ²⁰But, of course, some of them didn't listen and kept some of it until morning. By then it was full of maggots and had a terrible smell. And Moses was very angry with them.

²¹The people gathered the food morning by morning, each family according to its need. And as the sun became hot, the food they had not picked up melted and disappeared. ²²On the sixth day, there was twice as much as usual on the ground— four quarts* for each person instead of two. The leaders of the people came and asked

**16:1** Exod 17:1
Num 33:11-12

**16:2** Exod 14:11
1 Cor 10:10

**16:4** Deut 8:2, 16
Pss 78:24; 105:40
John 6:31
1 Cor 10:3

**16:5** Exod 16:22

**16:6** Exod 6:6

**16:7** Exod 16:12
Num 14:27; 16:11

**16:10** Num 16:19

**16:12** Exod 16:7

**16:13** Num 11:31
Pss 78:27-28;
105:40

**16:14** Num 11:7-9
Deut 8:3

**16:15** Exod 16:31
Neh 9:5
John 6:31
1 Cor 10:3

**16:16** Exod 16:33, 36

**16:18** 2 Cor 8:15

**16:19** Exod 12:10; 23:18

**16:22** Exod 16:5; 34:31

**16:1a** Not to be confused with the English word *sin.*   **16:1b** Hebrew *on the fifteenth day of the second month.* The Exodus had occurred on the fourteenth day of the first month (see 12:6).   **16:16** Hebrew *1 omer* [2 liters]; also in 16:18, 32, 33.   **16:22** Hebrew *2 omers* [4 liters].

**16:1** The Sin Desert was a vast and hostile environment of sand and stone. Its barren surroundings provided the perfect place for God to test and shape the character of his people.

**16:2, 3** It happened again. As the Israelites encountered danger, shortages, and inconvenience, they complained bitterly and longed to be back in Egypt. But as always, God provided for their needs. Difficult circumstances often lead to stress, and complaining is a natural response. The Israelites didn't really want to be back in Egypt; they just wanted life to get a little easier. In the pressure of the moment, they could not focus on the cause of their stress (in this case, lack of trust in God); they could only think about the quickest way of escape. When pres-

sure comes your way, resist the temptation to make a quick escape. Instead, focus on God's power and wisdom to help you deal with the cause of your stress.

**16:4, 5** God promised to meet the Hebrews' need for food in the desert, but he decided to test their obedience. God wanted to see if they would obey his detailed instructions. We can learn to trust him as our Lord only by following. We can learn to obey by taking small steps of obedience.

**16:14-16** Manna (16:31) appeared on the ground each day as thin flakes like frost. The people gathered it, ground it like grain, and made it into honey-tasting pancakes. For the Israelites the manna was a gift—it came every day and was just what they needed. It satisfied their temporary physical need. In John 6:48-51 Jesus compares himself to manna. Christ is our daily bread who satisfies our eternal, spiritual need.

**16:23**
Gen 2:3
Exod 20:8; 23:12
Neh 9:14

**16:24**
Exod 16:20

**16:28**
Ps 78:10

**16:31**
Num 11:7-9
Deut 8:3, 16

**16:33**
Heb 9:4
Rev 2:17

**16:34**
Exod 25:16, 21
Num 1:50

**16:35**
Josh 5:12
Neh 9:20-21

**17:1**
Exod 16:1; 19:2
Num 33:15

**17:2**
Exod 14:11-12
Num 20:3
Deut 6:16
1 Cor 10:10

Moses why this had happened. 23 He replied, "The LORD has appointed tomorrow as a day of rest, a holy Sabbath to the LORD. On this day we will rest from our normal daily tasks. So bake or boil as much as you want today, and set aside what is left for tomorrow."

24 The next morning the leftover food was wholesome and good, without maggots or odor. 25 Moses said, "This is your food for today, for today is a Sabbath to the LORD. There will be no food on the ground today. 26 Gather the food for six days, but the seventh day is a Sabbath. There will be no food on the ground for you on that day."

27 Some of the people went out anyway to gather food, even though it was the Sabbath day. But there was none to be found. 28 "How long will these people refuse to obey my commands and instructions?" the LORD asked Moses. 29 "Do they not realize that I have given them the seventh day, the Sabbath, as a day of rest? That is why I give you twice as much food on the sixth day, so there will be enough for two days. On the Sabbath day you must stay in your places. Do not pick up food from the ground on that day." 30 So the people rested on the seventh day.

31 In time, the food became known as manna.* It was white like coriander seed, and it tasted like honey cakes.

32 Then Moses gave them this command from the LORD: "Take two quarts of manna and keep it forever as a treasured memorial of the LORD's provision. By doing this, later generations will be able to see the bread that the LORD provided in the wilderness when he brought you out of Egypt."

33 Moses said to Aaron, "Get a container and put two quarts of manna into it. Then store it in a sacred place* as a reminder for all future generations." 34 Aaron did this, just as the LORD had commanded Moses. He eventually placed it for safekeeping in the Ark of the Covenant.* 35 So the people of Israel ate manna for forty years until they arrived in the land of Canaan, where there were crops to eat.

36 (The container used to measure the manna was an omer, which held about two quarts.)*

*Water from the Rock*

**17** At the LORD's command, the people of Israel left the Sin* Desert and moved from place to place. Eventually they came to Rephidim, but there was no water to be found there. 2 So once more the people grumbled and complained to Moses. "Give us water to drink!" they demanded.

"Quiet!" Moses replied. "Why are you arguing with me? And why are you testing the LORD?"

**16:31** *Manna* means "What is it?" See 13:15. **16:33** Hebrew *before the LORD.* **16:34** Hebrew *in front of the Testimony.* **16:36** Hebrew *An omer is one tenth of an ephah.* **17:1** Not to be confused with the English word *sin.*

---

**JOURNEY TO MOUNT SINAI**
God miraculously supplied food and water in the wilderness for the Israelites. In the Sin Desert, he provided manna (16). At Rephidim, he provided water from a rock (17:1–7). Finally God brought them to the foot of Mount Sinai, where he gave them his holy laws.

**16:23** The Israelites were not to work on the Sabbath—not even to cook food. Why? God knew that the busy routine of daily living could distract people from worshiping him. It is so easy to let work, family responsibilities, and recreation crowd our schedules so tightly that we don't take time to worship. Carefully guard your time with God.

**16:32** The Hebrews put some manna in a special jar as a reminder of the way God provided for them in the wilderness. Symbols have always been an important part of Christian worship also. We use special objects as symbols to remind us of God's work. Such symbols can be valuable aids to our worship as long as we are careful to keep them from becoming objects of worship.

**17:2** Again the people complained about their problem instead of praying. Some problems can be solved by careful thought or by rearranging our priorities. Some can be solved by discussion and good counsel. But some problems can be solved only by prayer. We should make a determined effort to pray when we feel like complaining because complaining only raises our level of stress. Prayer quiets our thoughts and emotions and prepares us to listen.

³But tormented by thirst, they continued to complain, "Why did you ever take us out of Egypt? Why did you bring us here? We, our children, and our livestock will all die!"

⁴Then Moses pleaded with the LORD, "What should I do with these people? They are about to stone me!"

⁵The LORD said to Moses, "Take your shepherd's staff, the one you used when you struck the water of the Nile. Then call some of the leaders of Israel and walk on ahead of the people. ⁶I will meet you by the rock at Mount Sinai.* Strike the rock, and water will come pouring out. Then the people will be able to drink." Moses did just as he was told; and as the leaders looked on, water gushed out.

⁷Moses named the place Massah—"the place of testing"—and Meribah—"the place of arguing"—because the people of Israel argued with Moses and tested the LORD by saying, "Is the LORD going to take care of us or not?"

### Israel Defeats the Amalekites

⁸While the people of Israel were still at Rephidim, the warriors of Amalek came to fight against them. ⁹Moses commanded Joshua, "Call the Israelites to arms, and fight the army of Amalek. Tomorrow, I will stand at the top of the hill with the staff of God in my hand."

¹⁰So Joshua did what Moses had commanded. He led his men out to fight the army of Amalek. Meanwhile Moses, Aaron, and Hur went to the top of a nearby hill. ¹¹As long as Moses held up the staff with his hands, the Israelites had the advantage. But whenever he lowered his hands, the Amalekites gained the upper hand. ¹²Moses' arms finally became too tired to hold up the staff any longer. So Aaron and Hur found a stone for him to sit on. Then they stood on each side, holding up his hands until sunset. ¹³As a result, Joshua and his troops were able to crush the army of Amalek.

¹⁴Then the LORD instructed Moses, "Write this down as a permanent record, and announce it to Joshua: I will blot out every trace of Amalek from under heaven." ¹⁵Moses built an altar there and called it "The LORD Is My Banner."* ¹⁶He said, "They have dared to raise their fist against the LORD's throne, so now* the LORD will be at war with Amalek generation after generation."

### Jethro's Visit to Moses

**18** Word soon reached Jethro, the priest of Midian and Moses' father-in-law, about all the wonderful things God had done for Moses and his people, the Israelites. He had heard about how the LORD had brought them safely out of Egypt.

²Some time before this, Moses had sent his wife, Zipporah, and his two sons to live with Jethro, his father-in-law. ³The name of Moses' first son was Gershom,* for Moses had said when the boy was born, "I have been a stranger in a foreign land." ⁴The name of his second son was Eliezer,* for Moses had said at his birth, "The God of my fathers was my helper; he delivered me from the sword of Pharaoh." ⁵Jethro now came to visit Moses, and he brought Moses' wife and two sons with him. They arrived while Moses and the people were camped near the mountain of God. ⁶Moses was told, "Jethro, your father-in-law, has come to visit you. Your wife and your two sons are with him."

⁷So Moses went out to meet his father-in-law. He bowed to him respectfully and

**Margin cross-references:**
17:3 Exod 16:2-3
17:4 Num 14:10; 16:19
17:5 Exod 7:20; 14:16
17:6 Num 20:8-10; Pss 78:15-16; 105:41; 1 Cor 10:4
17:7 Deut 6:16; 9:22; Pss 81:7; 95:8
17:8 Gen 36:12, 16; Num 24:20; Deut 25:17-19
17:9 Exod 24:13; Num 11:28
17:10 Exod 24:14; 31:2
17:12 Isa 35:3
17:14 Exod 24:4; 34:27; Num 33:2
17:15 Gen 22:14
18:1 Exod 2:16, 18; 3:1
18:2 Exod 2:21; 4:25
18:3 Exod 2:22; Acts 7:29
18:4 Gen 49:25
18:5 Exod 3:1
18:7 Gen 43:28

---

**17:6** Hebrew *Horeb*, another name for Sinai.   **17:15** Hebrew *Yahweh Nissi*.   **17:16** Or *Hands have been lifted up to the LORD's throne, and now.*   **18:3** *Gershom* sounds like a Hebrew term that means "a stranger there."   **18:4** *Eliezer* means "God is my helper."

---

**17:8** The Amalekites were descendants of Amalek, a grandson of Esau. They were a fierce nomadic tribe that lived in the desert region of the Dead Sea. They made part of their livelihood by conducting frequent raids on other settlements and carrying off booty. They killed for pleasure. One of the greatest insults in Israelite culture was to call someone "a friend of Amalek." When the Israelites entered the region, the Amalekites saw this as a perfect opportunity for both pleasure and profit. But this hostile tribe was moving in on the wrong group—a people led by God. For the Israelite slaves to defeat such a warlike nation was more than enough proof that God was with them as he had promised to be.

**17:9** Here we meet Joshua for the first time. Later he would become the great leader who brought God's people into the Promised Land. As a general of the Israelite army, he was gaining valuable experience for the greater battles to come.

**17:10-13** Aaron and Hur stood by Moses' side and held up his arms to ensure victory against Amalek. We need to "hold up the hands" of our spiritual leaders as well. Shouldering some responsibility, lending a word of encouragement, or offering a prayer are ways of refreshing spiritual leaders in their work.

**18:7** Jethro entered Moses' tent where the two talked. Tents were the homes of shepherds. In shape and design, they resembled the tents of today, but they were very large and made of a thick cloth woven from goat or camel hair. This fabric breathed in warm weather and contracted in stormy weather to offer protection from the winter winds and rains. The floor was often covered with animal-skin rugs, while curtains divided the inside space into rooms.

**18:8**
Exod 15:6, 16
Num 20:14

**18:9**
Isa 63:7-14

**18:10**
1 Kgs 8:56
Ps 68:19-20

**18:11**
Exod 12:12; 15:11

**18:12**
Gen 31:54
Exod 24:5

greeted him warmly. They asked about each other's health and then went to Moses' tent to talk further. [8]Moses told his father-in-law about everything the LORD had done to rescue Israel from Pharaoh and the Egyptians. He also told him about the problems they had faced along the way and how the LORD had delivered his people from all their troubles. [9]Jethro was delighted when he heard about all that the LORD had done for Israel as he brought them out of Egypt.

[10]"Praise be to the LORD," Jethro said, "for he has saved you from the Egyptians and from Pharaoh. He has rescued Israel from the power of Egypt! [11]I know now that the LORD is greater than all other gods, because his people have escaped from the proud and cruel Egyptians."

[12]Then Jethro presented a burnt offering and gave sacrifices to God. As Jethro was doing this, Aaron and the leaders of Israel came out to meet him. They all joined him in a sacrificial meal in God's presence.

### Jethro's Wise Advice

[13]The next day, Moses sat as usual to hear the people's complaints against each other. They were lined up in front of him from morning till evening.

[14]When Moses' father-in-law saw all that Moses was doing for the people, he said,

---

## JETHRO

People such as Jethro and Melchizedek—not Israelites, but nevertheless worshipers of the true God—play an important role in the Old Testament. They remind us of God's commitment to the world. God chose one nation through which to work, but his love and concern are for all nations!

Jethro's religious background prepared him for rather than prevented him from, responding in faith to God. When he saw and heard what God had done for the Israelites, he worshiped God wholeheartedly. We can guess that for 40 years as Moses' father-in-law, Jethro had been watching God at work, molding a leader. Moses' and Jethro's relationship must have been close, for Moses readily accepted his father-in-law's advice. Each benefited from knowing the other. Jethro met God through Moses, and Moses received hospitality, his wife, and wisdom from Jethro.

The greatest gift one person can give another is an introduction to God. But that gift is hindered if the believer's attitude is, "I have the greatest gift to pass on to you, while you have nothing to give me in return." Real friends give to and receive from each other. The importance of introducing a friend to God does not make the friend's gifts to us insignificant. Rather, the believer is doubly blessed—first by receiving the gifts the friend wishes to give; then by growing in knowledge of the Lord. For we discover that in introducing another person to God, we increase our own awareness of God. As we give God away, he gives himself even more to us.

Is all you know about God a miscellaneous collection of trivia, or do you have a living relationship with him? Only with a vital relationship can you pass on to others the excitement of allowing God to guide your life. Have you reached the point of saying, with Jethro, "I know now that the LORD is greater than all other gods" (Exodus 18:11)?

| | |
|---|---|
| **Strengths and accomplishments** | • As father-in-law to Moses, he came to recognize the one true God<br>• He was a practical troubleshooter and organizer |
| **Lessons from his life** | • Supervision and administration are team efforts<br>• God's plan includes all nations |
| **Vital statistics** | • Where: The land of Midian and the wilderness of Sinai<br>• Occupations: Shepherd, priest<br>• Relatives: Daughter: Zipporah. Son-in-law: Moses. Son: Hobab |
| **Key verse** | "Jethro was delighted when he heard about all that the LORD had done for Israel as he brought them out of Egypt" (Exodus 18:9). |

Jethro's story is told in Exodus 2:15—3:1; 18:1–27. He is also mentioned in Judges 1:16.

---

**18:8-11** Moses told his father-in-law all that God had done, convincing him that the Lord was greater than any other god. Our relatives are often the hardest people to tell about God. Yet we should look for opportunities to tell them what God is doing in our lives because we can have an important influence on them.

**18:12** This reunion turned into a large celebration. The Israelites frequently shared a sacrificial meal among themselves. A burnt offering was sacrificed to God, and then the meal taken from the sacrifice was dedicated to God and eaten ceremonially as a fellowship dinner.

**18:13-26** Moses was spending so much time and energy hearing the Hebrews' complaints that he could not get to other important work. Jethro suggested that Moses delegate most of this work to others and focus his efforts on jobs only he could do. People in positions of responsibility sometimes feel they are the only ones who can do necessary tasks, but others are capable of handling part of the load. Delegation relieved Moses' stress and improved the quality of the government. It helped prepare them for the system of government set up in Canaan. Proper delegation can multiply your effectiveness while giving others a chance to grow.

"Why are you trying to do all this alone? The people have been standing here all day to get your help."

[15] Moses replied, "Well, the people come to me to seek God's guidance. [16] When an argument arises, I am the one who settles the case. I inform the people of God's decisions and teach them his laws and instructions."

[17] "This is not good!" his father-in-law exclaimed. [18] "You're going to wear yourself out—and the people, too. This job is too heavy a burden for you to handle all by yourself. [19] Now let me give you a word of advice, and may God be with you. You should continue to be the people's representative before God, bringing him their questions to be decided. [20] You should tell them God's decisions, teach them God's laws and instructions, and show them how to conduct their lives. [21] But find some capable, honest men who fear God and hate bribes. Appoint them as judges over groups of one thousand, one hundred, fifty, and ten. [22] These men can serve the people, resolving all the ordinary cases. Anything that is too important or too complicated can be brought to you. But they can take care of the smaller matters themselves. They will help you carry the load, making the task easier for you. [23] If you follow this advice, and if God directs you to do so, then you will be able to endure the pressures, and all these people will go home in peace."

[24] Moses listened to his father-in-law's advice and followed his suggestions. [25] He chose capable men from all over Israel and made them judges over the people. They were put in charge of groups of one thousand, one hundred, fifty, and ten. [26] These men were constantly available to administer justice. They brought the hard cases to Moses, but they judged the smaller matters themselves.

[27] Soon after this, Moses said good-bye to his father-in-law, who returned to his own land.

## C. ISRAEL AT SINAI (19:1—40:38)

After escaping through the Red Sea, the Hebrews traveled through the wilderness and arrived at Sinai, God's holy mountain. There they received the Ten Commandments, as well as instructions for building a Tabernacle as a center of worship. Through Israel's experiences at Mount Sinai, we learn about the importance of obedience in our relationship with God. His laws help expose sin, and they give standards for righteous living.

### 1. Giving the law

**19** The Israelites arrived in the wilderness of Sinai exactly two months after they left Egypt.* [2] After breaking camp at Rephidim, they came to the base of Mount Sinai and set up camp there.

[3] Then Moses climbed the mountain to appear before God. The LORD called out to him from the mountain and said, "Give these instructions to the descendants of Jacob, the people of Israel: [4] 'You have seen what I did to the Egyptians. You know how I brought you to myself and carried you on eagle's wings. [5] Now if you will obey me and keep my

**19:1** Hebrew *in the third month . . . on the very day,* i.e., two lunar months to the day after leaving Egypt. This day of the Hebrew lunar calendar occurs in late May or early June; compare note on 13:4.

**18:15**
Num 9:8
Deut 17:8-13

**18:16**
Exod 24:14

**18:18**
Num 11:14, 17
Deut 1:9

**18:19-20**
Deut 1:18

**18:21**
Deut 1:13, 15
Ps 15:1-5

**18:22**
Num 11:17
Deut 1:17-18

**18:25**
Deut 1:15; 16:18

**18:26**
Deut 16:18

**18:27**
Num 10:29-30

**19:1**
Exod 12:51; 16:1

**19:3**
Exod 20:21
Acts 7:38

**19:4**
Deut 29:2
Isa 40:31; 63:9
Rev 12:14

**19:5**
Exod 15:26
Deut 10:14

---

**18:16** Moses not only decided these cases, he also taught the people God's laws. Whenever we help others settle disputes or resolve conflicts, we should also look for opportunities to teach about God.

**19:2, 3** Mount Sinai is one of the most sacred locations in Israel's history. Located in the south-central Sinai peninsula, this mountain is where Moses met God in a burning bush, God made his covenant with Israel, and Elijah heard God in the gentle whisper. Here God gave his people the laws and guidelines for right living. They learned the potential blessings of obedience (34:4-28) and the tragic consequences of disobedience (34:7).

**19:4-6** God had a reason for rescuing the Israelites from slavery. Now he was ready to tell them what it was: Israel was to become a kingdom of priests and a holy nation where anyone could approach God freely. It didn't take long, however, for the

people to corrupt God's plan. God then established Aaron's descendants from the tribe of Levi as priests (Leviticus 8, 9), representing what the entire nation should have been. But with the coming of Jesus Christ, God has once again extended his plan to all believers. We are to become holy, a "kingdom of priests" (1 Peter 2:9). The death and resurrection of Christ has allowed each of us to approach God freely.

**19:5** Why did God choose Israel as his nation? God knew that no nation on earth was good enough to deserve to be called his people, his "special treasure." He chose Israel, not because of anything they had done, but in his love and mercy he chose Israel in spite of the wrong the nation had done and would do. Why did he want to have a special nation on earth? To represent his way of life, to teach his Word, and to be an agent of salvation to the world. "All the nations of the earth" would be blessed through Abraham's descendants (Genesis

**19:6**
Lev 11:44-45
Deut 33:3
†1 Pet 2:5, 9
Rev 1:6; 5:10

**19:7**
Exod 4:29-30; 24:9

**19:8**
Exod 24:3, 7
Deut 5:27; 26:17

**19:9**
Exod 19:16; 24:15
Deut 4:11
Ps 99:7

**19:10**
Gen 35:2
Lev 11:44-45
Num 8:7; 19:19
Heb 10:22
Rev 22:14

**19:11**
Exod 19:16

**19:13**
†Heb 12:20

**19:15**
1 Sam 21:4
1 Cor 7:5

**19:16**
Exod 9:23; 20:18
Heb 12:18-19

**19:17**
Deut 4:11

**19:18**
Exod 24:17
Deut 5:4
Pss 68:7-8; 104:32

**19:19**
Ps 81:7

**19:20**
Exod 24:12
Neh 9:13

**19:21**
Exod 3:5

**19:22**
Lev 10:3; 21:6-8

**19:24**
Exod 24:1, 9

covenant, you will be my own special treasure from among all the nations of the earth; for all the earth belongs to me. 6And you will be to me a kingdom of priests, my holy nation.' Give this message to the Israelites."

7Moses returned from the mountain and called together the leaders of the people and told them what the LORD had said. 8They all responded together, "We will certainly do everything the LORD asks of us." So Moses brought the people's answer back to the LORD.

9Then the LORD said to Moses, "I am going to come to you in a thick cloud so the people themselves can hear me as I speak to you. Then they will always have confidence in you."

Moses told the LORD what the people had said. 10Then the LORD told Moses, "Go down and prepare the people for my visit. Purify them today and tomorrow, and have them wash their clothing. 11Be sure they are ready on the third day, for I will come down upon Mount Sinai as all the people watch. 12Set boundary lines that the people may not pass. Warn them, 'Be careful! Do not go up on the mountain or even touch its boundaries. Those who do will certainly die! 13Any people or animals that cross the boundary must be stoned to death or shot with arrows. They must not be touched by human hands.' The people must stay away from the mountain until they hear one long blast from the ram's horn. Then they must gather at the foot of the mountain."

14So Moses went down to the people. He purified them for worship and had them wash their clothing. 15He told them, "Get ready for an important event two days from now. And until then, abstain from having sexual intercourse."

16On the morning of the third day, there was a powerful thunder and lightning storm, and a dense cloud came down upon the mountain. There was a long, loud blast from a ram's horn, and all the people trembled. 17Moses led them out from the camp to meet with God, and they stood at the foot of the mountain. 18All Mount Sinai was covered with smoke because the LORD had descended on it in the form of fire. The smoke billowed into the sky like smoke from a furnace, and the whole mountain shook with a violent earthquake. 19As the horn blast grew louder and louder, Moses spoke, and God thundered his reply for all to hear. 20The LORD came down on the top of Mount Sinai and called Moses to the top of the mountain. So Moses climbed the mountain.

21Then the LORD told Moses, "Go back down and warn the people not to cross the boundaries. They must not come up here to see the LORD, for those who do will die. 22Even the priests who regularly come near to the LORD must purify themselves, or I will destroy them."

23"But, LORD, the people cannot come up on the mountain!" Moses protested. "You already told them not to. You told me to set boundaries around the mountain and to declare it off limits."

24But the LORD said, "Go down anyway and bring Aaron back with you. In the meantime, do not let the priests or the people cross the boundaries to come up here. If they do, I will punish them."

25So Moses went down to the people and told them what the LORD had said.

---

18:18). Gentiles and kings would come to the Lord through Israel, predicted Isaiah (Isaiah 60:3). Through the nation of Israel, the Messiah, God's chosen Son, would be born. God chose one nation and put it through a rigorous training program, so that one day it could be a channel for his blessings to the whole world.

**19:5-8** In Genesis 15 and 17, God made a covenant with Abraham, promising to make his descendants into a great nation. Now that promise was being realized as God restated his agreement with the Israelite nation, the descendants of Abraham. God promised to bless and care for them. The people promised to obey him. The covenant was thus sealed. But the good intentions of the people quickly wore off. Have you made a commitment to God? How are you holding up your end of the bargain?

**13:9-11** Moses was told to purify the people. This meant getting them physically and spiritually ready to meet God. The people were to set themselves apart from sin and even ordinary daily routine in order to dedicate themselves to God. The act of washing and preparing served to get their minds and hearts ready. When we meet God for worship, we should set aside the cares and preoccupations of everyday life. Use your time of physical preparation to get your mind ready to meet God.

## The Ten Commandments

**20** Then God instructed the people as follows:

²"I am the LORD your God, who rescued you from slavery in Egypt.

³"Do not worship any other gods besides me.

⁴"Do not make idols of any kind, whether in the shape of birds or animals or fish. ⁵You must never worship or bow down to them, for I, the LORD your God, am a jealous God who will not share your affection with any other god! I do not leave unpunished the sins of those who hate me, but I punish the children for the sins of their parents to the third and fourth generations. ⁶But I lavish my love on those who love me and obey my commands, even for a thousand generations.

⁷"Do not misuse the name of the LORD your God. The LORD will not let you go unpunished if you misuse his name.

⁸"Remember to observe the Sabbath day by keeping it holy. ⁹Six days a week are set apart for your daily duties and regular work, ¹⁰but the seventh day is a day of rest dedicated to the LORD your God. On that day no one in your household may do any kind of work. This includes you, your sons and daughters, your male and female servants, your livestock, and any foreigners living among you. ¹¹For in six days the LORD made the heavens, the earth, the sea, and everything in them; then he rested on the seventh day. That is why the LORD blessed the Sabbath day and set it apart as holy.

¹²"Honor your father and mother. Then you will live a long, full life in the land the LORD your God will give you.

¹³"Do not murder.

¹⁴"Do not commit adultery.

¹⁵"Do not steal.

¹⁶"Do not testify falsely against your neighbor.

**20:1-17** //Deut 5:6-21

**20:3** Exod 15:11; 20:23

**20:4** Lev 26:1

**20:5** Exod 23:13, 24; Num 14:18; Deut 4:24

**20:6** Exod 34:6-7; Deut 7:9

**20:7** Lev 19:12

**20:8** Exod 16:23

**20:11** Gen 2:2-3; †Acts 4:24

**20:12** †Matt 15:4; †Mark 7:10; †Luke 18:20; †Eph 6:2

**20:13** †Matt 5:21; 19:18; †Rom 13:9; †Jas 2:11

**20:14** †Matt 5:27

**20:15** †Matt 19:18; †Mark 10:19; †Luke 18:20

**20:16** Matt 19:18

**20:1ff** Why were the Ten Commandments necessary for God's new nation? At the foot of Mount Sinai, God showed his people the true function and beauty of his laws. The commandments were designed to lead Israel to a life of practical holiness. In them, people could see the nature of God and his plan for how they should live. The commands and guidelines were intended to direct the community to meet the needs of each individual in a loving and responsible manner. By Jesus' time, however, most people looked at the law the wrong way. They saw it as a means to prosperity in both this world and the next. And they thought that to obey every law was the way to earn God's protection from foreign invasion and natural disaster. Law keeping became an end in itself, not the means to fulfill God's ultimate law of love.

**20:1-6** The Israelites had just come from Egypt, a land of many idols and many gods. Because each god represented a different aspect of life, it was common to worship many gods in order to get the maximum number of blessings. When God told his people to worship and believe in him, that wasn't so hard for them—he was just one more god to add to the list. But when he said, "Worship only me," that was difficult for the people to accept. But if they didn't learn that the God who led them out of Egypt was the only true God, they could not be his people—no matter how faithfully they kept the other nine commandments. Thus, God made this his first commandment and emphasized it more than the others. Today we can allow many things to become gods to us. Money, fame, work, or pleasure can become gods when we concentrate too much on them for personal identity, meaning, and security. No one sets out with the intention of worshiping these things. But by the amount of time we devote to them, they can grow into gods that ultimately control our thoughts and energies. Letting God hold the central place in our lives keeps these things from turning into gods.

**20:7** God's name is special because it carries his personal identity. Using it frivolously or in a curse is so common today that we may fail to realize how serious it is. The way we use God's name conveys how we really feel about him. We should respect his name and use it appropriately, speaking it in praise or worship rather than in curse or jest. We should not take lightly the abuse or dishonor of his name.

**20:8-11** The Sabbath was a day set aside for rest and worship. God commanded a Sabbath because human beings need to spend unhurried time in worship and rest each week. A God who is concerned enough to provide a day each week for us to rest is indeed wonderful. To observe a regular time of rest and worship in our fast-paced world demonstrates how important God is to us, and it gives us the extra benefit of refreshing our spirits. Don't neglect God's provision.

**20:12** This is the first commandment with a promise attached. To live in peace for generations in the Promised Land, the Israelites would need to respect authority and build strong families. But what does it mean to "honor" parents? Partly, it means speaking well of them and politely to them. It also means acting in a way that shows them courtesy and respect (but not to obey them if this means disobedience to God). It means following their teaching and example of putting God first. Parents have a special place in God's sight. Even those who find it difficult to get along with their parents are still commanded to honor them.

**20:16** To testify falsely means lying in court. God knew that Israel could not survive unless its system of justice was incorruptible. We should be honest in our private dealings as well as in our public statements. In either situation, we "testify falsely" by leaving something out of a story, telling a half-truth, twisting the facts, or inventing a falsehood. God warns us against deception. Even though deception is a way of life for many people, God's people must not give in to it!

**20:17**
†Rom 7:7

17"Do not covet your neighbor's house. Do not covet your neighbor's wife, male or female servant, ox or donkey, or anything else your neighbor owns."

**20:18**
Exod 19:18
Heb 12:18

18When the people heard the thunder and the loud blast of the horn, and when they saw the lightning and the smoke billowing from the mountain, they stood at a distance, trembling with fear.

**20:19**
Deut 5:23-27

19And they said to Moses, "You tell us what God says, and we will listen. But don't let God speak directly to us. If he does, we will die!"

20"Don't be afraid," Moses said, "for God has come in this way to show you his awesome power. From now on, let your fear of him keep you from sinning!"

**20:21**
Deut 5:22
Ps 97:2

21As the people stood in the distance, Moses entered into the deep darkness where God was.

### Proper Use of Altars

**20:23**
Exod 32:4
Deut 29:17-18

22And the LORD said to Moses, "Say this to the people of Israel: You are witnesses that I have spoken to you from heaven. 23Remember, you must not make or worship idols of silver or gold.

---

**JESUS AND THE TEN COMMANDMENTS**

| The Ten Commandments said . . . | Jesus said . . . |
|---|---|
| Exodus 20:3 "Do not worship any other gods besides me.' | Matthew 4:10 "You must worship the Lord your God; serve only him." |
| Exodus 20:4 "Do not make idols of any kind." | Luke 16:13 "No one can serve two masters." |
| Exodus 20:7 "Do not misuse the name of the LORD your God." | Matthew 5:34 "But I say, don't make any vows! If you say, 'By heaven!' it is a sacred vow because heaven is God's throne." |
| Exodus 20:8 "Remember to observe the Sabbath day by keeping it holy.' | Mark 2:27, 28 "The Sabbath was made to benefit people and not people to benefit the Sabbath. And I, the Son of Man, am master even of the Sabbath!" |
| Exodus 20:12 "Honor your father and mother." | Matthew 10:37 "If you love your father or mother more than you love me, you are not worthy of being mine." |
| Exodus 20:13 "Do not murder." | Matthew 5:22 "If you are angry with someone, you are subject to judgment!" |
| Exodus 20:14 "Do not commit adultery." | Matthew 5:28 "Anyone who even looks at a woman with lust in his eye has already committed adultery with her in his heart." |
| Exodus 20:15 "Do not steal." | Matthew 5:40 "If you are ordered to court and your shirt is taken from you, give your coat, too." |
| Exodus 20:16 "Do not testify falsely against your neighbor." | Matthew 12:36 "You must give an account on judgment day of every idle word you speak." |
| Exodus 20:17 "Do not covet." | Luke 12:15 "Don't be greedy for what you don't have." |

---

**20:17** To covet is to wish to have the possessions of others. It goes beyond simply admiring someone else's possessions or thinking, "I'd like to have one of those." Coveting includes envy—resenting the fact that others have what you don't. God knows, however, that possessions never make anyone happy for long. Since only God can supply all our needs, true contentment is found only in him. When you begin to covet, try to determine if a more basic need is leading you to envy. For example, you may covet someone's success, not because you want to take it away from him, but because you would like to feel as appreciated by others as he is. If this is the case, pray that God will help you deal with your resentment and meet your basic needs.

**20:18** Sometimes God speaks to his people with a majestic display of power; at other times he speaks quietly. Why the difference? God speaks in the way that best accomplishes his purposes. At Sinai, the awesome display of light and sound

was necessary to show Israel God's great power and authority. Only then would they listen to Moses and Aaron.

**20:20** Throughout the Bible we find this phrase: "Don't be afraid." God wasn't trying to scare the people. He was showing his mighty power so the Israelites would know he was the true God and would therefore obey him. If they would do this, he would make his power available to them. God wants us to follow him out of love rather than fear. To overcome fear, we must think more about his love. First John 4:18 says, "Perfect love expels all fear."

²⁴"The altars you make for me must be simple altars of earth. Offer on such altars your sacrifices to me—your burnt offerings and peace offerings, your sheep and goats and your cattle. Build altars in the places where I remind you who I am, and I will come and bless you there. ²⁵If you build altars from stone, use only uncut stones. Do not chip or shape the stones with a tool, for that would make them unfit for holy use. ²⁶And you may not approach my altar by steps. If you do, someone might look up under the skirts of your clothing and see your nakedness.

### Fair Treatment of Slaves

**21** "Here are some other instructions you must present to Israel:
²"If you buy a Hebrew slave, he is to serve for only six years. Set him free in the seventh year, and he will owe you nothing for his freedom. ³If he was single when he became your slave and then married afterward, only he will go free in the seventh year. But if he was married before he became a slave, then his wife will be freed with him.

⁴"If his master gave him a wife while he was a slave, and they had sons or daughters, then the man will be free in the seventh year, but his wife and children will still belong to his master. ⁵But the slave may plainly declare, 'I love my master, my wife, and my children. I would rather not go free.' ⁶If he does this, his master must present him before God.* Then his master must take him to the door and publicly pierce his ear with an awl. After that, the slave will belong to his master forever.

⁷"When a man sells his daughter as a slave, she will not be freed at the end of six years as the men are. ⁸If she does not please the man who bought her, he may allow her to be bought back again. But he is not allowed to sell her to foreigners, since he is the one who broke the contract with her. ⁹And if the slave girl's owner arranges for her to marry his son, he may no longer treat her as a slave girl, but he must treat her as his daughter. ¹⁰If he himself marries her and then takes another wife, he may not reduce her food or clothing or fail to sleep with her as his wife. ¹¹If he fails in any of these three ways, she may leave as a free woman without making any payment.

### Cases of Personal Injury

¹²"Anyone who hits a person hard enough to cause death must be put to death. ¹³But if it is an accident and God allows it to happen, I will appoint a place where the slayer can run for safety. ¹⁴However, if someone deliberately attacks and kills another person, then the slayer must be dragged even from my altar and put to death.

¹⁵"Anyone who strikes father or mother must be put to death.

¹⁶"Kidnappers must be killed, whether they are caught in possession of their victims or have already sold them as slaves.

¹⁷"Anyone who curses father or mother must be put to death.

¹⁸"Now suppose two people quarrel, and one hits the other with a stone or fist, causing injury but not death. ¹⁹If the injured person is later able to walk again, even with a crutch, the assailant will be innocent. Nonetheless, the assailant must pay for time lost because of the injury and must pay for the medical expenses.

²⁰"If a male or female slave is beaten and dies, the owner must be punished. ²¹If the slave recovers after a couple of days, however, then the owner should not be punished, since the slave is the owner's property.

²²"Now suppose two people are fighting, and in the process, they hurt a pregnant

**21:6** Or *before the judges.*

---

**20:24**
Exod 10:25; 18:12; 24:5
Lev 1:2
Deut 12:5

**20:25**
Deut 27:5-6
Josh 8:31

**20:26**
Exod 28:42

**21:1**
Deut 4:14

**21:2-6**
Lev 25:39-41
//Deut 15:12-18

**21:2**
Jer 34:14

**21:5**
Deut 15:16

**21:6**
Exod 22:8-9

**21:7**
Neh 5:5

**21:10**
1 Cor 7:3, 5

**21:12**
Gen 9:6
Lev 24:21

**21:13**
Num 35:22
Deut 19:4-5
Josh 20:9

**21:14**
Num 35:30-31
1 Kgs 2:28-34

**21:16**
Deut 24:7

**21:17**
Lev 20:9
Deut 5:16
†Matt 15:4
†Mark 7:10

**21:21**
Lev 25:44-46

---

**20:24-26** Why were specific directions given for building altars? God's people had no Bible and few religious traditions to learn from. God had to start from scratch and teach them how to worship him. God gave specific instructions about building altars because he wanted to control the way sacrifices were offered. To prevent idolatry from creeping into worship, God did not allow the altar stones to be cut or shaped into any form. Nor did God let the people build an altar just anywhere. This was designed to prevent them from starting their own religions or making changes in the way God wanted things done. God is not against creativity, but he is against us creating our own religion.

**21:1ff** These laws were given because everything we do has consequences. It is vital to think before acting, to consider the effects of our choices. Think of your plans for today and consider what their long-range results will be. As we deal with others, we should keep the principles of these laws in mind. We should act responsibly and justly with all people—friends and enemies alike.

**21:2** The Hebrews, though freed from slavery, had slaves (or servants) themselves. A person could become a slave because of poverty, debt, or even crime. But Hebrew slaves were treated as humans, not property, and were allowed to work their way to freedom. The Bible acknowledges the existence of slavery but never encourages it.

woman so her child is born prematurely. If no further harm results, then the person responsible must pay damages in the amount the woman's husband demands and the judges approve. 23But if any harm results, then the offender must be punished according to the injury. If the result is death, the offender must be executed. 24If an eye is injured, injure the eye of the person who did it. If a tooth gets knocked out, knock out the tooth of the person who did it. Similarly, the payment must be hand for hand, foot for foot, 25burn for burn, wound for wound, bruise for bruise.

26"If an owner hits a male or female slave in the eye and the eye is blinded, then the slave may go free because of the eye. 27And if an owner knocks out the tooth of a male or female slave, the slave should be released in payment for the tooth.

28"If a bull gores a man or woman to death, the bull must be stoned, and its flesh may not be eaten. In such a case, however, the owner will not be held liable. 29Suppose, on the other hand, that the owner knew the bull had gored people in the past, yet the bull was not kept under control. If this is true and if the bull kills someone, it must be stoned, and the owner must also be killed. 30However, the dead person's relatives may accept payment from the owner of the bull to compensate for the loss of life. The owner will have to pay whatever is demanded.

31"The same principle applies if the bull gores a boy or a girl. 32But if the bull gores a slave, either male or female, the slave's owner is to be given thirty silver coins* in payment, and the bull must be stoned.

33"Suppose someone digs or uncovers a well and fails to cover it, and then an ox or a donkey falls into it. 34The owner of the well must pay in full for the dead animal but then gets to keep it.

35"If someone's bull injures a neighbor's bull and the injured bull dies, then the two owners must sell the live bull and divide the money between them. Each will also own half of the dead bull. 36But if the bull was known from past experience to gore, yet its owner failed to keep it under control, the money will not be divided. The owner of the living bull must pay in full for the dead bull but then gets to keep it.

### Protection of Property

**22** "A fine must be paid by anyone who steals an ox or sheep and then kills or sells it. For oxen the fine is five oxen for each one stolen. For sheep the fine is four sheep for each one stolen.

2"If a thief is caught in the act of breaking into a house and is killed in the process, the person who killed the thief is not guilty. 3But if it happens in daylight, the one who killed the thief is guilty of murder.

"A thief who is caught must pay in full for everything that was stolen. If payment is not made, the thief must be sold as a slave to pay the debt. 4If someone steals an ox or a donkey or a sheep and it is recovered alive, then the thief must pay double the value.

5"If an animal is grazing in a field or vineyard and the owner lets it stray into someone else's field to graze, then the animal's owner must pay damages in the form of high-quality grain or grapes.

6"If a fire gets out of control and goes into another person's field, destroying the sheaves or the standing grain, then the one who started the fire must pay for the lost crops.

**21:32** Hebrew *30 shekels of silver,* about 12 ounces or 342 grams in weight.

---

**Marginal references:**

21:23
Lev 24:19

21:24
Lev 24:20
†Matt 5:38

21:26
Job 31:13

21:28
Gen 9:5

21:32
Gen 37:28
Zech 11:12-13
Matt 26:15; 27:3, 9

21:33
Luke 14:5

22:1
Lev 6:1-7
2 Sam 12:6
Prov 6:31
Luke 19:8

22:2
Num 35:26-27

22:3
Exod 21:2

22:4
Prov 6:31
Jer 2:26
John 12:6

22:5
Exod 21:34

---

**21:24, 25** The "eye for an eye" rule was instituted as a guide for judges, not as a rule for personal relationships or to justify revenge. This rule made the punishment fit the crime, thereby preventing the cruel and barbaric punishments that characterized many ancient countries. Jesus used this principle to teach us not to retaliate (Matthew 5:38-48). Judges, parents, teachers, and others who work with people must make wise decisions in order for discipline to be effective. A punishment too harsh is unfair, and one too lenient is powerless to teach. Ask God for wisdom before you judge.

**22:1ff** These are not a collection of picky laws but are case studies of God's principles in action. God was taking potential situations and showing how his laws would work in the Israelites'

everyday lives. These case studies had several objectives: (1) to protect the nation, (2) to organize the nation, and (3) to focus the nation's attention on God. The laws listed here do not cover every possible situation but give practical examples that make it easier to decide what God wants.

**22:3ff** Throughout chapter 22 we find examples of the principle of restitution—making wrongs right. For example, if a man stole an animal, he had to repay double the beast's market value. If you have done someone wrong, perhaps you should go beyond what is expected to make things right. This will (1) help ease any pain you've caused, (2) help the other person be more forgiving, and (3) make you more likely to think before you do it again.

7 "Suppose someone entrusts money or goods to a neighbor, and they are stolen from the neighbor's house. If the thief is found, the fine is double the value of what was stolen. 8 But if the thief is not found, God* will determine whether or not it was the neighbor who stole the property.

9 "Suppose there is a dispute between two people as to who owns a particular ox, donkey, sheep, article of clothing, or anything else. Both parties must come before God* for a decision, and the person whom God declares* guilty must pay double to the other.

10 "Now suppose someone asks a neighbor to care for a donkey, ox, sheep, or any other animal, but it dies or is injured or gets away, and there is no eyewitness to report just what happened. 11 The neighbor must then take an oath of innocence in the presence of the LORD. The owner must accept the neighbor's word, and no payment will be required. 12 But if the animal or property was stolen, payment must be made to the owner. 13 If it was attacked by a wild animal, the carcass must be shown as evidence, and no payment will be required.

14 "If someone borrows an animal from a neighbor and it is injured or killed, and if the owner was not there at the time, the person who borrowed it must pay for it. 15 But if the owner is there, no payment is required. And no payment is required if the animal was rented because this loss was covered by the rental fee.

## Social Responsibility

16 "If a man seduces a virgin who is not engaged to anyone and sleeps with her, he must pay the customary dowry and accept her as his wife. 17 But if her father refuses to let her marry him, the man must still pay the money for her dowry.

18 "A sorceress must not be allowed to live.

19 "Anyone who has sexual relations with an animal must be executed.

20 "Anyone who sacrifices to any god other than the LORD must be destroyed.

21 "Do not oppress foreigners in any way. Remember, you yourselves were once foreigners in the land of Egypt.

22 "Do not exploit widows or orphans. 23 If you do and they cry out to me, then I will surely help them. 24 My anger will blaze forth against you, and I will kill you with the sword. Your wives will become widows, and your children will become fatherless.

25 "If you lend money to a fellow Hebrew in need, do not be like a money lender, charging interest. 26 If you take your neighbor's cloak as a pledge of repayment, you must return it by nightfall. 27 Your neighbor will need it to stay warm during the night. If you do not return it and your neighbor cries out to me for help, then I will hear, for I am very merciful.

28 "Do not blaspheme God* or curse anyone who rules over you.

29 "Do not hold anything back when you give me the tithe of your crops and your wine.

"You must make the necessary payment for redemption of your firstborn sons.

30 "You must also give me the firstborn of your cattle and sheep. Leave the newborn animal with its mother for seven days; then give it to me on the eighth day.

31 "You are my own holy people. Therefore, do not eat any animal that has been attacked and killed by a wild animal. Throw its carcass out for the dogs to eat.

**22:8** Or *the judges.*   **22:9a** Or *before the judges.*   **22:9b** Or *whom the judges declare.*   **22:28** Or *Do not revile your judges.*

**22:7**
Lev 6:1-7
**22:8**
Exod 21:6
Deut 17:8-9; 19:17
**22:9**
Deut 25:1
**22:13**
Gen 31:39
**22:16-17**
Deut 22:28-29
**22:18**
Lev 20:27
Deut 18:10
**22:19**
Lev 18:23; 20:15
**22:20**
Exod 32:8; 34:15
**22:21**
Lev 19:33
**22:22**
Deut 24:17-18
**22:25**
Lev 25:35-37
Deut 23:19-20
**22:26**
Deut 24:6, 10-13
**22:28**
Lev 24:15-16
Acts 23:5
**22:29**
Exod 13:2; 23:16, 19; 34:20
Deut 26:2
**22:30**
Gen 17:12
Lev 12:3; 22:27
**22:31**
Exod 19:6
Lev 7:24; 17:15; 22:8

**22:18** Why did God's laws speak so strongly against sorcery (Leviticus 19:31; 20:6, 27; Deuteronomy 18:10-12)? Sorcery was punishable by death because it was a crime against God himself. To invoke evil powers violated the first commandment to not worship any other god. Sorcery was rebellion against God and his authority. In essence, it was teaming up with Satan instead of with God.

**22:21** God warned the Israelites not to treat foreigners unfairly because they themselves were once foreigners in Egypt. It is not easy coming into a new environment where you feel alone and out of place. Are there foreigners in your corner of the world? refugees? new arrivals at school? immigrants from another country? Be sensitive to their struggles, and express God's love by your kindness and generosity.

**22:22-27** The Hebrew law code is noted for its fairness and social responsibility toward the poor. God insisted that the poor and powerless be well treated and given the chance to restore their fortunes. We should reflect God's concern for the poor by helping those less fortunate than ourselves.

**22:26** Why did the law insist on returning a person's cloak by nightfall? The cloak was one of an Israelite's most valuable possessions. Making clothing was difficult and time-consuming. As a result, cloaks were expensive, and most people owned only one. The cloak was used as a blanket, a sack to carry things in, a place to sit, a pledge for a debt, and, of course, clothing.

**22:29** The Israelites were to be prompt in giving God their offerings. The first of the harvest was to be dedicated to him. Since God doesn't send payment overdue notices, it is easy to take care of other financial responsibilities while letting our gifts to him slide. Giving to God first out of what he has allowed you to have demonstrates that he has first priority in your life.

## A Call for Justice

**23:1**
Exod 20:16
Ps 35:11

**23** "Do not pass along false reports. Do not cooperate with evil people by telling lies on the witness stand.

**23:2**
Deut 1:17; 16:19

2 "Do not join a crowd that intends to do evil. When you are on the witness stand, do not be swayed in your testimony by the opinion of the majority. 3 And do not slant your testimony in favor of a person just because that person is poor.

**23:4-5**
Deut 22:1-4

4 "If you come upon your enemy's ox or donkey that has strayed away, take it back to its owner. 5 If you see the donkey of someone who hates you struggling beneath a heavy load, do not walk by. Instead, stop and offer to help.

**23:6**
Exod 23:2-3

6 "Do not twist justice against people simply because they are poor,

**23:7**
Exod 20:13, 16
Deut 27:25

7 "Keep far away from falsely charging anyone with evil. Never put an innocent or honest person to death. I will not allow anyone guilty of this to go free.

**23:8**
Deut 16:19

8 "Take no bribes, for a bribe makes you ignore something that you clearly see. A bribe always hurts the cause of the person who is in the right.

**23:9**
Exod 22:21
Lev 19:33-34

9 "Do not oppress the foreigners living among you. You know what it is like to be a foreigner. Remember your own experience in the land of Egypt.

**23:10**
Lev 25:3

10 "Plant and harvest your crops for six years, 11 but let the land rest and lie fallow

**23:11**
Lev 25:1-7

during the seventh year. Then let the poor among you harvest any volunteer crop that may come up. Leave the rest for the animals to eat. The same applies to your vineyards and olive groves.

**23:12**
Exod 20:8-11

12 "Work for six days, and rest on the seventh. This will give your ox and your donkey a chance to rest. It will also allow the people of your household, including your slaves and visitors, to be refreshed.

**23:13**
Deut 4:9, 23

13 "Be sure to obey all my instructions. And remember, never pray to or swear by any other gods. Do not ever mention their names.

## Three Annual Festivals

**23:14**
Exod 34:23-24
Deut 16:16

14 "Each year you must celebrate three festivals in my honor. 15 The first is the Festival of Unleavened Bread. For seven days you are to eat bread made without yeast, just as I

**23:15**
Exod 12:15; 13:4
Lev 23:5

commanded you before. This festival will be an annual event at the appointed time in early spring,* for that is the anniversary of your exodus from Egypt. Everyone must

**23:16**
Exod 34:22
Lev 23:34
Deut 16:13

bring me a sacrifice at that time. 16 You must also celebrate the Festival of Harvest,* when you bring me the first crops of your harvest. Finally, you are to celebrate the Festival of the Final Harvest* at the end of the harvest season. 17 At these three times each year, every

**23:17**
Deut 16:16

man in Israel must appear before the Sovereign LORD.

**23:18**
Exod 12:8; 34:25
Lev 2:11

18 "Sacrificial blood must never be offered together with bread that has yeast in it. And no sacrificial fat may be left unoffered until the next morning.

**23:19**
Exod 22:29
Deut 14:21

19 "As you harvest each of your crops, bring me a choice sample of the first day's harvest. It must be offered to the LORD your God.

"You must not cook a young goat in its mother's milk.

## A Promise of the LORD's Presence

**23:20**
Exod 32:34

20 "See, I am sending my angel before you to lead you safely to the land I have prepared

**23:21**
Exod 3:14; 34:5
Num 14:10-11

for you. 21 Pay attention to him, and obey all of his instructions. Do not rebel against him,

**23:15** Hebrew *in the month of Abib.* This month of the Hebrew lunar calendar usually occurs in March and April.
**23:16a** Or *Festival of Weeks.* **23:16b** This was later called the Festival of Shelters; see Lev 23:33-36.

---

**23:1** Making up or spreading false reports was strictly forbidden by God. Gossip, slander, and false witnessing undermined families, strained neighborhood cooperation, and made chaos of the justice system. Destructive gossip still causes problems. Even if you do not initiate a lie, you become responsible if you pass it along. Don't circulate rumors; squelch them.

**23:2, 3** Justice is often perverted in favor of the rich. Here the people are warned against twisting justice in favor of the poor. Justice should be impartial, treating rich and poor alike. Giving special privileges to either rich or poor only makes justice for everyone more unlikely. Withstand the pressure of the crowd to sway your decision about a person. Let the fairness God shows to each of us guide your judgment.

**23:4, 5** The thought of being kind to enemies was new and

startling in a world where revenge was the common form of justice. God not only introduced this idea to the Israelites, he made it law! If a man found a lost animal owned by his enemy, he was to return it at once, even if his enemy might use it to harm him. Jesus clearly taught in Luke 10:30-37 to reach out to all people in need, even our enemies. Following the laws of right living is hard enough with friends. When we apply God's laws of fairness and kindness to our enemies, we show how different we are from the world.

**23:20, 21** Who was this angel that went with the Israelites? Most likely the angel was a manifestation of God. God was in the angel in the same way he was present in the pillars of cloud and fire (13:21, 22). "He bears my name" means the essential nature and power of God were made known in this angel.

around it. ¹²Cast four rings of gold for it, and attach them to its four feet, two rings on each side. ¹³Make poles from acacia wood, and overlay them with gold. ¹⁴Fit the poles into the rings at the sides of the Ark to carry it. ¹⁵These carrying poles must never be taken from the rings; they are to be left there permanently. ¹⁶When the Ark is finished, place inside it the stone tablets inscribed with the terms of the covenant,* which I will give to you.

¹⁷"Then make the Ark's cover—the place of atonement—out of pure gold. It must be 3¾ feet long and 2¼ feet wide. ¹⁸Then use hammered gold to make two cherubim, and place them at the two ends of the atonement cover. ¹⁹Attach the cherubim to each end of the atonement cover, making it all one piece. ²⁰The cherubim will face each other, looking down on the atonement cover with their wings spread out above it. ²¹Place inside the Ark the stone tablets inscribed with the terms of the covenant, which I will give to you. Then put the atonement cover on top of the Ark. ²²I will meet with you there and talk to you from above the atonement cover between the gold cherubim that hover over the Ark of the Covenant.* From there I will give you my commands for the people of Israel.

*Plans for the Table*

²³"Then make a table of acacia wood, 3 feet long, 1½ feet wide, and 2¼ feet high. ²⁴Overlay it with pure gold and run a molding of gold around it. ²⁵Put a rim about three inches* wide around the top edge, and put a gold molding all around the rim. ²⁶Make four gold rings, and put the rings at the four corners by the four legs, ²⁷close to the rim around the top. These rings will support the poles used to carry the table. ²⁸Make these poles from acacia wood and overlay them with gold. ²⁹And make gold plates and dishes, as well as pitchers and bowls to be used in pouring out drink offerings. ³⁰You must always keep the special Bread of the Presence on the table before me.

*Plans for the Lampstand*

³¹"Make a lampstand of pure, hammered gold. The entire lampstand and its decorations will be one piece—the base, center stem, lamp cups, buds, and blossoms. ³²It will have six branches, three branches going out from each side of the center stem. ³³Each of the six branches will hold a cup shaped like an almond blossom, complete with buds and petals. ³⁴The center stem of the lampstand will be decorated with four almond blossoms, complete with buds and petals. ³⁵One blossom will be set beneath each pair of branches where they extend from the center stem. ³⁶The decorations and branches must all be one piece with the stem, and they must be hammered from pure gold. ³⁷Then make the seven lamps for the lampstand, and set them so they reflect their light forward. ³⁸The lamp snuffers and trays must also be made of pure gold. ³⁹You will need seventy-five pounds* of pure gold for the lampstand and its accessories.

⁴⁰"Be sure that you make everything according to the pattern I have shown you here on the mountain.

*Plans for the Tabernacle*

**26** "Make the Tabernacle from ten sheets of fine linen. These sheets are to be decorated with blue, purple, and scarlet yarn, with figures of cherubim skillfully embroidered into them. ²Each sheet must be forty-two feet long and six feet wide.* All ten sheets must be exactly the same size. ³Join five of these sheets together into one set; then join the other five sheets into a second set. ⁴Put loops of blue yarn along the edge of the last sheet in each set. ⁵The fifty loops along the edge of one set are to match the fifty loops along the edge of the other. ⁶Then make fifty gold clasps to fasten the loops of the two sets of sheets together, making the Tabernacle a single unit.

⁷"Make heavy sheets of cloth from goat hair to cover the Tabernacle. There must be eleven of these sheets, ⁸each forty-five feet long and six feet wide. All eleven of these

**25:12**
Exod 26:29; 27:7;
37:5; 38:7

**25:15**
1 Kgs 8:8

**25:16**
Exod 16:34
Heb 9:4

**25:17**
Exod 37:6
Lev 16:13
Rom 3:25
Heb 9:5

**25:20**
1 Kgs 8:7
Heb 9:5

**25:21**
Exod 26:34

**25:22**
Exod 30:6, 36
Lev 1:1

**25:23-29**
∥Exod 37:10-16

**25:29**
Exod 37:16
Num 4:7

**25:30**
Exod 39:36; 40:23
Lev 24:5-9
Num 4:7

**25:31-39**
∥Exod 37:17-24

**25:31**
Exod 37:17
1 Kgs 7:49
Heb 9:2
Rev 1:12

**25:37**
Exod 27:21
Zech 4:2
Rev 1:4, 12, 20; 4:5

**25:40**
Acts 7:44
†Heb 8:5

**26:1-37**
∥Exod 36:8-38

**26:3**
Exod 36:10

**26:5**
Exod 36:12

**26:7**
Exod 36:14

**25:16** Hebrew *place inside it the Testimony*; also in 25:21. **25:22** Or *Ark of the Testimony.* **25:25** Hebrew *a hand-breadth* [8 centimeters]. **25:39** Hebrew *1 talent* [34 kilograms]. **26:2** Hebrew *28 cubits* [12.6 meters] *long and 4 cubits* [1.8 meters] *wide.* In this chapter, the distance measures are calculated from the Hebrew cubit at a ratio of 18 inches or 45 centimeters per cubit.

**25:17** The cover of the Ark of the Covenant was called the atonement cover. This is where, between the two golden cherubim (mighty angels), the presence of God would dwell in a cloud above their outstretched wings. The atonement cover was where the highest and most perfect act of atonement would be made when the high priest would enter the Most Holy Place on the Day of Atonement to atone for the sins of all the people (30:10).

sheets must be exactly the same size. [9]Join five of these together into one set, and join the other six into a second set. The sixth sheet of the second set is to be doubled over at the entrance of the sacred tent. [10]Put fifty loops along the edge of the last sheet in each

**26:11**
Exod 36:18

set, [11]and fasten them together with fifty bronze clasps. In this way, the two sets will become a single unit. [12]An extra half sheet of this roof covering will be left to hang over the back of the Tabernacle. [13]and the covering will hang down an extra eighteen inches

**26:14**
Exod 36:19

**26:15**
Exod 36:20-34

on each side. [14]On top of these coverings place a layer of tanned ram skins, and over them put a layer of fine goatskin leather. This will complete the roof covering.

[15]"The framework of the Tabernacle will consist of frames made of acacia wood. [16]Each frame must be 15 feet high and 2¼ feet wide. [17]There will be two pegs on each frame so they can be joined to the next frame. All the frames must be made this way. [18]Twenty of these frames will support the south side of the Tabernacle. [19]They will fit

**26:20**
Exod 36:23

into forty silver bases—two bases under each frame. [20]On the north side there will also be twenty of these frames, [21]with their forty silver bases, two bases for each frame. [22]On the west side there will be six frames, [23]along with an extra frame at each corner. [24]These corner frames will be connected at the bottom and firmly attached at the top with a single

**26:25**
Exod 36:30

ring, forming a single unit. Both of these corner frames will be made the same way. [25]So there will be eight frames on that end of the Tabernacle, supported by sixteen silver bases—two bases under each frame.

[26]"Make crossbars of acacia wood to run across the frames, five crossbars for the north side of the Tabernacle [27]and five for the south side. Also make five crossbars for the rear of the Tabernacle, which will face westward. [28]The middle crossbar, halfway up the frames, will run all the way from one end of the Tabernacle to the other. [29]Overlay the frames with gold and make gold rings to support the crossbars. Overlay the crossbars with gold as well.

**26:30**
Exod 25:9, 40
Acts 7:44
†Heb 8:5

[30]"Set up this Tabernacle according to the design you were shown on the mountain.

[31]"Across the inside of the Tabernacle hang a special curtain made of fine linen, with cherubim skillfully embroidered into the cloth using blue, purple, and scarlet yarn.

**26:31**
Exod 36:35
2 Chr 3:14
Matt 27:51
Heb 9:3

[32]Hang this inner curtain on gold hooks set into four posts made from acacia wood and overlaid with gold. The posts will fit into silver bases. [33]When the inner curtain is in place, put the Ark of the Covenant* behind it. This curtain will separate the Holy Place from the Most Holy Place.

**26:33**
Exod 25:16; 40:21
Heb 9:2-3

[34]"Then put the Ark's cover—the place of atonement—on top of the Ark of the Covenant inside the Most Holy Place. [35]Place the table and lampstand across the room from each other outside the inner curtain. The lampstand must be placed on the south side, and the table must be set toward the north.

**26:34**
Exod 25:21; 37:6
Heb 9:5

**26:36**
Exod 40:28

[36]"Make another curtain from fine linen for the entrance of the sacred tent, and embroider exquisite designs into it, using blue, purple, and scarlet yarn. [37]Hang this curtain on gold hooks set into five posts made from acacia wood and overlaid with gold. The posts will fit into five bronze bases.

**26:37**
Exod 36:38

### Plans for the Altar of Burnt Offering

**27:1-8**
//Exod 38:1-7

**27** "Using acacia wood, make a square altar 7½ feet wide, 7½ feet long, and 4½ feet high.* [2]Make a horn at each of the four corners of the altar so the horns and altar are all one piece. Overlay the altar and its horns with bronze. [3]The ash buckets, shovels,

**27:2**
Exod 29:12
Lev 4:7

**27:3**
Num 4:14

**26:33** Or *Ark of the Testimony;* also in 26:34.   **27:1** Hebrew *5 cubits* [2.3 meters] *wide, 5 cubits long, and 3 cubits* [1.4 meters] *high.* In this chapter, the distance measures are calculated from the Hebrew cubit at a ratio of 18 inches or 45 centimeters per cubit.

---

**26:31-33** This curtain separated the two sacred rooms in the Tabernacle—the Holy Place and the Most Holy Place. The priest entered the Holy Place each day to commune with God and to tend to the altar of incense, the lampstand, and the table with the Bread of the Presence. The Most Holy Place was where God himself dwelt, his presence resting on the atonement cover, which covered the Ark of the Covenant. Only the high priest could enter the Most Holy Place. Even he could do so only once a year (on the Day of Atonement) to make atonement for the sins of the nation as a whole. When Jesus Christ died on the cross, the curtain in the Temple (which had replaced the

Tabernacle) tore from top to bottom (Mark 15:38), symbolizing our free access to God because of Jesus' death. No longer did people have to approach God through priests and sacrifices.

**27:1** The altar of burnt offering was the first thing the Israelites saw as they entered the Tabernacle courtyard. Here sacrifices were constantly made. Its vivid presence constantly reminded the people that they could only come to God by means of the sacrifice. It was the only way their sins could be forgiven and taken away. In Hebrews 10:1-18, Jesus Christ is portrayed as the ultimate sacrifice.

basins, meat hooks, and firepans will all be made of bronze. ⁴Make a bronze grating, with a metal ring at each corner. ⁵Fit the grating halfway down into the firebox, resting it on the ledge built there. ⁶For moving the altar, make poles from acacia wood, and overlay them with bronze. ⁷To carry it, put the poles into the rings at two sides of the altar. ⁸The altar must be hollow, made from planks. Be careful to build it just as you were shown on the mountain.

**27:6**
Exod 25:13

**27:8**
Exod 25:40; 26:30

### Plans for the Courtyard

⁹"Then make a courtyard for the Tabernacle, enclosed with curtains made from fine linen. On the south side the curtains will stretch for 150 feet. ¹⁰They will be held up by twenty bronze posts that fit into twenty bronze bases. The curtains will be held up with silver hooks attached to the silver rods that are attached to the posts. ¹¹It will be the same on the north side of the courtyard—150 feet of curtains held up by twenty posts fitted into bronze bases, with silver hooks and rods. ¹²The curtains on the west end of the courtyard will be 75 feet long, supported by ten posts set into ten bases. ¹³The east end will also be 75 feet long. ¹⁴The courtyard entrance will be on the east end, flanked by two curtains. The curtain on the right side will be 22½ feet long, supported by three posts set into three bases. ¹⁵The curtain on the left side will also be 22½ feet long, supported by three posts set into three bases.

**27:9-19**
//Exod 38:9-20

**27:10**
Exod 38:17

**27:14**
Exod 38:15

¹⁶"For the entrance to the courtyard, make a curtain that is 30 feet long. Fashion it from fine linen, and decorate it with beautiful embroidery in blue, purple, and scarlet yarn. It will be attached to four posts that fit into four bases. ¹⁷All the posts around the courtyard must be connected by silver rods, using silver hooks. The posts are to be set in solid bronze bases. ¹⁸So the entire courtyard will be 150 feet long and 75 feet wide, with curtain walls 7½ feet high, made from fine linen. The bases supporting its walls will be made of bronze.

**27:16**
Exod 36:37

¹⁹"All the articles used in the work of the Tabernacle, including all the tent pegs used to support the Tabernacle and the courtyard curtains, must be made of bronze.

²⁰"Tell the people of Israel to bring you pure olive oil for the lampstand, so it can be kept burning continually. ²¹The lampstand will be placed outside the inner curtain of the Most Holy Place in the Tabernacle.* Aaron and his sons will keep the lamps burning in the LORD's presence day and night. This is a permanent law for the people of Israel, and it must be kept by all future generations.

**27:20-21**
//Lev 24:1-3
Zech 4:11-12

**27:21**
Exod 25:22
Lev 3:17; 16:34

### Clothing for the Priests

**28** "Your brother, Aaron, and his sons, Nadab, Abihu, Eleazar, and Ithamar, will be set apart from the common people. They will be my priests and will minister to me. ²Make special clothing for Aaron to show his separation to God—beautiful garments that will lend dignity to his work. ³Instruct all those who have special skills as tailors to make the garments that will set Aaron apart from everyone else, so he may serve me as a priest. ⁴They are to make a chestpiece, an ephod, a robe, an embroidered tunic, a turban, and a sash. They will also make special garments for Aaron's sons to wear when they serve as priests before me. ⁵These items must be made of fine linen cloth and embroidered with gold thread and blue, purple, and scarlet yarn.

**28:1**
Exod 24:1, 9
Num 18:7
Ps 99:6
Heb 5:1, 4

**28:2**
Exod 29:5, 9; 31:10
Lev 8:7, 30
Num 20:26

**28:5**
Exod 25:3-4

**27:21** Hebrew *in the Tent of Meeting, outside of the inner curtain, in front of the Testimony.*

---

**28:1ff** God was teaching his people how to worship him. To do so, he needed ministers to oversee the operations of the Tabernacle and to help the people maintain their relationship with God. These men were called priests and Levites, and they could only be members of the tribe of Levi. Chapters 28 and 29 give some details about priests. Not only was a priest from the tribe of Levi, but he also was a descendant of Aaron, Israel's first high priest. Priests had more responsibilities than Levites. As high priest, Aaron was in charge of all the priests and Levites. The priests performed the daily sacrifices, maintained the Tabernacle, and counseled the people on how to follow God. They were the people's representatives before God and thus were required to live worthy of their office. Jesus is now our High Priest (Hebrews 8). Daily sacrifices are no longer required because he sacrificed himself on the cross for our sins. Today ministers no longer sacrifice animals. Instead, ministers lead us in prayer and teach us about both the benefits and the commandments that characterize our new life as Christians.

**28:3** The tailors who made Aaron's garments were given wisdom by God in order to do their task. All of us have special skills. God wants to fill us with his Spirit so we will use them for his glory. Think about your special talents and abilities and the ways you could use them for God's work in the world. A talent must be used, or it will diminish.

### Design of the Ephod

**28:6-14**
//Exod 39:2-7

6 "The ephod must be made of fine linen cloth and skillfully embroidered with gold thread and blue, purple, and scarlet yarn. 7 It will consist of two pieces, front and back, joined at the shoulders with two shoulder-pieces. 8 And the sash will be made of the same materials: fine linen cloth embroidered with gold thread and blue, purple, and scarlet yarn. 9 Take two onyx stones and engrave on them the names of the tribes of Israel. 10 Six names will be on each stone, naming all the tribes in the order of their ancestors' births. 11 Engrave these names in the same way a gemcutter engraves a seal.

**28:12**
Exod 39:7

Mount the stones in gold settings. 12 Fasten the two stones on the shoulder-pieces of the ephod as memorial stones for the people of Israel. Aaron will carry these names before the LORD as a constant reminder. 13 The settings are to be made of gold filigree, 14 and two cords made of pure gold will be attached to the settings on the shoulders of the ephod.

### Design of the Chestpiece

**28:15-28**
//Exod 39:8-21

15 "Then, with the most careful workmanship, make a chestpiece that will be used to determine God's will. Use the same materials as you did for the ephod: fine linen cloth embroidered with gold thread and blue, purple, and scarlet yarn. 16 This chestpiece will

**28:17**
Exod 39:10

be made of two folds of cloth, forming a pouch nine inches* square. 17 Four rows of gemstones* will be attached to it. The first row will contain a red carnelian, a chrysolite, and an emerald. 18 The second row will contain a turquoise, a sapphire, and a white moonstone. 19 The third row will contain a jacinth, an agate, and an amethyst. 20 The fourth row will contain a beryl, an onyx, and a jasper. All these stones will be set in gold.

**28:21**
Exod 39:14

21 Each stone will represent one of the tribes of Israel, and the name of that tribe will be engraved on it as though it were a seal.

22 "To attach the chestpiece to the ephod, make braided cords of pure gold. 23 Then

**28:24**
Exod 39:17

**28:26**
Exod 39:17

make two gold rings and attach them to the top corners of the chestpiece. 24 The two gold cords will go through the rings on the chestpiece, 25 and the ends of the cords will be tied to the gold settings on the shoulder-pieces of the ephod. 26 Then make two more gold rings, and attach them to the two lower inside corners of the chestpiece next to the ephod. 27 And make two more gold rings and attach them to the ephod near the sash. 28 Then

**28:29**
Exod 28:12

attach the bottom rings of the chestpiece to the rings on the ephod with blue cords. This will hold the chestpiece securely to the ephod above the beautiful sash. 29 In this way, Aaron will carry the names of the tribes of Israel on the chestpiece over his heart when he goes into the presence of the LORD in the Holy Place. Thus, the LORD will be reminded

**28:30**
Lev 8:8
Num 27:21

of his people continually. 30 Insert into the pocket of the chestpiece the Urim and Thummim, to be carried over Aaron's heart when he goes into the LORD's presence. Thus, Aaron will always carry the objects used to determine the LORD's will for his people whenever he goes in before the LORD.

### Additional Clothing for the Priests

**28:31-43**
//Exod 39:22-31

31 "Make the robe of the ephod entirely of blue cloth, 32 with an opening for Aaron's head in the middle of it. The opening will be reinforced by a woven collar* so it will not tear. 33 Make pomegranates out of blue, purple, and scarlet yarn, and attach them to the hem of the robe, with gold bells between them. 34 The gold bells and pomegranates are to alternate all the way around the hem. 35 Aaron will wear this robe whenever he enters the Holy Place to minister to the LORD and the bells will tinkle as he goes in and out of the

**28:36**
Exod 39:30-31
Lev 8:9

LORD's presence. If he wears it, he will not die.

36 "Next make a medallion of pure gold. Using the techniques of an engraver, inscribe

**28:38**
Lev 10:17; 22:16
Num 18:1
Heb 9:28
1 Pet 2:24

it with these words: SET APART AS HOLY TO THE LORD. 37 This medallion will be attached to the front of Aaron's turban by means of a blue cord. 38 Aaron will wear it on his

28:16 Hebrew *1 span* [23 centimeters]. 28:17 The identification of some of these gemstones is uncertain.
28:32 The meaning of the Hebrew is uncertain

---

**28:6-13** The ephod was a kind of apron elaborately embroidered with two pieces, back and front, joined at the shoulder with a band at the waist. On each shoulder strap was a stone with 6 of the 12 tribes of Israel engraved on it. The priest symbolically carried the burden of the whole nation on his shoulders as he represented them before God.

**28:30** The Urim and the Thummim were used by the priest to make decisions. These names mean "Curses" and "Perfections" and refer to the nature of God whose will they revealed. They were kept in a pocket and taken out or shaken out to get either a yes or no decision.

forehead, thus bearing the guilt connected with any errors regarding the sacred offerings of the people of Israel. He must always wear it so the LORD will accept the people.

39"Weave Aaron's patterned tunic from fine linen cloth. Fashion the turban out of this linen as well. Also make him an embroidered sash.

40"Then for Aaron's sons, make tunics, sashes, and headdresses to give them dignity and respect. 41Clothe Aaron and his sons with these garments, and then anoint and ordain them. Set them apart as holy so they can serve as my priests. 42Also make linen underclothes for them, to be worn next to their bodies, reaching from waist to thigh. 43These must be worn whenever Aaron and his sons enter the Tabernacle* or approach the altar in the Holy Place to perform their duties. Thus they will not incur guilt and die. This law is permanent for Aaron and his descendants.

### Dedication of the Priests

**29** "This is the ceremony for the dedication of Aaron and his sons as priests: Take a young bull and two rams with no physical defects. 2Then using fine wheat flour and no yeast, make loaves of bread, thin cakes mixed with olive oil, and wafers with oil poured over them. 3Place these various kinds of bread in a single basket, and present them at the entrance of the Tabernacle, along with the young bull and the two rams.

4"Present Aaron and his sons at the entrance of the Tabernacle,* and wash them with water. 5Then put Aaron's tunic on him, along with the embroidered robe of the ephod, the ephod itself, the chestpiece, and the sash. 6And place on his head the turban with the gold medallion. 7Then take the anointing oil and pour it over his head. 8Next present his sons, and dress them in their tunics 9with their woven sashes and their headdresses. They will then be priests forever. In this way, you will ordain Aaron and his sons.

10"Then bring the young bull to the entrance of the Tabernacle, and Aaron and his sons will lay their hands on its head. 11You will then slaughter it in the LORD's presence at the entrance of the Tabernacle. 12Smear some of its blood on the horns of the altar with your finger, and pour out the rest at the base of the altar. 13Take all the fat that covers the internal organs, also the long lobe of the liver and the two kidneys with their fat, and burn them on the altar. 14Then take the carcass (including the skin and the dung) outside the camp, and burn it as a sin offering.

15"Next Aaron and his sons must lay their hands on the head of one of the rams 16as it is slaughtered. Its blood will be collected and sprinkled on the sides of the altar. 17Cut up the ram and wash off the internal organs and the legs. Set them alongside the head and the other pieces of the body, 18and burn them all on the altar. This is a burnt offering to the LORD, which is very pleasing to him.

19"Now take the other ram and have Aaron and his sons lay their hands on its head 20as it is slaughtered. Collect the blood and place some of it on the tip of the right earlobes of Aaron and his sons. Also put it on their right thumbs and the big toes of their right feet. Sprinkle the rest of the blood on the sides of the altar. 21Then take some of the blood from the altar and mix it with some of the anointing oil. Sprinkle it on Aaron and his sons and on their clothes. In this way, they and their clothing will be set apart as holy to the LORD.

22"Since this is the ram for the ordination of Aaron and his sons, take the fat of the ram, including the fat tail and the fat that covers the internal organs. Also, take the long

**28:40**
Exod 39:27-29
Lev 8:13

**28:41**
Exod 29:7-9
Lev 8:1-36
Heb 7:28

**28:42**
Lev 6:10; 16:4
Ezek 44:18

**28:43**
Exod 20:26; 27:21

**29:1-37**
/Lev 8:1-36

**29:2**
Lev 6:19-23

**29:4**
Exod 40:12
Heb 10:22

**29:5**
Exod 28:2, 5

**29:6**
Exod 28:36

**29:7**
Exod 28:41
Lev 8:12-13
Ps 133:2

**29:9**
Exod 40:15
Num 3:10; 18:7;
25:13
Deut 18:5

**29:10**
Lev 1:4; 8:14

**29:12**
Exod 27:2
Lev 8:15

**29:13**
Lev 3:3-5

**29:14**
Lev 4:11-12, 21
Heb 13:11

**29:15**
Exod 29:10

**29:18**
Gen 8:21

**29:21**
Exod 30:25, 31
Heb 9:22

**28:43** Hebrew *Tent of Meeting.*   **29:4** Hebrew *Tent of Meeting;* also in 29:10, 11, 30, 32, 42, 44.

---

**29:1ff** Why did God set up the priesthood? God had originally intended that his chosen people be a "kingdom of priests" with both the nation as a whole and each individual dealing directly with God. But the people's sin prevented this from happening because a sinful person is not worthy to approach a perfect God. God then appointed priests from the tribe of Levi and set up the system of sacrifices to help the people approach him. He promised to forgive the people's sins if they would offer certain sacrifices administered by the priests on behalf of the people. Through these priests and their work, God wished to prepare all people for the coming of Jesus Christ, who would once again offer a direct relationship with God for anyone who would come to him. But until Christ came, the priests were the

people's representatives before God. Through this Old Testament system, we can better understand the significance of what Christ did for us (see Hebrews 10:1-14).

**29:10-41** Why were there such detailed rituals in connection with these sacrifices? Partly it was for quality control. A centralized, standardized form of worship prevented problems of belief which could arise from individuals creating their own worship. Also, it differentiated the Hebrews from the pagan Canaanites they would meet in the Promised Land. By closely following God's instructions, the Hebrews could not possibly join the Canaanites in their immoral religious practices. Finally, it showed Israel that God was serious about his relationship with them.

**29:23**
Lev 8:26

**29:24**
Lev 7:30

**29:26**
Lev 7:31, 34; 8:29

**29:27**
Lev 7:31, 34
Num 18:11-12
Deut 18:3

**29:29**
Num 20:26, 28

**29:30**
Lev 8:35

**29:33**
Lev 22:10, 13

**29:34-35**
Lev 8:32-33

**29:36**
Exod 40:10
Heb 10:11

**29:37**
Exod 40:10
Matt 23:19

**29:38**
Num 28:3-31;
29:6-38
1 Chr 16:40
Dan 12:11

**29:41**
2 Kgs 16:15
Ezra 9:4-5
Ps 141:2

**29:42**
Exod 30:8

**29:43**
1 Kgs 8:11

**29:45**
Exod 25:8
Lev 26:12
Num 5:3
Deut 12:11
Ps 68:18
Zech 2:10
2 Cor 6:16
Rev 21:3

**29:46**
Exod 20:2

**30:1-5**
//Exod 37:25-28
1 Kgs 6:20
Rev 8:3

lobe of the liver, the two kidneys with their fat, and the right thigh. ²³Then take one loaf of bread, one cake mixed with olive oil, and one wafer from the basket of yeastless bread that was placed before the LORD. ²⁴Put all these in the hands of Aaron and his sons to be lifted up as a special gift to the LORD. ²⁵Afterward take the bread from their hands, and burn it on the altar as a burnt offering that will be pleasing to the LORD. ²⁶Then take the breast of Aaron's ordination ram, and lift it up in the LORD's presence as a special gift to him. Afterward keep it for yourself.

²⁷"Set aside as holy the parts of the ordination ram that belong to Aaron and his sons. This includes the breast and the thigh that were lifted up before the LORD in the ordination ceremony. ²⁸In the future, whenever the people of Israel offer up peace offerings or thanksgiving offerings to the LORD, these parts will be the regular share of Aaron and his descendants.

²⁹"Aaron's sacred garments must be preserved for his descendants who will succeed him, so they can be anointed and ordained in them. ³⁰Whoever is the next high priest after Aaron will wear these clothes for seven days before beginning to minister in the Tabernacle and the Holy Place.

³¹"Take the ram used in the ordination ceremony, and boil its meat in a sacred place. ³²Aaron and his sons are to eat this meat, along with the bread in the basket, at the Tabernacle entrance. ³³They alone may eat the meat and bread used for their atonement in the ordination ceremony. The ordinary people may not eat them, for these things are set apart and holy. ³⁴If any of the ordination meat or bread remains until the morning, it must be burned. It may not be eaten, for it is holy.

³⁵"This is how you will ordain Aaron and his sons to their offices. The ordination ceremony will go on for seven days. ³⁶Each day you must sacrifice a young bull as an offering for the atonement of sin. Afterward make an offering to cleanse the altar. Purify the altar by making atonement for it; make it holy by anointing it with oil. ³⁷Make atonement for the altar every day for seven days. After that, the altar will be exceedingly holy, and whatever touches it will become holy.

³⁸"This is what you are to offer on the altar. Offer two one-year-old lambs each day, ³⁹one in the morning and the other in the evening. ⁴⁰With one of them, offer two quarts of fine flour mixed with one quart of olive oil; also, offer one quart of wine* as a drink offering. ⁴¹Offer the other lamb in the evening, along with the same offerings of flour and wine as in the morning. It will be a fragrant offering to the LORD, an offering made by fire.

⁴²"This is to be a daily burnt offering given from generation to generation. Offer it in the LORD's presence at the Tabernacle entrance, where I will meet you and speak with you. ⁴³I will meet the people of Israel there, and the Tabernacle will be sanctified by my glorious presence. ⁴⁴Yes, I will make the Tabernacle and the altar most holy, and I will set apart Aaron and his sons as holy, that they may be my priests. ⁴⁵I will live among the people of Israel and be their God, ⁴⁶and they will know that I am the LORD their God. I am the one who brought them out of Egypt so that I could live among them. I am the LORD their God.

### Plans for the Incense Altar

**30** "Then make a small altar out of acacia wood for burning incense. ²It must be eighteen inches square and three feet high,* with horns at the corners carved from the same piece of wood as the altar. ³Overlay the top, sides, and horns of the altar with pure gold, and run a gold molding around the entire altar. ⁴Beneath the molding, on

**29:40** Hebrew *1/10 of an ephah* [2 liters] *of fine flour . . . 1/4 of a hin* [1 liter] *of olive oil . . . 1/4 of a hin of wine.*
**30:2** Hebrew *1 cubit* [45 centimeters] *square and 2 cubits* [90 centimeters] *high.*

---

**29:37** Notice the overwhelming emphasis on the holiness of God. The priests, the clothes, the Tabernacle, and the sacrifices had to be clean and consecrated, prepared to meet God. In contrast, today we tend to take God for granted, rushing into worship and treating him with almost casual disregard. But we worship the almighty Creator and Sustainer of the universe. Remember that profound truth when you pray or worship, and come before him with reverence and repentance.

**29:45, 46** God's action in bringing the Israelites out of Egypt showed his great desire to be with them and protect them. Throughout the Bible, God shows that he is not an absentee landlord. He wants to live among us, even in our hearts. Don't exclude God from your life. Allow him to be your God as you obey his Word and communicate with him in prayer. Let him be your resident landlord.

opposite sides of the altar, attach two gold rings to support the carrying poles. ⁵The poles are to be made of acacia wood and overlaid with gold. ⁶Place the incense altar just outside the inner curtain, opposite the Ark's cover—the place of atonement—that rests on the Ark of the Covenant.* I will meet with you there.

⁷"Every morning when Aaron trims the lamps, he must burn fragrant incense on the altar. ⁸And each evening when he tends to the lamps, he must again burn incense in the LORD's presence. This must be done from generation to generation. ⁹Do not offer any unholy incense on this altar, or any burnt offerings, grain offerings, or drink offerings.

¹⁰"Once a year Aaron must purify the altar by placing on its horns the blood from the offering made for the atonement of sin. This will be a regular, annual event from generation to generation, for this is the LORD's supremely holy altar."

### Money for the Tabernacle

¹¹And the LORD said to Moses, ¹²"Whenever you take a census of the people of Israel, each man who is counted must pay a ransom for himself to the LORD. Then there will be no plagues among the people as you count them. ¹³His payment to the LORD will be one-fifth of an ounce* of silver. ¹⁴All who have reached their twentieth birthday must give this offering to the LORD. ¹⁵When this offering is given to the LORD to make atonement for yourselves, the rich must not give more, and the poor must not give less. ¹⁶Use this money for the care of the Tabernacle.* It will bring you, the Israelites, to the LORD's attention, and it will make atonement for your lives."

### Plans for the Washbasin

¹⁷And the LORD said to Moses, ¹⁸"Make a large bronze washbasin with a bronze pedestal. Put it between the Tabernacle and the altar, and fill it with water. ¹⁹Aaron and his sons will wash their hands and feet there ²⁰before they go into the Tabernacle to appear before the LORD and before they approach the altar to burn offerings to the LORD. They must always wash before ministering in these ways, or they will die. ²¹This is a permanent law for Aaron and his descendants, to be kept from generation to generation."

### The Anointing Oil

²²Then the LORD said to Moses, ²³"Collect choice spices—12½ pounds of pure myrrh, 6¼ pounds* each of cinnamon and of sweet cane, ²⁴12½ pounds of cassia, and one gallon* of olive oil. ²⁵Blend these ingredients into a holy anointing oil. ²⁶Use this scented oil to anoint the Tabernacle, the Ark of the Covenant, ²⁷the table and all its utensils, the lampstand and all its accessories, the incense altar, ²⁸the altar of burnt offering with all its utensils, and the large washbasin with its pedestal. ²⁹Sanctify them to make them entirely holy. After this, whatever touches them will become holy. ³⁰Use this oil also to anoint Aaron and his sons, sanctifying them so they can minister before me as priests. ³¹And say to the people of Israel, 'This will always be my holy anointing oil. ³²It must never be poured on the body of an ordinary person, and you must never make any of it for yourselves. It is holy, and you must treat it as holy. ³³Anyone who blends scented oil like it or puts any of it on someone who is not a priest will be cut off from the community.'"

**30:6** Or *Ark of the Testimony;* also in 30:26, 36. **30:13** Hebrew *half a shekel* [6 grams], *according to the sanctuary shekel, 20 gerahs to each shekel.* **30:16** Hebrew *Tent of Meeting;* also in 30:18, 20, 26, 36. **30:23** Hebrew *500 shekels* [5.7 kilograms] *of pure myrrh, 250 shekels* [2.9 kilograms]. **30:24** Hebrew *500 shekels* [5.7 kilograms] *of cassia, according to the sanctuary shekel, and 1 hin* [3.8 liters].

Cross-references: 30:6 Exod 25:21-22; 30:7 Exod 27:21; 30:34-35; 1 Sam 2:28; Luke 1:9; 30:10 Lev 16:8; 30:12 Exod 38:25-26; Num 1:2; 26:2; 2 Sam 24:1; Matt 20:28; 30:13 Matt 17:24; 30:15 Prov 22:2; 30:18 Exod 38:8; 40:7, 30; 30:19 Exod 40:31-32; 30:21 Exod 28:43; 30:25 Exod 37:29; 40:9; 30:26 Lev 8:10; Num 7:1; 30:29 Exod 29:37; 30:30 Lev 8:2, 12, 30; 30:33 Gen 17:14; Exod 12:15; Lev 7:20-21

**30:10** This once-a-year ceremony was called the Day of Atonement. On this day a sacrifice was made for the sins of the entire Israelite nation. This was the only day the high priest could enter the Most Holy Place, the innermost room of the Tabernacle. Here he asked God to forgive the people. The Day of Atonement served as a reminder that the daily, weekly, and monthly sacrifices could cover sins only temporarily. It pointed toward Jesus Christ, the perfect atonement, who could remove sins forever.

**30:11-16** This money was like a census tax. It continued the principle that all the people belonged to God and therefore needed to be redeemed by a sacrifice. Whenever a census took place, everyone, both rich and poor, was required to pay a ransom. God does not discriminate between people (see Acts 10:34; Galatians 3:28). All of us need mercy and forgiveness because of our sinful thoughts and actions. There is no way the rich person can buy off God, and no way the poor can avoid paying. God's demand is that all of us come humbly before him to be forgiven and brought into his family.

### The Incense

**30:36**
Exod 29:42
Lev 2:3

34 These were the LORD's instructions to Moses concerning the incense: "Gather sweet spices—resin droplets, mollusk scent, galbanum, and pure frankincense—weighing out the same amounts of each. 35 Using the usual techniques of the incense maker, refine it to produce a pure and holy incense. 36 Beat some of it very fine and put some of it in front of the Ark of the Covenant, where I will meet with you in the Tabernacle. This incense is most holy. 37 Never make this incense for yourselves. It is reserved for the LORD, and you must treat it as holy. 38 Those who make it for their own enjoyment will be cut off from the community."

### Craftsmen: Bezalel and Oholiab

**31:2-6**
//Exod 35:30—36:1
1 Chr 2:20

**31:3**
1 Kgs 7:14

**31:6**
Exod 35:34; 36:1

**31:7**
Exod 37:1-9

**31:8**
Exod 37:10-16
Lev 24:4

**31:11**
Exod 30:23-32

**31** The LORD also said to Moses, 2 "Look, I have chosen Bezalel son of Uri, grandson of Hur, of the tribe of Judah. 3 I have filled him with the Spirit of God, giving him great wisdom, intelligence, and skill in all kinds of crafts. 4 He is able to create beautiful objects from gold, silver, and bronze. 5 He is skilled in cutting and setting gemstones and in carving wood. Yes, he is a master at every craft!

6 "And I have appointed Oholiab son of Ahisamach, of the tribe of Dan, to be his assistant. Moreover, I have given special skill to all the naturally talented craftsmen so they can make all the things I have instructed you to make: 7 the Tabernacle itself; the Ark of the Covenant;* the Ark's cover—the place of atonement; all the furnishings of the Tabernacle; 8 the table and all its utensils; the gold lampstand with all its accessories; the incense altar; 9 the altar of burnt offering with all its utensils; the washbasin and its pedestal; 10 the beautifully stitched, holy garments for Aaron the priest, and the garments for his sons to wear as they minister as priests; 11 the anointing oil; and the special incense for the Holy Place. They must follow exactly all the instructions I have given you."

### Instructions for the Sabbath

**31:13**
Lev 19:3, 30
Ezek 20:12-13

**31:14**
Exod 16:23; 35:2
John 7:23

**31:16**
Exod 20:8

**31:17**
Gen 2:2-3
Exod 20:11

**31:18**
Exod 24:12;
32:15-16; 34:1, 28

12 The LORD then gave these further instructions to Moses: 13 "Tell the people of Israel to keep my Sabbath day, for the Sabbath is a sign of the covenant between me and you forever. It helps you to remember that I am the LORD, who makes you holy. 14 Yes, keep the Sabbath day, for it is holy. Anyone who desecrates it must die; anyone who works on that day will be cut off from the community. 15 Work six days only, but the seventh day must be a day of total rest. I repeat: Because the LORD considers it a holy day, anyone who works on the Sabbath must be put to death. 16 The people of Israel must keep the Sabbath day forever. 17 It is a permanent sign of my covenant with them. For in six days the LORD made heaven and earth, but he rested on the seventh day and was refreshed."

18 Then as the LORD finished speaking with Moses on Mount Sinai, he gave him the two stone tablets inscribed with the terms of the covenant,* written by the finger of God.

**31:7** Hebrew *the Tent of Meeting; the Ark of the Testimony.*   **31:18** Hebrew *the Testimony.*

---

**30:34-38** The Israelites often burned incense, but this holy incense could be burned only in the Tabernacle. Here God gave the recipe for this special incense. The sweet-smelling incense was burned in shallow dishes called incense burners and was used to show honor and reverence to God. It was like prayer lifting up to God. It was also a vital part of the sacred ceremony on the Day of Atonement, when the high priest carried his smoking censer into the Most Holy Place. This incense, like the sacred anointing oil, was so holy that the people were strictly forbidden to copy it for personal use.

**31:1-11** God regards all the skills of his people, not merely those with theological or ministerial abilities. Our tendency is to regard only those who are up front and in leadership roles. God gave Bezalel and Oholiab Spirit-filled abilities in artistic craftsmanship. Take notice of all the abilities God gives his people. Don't diminish your skills if they are not like Moses' and Aaron's.

**31:12-17** The Sabbath had two purposes: It was a time *to rest* and a time *to remember* what God had done. We need

rest. Without time out from the bustle, life loses its meaning. In our day, as in Moses' day, taking time out is not easy. But God reminds us that without Sabbaths we will forget the purpose for all of our activity and lose the balance crucial to a faithful life. Make sure your Sabbath provides a time of both refreshment and remembrance of God.

**31:18** The two stone tablets contained the Ten Commandments. These were not the only code of laws in the ancient world. Other law codes had come into existence when cities or nations decided that there must be standards of judgment, ways to correct specific wrongs. But God's laws for Israel were unique: (1) They alleviated the harsh judgments typical of the day; (2) they were egalitarian—the poor and the powerful received the same punishment; (3) they did not separate religious and social law. All law rested on God's authority.

## 3. Breaking the law

*The Calf of Gold*

**32** When Moses failed to come back down the mountain right away, the people went to Aaron. "Look," they said, "make us some gods who can lead us. This man Moses, who brought us here from Egypt, has disappeared. We don't know what has happened to him."

**32:1**
Exod 24:18
Deut 9:9-12
†Acts 7:40

²So Aaron said, "Tell your wives and sons and daughters to take off their gold earrings, and then bring them to me."

**32:2**
Exod 35:22

³All the people obeyed Aaron and brought him their gold earrings. ⁴Then Aaron took the gold, melted it down, and molded and tooled it into the shape of a calf. The people exclaimed, "O Israel, these are the gods who brought you out of Egypt!"

**32:4**
Exod 20:23
Deut 9:16
Ps 106:19
Acts 7:41

⁵When Aaron saw how excited the people were about it, he built an altar in front of the calf and announced, "Tomorrow there will be a festival to the LORD!"

⁶So the people got up early the next morning to sacrifice burnt offerings and peace offerings. After this, they celebrated with feasting and drinking, and indulged themselves in pagan revelry.

**32:6**
Num 25:2
Acts 7:41
†1 Cor 10:7

⁷Then the LORD told Moses, "Quick! Go down the mountain! The people you brought from Egypt have defiled themselves. ⁸They have already turned from the way I commanded them to live. They have made an idol shaped like a calf, and they have worshiped and sacrificed to it. They are saying, 'These are your gods, O Israel, who brought you out of Egypt.'"

**32:7**
Exod 19:24; 33:1
Deut 9:12

**32:8**
Exod 22:20; 34:15
Deut 32:17

⁹Then the LORD said, "I have seen how stubborn and rebellious these people are. ¹⁰Now leave me alone so my anger can blaze against them and destroy them all. Then I will make you, Moses, into a great nation instead of them."

**32:9**
Exod 33:5
Num 14:11
Acts 7:51

**32:10**
Num 14:12
Deut 9:14

¹¹But Moses pleaded with the LORD his God not to do it. "O LORD!" he exclaimed. "Why are you so angry with your own people whom you brought from the land of Egypt with such great power and mighty acts? ¹²The Egyptians will say, 'God tricked them into coming to the mountains so he could kill them and wipe them from the face of the earth.' Turn away from your fierce anger. Change your mind about this terrible disaster you are planning against your people! ¹³Remember your covenant with your servants—Abraham, Isaac, and Jacob.* You swore by your own self, 'I will make your descendants as numerous as the stars of heaven. Yes, I will give them all of this land that I have promised to your descendants, and they will possess it forever.'"

**32:11**
Deut 9:18, 26
Ps 106:23

**32:12**
Num 14:13-16
Deut 9:28

**32:13**
Gen 15:5; 22:16-18
Heb 6:13

¹⁴So the LORD withdrew his threat and didn't bring against his people the disaster he had threatened.

**32:14**
2 Sam 24:16
Ps 106:45

**32:13** Hebrew *Israel.*

---

**32:1-10** Idols again! Even though Israel had seen the invisible God in action, they still wanted the familiar gods they could see and shape into whatever image they desired. How much like them we are! Our great temptation is still to shape God to our liking, to make him convenient to obey or ignore. God responds in great anger when his mercy is trampled on. The gods we create blind us to the love that our loving God wants to shower on us. God cannot work in us when we elevate anyone or anything above him. What false gods in your life are preventing the true God from living in you?

**32:4, 5** Two popular Egyptian gods, Hapi (Apis) and Hathor, were thought of as a bull and a heifer. The Canaanites around them worshiped Baal, thought of as a bull. Baal was their sacred symbol of power and fertility and was closely connected to immoral sexual practices. No doubt the Israelites, fresh from Egypt, found it quite natural to make a golden calf to represent the God that had just delivered them from their oppressors. They were weary of a god without a face. But in doing so, they were ignoring the command he had just given them: "Do not make idols of any kind" (20:4). They may even have thought they were worshiping God. Their apparent sincerity was no substitute for obedience or excuse for disobedience.

Even if we do not make idols, we are often guilty of trying to make God in our image, molding him to fit our expectations,

desires, and circumstances. When we do this, we end up worshiping ourselves rather than the God who created us—and self-worship, today as in the Israelites' time, leads to all kinds of immorality. What is your favorite image of God? Is it biblical? Is it adequate? Do you need to destroy it in order to worship the immeasurably powerful God who delivered you from bondage to sin?

**32:9-14** God was ready to destroy the whole nation because of their sin. But Moses pleaded for mercy, and God spared them. This is one of the countless examples in the Bible of God's mercy. Although we deserve his anger, he is willing to forgive and restore us to himself. We can receive God's forgiveness from sin by asking him. Like Moses, we can pray that he will forgive others and use us to bring them the message of his mercy.

**32:14** How could God relent? God did not change his mind in the same way that a parent decides not to discipline a child. Instead, God changed his behavior to remain consistent with his nature. When God first wanted to destroy the people, he was acting consistently with his justice. When Moses interceded for the people, God relented in order to act consistently with his mercy. God had often told the people that if they changed their ways, he would not condemn them. They changed, and God did as he promised.

**32:15**
Exod 24:18
Deut 9:15

**32:16**
Exod 31:18

**32:19**
Exod 32:6
Deut 9:16-17

**32:20**
Deut 9:21

**32:22**
Deut 9:24

**32:23**
Exod 32:1

¹⁵Then Moses turned and went down the mountain. He held in his hands the two stone tablets inscribed with the terms of the covenant.* They were inscribed on both sides, front and back. ¹⁶These stone tablets were God's work; the words on them were written by God himself.

¹⁷When Joshua heard the noise of the people shouting below them, he exclaimed to Moses, "It sounds as if there is a war in the camp!"

¹⁸But Moses replied, "No, it's neither a cry of victory nor a cry of defeat. It is the sound of a celebration."

¹⁹When they came near the camp, Moses saw the calf and the dancing. In terrible anger, he threw the stone tablets to the ground, smashing them at the foot of the mountain. ²⁰He took the calf they had made and melted it in the fire. And when the metal had cooled, he ground it into powder and mixed it with water. Then he made the people drink it.

²¹After that, he turned to Aaron. "What did the people do to you?" he demanded. "How did they ever make you bring such terrible sin upon them?"

²²"Don't get upset, sir," Aaron replied. "You yourself know these people and what a wicked bunch they are. ²³They said to me, 'Make us some gods to lead us, for something has happened to this man Moses, who led us out of Egypt.' ²⁴So I told them, 'Bring me

**32:15** Hebrew *the Testimony.*

---

# AARON

Effective teamwork happens when each team member uses his or her special skills. Ideally each member's strengths will contribute something important to the team effort. In this way, members make up for one another's weaknesses. Aaron made a good team with Moses. He provided Moses with one skill Moses lacked—effective public speaking. But while Aaron was necessary to Moses, he needed Moses as well. Without a guide, Aaron had little direction of his own. There was never any doubt as to who God's chosen and trained leader was. The pliability that made Aaron a good follower made him a weak leader. His major failures were caused by his inability to stand alone. His yielding to public pressure and making an idol was a good example of this weakness.

Most of us have more of the follower than the leader in us. We may even be good followers, following a good leader. But no leader is perfect, and no human deserves our complete allegiance. Only God deserves our complete loyalty and obedience. We need to be effective team members in using the skills and abilities God has given us. But if the team or the leader goes against God's Word, we must be willing to stand alone.

| | |
|---|---|
| **Strengths and accomplishments** | • First high priest of God in Israel<br>• Effective communicator; Moses' mouthpiece |
| **Weaknesses and mistakes** | • Pliable personality; gave in to people's demands for a golden calf<br>• Joined with Moses in disobeying God's orders about the water-giving rock<br>• Joined sister Miriam in complaining against Moses |
| **Lessons from his life** | • God gives individuals special abilities, which he weaves together for his use<br>• The very skills that make a good team player sometimes also make a poor leader |
| **Vital statistics** | • Where: Egypt, wilderness of Sinai<br>• Occupations: Priest; Moses' second in command<br>• Relatives: Brother: Moses. Sister: Miriam. Sons: Nadab, Abihu, Eleazar, and Ithamar |
| **Key verses** | "Then the LORD became angry with Moses. 'All right, he said. 'What about your brother, Aaron the Levite? He is a good speaker. And look! He is on his way to meet you now. And when he sees you, he will be very glad. . . . Aaron will be your spokesman to the people, and you will be as God to him, telling him what to say' " (Exodus 4:14, 16). |

Aaron's story is told in Exodus—Deuteronomy 10:6. He is also mentioned in Hebrews 7:11.

---

**32:19, 20** Overwhelmed by the actual sight of the blatant idolatry and revelry, Moses broke the tablets containing the commandments which had already been broken in the hearts and actions of the people. There is a place for righteous anger. However angry Moses might have been, God was angrier still—he wanted to kill all the people. Anger at sin is a sign of spiritual vitality. Don't squelch this kind of anger. But when you are justifiably angry at sin, be careful not to do anything that you will regret later.

**32:21-24** Aaron's decision nearly cost him his life. His absurd excuse shows the spiritual decline in his leadership and in the people. Those who function as spokespersons and assistants need to be doubly sure their theology and morality are in tune with God so they will not be influenced by pressure from people. For more information on Aaron, see his Profile in chapter 32.

your gold earrings.' When they brought them to me, I threw them into the fire—and out came this calf!"

25 When Moses saw that Aaron had let the people get completely out of control—and much to the amusement of their enemies—26 he stood at the entrance to the camp and shouted, "All of you who are on the LORD's side, come over here and join me." And all the Levites came.

27 He told them, "This is what the LORD, the God of Israel, says: Strap on your swords! Go back and forth from one end of the camp to the other, killing even your brothers, friends, and neighbors." 28 The Levites obeyed Moses, and about three thousand people died that day.

29 Then Moses told the Levites, "Today you have been ordained for the service of the LORD, for you obeyed him even though it meant killing your own sons and brothers. Because of this, he will now give you a great blessing."

### Moses Intercedes for Israel

30 The next day Moses said to the people, "You have committed a terrible sin, but I will return to the LORD on the mountain. Perhaps I will be able to obtain forgiveness for you."

31 So Moses returned to the LORD and said, "Alas, these people have committed a terrible sin. They have made gods of gold for themselves. 32 But now, please forgive their sin—and if not, then blot me out of the record you are keeping."

33 The LORD replied to Moses, "I will blot out whoever has sinned against me. 34 Now go, lead the people to the place I told you about. Look! My angel will lead the way before you! But when I call the people to account, I will certainly punish them for their sins."

35 And the LORD sent a great plague upon the people because they had worshiped the calf Aaron had made.

**33** The LORD said to Moses, "Now that you have brought these people out of Egypt, lead them to the land I solemnly promised Abraham, Isaac, and Jacob. I told them long ago that I would give this land to their descendants. 2 And I will send an angel before you to drive out the Canaanites, Amorites, Hittites, Perizzites, Hivites, and Jebusites. 3 Theirs is a land flowing with milk and honey. But I will not travel along with you, for you are a stubborn, unruly people. If I did, I would be tempted to destroy you along the way."

4 When the people heard these stern words, they went into mourning and refused to wear their jewelry and ornaments. 5 For the LORD had told Moses to tell them, "You are an unruly, stubborn people. If I were there among you for even a moment, I would destroy you. Remove your jewelry and ornaments until I decide what to do with you." 6 So from the time they left Mount Sinai,* the Israelites wore no more jewelry.

7 It was Moses' custom to set up the tent known as the Tent of Meeting far outside the camp. Everyone who wanted to consult with the LORD would go there.

8 Whenever Moses went out to the Tent of Meeting, all the people would get up and stand in their tent entrances. They would all watch Moses until he disappeared inside. 9 As he went into the tent, the pillar of cloud would come down and hover at the entrance while the LORD spoke with Moses. 10 Then all the people would stand and bow low at their tent entrances. 11 Inside the Tent of Meeting, the LORD would speak to Moses face to face, as a man speaks to his friend. Afterward Moses would return to the camp, but the young man who assisted him, Joshua son of Nun, stayed behind in the Tent of Meeting.

**33:6** Hebrew *Horeb,* another name for Sinai.

---

**32:25**
1 Kgs 12:28-30

**32:26**
2 Sam 20:11

**32:27**
Num 25:5
Deut 33:9

**32:28**
Num 16:32; 25:9

**32:29**
Deut 13:6; 33:9

**32:31**
Exod 20:23

**32:32**
Dan 12:1
Mal 3:16-17
Phil 4:3
Rev 3:5; 21:27

**32:33**
Deut 29:20
Ps 9:5
Rev 3:5

**32:34**
Exod 3:17; 23:20
Ps 99:8

**33:1**
Gen 12:7
Exod 32:7, 13

**33:2**
Exod 23:27-31

**33:3**
Exod 3:8, 17;
32:9-10

**33:4**
Num 14:1, 39

**33:5**
Exod 33:3

**33:7**
Exod 29:42-43

**33:8**
Num 16:27

**33:9**
Exod 13:21; 19:9;
25:22
Ps 99:7

**33:11**
Num 12:8
Deut 34:10

---

**33:5, 6** This ban on ornaments was not a permanent ban on all jewelry. It was a temporary sign of repentance and mourning. In 35:22 we read that the people had jewelry.

**33:11** God and Moses talked face to face in the Tent of Meeting, just as friends do. Why did Moses find such favor with God? It certainly was not because he was perfect, gifted, or powerful. Rather, it was because God chose Moses, and Moses in turn relied wholeheartedly on God's wisdom and direction. Friendship

with God was a true privilege for Moses, out of reach for the other Hebrews. But it is not out of reach for us today. Jesus called his disciples—and, by extension, all of his followers—his friends (John 15:15). He has called you to be his friend. Will you trust him as Moses did?

**33:11** Joshua, Moses' aide, did not leave the Tent of Meeting, probably because he was guarding it. No doubt there were curious people who would have dared to go inside.

## Moses Sees the LORD's Glory

**33:12**
Exod 3:10; 32:34
John 10:14-15
2 Tim 2:19

12Moses said to the LORD, "You have been telling me, 'Take these people up to the Promised Land.' But you haven't told me whom you will send with me. You call me by name and tell me I have found favor with you. 13Please, if this is really so, show me your intentions so I will understand you more fully and do exactly what you want me to do. Besides, don't forget that this nation is your very own people."

**33:13**
Exod 34:9
Pss 25:4; 27:11

**33:14**
Exod 13:21
Josh 22:4
Isa 63:9

14And the LORD replied, "I will personally go with you, Moses. I will give you rest—everything will be fine for you."

**33:16**
Exod 34:10
Lev 20:24, 26
Num 14:14

15Then Moses said, "If you don't go with us personally, don't let us move a step from this place. 16If you don't go with us, how will anyone ever know that your people and I have found favor with you? How else will they know we are special and distinct from all other people on the earth?"

**33:17**
Exod 33:12

17And the LORD replied to Moses, "I will indeed do what you have asked, for you have found favor with me, and you are my friend."

**33:18**
Exod 33:20, 23

18Then Moses had one more request. "Please let me see your glorious presence," he said.

**33:19**
†Rom 9:15

19The LORD replied, "I will make all my goodness pass before you, and I will call out my name, 'the LORD,' to you. I will show kindness to anyone I choose, and I will show mercy to anyone I choose. 20But you may not look directly at my face, for no one may see me and live." 21The LORD continued, "Stand here on this rock beside me. 22As my glorious presence passes by, I will put you in the cleft of the rock and cover you with my hand until I have passed. 23Then I will remove my hand, and you will see me from behind. But my face will not be seen."

**33:20**
Isa 6:5
John 1:18
1 Tim 6:16

**33:22**
Ps 91:1, 4
Isa 49:2; 51:16

**33:23**
John 1:18

## A New Copy of the Covenant

**34:1**
Exod 24:12; 32:19
Deut 10:2, 4

**34** The LORD told Moses, "Prepare two stone tablets like the first ones. I will write on them the same words that were on the tablets you smashed. 2Be ready in the morning to come up Mount Sinai and present yourself to me there on the top of the mountain. 3No one else may come with you. In fact, no one is allowed anywhere on the mountain. Do not even let the flocks or herds graze near the mountain."

**34:3**
Exod 19:12-13

4So Moses cut two tablets of stone like the first ones. Early in the morning he climbed Mount Sinai as the LORD had told him, carrying the two stone tablets in his hands.

**34:5**
Exod 33:19

5Then the LORD came down in a pillar of cloud and called out his own name, "the LORD," as Moses stood there in his presence. 6He passed in front of Moses and said, "I am the LORD, I am the LORD, the merciful and gracious God. I am slow to anger and rich in unfailing love and faithfulness. 7I show this unfailing love to many thousands by forgiving every kind of sin and rebellion. Even so I do not leave sin unpunished, but I punish the children for the sins of their parents to the third and fourth generations."

**34:6**
Num 14:18
Neh 9:17
Pss 86:15; 103:8

**34:7**
Exod 20:6-7
Deut 5:10
Nah 1:3

**34:9**
Num 14:19
Deut 4:20; 32:9
Ps 25:11

8Moses immediately fell to the ground and worshiped. 9And he said, "If it is true that I have found favor in your sight, O Lord, then please go with us. Yes, this is an unruly and stubborn people, but please pardon our iniquity and our sins. Accept us as your own special possession."

**34:10**
Deut 5:2-3
Pss 72:18; 136:4

10The LORD replied, "All right. This is the covenant I am going to make with you. I will perform wonders that have never been done before anywhere in all the earth or in any nation. And all the people around you will see the power of the LORD—the awesome

---

**33:18-23** Moses' prayer was to see the manifest glory of God. He wanted assurance of God's presence with him. Aaron, and Joshua, and also he desired to know that presence experientially. Because we are finite and morally imperfect, we cannot exist and see God as he is. To see God's back means we can only see where God has passed by. We can only know him by what he does and how he acts. We cannot comprehend God as he really is apart from Jesus Christ (John 14:9). Jesus promised to show himself to those who believe (John 14:21).

**34:6, 7** Moses had asked to see God's glorious presence (33:18), and this was God's response. What is God's glory? It is his character, his nature, his way of relating to his creatures. Notice that God did not give Moses a vision of his power and majesty, but rather of his love. God's glory is revealed in his

mercy, grace, compassion, faithfulness, forgiveness, and justice. God's love and mercy are truly wonderful, and we benefit from them. We can respond and give glory to God when our characters resemble his.

**34:7** Why would sins affect grandchildren and great-grand-children? This is no arbitrary punishment. Children still suffer for the sins of their parents. Consider child abuse or alcoholism, for example. While these sins are obvious, sins like selfishness and greed can be passed along as well. The dire consequences of sin are not limited to the individual family member. Be careful not to treat sin casually, but repent and turn from it. The sin may cause you little pain now, but it could sting in a most tender area of your life later—your children and grandchildren.

10"Come, all of you who are gifted craftsmen. Construct everything that the LORD has commanded: 11 the entire Tabernacle, including the sacred tent and its coverings, the clasps, frames, crossbars, posts, and bases; 12 the Ark and its poles; the Ark's cover—the place of atonement; the inner curtain to enclose the Ark in the Most Holy Place; 13 the table, its carrying poles, and all of its utensils; the Bread of the Presence; 14 the lampstand and its accessories; the lamp cups and the oil for lighting; 15 the incense altar and its carrying poles; the anointing oil and fragrant incense; the curtain for the entrance of the Tabernacle; 16 the altar of burnt offering; the bronze grating of the altar and its carrying poles and utensils; the large washbasin with its pedestal; 17 the curtains for the walls of the courtyard; the posts and their bases; the curtain for the entrance to the courtyard; 18 the tent pegs of the Tabernacle and courtyard and their cords; 19 the beautifully stitched clothing for the priests to wear while ministering in the Holy Place; the sacred garments for Aaron and his sons to wear while officiating as priests."

20 So all the people left Moses and went to their tents to prepare their gifts. 21 If their hearts were stirred and they desired to do so, they brought to the LORD their offerings of materials for the Tabernacle* and its furnishings and for the holy garments. 22 Both men and women came, all whose hearts were willing. Some brought to the LORD their offerings of gold—medallions, earrings, rings from their fingers, and necklaces. They presented gold objects of every kind to the LORD. 23 Others brought blue, purple, and scarlet yarn, fine linen, or goat hair for cloth. Some gave tanned ram skins or fine goatskin leather. 24 Others brought silver and bronze objects as their offering to the LORD. And those who had acacia wood brought it.

25 All the women who were skilled in sewing and spinning prepared blue, purple, and scarlet yarn, and fine linen cloth, and they brought them in. 26 All the women who were willing used their skills to spin and weave the goat hair into cloth. 27 The leaders brought onyx stones and the other gemstones to be used for the ephod and the chestpiece. 28 They also brought spices and olive oil for the light, the anointing oil, and the fragrant incense. 29 So the people of Israel—every man and woman who wanted to help in the work the LORD had given them through Moses—brought their offerings to the LORD.

30 And Moses told them, "The LORD has chosen Bezalel son of Uri, grandson of Hur, of the tribe of Judah. 31 The LORD has filled Bezalel with the Spirit of God, giving him great wisdom, intelligence, and skill in all kinds of crafts. 32 He is able to create beautiful objects from gold, silver, and bronze. 33 He is skilled in cutting and setting gemstones and in carving wood. In fact, he has every necessary skill. 34 And the LORD has given both him and Oholiab son of Ahisamach, of the tribe of Dan, the ability to teach their skills to others. 35 The LORD has given them special skills as jewelers, designers, weavers, and embroiderers in blue, purple, and scarlet yarn on fine linen cloth. They excel in all the crafts needed for the work.

**36** "Bezalel, Oholiab, and the other craftsmen whom the LORD has gifted with wisdom, skill, and intelligence will construct and furnish the Tabernacle, just as the LORD has commanded."

35:21 Hebrew *Tent of Meeting.*

**35:10-19**
//Exod 39:32-41

**35:21**
Exod 25:2; 35:5

**35:23**
Exod 39:1

**35:25**
Exod 28:3

**35:27**
1 Chr 29:6
Ezra 2:68

**35:29**
1 Chr 29:9

**35:30-35**
//Exod 31:2-6

**35:34**
Exod 31:6

**35:35**
Exod 31:3, 6; 35:31
1 Kgs 7:14

**36:1**
Exod 25:8

---

**35:10-19** Moses asked people with various abilities to help with the Tabernacle. Every one of God's people has been given special abilities. We are responsible to develop these abilities—even the ones not considered religious—and to use them for God's glory. We can become skilled through study, by watching others, and through practice. Work on your skills or abilities that could help your church or community.

**35:20-24** Where did the Israelites, who were once Egyptian slaves, get all this gold and jewelry? When the Hebrews left Egypt, they took with them the spoils from the land—all the booty they could carry (12:35, 36). This included gold, silver, jewels, linen, skins, and other valuables.

**35:21, 22** Those whose hearts were stirred gave willingy to the Tent of Meeting (also called the Tabernacle). With great enthusiasm they gave because they knew how important their giving was to the completion of God's house. Airline pilots and computer operators can push test buttons to see if their equipment is functioning properly. God has a quick test button he can push to see the level of our commitment—our pocketbooks. Generous people aren't necessarily faithful to God. But faithful people are always generous.

**35:26** Those who spun cloth made a beautiful contribution to the Tabernacle. Good workers take pride in the quality and beauty of their work. God is concerned with the quality and beauty of what you do. Whether you are a corporate executive or a drugstore cashier, your work should reflect the creative abilities God has given you.

**36:2**
Exod 35:21, 26
1 Chr 29:5

**36:5**
2 Chr 24:14;
31:6-10
2 Cor 8:2-3

**36:7**
1 Kgs 8:64

**36:8-38**
//Exod 26:1-37

**36:14**
Exod 26:7

**36:20-34**
Exod 26:15-29;
40:18-19

**36:35-38**
Exod 26:31-37

[2] So Moses told Bezalel and Oholiab to begin the work, along with all those who were specially gifted by the LORD. [3] Moses gave them the materials donated by the people for the completion of the sanctuary. Additional gifts were brought each morning. [4] But finally the craftsmen left their work to meet with Moses. [5] "We have more than enough materials on hand now to complete the job the LORD has given us to do!" they exclaimed.

[6] So Moses gave the command, and this message was sent throughout the camp: "Bring no more materials! You have already given more than enough." So the people stopped bringing their offerings. [7] Their contributions were more than enough to complete the whole project.

*Building the Tabernacle*

[8] The skilled weavers first made ten sheets from fine linen. One of the craftsmen then embroidered blue, purple, and scarlet cherubim into them. [9] Each sheet was exactly the same size—forty-two feet long and six feet wide.* [10] Five of these sheets were joined together to make one set, and a second set was made of the other five. [11] Fifty blue loops were placed along the edge of the last sheet in each set. [12] The fifty loops along the edge of the first set of sheets matched the loops along the edge of the second set. [13] Then fifty gold clasps were made to connect the loops on the edge of each set. Thus the Tabernacle was joined together in one piece.

[14] Above the Tabernacle, a roof covering was made from eleven sheets of cloth made from goat hair. [15] Each sheet was exactly the same size—forty-five feet long and six feet wide. [16] The craftsmen joined five of these sheets together to make one set, and the six remaining sheets were joined to make a second set. [17] Then they made fifty loops along the edge of the last sheet in each set. [18] They also made fifty small bronze clasps to couple the loops, so the two sets of sheets were firmly attached to each other. In this way, the roof covering was joined together in one piece. [19] Then they made two more layers for the roof covering. The first was made of tanned ram skins, and the second was made of fine goatskin leather.

[20] For the framework of the Tabernacle, they made frames of acacia wood standing on end. [21] Each frame was 15 feet high and 2¼ feet wide. [22] There were two pegs on each frame so they could be joined to the next frame. All the frames were made this way. [23] They made twenty frames to support the south side, [24] along with forty silver bases, two for each frame. [25] They also made twenty frames for the north side of the Tabernacle, [26] along with forty silver bases, two for each frame. [27] The west side of the Tabernacle, which was its rear, was made from six frames, [28] plus an extra frame at each corner. [29] These corner frames were connected at the bottom and firmly attached at the top with a single ring, forming a single unit from top to bottom. They made two of these, one for each rear corner. [30] So for the west side they made a total of eight frames, along with sixteen silver bases, two for each frame.

[31] Then they made five crossbars from acacia wood to tie the frames on the south side together. [32] They made another five for the north side and five for the west side. [33] The middle crossbar of the five was halfway up the frames, along each side, running from one end to the other. [34] The frames and crossbars were all overlaid with gold. The rings used to hold the crossbars were made of pure gold.

[35] The inner curtain was made of fine linen cloth, and cherubim were skillfully embroidered into it with blue, purple, and scarlet yarn. [36] This curtain was then attached to four gold hooks set into four posts of acacia wood. The posts were overlaid with gold and set into four silver bases.

[37] Then they made another curtain for the entrance to the sacred tent. It was made of fine linen cloth and embroidered with blue, purple, and scarlet yarn. [38] This curtain was

**36:9** Hebrew *28 cubits* [12.6 meters] *long and 4 cubits* [1.8 meters] *wide.* In this chapter, the distance measures are calculated from the Hebrew cubit at a ratio of 18 inches or 45 centimeters per cubit.

**36:8, 9** Making cloth (spinning and weaving) took a great deal of time in Moses' day. To own more than two or three charges of clothes was a sign of wealth. The effort involved in making enough cloth for the Tabernacle was staggering. The Tabernacle would never have been built without tremendous community involvement. Today, churches and neighborhoods often require this same kind of pulling together. Without it, many essential services wouldn't get done.

**36:35** Cherubim are mighty angels.

connected by five hooks to five posts. The posts with their decorated tops and bands were overlaid with gold. The five bases were molded from bronze.

## Building the Ark

**37** Next Bezalel made the Ark out of acacia wood. It was 3¾ feet long, 2¼ feet wide, and 2¼ feet high.* ²It was overlaid with pure gold inside and out, and it had a molding of gold all the way around. ³Four gold rings were fastened to its four feet, two rings at each side. ⁴Then he made poles from acacia wood and overlaid them with gold. ⁵He put the poles into the rings at the sides of the Ark to carry it.

⁶Then, from pure gold, he made the Ark's cover—the place of atonement. It was 3¾ feet long and 2¼ feet wide. ⁷He made two figures of cherubim out of hammered gold and placed them at the two ends of the atonement cover. ⁸They were made so they were actually a part of the atonement cover—it was all one piece. ⁹The cherubim faced each other as they looked down on the atonement cover, and their wings were stretched out above the atonement cover to protect it.

## Building the Table

¹⁰Then he made a table out of acacia wood, 3 feet long, 1½ feet wide, and 2¼ feet high. ¹¹It was overlaid with pure gold, with a gold molding all around the edge. ¹²A rim about 3 inches* wide was attached along the edges of the table, and a gold molding ran around the rim. ¹³Then he cast four rings of gold and attached them to the four table legs ¹⁴next to the rim. These were made to hold the carrying poles in place. ¹⁵He made the carrying poles of acacia wood and overlaid them with gold. ¹⁶Next, using pure gold, he made the plates, dishes, bowls, and pitchers to be placed on the table. These utensils were to be used in pouring out drink offerings.

## Building the Lampstand

¹⁷Then he made the lampstand, again using pure, hammered gold. Its base, center stem, lamp cups, blossoms, and buds were all of one piece. ¹⁸The lampstand had six branches, three going out from each side of the center stem. ¹⁹Each of the six branches held a cup shaped like an almond blossom, complete with buds and petals. ²⁰The center stem of the lampstand was also decorated with four almond blossoms. ²¹One blossom was set beneath each pair of branches, where they extended from the center stem. ²²The decorations and branches were all one piece with the stem, and they were hammered from pure gold. ²³He also made the seven lamps, the lamp snuffers, and the trays, all of pure gold. ²⁴The entire lampstand, along with its accessories, was made from seventy-five pounds* of pure gold.

## Building the Incense Altar

²⁵The incense altar was made of acacia wood. It was eighteen inches square and three feet high, with its corner horns made from the same piece of wood as the altar itself. ²⁶He overlaid the top, sides, and horns of the altar with pure gold and ran a gold molding around the edge. ²⁷Two gold rings were placed on opposite sides, beneath the molding, to hold the carrying poles. ²⁸The carrying poles were made of acacia wood and were overlaid with gold.

²⁹Then he made the sacred oil, for anointing the priests, and the fragrant incense, using the techniques of the most skilled incense maker.

## Building the Altar of Burnt Offering

**38** The altar for burning animal sacrifices also was constructed of acacia wood. It was 7½ feet square at the top and 4½ feet high.* ²There were four horns, one at each of the four corners, all of one piece with the rest. This altar was overlaid with

**37:1-9**
//Exod 25:10-20

**37:1**
Deut 10:3

**37:10-16**
//Exod 25:23-29;
40:22

**37:17-24**
//Exod 25:31-39;
40:24

**37:17**
Heb 9:2
Rev 1:12

**37:25-28**
//Exod 30:1-5

**37:25**
Heb 9:4
Rev 8:3

**37:29**
Exod 30:22-23;
40:9
Lev 8:10

**38:1-7**
//Exod 27:1-8;
40:10, 29

**37:1** Hebrew 2½ cubits [1.1 meters] long, 1½ cubits [0.7 meters] wide, and 1½ cubits high. In this chapter, the distance measures are calculated from the Hebrew cubit at a ratio of 18 inches or 45 centimeters per cubit. **37:12** Hebrew a handbreadth [8 centimeters]. **37:24** Hebrew 1 talent [34 kilograms]. **38:1** Hebrew 5 cubits [2.3 meters] square at the top, and 3 cubits [1.4 meters] high. In this chapter, the distance measures are calculated from the Hebrew cubit at a ratio of 18 inches or 45 centimeters per cubit.

**37:1** The Ark (also called the Ark of the Covenant) was built to hold the Ten Commandments. It symbolized God's covenant with his people. Two gold angels called cherubim were placed on its top. The Ark was Israel's most sacred object and was kept in the Most Holy Place in the Tabernacle. Only once each year, the high priest entered the Most Holy Place to sprinkle blood on the top of the Ark (called the atonement cover) to atone for the sins of the entire nation.

bronze. ³Then he made all the bronze utensils to be used with the altar—the ash buckets, shovels, basins, meat hooks, and firepans. ⁴Next he made a bronze grating that rested on a ledge about halfway down into the firebox. ⁵Four rings were cast for each side of the grating to support the carrying poles. ⁶The carrying poles themselves were made of acacia wood and were overlaid with bronze. ⁷These poles were inserted into the rings at the side of the altar. The altar was hollow and was made from planks.

### Building the Washbasin

**38:8**
Exod 30:18

⁸The bronze washbasin and its bronze pedestal were cast from bronze mirrors donated by the women who served at the entrance of the Tabernacle.*

### Building the Courtyard

**38:9-20**
//Exod 27:9-19; 40:8

⁹Then he constructed the courtyard. The south wall was 150 feet long. It consisted of curtains made of fine linen. ¹⁰There were twenty posts, each with its own bronze base, and there were silver hooks and rods to hold up the curtains. ¹¹The north wall was also 150 feet long, with twenty bronze posts and bases and with silver hooks and rods. ¹²The west end was 75 feet wide. The walls were made from curtains supported by ten posts and bases and with silver hooks and rods. ¹³The east end was also 75 feet wide.

¹⁴The courtyard entrance was on the east side, flanked by two curtains. The curtain on the right side was 22½ feet long and was supported by three posts set into three bases. ¹⁵The curtain on the left side was also 22½ feet long and was supported by three posts set into three bases. ¹⁶All the curtains used in the courtyard walls were made of fine linen. ¹⁷Each post had a bronze base and all the hooks and rods were silver. The tops of the posts were overlaid with silver, and the rods to hold up the curtains were solid silver.

¹⁸The curtain that covered the entrance to the courtyard was made of fine linen cloth and embroidered with blue, purple, and scarlet yarn. It was 30 feet long and 7½ feet high, just like the curtains of the courtyard walls. ¹⁹It was supported by four posts set into four bronze bases. The tops of the posts were overlaid with silver, and the hooks and rods were also made of silver.

²⁰All the tent pegs used in the Tabernacle and courtyard were made of bronze.

### Inventory of Materials

²¹Here is an inventory of the materials used in building the Tabernacle of the Covenant.* Moses directed the Levites to compile the figures, and Ithamar son of Aaron the priest served as recorder. ²²Bezalel son of Uri, grandson of Hur, of the tribe of Judah, was in charge of the whole project, just as the LORD had commanded Moses. ²³He was assisted by Oholiab son of Ahisamach, of the tribe of Dan, a craftsman expert at engraving, designing, and embroidering blue, purple, and scarlet yarn on fine linen cloth.

²⁴The people brought gifts of gold totaling about 2,200 pounds,* all of which was used throughout the Tabernacle.

**38:25-26**
Exod 12:37;
30:11-16
Num 1:46; 26:51

²⁵The amount of silver that was given was about 7,545 pounds.* ²⁶It came from the tax of one-fifth of an ounce of silver* collected from each of those registered in the census. This included all the men who were twenty years old or older, 603,550 in all. ²⁷The 100 bases for the frames of the sanctuary walls and for the posts supporting the inner curtain required 7,500 pounds of silver, about 75 pounds for each base.* ²⁸The rest of the silver, about 45 pounds,* was used to make the rods and hooks and to overlay the tops of the posts.

²⁹The people also brought 5,310 pounds* of bronze, ³⁰which was used for casting the

**38:8** Hebrew *Tent of Meeting;* also in 38:30.     **38:21** Hebrew *the Tabernacle, the Tabernacle of the Testimony.*
**38:24** Hebrew *29 talents* [2,175 pounds or 986 kilograms] *and 730 shekels* [18.3 pounds or 8.3 kilograms], *according to the sanctuary shekel.*     **38:25** Hebrew *100 talents* [7,500 pounds or 3,400 kilograms] *and 1,775 shekels* [44.4 pounds or 20.2 kilograms], *according to the sanctuary shekel.*     **38:26** Hebrew *1 beka* [6 grams] *per person, that is, half a shekel, according to the sanctuary shekel.*     **38:27** Hebrew *100 talents* [3,400 kilograms] *of silver, 1 talent* [34 kilograms] *for each base.*     **38:28** Hebrew *1,775 shekels* [20.2 kilograms].     **38:29** Hebrew *70 talents* [5,250 pounds or 2,380 kilograms] *and 2,400 shekels* [60 pounds or 27.4 kilograms].

**38:21**  In the building of the Tabernacle, Moses laid out the steps, but Ithamar supervised the project. We all have different talents and abilities. God didn't ask Moses to build the Tabernacle but to motivate the experts to do it. Look for the areas where God has gifted you and then seek opportunities to allow God to use your gifts.

bases for the posts at the entrance to the Tabernacle, and for the bronze altar with its bronze grating and altar utensils. [31]Bronze was also used to make the bases for the posts that supported the curtains around the courtyard, the bases for the curtain at the entrance of the courtyard, and all the tent pegs used to hold the curtains of the courtyard in place.

## Clothing for the Priests

**39** For the priests, the craftsmen made beautiful garments of blue, purple, and scarlet cloth—clothing to be worn while ministering in the Holy Place. This same cloth was used for Aaron's sacred garments, just as the LORD had commanded Moses.

**39:1**
Exod 35:23

## Making the Ephod

[2]The ephod was made from fine linen cloth and embroidered with gold thread and blue, purple, and scarlet yarn. [3]A skilled craftsman made gold thread by beating gold into thin sheets and cutting it into fine strips. He then embroidered it into the linen with the blue, purple, and scarlet yarn.

[4]They made two shoulder-pieces for the ephod, which were attached to its corners so it could be tied down. [5]They also made an elaborate woven sash of the same materials: fine linen cloth; blue, purple, and scarlet yarn; and gold thread, just as the LORD had commanded Moses. [6]The two onyx stones, attached to the shoulder-pieces of the ephod, were set in gold filigree. The stones were engraved with the names of the tribes of Israel, just as initials are engraved on a seal. [7]These stones served as reminders to the LORD concerning the people of Israel. All this was done just as the LORD had commanded Moses.

**39:2-7**
//Exod 28:6-14

## Making the Chestpiece

[8]The chestpiece was made in the same style as the ephod, crafted from fine linen cloth and embroidered with gold thread and blue, purple, and scarlet yarn. [9]It was doubled over to form a pouch, nine inches* square. [10]Four rows of gemstones* were set across it. In the first row were a red carnelian, a chrysolite, and an emerald. [11]In the second row were a turquoise, a sapphire, and a white moonstone. [12]In the third row were a jacinth, an agate, and an amethyst. [13]In the fourth row were a beryl, an onyx, and a jasper. Each of these gemstones was set in gold. [14]The stones were engraved like a seal, each with the name of one of the twelve tribes of Israel.

**39:8-21**
//Exod 28:15-28

**39:14**
Rev 21:12

[15]To attach the chestpiece to the ephod, they made braided cords of pure gold. [16]They also made two gold rings and attached them to the top corners of the chestpiece. [17]The two gold cords were put through the gold rings on the chestpiece, [18]and the ends of the cords were tied to the gold settings on the shoulder-pieces of the ephod. [19]Two more gold rings were attached to the lower inside corners of the chestpiece next to the ephod. [20]Then two gold rings were attached to the ephod near the sash. [21]Blue cords were used to attach the bottom rings of the chestpiece to the rings on the ephod. In this way, the chestpiece was held securely to the ephod above the beautiful sash. All this was done just as the LORD had commanded Moses.

## Additional Clothing for the Priests

[22]The robe of the ephod was woven entirely of blue yarn, [23]with an opening for Aaron's head in the middle of it. The edge of this opening was reinforced with a woven collar,* so it would not tear. [24]Pomegranates were attached to the bottom edge of the robe. These were finely crafted of blue, purple, and scarlet yarn. [25]Bells of pure gold were placed between the pomegranates along the hem of the robe, [26]with bells and pomegranates

**39:22-31**
//Exod 28:31-43

**39:9** Hebrew *1 span* [23 centimeters].   **39:10** The identification of some of these gemstones is uncertain.   **39:23** The meaning of the Hebrew is uncertain.

**39:1-21** The priests wore a uniform to the Tabernacle each day. Some of the pieces of their uniform were not only beautiful but also significant. Two parts of the high priest's uniform were the ephod and chestpiece. The ephod looked like a vest and was worn over the outer clothing. The chestpiece was fitted to the ephod (and sometimes was called the ephod). The chestpiece was made of colored linens about nine inches square. On its front were attached 12 gemstones, each inscribed with the name of a tribe of Israel. This symbolized how the high priest represented all the people before God. The chestpiece also contained pockets that held two stones or plates called the Urim and Thummim. The high priest could determine God's will for the nation by consulting the Urim and Thummim. (See the notes on 28:30 and Leviticus 8:8.)

alternating all around the hem. This robe was to be worn when Aaron ministered to the LORD, just as the LORD had commanded Moses.

**39:27**
Exod 28:39-40, 42

²⁷Tunics were then made for Aaron and his sons from fine linen cloth. ²⁸The turban, the headdresses, and the underclothes were all made of this fine linen. ²⁹The sashes were made of fine linen cloth and embroidered with blue, purple, and scarlet yarn, just as the LORD had commanded Moses. ³⁰Finally, they made the sacred medallion of pure gold to be worn on the front of the turban. Using the techniques of an engraver, they inscribed it with these words: SET APART AS HOLY TO THE LORD. ³¹This medallion was tied to the turban with a blue cord, just as the LORD had commanded Moses.

**39:30**
Exod 28:36-37

### Moses Inspects the Work

**39:32-41**
//Exod 35:10-19

³²And so at last the Tabernacle* was finished. The Israelites had done everything just as the LORD had commanded Moses. ³³And they brought the entire Tabernacle to Moses: the sacred tent with all its furnishings, the clasps, frames, crossbars, posts, and bases; ³⁴the layers of tanned ram skins and fine goatskin leather; the inner curtain that enclosed the Most Holy Place; ³⁵the Ark of the Covenant* and its carrying poles; the Ark's cover—the place of atonement; ³⁶the table and all its utensils; the Bread of the Presence; ³⁷the gold lampstand and its accessories; the lamp cups and the oil for lighting; ³⁸the gold altar; the anointing oil; the fragrant incense; the curtain for the entrance of the sacred tent; ³⁹the bronze altar; the bronze grating; its poles and utensils; the large washbasin and its pedestal; ⁴⁰the curtains for the walls of the courtyard and the posts and bases holding them up; the curtain at the courtyard entrance; the cords and tent pegs; all the articles used in the operation of the Tabernacle; ⁴¹the beautifully crafted garments to be worn while ministering in the Holy Place—the holy garments for Aaron the priest and for his sons to wear while on duty.

**39:43**
Lev 9:22-23
Num 6:23-26
1 Kgs 8:14
2 Chr 30:27

⁴²So the people of Israel followed all of the LORD's instructions to Moses. ⁴³Moses inspected all their work and blessed them because it had been done as the LORD had commanded him.

### The Tabernacle Completed

**40:2**
Exod 12:2; 19:1;
40:17
Num 1:1

**40** The LORD now said to Moses, ²"Set up the Tabernacle* on the first day of the new year.* ³Place the Ark of the Covenant* inside, and install the inner curtain to enclose the Ark within the Most Holy Place. ⁴Then bring in the table, and arrange the utensils on it. And bring in the lampstand, and set up the lamps.

**40:3**
Exod 26:33;
40:21-30
Num 4:5

⁵"Place the incense altar just outside the inner curtain, opposite the Ark of the Covenant. Set up the curtain made for the entrance of the Tabernacle. ⁶Place the altar of burnt offering in front of the Tabernacle entrance. ⁷Set the large washbasin between the Tabernacle* and the altar and fill it with water. ⁸Then set up the courtyard around the outside of the tent, and hang the curtain for the courtyard entrance.

**40:4**
Exod 25:30

**40:7**
Exod 30:18

**40:9**
Exod 30:26

⁹"Take the anointing oil and sprinkle it on the Tabernacle and on all its furnishings to make them holy. ¹⁰Sprinkle the anointing oil on the altar of burnt offering and its

**39:32** Hebrew *the Tabernacle, the Tent of Meeting;* also in 39:40.   **39:35** Or *Ark of the Testimony.*   **40:2a** Hebrew *the Tabernacle, the Tent of Meeting;* also in 40:6, 29.   **40:2b** Hebrew *the first day of the first month.* This day of the Hebrew lunar calendar occurs in March or early April.   **40:3** Or *Ark of the Testimony;* also in 40:5, 21.   **40:7** Hebrew *Tent of Meeting;* also in 40:12, 22, 24, 26, 30, 32, 34, 35.

**39:32** The Tabernacle was finally complete to the last detail. God was keenly interested in every minute part. The Creator of the universe was concerned about even the little things. Matthew 10:30 says that God knows the number of hairs on our heads. This shows that God is greatly interested in you. Don't be afraid to talk with him about any of your concerns—no matter how small or unimportant they might seem.

**39:42** Moses had learned his management lesson well. He gave important responsibilities to others and then trusted them to do the job. Great leaders, like Moses, give plans and direction while letting others participate on the team. If you are a leader, trust your assistants with key responsibilities.

**39:43** Moses inspected the finished work, saw that it was done the way God wanted, and then blessed the people. A good leader follows up on assigned tasks and gives rewards for good work. In whatever responsible position you find yourself, follow up to make sure that tasks are completed as intended, and show your appreciation to the people who have helped.

**40:1ff** Moses was careful to obey God's instructions in the smallest detail. Notice that he didn't make a reasonable facsimile of God's description, but an exact copy. We should follow Moses' example and be fastidious about our obedience. If God has told you to do something, do it, do it right, and do it completely.

# LEVITICUS

## VITAL STATISTICS

**PURPOSE:**
A handbook for the priests and Levites outlining their duties in worship, and a guidebook of holy living for the Hebrews

**AUTHOR:**
Moses

**DATE OF EVENTS:**
1445–1444 B.C.

**SETTING:**
At the foot of Mount Sinai. God is teaching the Israelites how to live as holy people.

**KEY VERSE:**
"You must be holy because I, the LORD your God, am holy" (19:2).

**KEY PEOPLE:**
Moses, Aaron, Nadab, Abihu, Eleazar, Ithamar

**KEY PLACE:**
Mount Sinai

**SPECIAL FEATURE:**
Holiness is mentioned more times (152) than in any other book of the Bible.

"GOD seems so far away . . . if only I could see or hear him." Have you ever felt this way—struggling with sin, loneliness, burdened by despair, riddled with sin, overwhelmed by problems? Made in God's image, we were created to have a close relationship with him; and when fellowship is broken, we are incomplete and need restoration. Communion with the living God is the essence of worship. It is vital, touching the very core of our lives. Perhaps this is why a whole book of the Bible is dedicated to worship. After Israel's dramatic exit from Egypt, the nation was camped at the foot of Mount Sinai for two years to listen to God (Exodus 19 to Numbers 10). It was a time of resting, teaching, building, and meeting with him face to face. Redemption in Exodus is the foundation for cleansing, worship, and service in Leviticus.

The overwhelming message of Leviticus is the holiness of God—"You must be holy because I, the LORD your God, am holy" (19:2). But how can unholy people approach a holy God? The answer—first sin must be dealt with. Thus the opening chapters of Leviticus give detailed instructions for offering sacrifices, which were the active symbols of repentance and obedience. Whether bulls, grain, goats, or sheep, the sacrificial offerings had to be perfect, with no defects or bruises—pictures of the ultimate sacrifice to come, Jesus, the Lamb of God. Jesus has come and opened the way to God by giving up his life as the final sacrifice in our place. True worship and oneness with God begin as we confess our sin and accept Christ as the only one who can redeem us from sin and help us approach God.

In Leviticus, sacrifices, priests, and the sacred Day of Atonement opened the way for the Israelites to come to God. God's people were also to worship him with their lives. Thus we read of purity laws (chapters 11—15) and rules for daily living concerning family responsibilities, sexual conduct, relationships, worldliness (chapters 18—20), and vows (chapter 27). These instructions involve one's holy walk with God, and the patterns of spiritual living still apply today. Worship, therefore, has a horizontal aspect—that is, God is honored by our lives as we relate to others.

The final emphasis in Leviticus is celebration. The book gives instructions for the feasts. These were special, regular, and corporate occasions for remembering what God had done, giving thanks to him, and rededicating lives to his service (chapter 23). Our Christian traditions and holidays are different, but they are necessary ingredients of worship. We, too, need special days of worship and celebration with our brothers and sisters to remember God's goodness in our lives.

As you read Leviticus, rededicate yourself to holiness, worshiping God in private confession, public service, and group celebration.

## THE BLUEPRINT

A. WORSHIPING A HOLY GOD
   (1:1—17:16)
   1. Instructions for the offerings
   2. Instructions for the priests
   3. Instructions for the people
   4. Instructions for the altar

God provided specific directions for the kind of worship that would be pleasing to him. These instructions teach us about the nature of God and can help us develop a right attitude toward worship. Through the offerings we learn of the seriousness of sin and the importance of bringing our sins to God for forgiveness.

B. LIVING A HOLY LIFE (18:1—27:34)
   1. Standards for the people
   2. Rules for priests
   3. Seasons and festivals
   4. Receiving God's blessing

God gave clear standards to the Israelites for living a holy life. They were to be separate and distinct from the pagan nations around them. In the same way, all believers should be separated from sin and dedicated to God. God still wants to remove sin from the lives of his people.

## MEGATHEMES

| THEME | EXPLANATION | IMPORTANCE |
| --- | --- | --- |
| *Sacrifice/Offering* | There are five kinds of offerings that fulfill two main purposes: one to show praise, thankfulness, and devotion; the other for atonement, the covering and removal of guilt and sin. Animal offerings demonstrated that the person was giving his or her life to God by means of the life of the animal | The sacrifices (offerings) were for worship and forgiveness of sin. Through them we learn about the cost of sin, for we see that we cannot forgive ourselves. God's system says that a life must be given for a life. In the Old Testament, an animal's life was given to save the life of a person. But this was only a temporary measure until Jesus' death paid the penalty of sin for all people forever. |
| *Worship* | Seven festivals were designated as religious and national holidays. They were often celebrated in family settings. These events teach us much about worshiping God in both celebration and quiet dedication. | God's rules about worship set up an orderly, regular pattern of fellowship with him. They allowed times for celebration and thanksgiving as well as for reverence and rededication. Our worship should demonstrate our deep devotion. |
| *Health* | Civil rules for handling food, disease, and sex were taught. In these physical principles, many spiritual principles were suggested. Israel was to be different from the surrounding nations. God was preserving Israel from disease and community health problems. | We are to be different morally and spiritually from the unbelievers around us. Principles for healthy living are as important today as in Moses' time. A healthy environment and a healthy body make our service to God more effective. |
| *Holiness* | *Holy* means "separated" or "devoted." God removed his people from Egypt; now he was removing Egypt from the people. He was showing them how to exchange Egyptian ways of living and thinking for his ways. | We must devote every area of life to God. God desires absolute obedience in motives as well as practices. Though we do not observe all the worship practices of Israel, we are to have the same spirit of preparation and devotion. |
| *Levites* | The Levites and priests instructed the people in their worship. They were the ministers of their day. They also regulated the moral, civil, and ceremonial laws and supervised the health, justice, and welfare of the nation. | The Levites were servants who showed Israel the way to God. They provide the historical backdrop for Christ, who is our High Priest and yet our Servant. God's true servants care for all the needs of their people. |

## A. WORSHIPING A HOLY GOD (1:1—17:16)

The Israelites have arrived safely at the foot of Mount Sinai, and the Tabernacle has been completed. The people will spend a great deal of time here as God shows them a new way of life with clear instructions on how sinful people can relate to a holy God. These instructions help us avoid taking our relationship with the same holy God too lightly. We learn about the holiness and majesty of the God with whom we are allowed to have a personal relationship.

### 1. Instructions for the offerings

*Procedures for the Burnt Offering*

1 The LORD called to Moses from the Tabernacle* and said to him, ²"Give the following instructions to the Israelites: Whenever you present offerings to the LORD, you must bring animals from your flocks and herds.

³"If your sacrifice for a whole burnt offering is from the herd, bring a bull with no

1:1 Hebrew *Tent of Meeting;* also in 1:3, 5.

**1:1**
Exod 25:22
Num 7:89

**1:2**
Lev 6:9-13; 17:1-8

**1:3**
Heb 9:14

---

**THE ISRAELITES AT MOUNT SINAI**
Throughout the book of Leviticus, the Israelites were camped at the foot of Mount Sinai. It was time to regroup as a nation and learn the importance of following God as they prepared to march toward the Promised Land.

**1:1** The book of Leviticus begins where the book of Exodus ends—at the foot of Mount Sinai. The Tabernacle was just completed (Exodus 35—40), and God was ready to teach the people how to worship there.

**1:1** The "Tabernacle" where God met with Moses was actually the Tent of Meeting, a smaller structure inside the larger Tabernacle. The Tent of Meeting contained the sanctuary in one part and the Most Holy Place with the Ark in another part. These two sections were separated by a curtain. God revealed himself to Moses in the Most Holy Place. Exodus 33:7 mentions a "Tent of Meeting" where Moses met God before the Tabernacle was constructed. Many believe it served the same function as the one described here.

**1:1ff** We may be tempted to dismiss Leviticus as a record of bizarre rituals of a different age. But its practices made sense to the people of the day and offer important insights for us into God's nature and character. Animal sacrifice seems obsolete and repulsive to many people today, but animal sacrifices were practiced in many cultures in the Middle East. God used the form of sacrifice to teach his people about faith. Sin needed to be taken seriously. When people saw the sacrificial animals being killed, they were sensitized to the importance of their sin and guilt. Our culture's casual attitude toward sin ignores the cost of sin and need for repentance and restoration. Although many of the rituals of Leviticus were designed for the culture of the day, their purpose was to reveal a high and holy God who should be loved, obeyed, and worshiped. God's laws and sacrifices were intended to bring out true devotion of the heart. The ceremonies and rituals were the best way for the Israelites to focus their lives on God.

**1:2** Was there any difference between a sacrifice and an offering? In Leviticus the words are interchanged. Usually a specific sacrifice is called an offering (burnt offering, grain offering, peace offering). Offerings in general are called sacrifices. The point is that each person *offered* a gift to God by *sacrificing* it on the altar. In the Old Testament, the sacrifice was the only way to approach God and restore a relationship with him. There was more than one kind of offering or sacrifice. The variety of sacrifices made them more meaningful because each one related to a specific life situation. Sacrifices were given in praise, worship, and thanksgiving, as well as for forgiveness and fellowship. The first seven chapters of Leviticus describe the variety of offerings and how they were to be used.

**1:2** When God taught his people to worship him, he placed great emphasis on sacrifices. Why? Sacrifices were God's Old Testament way for people to ask for forgiveness for their sins. Since Creation, God has made it clear that sin separates people from him, and that those who sin deserve to die. Because "all have sinned" (Romans 3:23), God designed sacrifice as a way to seek forgiveness and restore a relationship with him. Because he is a God of love and mercy, God decided from the very first that he would come into our world and die to pay the penalty for all humans. This he did in his Son, who, while still God, became a human being. In the meantime, before God gave this ultimate sacrifice of his Son, he instructed people to kill animals as sacrifices for sin.

Animal sacrifice accomplished two purposes: (1) The animal symbolically took the sinner's place and paid the penalty for sin, and (2) the animal's death represented one life given so that another life could be saved. This method of sacrifice continued throughout Old Testament times. It was effective in teaching and guiding the people and bringing them back to God. But in New Testament times, Christ's death became the last sacrifice needed. He took our punishment once and for all. Animal sacrifice is no longer required. Now all people can be freed from the penalty of sin by simply believing in Jesus and accepting the forgiveness he offers.

**1:3, 4** The first offering God describes is the burnt offering. A person who had sinned brought an animal with no defects to a priest. The unblemished animal symbolized the moral perfection demanded by a holy God and the perfect nature of the real sacrifice to come—Jesus Christ. The person then laid his hand on the head of the animal to symbolize the person's complete identification with the animal as his substitute. Then he killed the animal, and the priest sprinkled the blood. He symbolically transferred his sins to the animal, and thus his sins were taken away (atonement). Finally the animal (except for the blood and skin) was burned on the altar, signifying the person's complete dedication to God. God required more than a sacrifice, of course. He also asked the sinner to have an attitude of repentance. The outward symbol (the sacrifice) and the inner change (repentance) were to work together. But it is important to remember that neither sacrifice nor repentance actually caused the sin to be taken away. God alone forgives sin. Fortunately for us, forgiveness is part of God's loving nature. Have you come to him to receive forgiveness?

**1:4**
Exod 29:10, 15, 19
Lev 4:13-35
Num 8:10-12; 15:25
2 Chr 29:23-24

**1:5**
Lev 1:11; 3:8
Heb 12:24

**1:6**
Lev 7:8

**1:8**
Exod 29:13

**1:9**
Gen 8:21
Exod 29:17
Eph 5:2

**1:14**
Gen 15:9
Lev 12:8

**1:15**
Lev 5:9

physical defects to the entrance of the Tabernacle so it will be accepted by the LORD. ⁴Lay your hand on its head so the LORD will accept it as your substitute, thus making atonement for you. ⁵Then slaughter the animal in the LORD's presence, and Aaron's sons, the priests, will present the blood by sprinkling it against the sides of the altar that stands in front of the Tabernacle. ⁶When the animal has been skinned and cut into pieces, ⁷the sons of Aaron the priest will build a wood fire on the altar. ⁸Aaron's sons will then put the pieces of the animal, including its head and fat, on the wood fire. ⁹But the internal organs and legs must first be washed with water. Then the priests will burn the entire sacrifice on the altar. It is a whole burnt offering made by fire, very pleasing to the LORD.

¹⁰"If your sacrifice for a whole burnt offering is from the flock, bring a male sheep or goat with no physical defects. ¹¹Slaughter the animal on the north side of the altar in the LORD's presence. Aaron's sons, the priests, will sprinkle its blood against the sides of the altar. ¹²Then you must cut the animal in pieces, and the priests will lay the pieces of the sacrifice, including the head and fat, on top of the wood fire on the altar. ¹³The internal organs and legs must first be washed with water. Then the priests will burn the entire sacrifice on the altar. It is a whole burnt offering made by fire, very pleasing to the LORD.

¹⁴"If you bring a bird as a burnt offering to the LORD, choose either a turtledove or a young pigeon. ¹⁵The priest will take the bird to the altar, twist off its head, and burn the head on the altar. He must then let its blood drain out against the sides of the altar. ¹⁶The priest must remove the crop and the feathers* and throw them to the east side of the altar among the ashes. ¹⁷Then, grasping the bird by its wings, the priest will tear the bird apart, though not completely. Then he will burn it on top of the wood fire on the altar. It is a whole burnt offering made by fire, very pleasing to the LORD.

**1:16** Or *the crop and its contents.* The meaning of the Hebrew is uncertain.

---

**THE OFFERINGS**
Listed here are the five key offerings the Israelites made to God. They made these offerings in order to have their sins forgiven and to restore their fellowship with God. The death of Jesus Christ made these sacrifices unnecessary. Because of his death, our sins were completely forgiven, and fellowship with God has been restored.

| Offering | Purpose | Significance | Christ, the Perfect Offering |
|---|---|---|---|
| Burnt Offering (Lev. 1—voluntary) | To make payment for sins in general | Showed a person's devotion to God | Christ's death was the perfect offering |
| Grain Offering (Lev. 2—voluntary) | To show honor and respect to God in worship | Acknowledged that all we have belongs to God | Christ was the perfect man, who gave all of himself to God and others |
| Peace Offering (Lev. 3—voluntary) | To express gratitude to God | Symbolized peace and fellowship with God | Christ is the only way to fellowship with God |
| Sin Offering (Lev. 4—required) | To make payment for unintentional sins of uncleanness, neglect, or thoughtlessness | Restored the sinner to fellowship with God; showed seriousness of sin | Christ's death restores our fellowship with God |
| Guilt Offering (Lev. 5—required) | To make payment for sins against God and others. A sacrifice was made to God, and the injured person was repaid or compensated | Provided compensation for injured parties | Christ's death takes away the deadly consequences of sin |

---

**1:3ff** What did sacrifices teach the people? (1) By requiring perfect animals and holy priests, they taught reverence for a holy God. (2) By demanding exact obedience, they taught total submission to God's laws. (3) By requiring an animal of great value, they showed the high cost of sin and demonstrated the sincerity of their commitment to God.

**1:3-13** Why are there such detailed regulations for each offering? God had a purpose in giving these commands. Starting from scratch, he was teaching his people a whole new way of life, cleansing them from the many pagan practices they had learned in Egypt and restoring true worship of himself. The strict details kept Israel from slipping back into their old life-

style. In addition, each law paints a graphic picture of the seriousness of sin and of God's great mercy in forgiving sinners.

**1:4ff** Israel was not the only nation to sacrifice animals. Many other religions did it as well to try to please their gods. Some cultures even included human sacrifice, which was strictly forbidden by God. However, the meaning of Israel's animal sacrifices was clearly different from that of their pagan neighbors' sacrifices. Israelites sacrificed animals, not just to appease God's wrath, but as a substitute for the punishment they deserved for their sins. A sacrifice showed faith in God and commitment to his laws. Most important, this system foreshadowed the day when the Lamb of God (Jesus Christ) would die and conquer sin once and for all.

before the LORD in front of the inner curtain. [18] He will then put some of the blood on the horns of the incense altar that stands in the LORD's presence in the Tabernacle. The rest of the blood must then be poured out at the base of the altar of burnt offerings at the entrance of the Tabernacle. [19] The priest must remove all the animal's fat and burn it on the altar, [20] following the same procedure as with the sin offering for the priest. In this way, the priest will make atonement for the people, and they will be forgiven. [21] The priest must then take what is left of the bull outside the camp and burn it there, just as is done with the sin offering for the high priest. This is a sin offering for the entire community of Israel.

[22] "If one of Israel's leaders does something forbidden by the LORD his God, he will be guilty even if he sinned unintentionally. [23] When he becomes aware of his sin, he must bring as his offering a male goat with no physical defects. [24] He is to lay his hand on the goat's head and slaughter it before the LORD at the place where burnt offerings are slaughtered. This will be his sin offering. [25] Then the priest will dip his finger into the blood of the sin offering, put it on the horns of the altar of burnt offerings, and pour out the rest of the blood at the base of the altar. [26] He must burn all the goat's fat on the altar, just as is done with the peace offering. In this way, the priest will make atonement for the leader's sin, and he will be forgiven.

[27] "If any of the citizens of Israel* do something forbidden by the LORD, they will be guilty even if they sinned unintentionally. [28] When they become aware of their sin, they must bring as their offering a female goat with no physical defects. It will be offered for their sin. [29] They are to lay a hand on the head of the sin offering and slaughter it at the place where burnt offerings are slaughtered. [30] The priest will then dip his finger into the blood, put the blood on the horns of the altar of burnt offerings, and pour out the rest of the blood at the base of the altar. [31] Those who are guilty must remove all the goat's fat, just as is done with the peace offering. Then the priest will burn the fat on the altar, and it will be very pleasing to the LORD. In this way, the priest will make atonement for them, and they will be forgiven.

[32] "If any of the people bring a sheep as their sin offering, it must be a female with no physical defects. [33] They are to lay a hand on the head of the sin offering and slaughter it at the place where the burnt offerings are slaughtered. [34] The priest will then dip his finger into the blood, put it on the horns of the altar of burnt offerings, and pour out the rest of the blood at the base of the altar. [35] Those who are guilty must remove all the sheep's fat, just as is done with a sheep presented as a peace offering. Then the priest will burn the fat on the altar on top of the offerings given to the LORD by fire. In this way, the priest will make atonement for them, and they will be forgiven.

*Sins Requiring a Sin Offering*

**5** "If any of the people are called to testify about something they have witnessed, but they refuse to testify, they will be held responsible and be subject to punishment.

[2] "Or if they touch something that is ceremonially unclean, such as the dead body of an animal that is ceremonially unclean—whether a wild animal, a domesticated animal, or an animal that scurries along the ground—they will be considered ceremonially unclean and guilty, even if they are unaware of their defilement.

[3] "Or if they come into contact with any source of human defilement, even if they don't

**4:27** Hebrew *people of the land.*

---

**5:4** Have you ever sworn to do or not do something and then realized how foolish your promise was? God's people are called to keep their word, even if they make promises that are tough to keep. Jesus was warning against swearing (in the sense of making vows or oaths) when he said, "Just say a simple, 'Yes, I will,' or 'No, I won't.' Your word is enough. To strengthen your promise with a vow shows that something is wrong" (Matthew 5:37). Our word should be enough. If we feel we have to strengthen it with an oath, something is wrong with our sincerity. The only promises we ought not to keep are promises that lead to sin. A wise and self-controlled person avoids making rash promises.

**5:5** The entire system of sacrifices could not help a sinner unless he brought his offering with an attitude of repentance and a willingness to confess sin. Today, because of Christ's death on the cross, we do not have to sacrifice animals. But it is still vital to confess sin, because confession shows realization of sin, awareness of God's holiness, humility before God, and willingness to turn from this sin (Psalm 51:16, 17). Even Jesus' death will be of little value to us if we do not repent and follow him. It is like a vaccine for a dangerous disease—it won't help unless it enters the bloodstream.

realize they have been defiled, they will be considered guilty as soon as they become aware of it.

4"Or if they make a rash vow of any kind, whether its purpose is for good or bad, they will be considered guilty even if they were not fully aware of what they were doing at the time.

5"When any of the people become aware of their guilt in any of these ways, they must confess their sin 6and bring to the LORD as their penalty a female from the flock, either a sheep or a goat. This will be a sin offering to remove their sin, and the priest will make atonement for them.

7"If any of them cannot afford to bring a sheep, they must bring to the LORD two young turtledoves or two young pigeons as the penalty for their sin. One of the birds will be a sin offering, and the other will be a burnt offering. 8They must bring them to the priest, who will offer one of the birds as the sin offering. The priest will wring its neck but without severing its head from the body. 9Then he will sprinkle some of the blood of the sin offering against the sides of the altar, and the rest will be drained out at the base of the altar. 10The priest will offer the second bird as a whole burnt offering, following all the procedures that have been prescribed. In this way, the priest will make atonement for those who are guilty, and they will be forgiven.

11"If any of the people cannot afford to bring young turtledoves or pigeons, they must bring two quarts* of choice flour for their sin offering. Since it is a sin offering, they must not mix it with olive oil or put any incense on it. 12They must take the flour to the priest, who will scoop out a handful as a token portion. He will burn this flour on the altar just like any other offering given to the LORD by fire. This will be their sin offering. 13In this way, the priest will make atonement for those who are guilty, and they will be forgiven. The rest of the flour will belong to the priest, just as with the grain offering."

### Procedures for the Guilt Offering

14Then the LORD said to Moses, 15"If any of the people sin by unintentionally defiling the LORD's sacred property, they must bring to the LORD a ram from the flock as their guilt offering. The animal must have no physical defects, and it must be of the proper value in silver as measured by the standard sanctuary shekel.* 16They must then make restitution for whatever holy things they have defiled by paying for the loss, plus an added penalty of 20 percent. When they give their payments to the priest, he will make atonement for them with the ram sacrificed as a guilt offering, and they will be forgiven.

17"If any of them sin by doing something forbidden by the LORD, even if it is done unintentionally, they will be held responsible. When they become aware of their guilt, 18they must bring to the priest a ram from the flock as a guilt offering. The animal must have no physical defects, and it must be of the proper value. In this way, the priest will make atonement for those who are guilty, and they will be forgiven. 19This is a guilt offering, for they have been guilty of an offense against the LORD."

### Sins Requiring a Guilt Offering

**6** And the LORD said to Moses, 2"Suppose some of the people sin against the LORD by falsely telling their neighbor that an item entrusted to their safekeeping has been lost or stolen. Or suppose they have been dishonest with regard to a security deposit, or they have taken something by theft or extortion. 3Or suppose they find a lost item and lie about it, or they deny something while under oath, or they commit any other similar sin. 4If they have sinned in any of these ways and are guilty, they must give back whatever they have taken by theft or extortion, whether a security deposit, or property

5:11 Hebrew *1/10 of an ephah* [2 liters]. 5:15 Each sanctuary shekel was about 0.4 ounces or 11 grams in weight.

**Cross references (left margin):**

5:4 Num 30:6-8

5:5 Lev 16:21; Num 5:7; Josh 7:19

5:6 Lev 4:28, 32

5:7 Lev 12:8; Luke 2:24

5:8 Lev 1:15, 17

5:9 Lev 4:7; 7:2

5:10 Lev 1:14-17

5:11 Lev 14:21; †Luke 2:24

5:15 Exod 30:13; Lev 6:6; 7:1-10; 22:14

5:16 Lev 6:5; 22:14

5:17 Lev 5:15

6:2 Exod 22:7-15; Num 5:6; Col 3:9

6:3 Deut 22:1-3

**5:14-19** The guilt offering was a way of taking care of sin committed unintentionally. It was for those who sinned in some way against "sacred property"—the Tabernacle or the priesthood—as well as for those who unintentionally sinned against someone. In either case, a ram with no defects had to be sacrificed, plus those harmed by the sin had to be compensated for their loss, plus a 20 percent penalty. Even though Christ's death has made guilt offerings unnecessary for us today, we still need to make things right with those we hurt.

**6:1-7** Here we discover that stealing involves more than just taking from someone. Finding something and not returning it or refusing to return something borrowed are other forms of stealing. These are sins against God and not just your neighbor, a stranger, or a large business. If you have gotten something deceitfully, then confess your sin to God, apologize to the owner, and return the stolen items—with interest.

by a wild animal may never be eaten, though it may be used for any other purpose. 25Anyone who eats fat from an offering given to the LORD by fire must be cut off from the community. 26Even in your homes, you must never eat the blood of any bird or animal. 27Anyone who eats blood must be cut off from the community."

*A Portion for the Priests*

28Then the LORD said to Moses, 29"Give these further instructions to the Israelites: When you present a peace offering to the LORD, bring part of it as a special gift to the LORD. 30Present it to him with your own hands as an offering given to the LORD by fire. Bring the fat of the animal, together with the breast, and present it to the LORD by lifting it up before him. 31Then the priest will burn the fat on the altar, but the breast will belong to Aaron and his sons. 32You are to give the right thigh of your peace offering to the priest as a gift. 33The right thigh must always be given to the priest who sprinkles the blood and offers the fat of the peace offering. 34For I have designated the breast and the right thigh for the priests. It is their regular share of the peace offerings brought by the Israelites. 35This is their share. It has been set apart for Aaron and his descendants from the offerings given to the LORD by fire from the time they were appointed to serve the LORD as priests. 36The LORD commanded that the Israelites were to give these portions to the priests as their regular share from the time of the priests' anointing. This regulation applies throughout the generations to come."

37These are the instructions for the whole burnt offering, the grain offering, the sin offering, the guilt offering, the ordination offering, and the peace offering. 38The LORD gave these instructions to Moses on Mount Sinai when he commanded the Israelites to bring their offerings to the LORD in the wilderness of Sinai.

## 2. Instructions for the priests

*Ordination of the Priests*

**8** The LORD said to Moses, 2"Now bring Aaron and his sons, along with their special clothing, the anointing oil, the bull for the sin offering, the two rams, and the basket of unleavened bread 3to the entrance of the Tabernacle.* Then call the entire community of Israel to meet you there."

4So Moses followed the LORD's instructions, and all the people assembled at the Tabernacle entrance. 5Moses announced to them, "The LORD has commanded what I am

8:3 Hebrew *Tent of Meeting;* also in 8:4, 31, 33, 35.

**7:26**
Gen 9:4
Lev 17:10-14
Acts 15:20, 29

**7:29**
Lev 3:1

**7:30**
Exod 29:26-27
Lev 8:29
Num 6:20

**7:31**
Lev 7:34
Num 18:11

**7:32**
Num 18:18

**7:34**
Exod 29:22
Lev 10:15

**7:36**
Exod 29:22-34;
40:13-15

**7:38**
Lev 26:46

**8:2**
Exod 28:1

---

**7:28-30** God told the people of Israel to bring their peace offerings personally, with their own hands. They were to take time and effort to express thanks to God. You are the only person who can express your thankfulness to God and to others. Do you leave it to others to express thanks for what people have done? Do you rely on the one leading the prayer to thank God for you? Take time yourself to express thanks both to God and to others who have helped and blessed you.

**7:31-36** Part of the offering was designated for the priests. This food helped to care for the priests, who cared for God's house. The New Testament teaches that ministers should be paid by the people they serve (1 Corinthians 9:14). We should give generously to those who minister to us.

**7:37** The ordination offering refers to the offering given at the ceremony when priests were inducted into office (8:22).

**7:38** God gave his people many rituals and instructions to follow. All the rituals in Leviticus were meant to teach the people valuable lessons. But over time, the people became indifferent to the meanings of these rituals, and they began to lose touch with God. When your church appears to be conducting dry, meaningless rituals, try rediscovering the original meaning and purpose behind each. Your worship will be revitalized.

**8:1ff** Why did Aaron and his sons need to be cleansed and set apart? Although all the men from the tribe of Levi were dedicated for service to God, only Aaron's descendants could be priests. They alone had the honor and responsibility of performing the

sacrifices. These priests had to cleanse and dedicate themselves before they could help the people do the same.

The ceremony described in Leviticus 8 and 9 was their ordination ceremony. Aaron and his sons were washed with water (8:6), clothed with special garments (8:7-9, 13), and anointed with oil (8:12). They placed their hands on a young bull as it was killed (8:14, 15), and on two rams as they were killed (8:18, 19, 22, 23). This showed that holiness came from God alone, not from the priestly role. Similarly, we are not spiritually cleansed because we have a religious position. Spiritual cleansing comes only from God. No matter how high our position or how long we have held it, we must depend on God for spiritual vitality.

**8:2, 3** Why were priests needed in Israel? In Exodus 19:6, the Israelites were instructed to be a kingdom of priests; ideally they would all be holy and relate to God. But from the time of Adam's fall, sin has separated man and God, and people have needed mediators to help them find forgiveness. At first, the patriarchs—heads of households like Abraham and Job—were priests of the house or clan and made sacrifices for the family. When the Israelites left Egypt, the descendants of Aaron were chosen to serve as priests for the nation. The priests stood in the gap between God and man. They were the full-time spiritual leaders and over-seers of offerings. The priestly system was a concession to people's inability, because of sin, to confront and relate to God individually and corporately. In Christ, this imperfect system was transformed. Jesus Christ himself is our High Priest. Now all believers can approach God through him.

**8:6**
Exod 29:3-4

**8:8**
Exod 28:30-31
Ezra 2:63

**8:9**
Exod 28:4, 36-38

**8:10**
Exod 30:26-33

**8:11**
Exod 29:37
Lev 16:14

**8:12**
Exod 28:41; 30:30
Lev 21:10-12

**8:13**
Exod 28:4, 39

**8:14**
Exod 29:10-14
Lev 4:4

**8:15**
Lev 4:7

**8:17**
Lev 4:11

**8:18**
Exod 29:15-19

**8:22**
Exod 29:31

**8:23**
Exod 29:20-21

**8:25**
Exod 29:22

**8:26**
Exod 29:23

**8:27**
Exod 29:24

**8:28**
Exod 29:25

**8:29**
Exod 29:26
Lev 7:31-34

**8:30**
Exod 29:21

now going to do!" 6 Then he presented Aaron and his sons and washed them with water. 7 He clothed Aaron with the embroidered tunic and tied the sash around his waist. He dressed him in the robe of the ephod, along with the ephod itself, and attached the ephod with its decorative sash. 8 Then Moses placed the chestpiece on Aaron and put the Urim and the Thummim inside it. 9 He placed on Aaron's head the turban with the gold medallion at its front, just as the LORD had commanded him.

10 Then Moses took the anointing oil and anointed the Tabernacle and everything in it, thus making them holy. 11 He sprinkled the altar seven times, anointing it and all its utensils and the washbasin and its pedestal, making them holy. 12 Then he poured some of the anointing oil on Aaron's head, thus anointing him and making him holy for his work. 13 Next Moses presented Aaron's sons and clothed them in their embroidered tunics, their sashes, and their turbans, just as the LORD had commanded him.

14 Then Moses brought in the bull for the sin offering, and Aaron and his sons laid their hands on its head 15 as Moses slaughtered it. Moses took some of the blood, and with his finger he put it on the four horns of the altar to purify it. He poured out the rest of the blood at the base of the altar. In this way, he set the altar apart as holy and made atonement for it.* 16 He took all the fat around the internal organs, the lobe of the liver, and the two kidneys and their fat, and he burned them all on the altar. 17 The rest of the bull, including its hide, meat, and dung, was burned outside the camp, just as the LORD had commanded Moses.

18 Then Moses presented the ram to the LORD for the whole burnt offering, and Aaron and his sons laid their hands on its head 19 as Moses slaughtered it. Then Moses took the ram's blood and sprinkled it against the sides of the altar. 20 Next he cut the ram into pieces and burned the head, some of its pieces, and the fat on the altar. 21 After washing the internal organs and the legs with water, Moses burned the entire ram on the altar as a whole burnt offering. It was an offering given to the LORD by fire, very pleasing to the LORD. All this was done just as the LORD had commanded Moses.

22 Next Moses presented the second ram, which was the ram of ordination. Aaron and his sons laid their hands on its head 23 as Moses slaughtered it. Then Moses took some of its blood and put it on the lobe of Aaron's right ear, the thumb of his right hand, and the big toe of his right foot. 24 Next he presented Aaron's sons and put some of the blood on the lobe of their right ears, the thumb of their right hands, and the big toe of their right feet. He then sprinkled the rest of the blood against the sides of the altar.

25 Next he took the fat, including the fat from the tail, the fat around the internal organs, the lobe of the liver, and the two kidneys with their fat, along with the right thigh. 26 On top of these he placed a loaf of unleavened bread, a cake of unleavened bread soaked with olive oil, and a thin wafer spread with olive oil. All these were taken from the basket of bread made without yeast that was placed in the LORD's presence. 27 He gave all of these to Aaron and his sons, and he presented the portions by lifting them up before the LORD. 28 Moses then took all the offerings back and burned them on the altar on top of the burnt offering as an ordination offering. It was an offering given to the LORD by fire, very pleasing to the LORD. 29 Then Moses took the breast and lifted it up in the LORD's presence. This was Moses' share of the ram of ordination, just as the LORD had commanded him.

30 Next Moses took some of the anointing oil and some of the blood that was on the altar, and he sprinkled them on Aaron and his clothing and on his sons and their clothing. In this way, he made Aaron and his sons and their clothing holy.

**8:15** Or *that atonement may be made on it.*

---

**8:8** What were the Urim and Thummim? Little is known about them, but they were probably precious stones or flat objects that God used to give guidance to his people. The high priest kept them in a pocket attached to his chestpiece. Some scholars think the Urim may have been the *no* answer and the Thummim the *yes* answer. After a time of prayer for guidance, the priest would shake the stones and God would cause the proper one to fall out. Another view is that the Urim and Thummim were small flat objects, each with a *yes* side and a *no* side. The priest spilled both from his pouch. If both landed on their *yes* sides, God's answer was positive. Two *no* sides were negative. A *yes* and a *no* meant no

reply. God had a specific purpose for using this method of guidance—he was teaching a nation the principles of following him. Our situation is not the same, however, so we must not invent ways like this for God to guide us.

**8:12** What was the significance of anointing Aaron as high priest? The high priest had special duties that no other priest had. He alone could enter the Most Holy Place in the Tabernacle on the yearly Day of Atonement to atone for the sins of the nation. Therefore, he was in charge of all the other priests. The high priest was a picture of Jesus Christ, who is our High Priest (Hebrews 7:26-28).

<sup>31</sup>Then Moses said to Aaron and his sons, "Boil the rest of the meat at the Tabernacle entrance, and eat it along with the bread that is in the basket of ordination offerings, just as I commanded you. <sup>32</sup>Any meat or bread that is left over must then be burned up. <sup>33</sup>Do not leave the Tabernacle entrance for seven days, for that is the time it will take to complete the ordination ceremony. <sup>34</sup>What has been done today was commanded by the LORD in order to make atonement for you. <sup>35</sup>Remember, you must stay at the entrance of the Tabernacle day and night for seven days, doing everything the LORD requires. If you fail in this, you will die. This is what the LORD has said." <sup>36</sup>So Aaron and his sons did everything the LORD had commanded through Moses.

### The Priests Begin Their Work

**9** After the ordination ceremony, on the eighth day, Moses called together Aaron and his sons and the leaders of Israel. <sup>2</sup>He said to Aaron, "Take a young bull for a sin offering and a ram for a whole burnt offering, both with no physical defects, and present them to the LORD. <sup>3</sup>Then tell the Israelites to take a male goat for a sin offering for themselves and a year-old calf and a year-old lamb for a whole burnt offering, each with no physical defects. <sup>4</sup>Also tell them to take a bull* and a ram for a peace offering and flour mixed with olive oil for a grain offering. Tell them to present all these offerings to the LORD because the LORD will appear to them today."

<sup>5</sup>So the people brought all of these things to the entrance of the Tabernacle,* just as Moses had commanded, and the whole community came and stood there in the LORD's presence. <sup>6</sup>Then Moses told them, "When you have followed these instructions from the LORD, the glorious presence of the LORD will appear to you."

<sup>7</sup>Then Moses said to Aaron, "Approach the altar and present your sin offering and your whole burnt offering to make atonement for yourself. Then present the offerings to make atonement for the people, just as the LORD has commanded."

<sup>8</sup>So Aaron went to the altar and slaughtered the calf as a sin offering for himself. <sup>9</sup>His sons brought him the blood, and he dipped his finger into it and put it on the horns of the altar. He poured out the rest of the blood at the base of the altar. <sup>10</sup>Then he burned on the altar the fat, the kidneys, and the lobe of the liver from the sin offering, just as the LORD had commanded Moses. <sup>11</sup>The meat and the hide, however, he burned outside the camp.

<sup>12</sup>Next Aaron slaughtered the animal for the whole burnt offering. His sons brought him the blood, and he sprinkled it against the sides of the altar. <sup>13</sup>They handed the animal to him piece by piece, including the head, and he burned each part on the altar. <sup>14</sup>Then he washed the internal organs and the legs and also burned them on the altar as a whole burnt offering.

<sup>15</sup>Next Aaron presented the sacrifices for the people. He slaughtered the people's goat and presented it as their sin offering, just as he had done previously for himself. <sup>16</sup>Then he brought the whole burnt offering and presented it in the prescribed way. <sup>17</sup>He also brought the grain offering, burning a handful of the flour on the altar, in addition to the regular morning burnt offering.

<sup>18</sup>Then Aaron slaughtered the bull and the ram for the people's peace offering. His sons brought him the blood, and he sprinkled it against the sides of the altar. <sup>19</sup>Then he took the fat of the bull and the ram—the fat from the tail and from around the internal organs—along with the kidneys and the lobe of the liver. <sup>20</sup>He placed these fat parts on top of the breasts of these animals and then burned them on the altar. <sup>21</sup>Aaron then lifted up the breasts and right thighs as an offering to the LORD, just as Moses had commanded.

<sup>22</sup>After that, Aaron raised his hands toward the people and blessed them. Then, after

**9:4** Or *cow;* also in 9:18, 19.    **9:5** Hebrew *Tent of Meeting;* also in 9:23.

**8:31** Exod 29:31-32
**8:32** Exod 29:34
**8:33** Exod 29:35
**8:34** Heb 7:16
**8:35** Num 3:7; 9:19 Deut 11:1 1 Kgs 2:3 Ezek 48:11
**9:3** Lev 4:3
**9:4** Exod 29:43
**9:6** Lev 9:23
**9:7** Heb 5:1-3; 7:27
**9:9** Lev 4:6-7
**9:15** Lev 4:27-31; 9:3
**9:16** Lev 1:3, 10
**9:17** Lev 2:1-3; 3:5
**9:18** Lev 3:1-11
**9:19** Lev 3:9
**9:21** Lev 7:30, 32
**9:22** Num 6:24-26

**8:36** Aaron and his sons did "everything the LORD had commanded." Considering the many detailed lists of Leviticus, that was a remarkable feat. They knew what God wanted, how he wanted it done, and with what attitude it was to be carried out. This can serve as a model for how carefully we ought to obey God. God wants us to be thoroughly holy people, not a rough approximation of the way his followers should be.

**9:22, 23** In 9:6 Moses said to the people, "When you have followed these instructions from the LORD, the glorious presence of the LORD will appear to you." Moses, Aaron, and the people then got to work and followed God's instructions. Soon after, the glory of the Lord appeared. Often we look for God's glorious acts without concern for following his instructions. Do you serve God in the daily routines of life, or do you wait for him to do a mighty act? If you depend on his glorious acts, you may find yourself sidestepping your everyday duty to obey.

**9:23**
Num 16:19, 42

**9:24**
1 Kgs 18:38

presenting the sin offering, the whole burnt offering, and the peace offering, he stepped down from the altar. ²³Next Moses and Aaron went into the Tabernacle, and when they came back out, they blessed the people again, and the glorious presence of the LORD appeared to the whole community. ²⁴Fire blazed forth from the LORD's presence and consumed the burnt offering and the fat on the altar. When the people saw all this, they shouted with joy and fell face down on the ground.

*The Sin of Nadab and Abihu*

**10:1**
Exod 6:23
Num 3:2

**10:2**
Num 26:61

**10** Aaron's sons Nadab and Abihu put coals of fire in their incense burners and sprinkled incense over it. In this way, they disobeyed the LORD by burning before him a different kind of fire than he had commanded. ²So fire blazed forth from the LORD's presence and burned them up, and they died there before the LORD.

---

**NADAB/ABIHU**

Some brothers, like Cain and Abel or Jacob and Esau, get each other in trouble. Nadab and Abihu got in trouble together.

Although little is known of their early years, the Bible gives us an abundance of information about the environment in which they grew up. Born in Egypt, they were eyewitnesses of God's mighty acts of the Exodus. They saw their father, Aaron, their uncle, Moses, and their aunt, Miriam, in action many times. They had firsthand knowledge of God's holiness as few men have ever had, and for a while at least, they followed God wholeheartedly (Leviticus 8:36). But at a crucial moment they chose to treat with indifference the clear instructions from God. The consequence of their sin was fiery, instant, and shocking to all.

We are in danger of making the same mistake as these brothers when we treat lightly the justice and holiness of God. We must draw near to God while realizing that there is a proper fear of God. Don't forget that the opportunity to know God personally is based on his gracious invitation to an always unworthy people, not a gift to be taken for granted. Do your thoughts about God include a humble recognition of his great holiness?

**Strengths and accomplishments**
• Oldest sons of Aaron
• Primary candidates to become high priest after their father
• Involved with the original consecration of the Tabernacle
• Commended for doing "everything the LORD had commanded" (Leviticus 8:36)

**Weakness and mistake**
• Treated lightly God's direct commands

**Lesson from their lives**
• Sin has deadly consequences

**Vital statistics**
• Where: The Sinai peninsula
• Occupation: Priests-in-training
• Relatives: Father: Aaron. Uncle and Aunt: Moses and Miriam. Brothers: Eleazar and Ithamar

**Key verses**
"Aaron's sons Nadab and Abihu put coals of fire in their incense burners and sprinkled incense over it. In this way, they disobeyed the LORD by burning before him a different kind of fire than he had commanded. So fire blazed forth from the LORD's presence and burned them up, and they died there before the LORD" (Leviticus 10:1, 2).

The story of Nadab and Abihu is told in Leviticus 8—10. They are also mentioned in Exodus 24:1, 9; 28:1; Numbers 3:2–4; 26:60, 61.

---

**9:24** As a display of his mighty power, God sent fire from the sky to consume Aaron's offering. The people fell to the ground in awe. Some people wonder if God really exists because they don't see his activity in the world. But God is at work in today's world just as he was in Moses' world. Where a large body of believers is active for him, God tends not to display his power in the form of mighty physical acts. Instead, he works to change the world through the work of these believers. When you realize that, you will begin to see acts of love and faith that are just as supernatural.

**10:1** What was the different kind of fire that Nadab and Abihu offered before the Lord? The fire on the altar of burnt offering was never to go out (6:12, 13), implying that it was holy. It is possible that Nadab and Abihu brought coals of fire to the altar from another source, making the sacrifice unholy. It has also been suggested that the two priests gave an offering at an unprescribed time.

Whatever explanation is correct, the point is that Nadab and Abihu abused their office as priests in a flagrant act of disrespect to God, who had just reviewed with them precisely how they were to conduct worship. As leaders, they had special responsibility to obey God. In their position, they could easily lead many people astray. If God has commissioned you to lead or teach others, be sure to stay close to him and follow his instructions.

**10:2** Aaron's sons were careless about following the laws for sacrifices. In response, God destroyed them with a blast of fire. Performing the sacrifices was an act of obedience. Doing them correctly showed respect for God. It is easy for us to grow careless about obeying God, to live our way instead of God's. But if one way were just as good as another, God would not have commanded us to live his way. He always has good reasons for his commands, and we always place ourselves in danger when we consciously or carelessly disobey them.

3 Then Moses said to Aaron, "This is what the LORD meant when he said,

'I will show myself holy
    among those who are near me.
I will be glorified
    before all the people.'"

And Aaron was silent.

4 Then Moses called for Mishael and Elzaphan, Aaron's cousins, the sons of Aaron's uncle Uzziel. He said to them, "Come and carry the bodies of your relatives away from the sanctuary to a place outside the camp." 5 So they came forward and carried them out of the camp by their tunics as Moses had commanded.

6 Then Moses said to Aaron and his sons Eleazar and Ithamar, "Do not mourn by letting your hair hang loose* or by tearing your clothes. If you do, you will die, and the LORD will be angry with the whole community of Israel. However, the rest of the Israelites, your relatives, may mourn for Nadab and Abihu, whom the LORD has destroyed by fire. 7 But you are not to leave the entrance of the Tabernacle,* under penalty of death, for the anointing oil of the LORD is upon you." So they did as Moses commanded.

## Instructions for Priestly Conduct

8 Then the LORD said to Aaron, 9 "You and your descendants must never drink wine or any other alcoholic drink before going into the Tabernacle. If you do, you will die. This is a permanent law for you, and it must be kept by all future generations. 10 You are to distinguish between what is holy and what is ordinary, what is ceremonially unclean and what is clean. 11 And you must teach the Israelites all the laws that the LORD has given through Moses."

12 Then Moses said to Aaron and his remaining sons, Eleazar and Ithamar, "Take what is left of the grain offering after the handful has been presented to the LORD by fire. Make sure there is no yeast in it, and eat it beside the altar, for it is most holy. 13 It must be eaten in a sacred place, for it has been given to you and your descendants as your regular share of the offerings given to the LORD by fire. These are the commands I have been given. 14 But the breast and thigh that were lifted up may be eaten in any place that is ceremonially clean. These parts have been given to you and to your sons and daughters as your regular share of the peace offerings presented by the people of Israel. 15 The thigh and breast that are lifted up must be lifted up to the LORD along with the fat of the offerings given by fire. Then they will belong to you and your descendants forever, just as the LORD has commanded."

16 When Moses demanded to know what had happened to the goat of the sin offering, he discovered that it had been burned up. As a result, he became very angry with Eleazar and Ithamar, Aaron's remaining sons. 17 "Why didn't you eat the sin offering in the sanctuary area?" he demanded. "It is a holy offering! It was given to you for removing the guilt of the community and for making atonement for the people before the LORD. 18 Since the animal's blood was not taken into the Holy Place, you should have eaten the meat in the sanctuary area as I ordered you."

19 Then Aaron answered Moses on behalf of his sons. "Today my sons presented both

**10:3** Exod 19:22; Ezek 38:16
**10:4** Exod 6:18
**10:6** Lev 21:1-15; Num 1:53; 16:22; Josh 7:1
**10:7** Lev 21:12
**10:9** Ezek 44:21
**10:10** Lev 11:47; Ezek 22:26
**10:11** Deut 33:10
**10:12** Lev 21:22; Num 3:2
**10:14** Lev 7:28-36
**10:15** Lev 7:30-34
**10:16** Lev 9:3
**10:17** Lev 6:24-30
**10:18** Lev 6:30
**10:19** Lev 9:8, 12

**10:6** Or by uncovering your heads.   **10:7** Hebrew Tent of Meeting; also in 10:9.

**10:8-11** The priests were not to drink wine or other alcoholic beverages before going into the Tabernacle. If their senses were dulled by alcohol, they might repeat Nadab and Abihu's sin and bring something unholy into the worship ceremony. In addition, drinking would disqualify them to teach the people God's requirements of self-discipline. Drunkenness was associated with pagan practices and the Jewish priests were supposed to be distinctively different.

**10:10, 11** This passage (along with 19:1, 2) shows the focus of Leviticus. The Ten Commandments recorded in Exodus 20 were God's fundamental laws. Leviticus explained and supplemented those laws with many other guidelines and principles that helped

the Israelites put them into practice. The purpose of God's laws was to teach people how to distinguish right from wrong, the holy from the common. The nation who lived by God's laws would obviously be set apart, dedicated to his service.

**10:16-20** The priest who offered the sin offering was supposed to eat a portion of the animal and then burn the rest (6:24-30). Moses was angry because Eleazar and Ithamar burned the sin offering but did not eat any of it. Aaron explained to Moses that his two sons did not feel it appropriate to eat the sacrifice after their two brothers, Nadab and Abihu, had just been killed for sacrificing wrongly. Moses then understood that Eleazar and Ithamar were not trying to disobey God. They were simply afraid and upset over what had just happened to their brothers.

place designated as ceremonially unclean. 46Anyone who enters the house while it is closed will be considered ceremonially unclean until evening. 47All who sleep or eat in the house must wash their clothing.

48"But if the priest returns for his inspection and finds that the affected areas have not reappeared after the fresh plastering, then he will pronounce the house clean because the infectious mildew is clearly gone. 49To purify the house the priest will need two birds, some cedarwood, a scarlet cloth, and a hyssop branch. 50He will slaughter one of the birds over a clay pot that is filled with fresh springwater. 51Then he will dip the cedarwood, the hyssop branch, the scarlet cloth, and the living bird into the blood of the slaughtered bird, and he will sprinkle the house seven times. 52After he has purified the house in this way, 53he will release the living bird in the open fields outside the town. In this way, the priest will make atonement for the house, and it will be ceremonially clean.

54"These are the instructions for dealing with the various kinds of contagious skin disease* and infectious mildew,* 55whether in clothing, in a house, 56in a swollen area of skin, in a skin rash, or in a shiny patch of skin. 57These instructions must be followed when dealing with any contagious skin disease or infectious mildew, to determine when something is ceremonially clean or unclean."

*Bodily Discharges*

**15** The LORD said to Moses and Aaron. 2"Give these further instructions to the Israelites: Any man who has a genital discharge* is ceremonially unclean because of it. 3This defilement applies whether the discharge continues or is stopped up. In either case the man is unclean. 4Any bedding on which he lies and anything on which he sits will be defiled.

5"So if you touch the man's bedding, you will be required to wash your clothes and bathe in water, and you will remain ceremonially defiled until evening. 6If you sit where the man with the discharge has sat, you will be required to wash your clothes and bathe in water. You will then remain defiled until evening. 7The same instructions apply if you touch the man who has the unclean discharge. 8And if he spits on you, you must undergo the same procedure. 9Any blanket on which the man rides will be defiled. 10If you touch or carry anything that was under him, you will be required to wash your clothes and bathe in water, and you will remain defiled until evening. 11If the man touches you without first rinsing his hands, then you will be required to wash your clothes and bathe in water, and you will remain defiled until evening. 12Any clay pot touched by the man with the discharge must be broken, and every wooden utensil he touches must be rinsed with water.

13"When the man's discharge heals, he must count off a period of seven days. During that time, he must wash his clothes and bathe in fresh springwater. Then he will be ceremonially clean. 14On the eighth day he must bring two turtledoves or two young pigeons and present himself to the LORD at the entrance of the Tabernacle* and give his offerings to the priest. 15The priest will present the offerings there, one for a sin offering and the other for a whole burnt offering. In this way, the priest will make atonement for the man before the LORD for his discharge.

16"Whenever a man has an emission of semen, he must wash his entire body, and he will remain ceremonially defiled until evening. 17Any clothing or leather that comes in

**14:49**
Lev 14:4
Num 19:6

**14:56**
Lev 13:2

**15:2**
Lev 22:4
Num 5:2

**15:12**
Lev 6:28; 11:32-33

**15:13**
Lev 15:28

**15:15**
Lev 14:30-31

**15:16**
Lev 22:4
Deut 23:10-11

14:54 Traditionally rendered *leprosy*. See notes at 13:2 and 13:47.   15:2 Hebrew *a discharge from his flesh;* also in 15:32.   15:14 Hebrew *Tent of Meeting;* also in 15:29.

**14:54-57** God told the Israelites how to diagnose contagious skin diseases and mildew so they could avoid them or treat them. These laws were given for the people's health and protection. They helped the Israelites avoid diseases that were serious threats in that time and place. Although they wouldn't have understood the medical reasons for some of these laws, their obedience to them made them healthier. Many of God's laws must have seemed strange to the Israelites. His laws, however, helped them avoid not only physical contamination but also moral and spiritual infection.

The Word of God still provides a pattern for physically, spiritually, and morally healthy living. We may not always understand the wisdom of God's laws, but if we obey them, we will thrive.

Does this mean we are to follow the Old Testament health and dietary restrictions? In general, the basic principles of health and cleanliness are still healthful practices, but it would be legalistic, if not wrong, to adhere to each specific restriction today. Some of these regulations were intended to mark the Israelites as different from the wicked people around them. Others were given to prevent God's people from becoming involved in pagan religious practices, one of the most serious problems of the day. Still others related to quarantines in a culture where exact medical diagnosis was impossible. Today, for example, physicians can diagnose the different forms of leprosy, and they know which ones are contagious. Treatment methods have greatly improved, and quarantine for leprosy is rarely necessary.

33"Do not exploit the foreigners who live in your land. 34They should be treated like everyone else, and you must love them as you love yourself. Remember that you were once foreigners in the land of Egypt. I, the LORD, am your God.

35"Do not use dishonest standards when measuring length, weight, or volume. 36Your scales and weights must be accurate. Your containers for measuring dry goods or liquids must be accurate.* I, the LORD, am your God, who brought you out of the land of Egypt. 37You must be careful to obey all of my laws and regulations, for I am the LORD."

### Punishments for Disobedience

**20** The LORD said to Moses, 2"Give the Israelites these instructions, which apply to those who are Israelites by birth as well as to the foreigners living among you. If any among them devote their children as burnt offerings to Molech, they must be stoned to death by people of the community. 3I myself will turn against them and cut them off from the community, because they have defiled my sanctuary and profaned my holy name by giving their children to Molech. 4And if the people of the community ignore this offering of children to Molech and refuse to execute the guilty parents, 5then I myself will turn against them and cut them off from the community, along with all those who commit prostitution by worshiping Molech.

6"If any among the people are unfaithful by consulting and following mediums or psychics, I will turn against them and cut them off from the community. 7So set yourselves apart to be holy, for I, the LORD, am your God. 8Keep all my laws and obey them, for I am the LORD, who makes you holy.

9"All who curse their father or mother must be put to death. They are guilty of a capital offense.

10"If a man commits adultery with another man's wife, both the man and the woman must be put to death. 11If a man has intercourse with his father's wife, both the man and the woman must die, for they are guilty of a capital offense. 12If a man has intercourse with his daughter-in-law, both must be put to death. They have acted contrary to nature and are guilty of a capital offense.

13"The penalty for homosexual acts is death to both parties. They have committed a detestable act and are guilty of a capital offense. 14If a man has intercourse with both a woman and her mother, such an act is terribly wicked. All three of them must be burned to death to wipe out such wickedness from among you.

**19:36** Hebrew Use an honest ephah [a dry measure] and an honest hin [a liquid measure].

**19:34**
Lev 19:18

**19:35**
Deut 25:13-16

**19:36**
Deut 25:13-15
Prov 20:10

**20:2**
Lev 18:21; 24:14-23

**20:3**
Lev 18:21
Num 19:20
Ezek 5:11

**20:6**
Lev 19:26, 31

**20:7**
Lev 11:44-45
†1 Pet 1:16

**20:9**
Exod 21:17
Deut 27:16
†Matt 15:4

**20:10**
Exod 20:14
Deut 22:22

**20:11**
Lev 18:7-8
Deut 27:20

**20:12**
Lev 18:15

**20:13**
Lev 18:22

**20:14**
Lev 18:17
Deut 27:23

---

**19:33, 34** How do you feel when you encounter foreigners, especially those who don't speak your language? Are you impatient? Do you think or act as if they should go back where they came from? Are you tempted to take advantage of them? God says to treat foreigners as you'd treat fellow countrymen, to love them as you love yourself. In reality, we are all foreigners in this world because it is only our temporary home. View strangers, newcomers, and foreigners as opportunities to demonstrate God's love.

**20:1-3** Sacrificing children to the gods was a common practice in ancient religions. The Ammonites, Israel's neighbors, made child sacrifice to Molech (their national god) a vital part of their religion. They saw this as the greatest gift they could offer to ward off evil or appease angry gods. God made it clear that this practice was detestable and strictly forbidden. In Old Testament times as well as New, his character made human sacrifice unthinkable. (1) Unlike the pagan gods, he is a God of love, who does not need to be appeased (Exodus 34:6). (2) He is a God of life, who prohibits murder and encourages practices that lead to health and happiness (Deuteronomy 30:15, 16). (3) He is God of the helpless, who shows special concern for children (Psalm 72:4). (4) He is a God of unselfishness, who instead of demanding blood gives his life for others (Isaiah 53:4, 5).

**20:6** Everyone is interested in what the future holds, and we often look to others for guidance. But God warned about looking to the occult for advice. Mediums and psychics were outlawed because God was not the source of their information.

At best, occult practitioners are fakes whose predictions cannot be trusted. At worst, they are in contact with evil spirits and are thus extremely dangerous. We don't need to look to the occult for information about the future. God has given us the Bible so that we may obtain all the information we need— and the Bible's teaching is trustworthy.

**20:10-21** This list of commands against sexual sins includes extremely harsh punishments. Why? God had no tolerance for such acts for the following reasons: (1) They shatter the mutual commitment of married partners; (2) they destroy the sanctity of the family; (3) they twist people's mental well-being; and (4) they spread disease. Sexual sin has always been widely available, but the glorification of sex between people who are not married to each other often hides deep tragedy and hurt behind the scenes. When society portrays sexual sins as attractive, it is easy to forget the dark side. God had good reasons for prohibiting sexual sins: He loves us and wants the very best for us.

**20:10-21** The detestable acts listed here were very common in the pagan nations of Canaan; their religions were rampant with sex goddesses, temple prostitution, and other gross sins. The Canaanites' immoral religious practices reflected a decadent culture that tended to corrupt whoever came in contact with it. By contrast, God was building a nation to make a positive influence on the world. He did not want the Israelites to adopt the Canaanites' practices and slide into debauchery. So he prepared the people for what they would face in the Promised Land by commanding them to steer clear of sexual sins.